# Nevada

UPPER RIM GREAT BASIN LAKES

Upper and Lower Angora lakes are in the foreground, Fallen Leaf Lake in the middle background, and Lake Tahoe in the background. The mountains in the distance are in Nevada.

# NEVADA

## a history of the state
### from the earliest times
### through the Civil War

by
EFFIE MONA MACK, PH.D.

THE ARTHUR H. CLARK COMPANY
Glendale, California, U.S.A.
1936

To
SARAH EMELINE MACK
My Mother

O North! give him beauty for rags,
  And honor, O South! for his shame;
Nevada! coin thy golden crags,
  With Freedom's image and name.

  "Boston Hymn," by Ralph Waldo Emerson
  (Read in Music Hall, January 1, 1863)

# Contents

# Illustrations and Maps

# Preface

Nevada, the third state west of the Rocky mountains to be admitted to the Union, is little known except through drama and fiction. From its earliest history, the romance and tragedy which have attended its development, stories of the frontier and mining days, have been over-emphasized in books on the history of this state, entirely provincial in quality; they have related a purely local narrative. This volume aims to draw attention to the fact that Nevada played an important part in the history of the United States during the middle of the nineteenth century, not only in the development of the West, but also in the assistance it gave to the Union during the Civil War. In the settlement of the region and the organization of the territory and state, Nevada had many important relations with the federal government. Certain principles established in our national policy found their origins in the facts peculiar to the history of this region. For these reasons federal relations with Nevada between 1850 and 1866, which have never before been presented in one book, are here treated in general perspective. In order to understand more fully the difficult problems the federal government had to meet in adjusting these relations, it is necessary to present in several introductory chapters, the historical background, the setting of the dramatic entry of the state into the Union.

Within the memory of a few illiterate Indians still living, there wandered through the Great American Desert, out of which Nevada was carved, a growing stream of trappers, explorers, and pathfinders. Then the great army of gold seekers began to trek through the area before there was a single permanent settlement in it. The Mormons, zealously wishing to found a new Zion, established colonies around the rim of the Great Basin, and set up trading posts on the emigrant trails. One of these, Genoa, was the first permanent settlement in Nevada. The silver rush to Washoe, backwash of the gold rush to California, led directly to the formation of the state.

In many ways this story is unique. Most of the states of the Union developed gradually; Nevada came of age suddenly. No other one, perhaps, made so many demands on the federal government in so short a time. The establishment of political institutions, the provision for adequate means of transportation and communication, the disposition of the public lands, the settlement of the Indian question, and the adoption of a national mining code were some of the problems which the territory and state of Nevada petitioned the federal government to solve. It was the national exigency of civil war which made possible admission of the scantily populated territory into the family of states; the way thereto was smoothed by a group of astute political leaders.

The formative years lying between 1850 and 1866 have been selected for emphasis in this study. In 1850, the territories of Utah and New Mexico, parts of both of which were included in Nevada territory, were organized. By 1866, most of the important questions facing the new state had been settled – the limits of its boundaries were fixed, the disturbing question of legal mining titles was ended by the passage of the National Mining Act of 1866, the Indians were subdued by the establishment of a number of forts, the period of slow and painful transportation was at an end, the first rush of new population was spent – and from that year Nevada settled down to a more unvaried existence.

This book is the result of many years of formal and creative research on the part of the writer. For the critical relations between nation and state, federal and state documents have been winnowed as the most reliable sources. The volumes of Hubert Howe Bancroft have been used as a guide for much hitherto inarticulated manuscript and source material. The records of the territorial period, preserved in manuscript form in the office of the secretary of state of Nevada, were used freely for their first-hand information on the correspondence between the government and territorial officers. Photostatic copies of the reports of the mili-

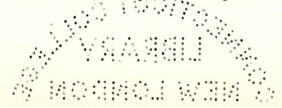

tary activities in Nevada, hitherto unexploited, were obtained from the war department. From her conversations with many of the pioneers, from her journeys over the state, and from her personal visits to many of the settlements which made important contributions to the territorial period, the writer has been able to piece together many fragments of the early history of the state and present them for the first time in an orderly array.

Because many of the sources of Nevada history are beyond the reach of many readers, frequent quotations from earlier books, as well as occasional well-formulated opinions in old and now rare newspapers, are inserted at some length in several of the chapters. A number of illustrations and several maps, many of them rare and never published heretofore, are included to interpret the stirring activities of these times. But since the book is written for students as well as for the general public, the canons of sound scholarship have been rigorously followed, and no attempt made to color any part of the story. Generalizations, which might seem at first glance sweeping, have been supported by standard authority although a minimum of footnotes has been used except where references are made to federal and state documents. A carefully selected bibliography for further reading has been included.

The writer wishes to express her thanks to the persons who have aided in the preparation of this work. Through the guidance and direction of Herbert Ingram Priestley, professor of history, University of California, the writer has gained invaluable counsel and suggestions. An appreciation of the importance of the history of the West and the responsibility of the residents of each section to write its own history was forcefully brought to the attention of the writer by Herbert Eugene Bolton, Sather professor of history, University of California. Through the efforts of Tasker L. Oddie, United States senator from Nevada, valuable material was obtained from the government archives in Washington. The writer is indebted to Mr. W. G. Greathouse, secretary of state of Nevada, for the use of the territorial records. Miss Edna Rodden Martin, of the staff of the Bancroft Library, University of California, brought important material to the attention of the writer. Don Harvey Bell, instructor of English, Reno High School, read the manuscript. He assisted greatly with historical comment and pertinent criticisms. Lastly, to the pioneers of Nevada themselves, the book owes whatever of human interest its pages reveal.

EFFIE MONA MACK

Reno, Nevada
July 1, 1935

# The Land Nevada

The coincidence of two unusual circumstances occurring about the same time in the history of the United States — discovery of the Comstock Lode and the Civil War — made it possible for the state of Nevada to be admitted to the Union. Certain established facts peculiar to the organization and development of this area are found in our national policy. Because Nevada shared largely in the nationalizing process which linked the East to the West, this volume emphasizes the more important relations of the state with the federal government between 1850 and 1866. In order that the problems the national government faced with regard to Nevada may be understood, her physical features, aboriginal culture, and early history must be kept in mind.

Nevada is a land of variations. The native life, the exploration and settlement of the state, were all limited by its odd formations. It is a land of physical opposites and extremes in climate and soil, in arid wastes and humid sinks, in mountain steeps and valley depressions. Some of the most barren parts yield the greatest wealth; and from the unbasked brows of her mountains bare, beetling, one may see some of the most fertile valleys in America as well as deserts where death finds nothing to destroy. Even the scenery of these wastes contrasts sharply with the fruitful areas along the slender margins of the streams; the brilliant colors of the naked rocks stand out sharply against the silvery sagebrush background.

With the exception of two small areas in northeastern and southeastern parts, Nevada, 110,690 square miles in extent, lies entirely within the western part of the broad elevated region between the Sierra Nevada range and the Wasatch mountains. In 1844, although John Charles Frémont had been around only the rim of it, he gave it the name, "Great

Basin." [1] The parallel of the 42nd degree north latitude forms the northern boundary between Nevada and the states of Oregon and Idaho; the eastern boundary, separating Nevada from Utah, is four miles west of and parallel to the 114th meridian; the Colorado river forms the southeastern boundary line between Arizona and Nevada for a distance of nearly one hundred and fifty miles; and the western boundary line, between California and Nevada, extends obliquely northwest from the point where the 35th parallel crosses the Colorado river to the point where it makes a junction with the 120th meridian; and follows northward along this line to the 42nd parallel north latitude.

Nevada, having the refreshing name of "snow-covered," is ribbed by over a hundred mountain ranges having a general northerly and southerly trend with a rise from one to ten thousand feet above the level of the basin floor. Between each of these ranges are valleys which vary from five to twenty-five miles in width and from fifteen to one hundred and fifty miles in length. The floor of the Great Basin, averaging about forty-five hundred feet above the level of the sea, has a gentle rise toward the east; it reaches its summit in the Humboldt range, sixty miles from the Utah-Nevada line. The difference in elevation ranging from Boundary Peak, Esmeralda county, 13,145 feet,[2] to the depressions in Clark county of 300 feet, allows for great topographical variations.

One of the strangest and most awe-inspiring sights in North America may be viewed from the summits of the mountains located on the boundary line between California and Nevada. From these heights one may look down into Death Valley, whose colors, beauty, and desolation no painter has been able to put on canvas; he may experience a loneliness which no poet has been able to describe; he may see shapes molded in the tawny sands by the capricious hands of the wind and storm which no sculptor has been able to reproduce; he may hear mystic symphonic sounds which no

1 Hubert Howe Bancroft, *History of Nevada, Colorado, and Wyoming*, 2.
2 Wheeler Peak, White Pine county, 13,058 feet in height, has been regarded generally the highest peak in the state. The elevations of the leading peaks in Nevada are given in the *Biennial Report,* surveyor-general of Nevada, 1932, 21.

musician has been able to imitate, and, then he may look up
to the majestic heights of the perennially snowclad peak of
Mount Whitney.[3]

While it is not within the scope of this volume to describe
the geological changes that have brought about the many
topographical variations mentioned,[4] a few generalizations
are necessary in order to show their bearing on the state's
history. It is supposed that at the beginning of the glacial
period, the Great Basin was a simple tableland, comparatively bald and featureless, bounded on the east and west by
lofty mountain ranges; then, this tableland was later covered
with ice which discharged its waters northward and southward, carving the interior ranges and valleys, and leaving its
detritus at the end of the ranges in the form of double and
terminal moraines; and finally as the "glacial winter" came
to a close the lowest portions became immense lakes in the
midst of which many of the interior ranges stood as islands.
A period of dessication then followed, wherein the large
lakes became separated into many smaller ones whose waters
no longer flowed to the sea. By the filling of their basins
with detritus, many of these smaller lakes have entirely
disappeared. The continued dryness and decay have left the
present conditions of sage and sand.[5]

Lake Lahontan,[6] the greatest lake left in the Nevada
portion of the Great Basin, drained the largest area within
the state. It spread over the valleys of the northern and
western parts of the state, being fed from the west by the
Walker, Carson, and Truckee rivers, each of which descended from the glacier-covered Sierra Nevada. The Humboldt river was the greatest contributary to Lake Lahontan
from the eastern rim of the basin. When the water supply

[3] Death Valley and Mount Whitney are the lowest and highest points in
the United States.

[4] For further details regarding the mountains in the Great Basin, see
George Louderback, "Basin Range Structures in the Great Basin," Uni-
versity of California Publications, Bulletin of the Department of Geological
Sciences, vol. 14.

[5] John Muir, Steep Trails, California, Utah, Nevada, Washington, Oregon,
the Grand Canyon, 184-194.

[6] The lake was named for Baron de Armand Louis de Delondarce Lahontan,
a French soldier in North America during the French and Indian War.

from the mountains was in excess of the evaporation in the valleys, the overflow from the larger basins to the smaller ones made up the great Lake Lahontan.[7] The ancient boundaries of this lake have been traced and studied carefully. It is now known that during its high water state it was second only to Lake Bonneville,[8] its complement in the eastern area of the Great Basin. Lake Lahontan, two hundred miles from north to south and one hundred and eighty miles from east to west, had a hydrographic basin of about 45,000 square miles. It was an exceedingly irregular lake, however, for it was broken up by mountain ranges into many long and narrow arms, with deep bays and long peninsulas, one arm reaching as far westward as Honey Lake Valley, California, and another extending into southern Oregon. The late J. Claude Jones, professor of geology at the University of Nevada for twenty-three years, received international recognition for his studies of the Lahontan Basin. He placed its age at about 2,400 years [9] and believed it reached its highest

---

[7] The United States government became interested in this area and a series of official expeditions followed, some reports of which are to be found in Frémont, *Memoirs,* 2 vols.; a summary of the results of exploration in this region previous to 1857, written by Lieutenant G. K. Warren in *Pacific Railroad Explorations,* XL; a brief account of the Great Basin in *Geological Survey of California,* vol. I, by J. D. Whitney; the United States geological exploration of the 40th parallel in charge of Clarence King, mapped the geology of a belt one hundred miles wide across the northern portion; surveys in charge of Captain George Wheeler and Major J. W. Powell mapped large portions of the basin; Captain E. G. Beckwith crossed the northern part of the Lahontan Basin in the region of the Black Rock Desert and Smoke Creek Desert in search of a northern route for a railroad and made an excellent report on the area; Captain R. Ingalls crossed the Great Basin in 1855. His report may be found in 34 Cong., 1 sess., *H. Ex. Doc.* no. 1, part 2, p. 152; and Captain J. H. Simpson entered the Great Basin at Sand Springs Pass in June, 1859, to survey a central road across Nevada. He gave many names to mountains, rivers, and valleys in the state. Simpson, *Explorations across the Great Basin.*

[8] Great Salt Lake is the largest remaining pool of Lake Bonneville. It was first named for Captain B. L. D. Bonneville. He made a partial survey of the lake in 1833.

[9] J. Claude Jones, "The Geologic History of Lake Lahontan," *The University of Chicago Abstracts of Theses Science Series,* I, 289-296; "Age of Lake Lahontan," *Bulletin of the Geological Society of America,* vol. 40, pp. 433-540, September 30, 1929.

water stage about 100 A.D. at which time it covered 8,000 square miles.[10]

As time passed and precipitation decreased in the Great Basin area, the supplying streams became smaller, and Lake Lahontan began to shrink. The basins, connected at high water periods, were separated; deserts, sinks, and lakes were left, the waters of the lake receded by stages, at every recession a well-defined bench was left. These old beach terraces are among the most striking features of the region of the old lake bed. One may travel over the desert for many miles with the old wave-cut benches circling the mountains far above him. Fossils are found in abundance along these old shore lines.

The floors left by the receding waters of Lake Lahontan are called sinks, dry lakes, alkali washes, and salt or borax marshes. These depressions receive all the alkaline waters which drain from the higher regions above them; and, since these sinks have no outlet, each becomes a lake or playa during the rainy season, and a hard sun-baked expanse of clay during the remainder of the year. They are bare of vegetation; even the hardy desert plants cannot survive the intermittent floods and excessive deposits of alkali.

The largest of these playas are Black Rock, Smoke Creek, and San Mateo deserts, which join in one great expanse of alkaline soil extending north of Pyramid and Winnemucca lakes. This great desert has genuine high mountains surrounding it and imaginary hills and even cities in their ever present mirages. The name "Black Rock" was given to this desert by the early emigrants, who could see the large jutting black rock on the edge of the desert long before they reached it. Not far from this Black Rock Desert country lie the "bad lands" of Nevada, a broken range cut up into gullies and cañons, a region ever the dread of cattle and sheep men, where visibility is not more than fifty yards in any direction. These lands harbor not only much game, but large bands of cattle and horses that have gone wild find a safe retreat within them.

[10] Israel Cook Russell, "Geological History of Lake Lahontan," *United States Geological Survey,* 11.

Still other desert areas impeded travel across the state, and made it dangerous and tedious to the early emigrants. A portion of the Great Salt Desert extends into northeastern Nevada. This desert, however, may be avoided by going to the north or to the south of the Great Salt Lake. Another desert, which could not be escaped on the Humboldt or northern route, was known as the "Forty-mile Desert." This long stretch of deep sandy soil, almost completely devoid of water between the Humboldt and the Carson rivers, was the grave-yard for hundreds of weary animals already worn down by many months of travel.

Mirages and giant whirlwinds are not unusual spectacles of the Nevada deserts. During the summer months, the former may appear across a perfectly level floor. There may not be a single object in a cerulescent sky to cast a shadow on the oceanlike expanse, and yet, limpid waters and placid lakes abounding with beautiful islands and picturesque headlands may be seen in the distance. These deceptive illusions proved disastrous to many an early traveler for they often led him on to false hopes of water and shade. One observing emigrant, while crossing the Forty-mile Desert between the Humboldt Sink and the Carson river, witnessed the phenomenon. He wrote: "The illusion was so complete on the east side of the desert as to draw stock toward it, as may be seen by the greater number of bones on the east side of the sink." The giant whirlwinds are minia-ture cyclones of sand and dirt, which twist and gyrate in huge columns. These "whirling dervishes" sweep along the ground for many miles until their force is spent. A half dozen may be seen in the air at a given time; they continue through-out the dry season.

The "cloudburst" is another phenomena of the Nevada desert. Upon bare plateaus or on the rocky summit of a range of mountains, clouds ascend, and almost instantly, the cañons leading to the lower ground are filled with a rush of water. If the cañon is narrow, the water will rise many feet, carrying an immense load of boulders and detritus with it. As the water leaves the cañon, it spreads out into a fan-shaped delta on the plains below.[11] Such conditions as these

[11] B. W. Currie, "Surprises of the Nevada Desert," *Harper's Weekly,* February 23, 1907.

INTERIOR OF LEHMAN CAVE, WHITE PINE COUNTY

made travel for the emigrants particularly hazardous and slow.

While the surface of the Great Basin was being changed, subterranean disturbances were forming caverns under the mountains. Caves of all sizes and descriptions are found all over Nevada, but they occur in such sizes and numbers in the eastern part of the state that the region is known as "Nevada's Caveland." [12] The largest one, Lehman Cave, is located near the foot of Mount Wheeler.[13] It is an underground fairyland of elfin castles, crags, temples, and palaces of stone. The constant dropping of calcareous water has produced the most realistic shapes and formations in stalagmites and stalactites. The entrance to the cave is through a "Gothic Palace," where great white columns rise from floor to roof. The slow but continuous work of the ages has reproduced fantastic shapes. In one part, a garden of plants with buds and flowers occurs; and in another, masses of coral stand out. The walls and roofs are covered with a formation of pure white which resembles popcorn kernels; others hang in clusters like grapes. Chamber after chamber extends through this enormous cavern, each one a new wonderland. "Angel's Wing," "Liberty Bell," "Tower of Jewels," "Parachute," "The Crystal Hyacinth," and the "Caveman's Den," are some of the realistic sights of the cave. The "Navajo Blanket" hangs in graceful folds, so thin that a light held behind it reveals the beautiful stripes of onyx in it. "The Pipe Organ" with flutes, made of massive stalactites, gives forth pure and melodious tones when struck with a stick.

In all this land with its oddities and peculiarities, there is nothing so unusual as the drainage systems. The Great Basin, of which Nevada is the larger part, is turned upside down. The rivers flow inward, instead of outward. This inversion of the streams is caused by the elevated center of

[12] Whipple Cave is another wonder in this caveland, chief attraction of which is an immense room 500 feet in length and 100 feet in width and height. In the center of this room, one massive column five feet in diameter reaches from the floor to the roof. In many of the caves in this region writings and remains of an ancient race are found.

[13] Lehman Cave was discovered by a man riding on horseback. The hoofs of the horse broke through the thin, crustlike covering and plunged its rider into the cavern.

the Great Basin, and the high mountains around the rim of
it. The greater portion of northern Nevada is drained into
the remaining pools of Lake Lahontan, Walker, Pyramid,
Winnemucca, Carson, and Humboldt lakes. Because these
lakes have no outlet their waters are brackish and their
sandy shore lines have little or no vegetation. Although
Carson and Humboldt lakes receive the water of the Carson
and Humboldt rivers, it sinks and evaporates rapidly. In
particularly dry years there is little or no water in them
during the summer months. Pyramid and Walker lakes are
fed by the Truckee and Walker rivers respectively; they are
deep desert lakes. The former is the largest, deepest and
most picturesque of all of the lakes in western Nevada. It
was first discovered and named by Captain John Charles
Frémont in his first expedition to Nevada, when he and Kit
Carson came over the pass in the mountains bordering the
east side of the lake and saw the large pyramid which suggested its name.[14] There are, also, many other strange appearing tufa deposits on the shores of the lake. The smaller
ones bear a striking resemblance to great thick mushrooms
with a concentric structure. When the lake is disturbed by
a strong wind, it exhibits a riot of colors. At the north end
of the lake a rugged cape known as the "Needles" projects
a mile or more into the water. On this cape the tufa deposits
take fantastic shapes such as domes, spires, and crags.

Upon the upper rim of the basin facing Nevada on the
west, a number of lakes are found. The largest of these,
Lake Tahoe, about one-third of which is in Nevada, receives
its water from the Sierra Nevada mountains, and discharges
its contents through the Truckee river for a distance of some
eighty miles to Pyramid Lake. There are small pools and
lakes occurring at the base of many of the mountains throughout the state, but few of them attain any size, even during
the rainy season.

In addition to the drainage systems of old Lake Lahontan,
there are several other smaller ones. The most southeast-
erly one is drained through the confluence of the Muddy and
Virgin rivers for a distance of sixty miles to the Colorado
river. A still smaller area drains away to the southwest into

14 Frémont, *Exploring Expedition*, 216-217.

Death Valley by way of the Amargosa river. This river truly belongs to this land of contradictions. For many miles there is not a sign of water on the surface; yet, it can be found by breaking through the shallow crust. In the spring of the year it will wind its way along the surface; then, it will sink out of sight for several hundred yards, only to appear again; finally, it loses itself in the absorbing sands of Death Valley. Another drainage system in northeastern Nevada sends its water to the Pacific by way of the Owyhee river,[15] which flows into the Snake, tributary of the Columbia river. Broken and ill-defined, an unnamed range of highlands with an easterly and westerly trend forms the watershed between the tributaries of the Humboldt and the Snake rivers.

From the Sierra Nevada range eastward, one mountain range after another continues across the state. During the day the clearness of the desert air makes the distance deceptive; each mountain range stands out in bold relief; but when the sun sets, every ravine and every cañon becomes a fathomless abyss of purple haze. Most of these mountain ranges have a culminating peak, some of which rise to a height of 13,000 feet. On the steep slopes deep gorges are cut, each of which is rich in glacial records. Through these cañons, the waters from the melting snows rush down to the valleys below, carrying heavy loads of detritus. Because most of these clefts presented a uniform appearance they often led the emigrant in the wrong direction. The swift streams have cut narrow cañons for long distances, such as the Truckee and Walker river cañons, and the palisades on the Humboldt river. Deepest of all, however, are the Boulder, Black, and Eldorado cañons cut by the Colorado river as it rushed along the border between Arizona and Nevada.

At the base of each of the ranges throughout the state a fertile valley lies, each watered by the streams which descend

15 The name of "Owyhee" was given to the river by two Kanakas, native Hawaiians, in the service of the Hudson's Bay Company while trading with the Shoshone Indians. Bancroft, *History of Washington, Idaho, and Montana*, 444. When Captain James Cook discovered the Sandwich Islands in 1778, he gave the largest island in the group the name of "Owyhee." When the American missionaries reduced the native tongue of the islanders to a written language the name Owyhee became "Hawaii." The river, however, retained the original spelling.

from their icy fountains into the desert like angels of mercy.
The most extensive of these valleys are at the base of the
Sierra Nevada mountains. The waters from the principal
rivers have been diverted so as to reclaim large areas along
the borders of these streams. The Humboldt, with its tributaries, forms the most important and largest river system in
the state. This river rises on the southwesterly slope of the
continental divide in northeastern Nevada and flows in a
south-southwest direction to the Humboldt Sink in Pershing
county. It is about six hundred miles in length with a total
watershed, however, of approximately 14,000 square miles.
Every rivulet and every rill in the state has been claimed,
and its waters put to use for irrigation.

Many springs occur throughout the Great Basin area;
there are evidences that at one time there were many more
of them. These springs may be grouped conveniently into two
classes – hillside and fissure springs. The former are found
on hillsides or in the cañons of the mountains. The source
of the water, deliciously cold and pure, is from the rainfall
in the immediate neighborhood. The lives of many of the
early emigrants were saved by the water from these springs.
So many of them occur in the northeastern part of Elko
county as to have the region known as the "Thousand Springs
Valley." The fissure springs are found where the earth's
crust has been broken, usually by some displacement, to a
great depth. Their water supply is derived from the same
source as the hillside springs, but owing to the depth to
which these springs descend, the water often reaches the
surface with a boiling temperature. Although hot springs are
found in many places in the state, the Devil's Punch Bowl
in Nye county, and Steamboat Springs near Reno are well
known examples of them.

A number of scenic phenomena occur in this land of contrasts, among them the Cathedral Gorge and the Valley of
Fire. The former, situated near a tributary of the Muddy
river, two miles from the present town of Panaca, is made up
of myriad cathedral-like spires of colored clay, impossible
to scale and wonderful to behold. They rise in some places
to a height of one hundred feet. The Valley of Fire is a
remarkable formation near the picturesque village of St.

Thomas, an early Mormon settlement in Clark county. The brilliant and lurid coloring of the sandstone, as red as a mass of flames, accounts for its name. A distinctive feature of it is the unusual number of "Pot Holes" which have been cut into the boulders by the sand blasts. These vary in depth from a few inches to several feet, and in some cases to the proportions of small caves. Mysterious records of a prehistoric race are written on some of these larger stones. The most conspicuous of these inscriptions, on "Atl-Atl Rock," records undoubtedly some episode in the life of an ancient race which once made its home in this valley.[16]

There is no set of climatic conditions applicable to the whole of the state of Nevada.[17] The great differences in altitude and topography cause wide variations in the climate of a given locality. In general, however, the air is characterized as light and dry, the sunshine constant. Everywhere the phenomenon of evaporation obtains to the greatest extent. The high Sierra blocks the moisture-laden aerial currents from the Pacific ocean and makes the annual rainfall one of absolute minimum. The climate varies from semitropical sections in southern Nevada, where a freezing temperature is almost unknown, to points in the northeastern part of the state, where the thermometer often falls to forty degrees below zero.[18]

Nevada abounds in minerals. Nature seemingly tried to balance the aridity of her climate and the sterility of her soil with a variety of precious and base metals which have brought Nevada worldwide fame. To the lure of the precious metal the state owes its creation. The development in farming, the increase in transportation facilities, and the growth of her population have depended largely upon the mining industry. While the state is best known for its valuable deposits of gold and silver, yet copper, lead, and zinc are

[16] Philip Johnston, "The Valley of Fire," *Touring Topics*, vol. 21, no. 1, Jan., 1929, 29-31.

[17] W. A. Glassford, "Report on the climate of California and Nevada with particular reference to questions of irrigation and water storage in the arid region," *H. Ex. Doc.* no. 287, 51 Cong., 2 sess., 12, 31.

[18] The highest temperature of 119 degrees recorded in the state was at Logandale in southeastern Nevada and the lowest of 45 degrees below zero was recorded at San Jacinto in northern Nevada. *Reno Evening Gazette*, August 25, 1932.

found in large quantities. Of the non-metallic minerals, Nevada is rich in gypsum, sulphur, salt, borax, and soda. Building stones in the form of marble, granite, sandstone, travertine, and slate, are valuable resources, while opal, turquoise, variscite, malachite, and azurite of remarkable beauty, find a ready market for semi-precious gems.

The highly mineralized character of the surrounding mountains has made the soils of the valleys vary, even as the rocks in them differ one from the other. With the exception of a few strictly desert areas, Nevada is covered with some kind of vegetation. In the drier parts the plants do not attain much growth; and when they die, most of them dry up instead of decaying as they would in a moister climate. However, on the lowlands surrounding some of the shallow lakes or sinks, the plants decay and form a deep, rich, black soil. The presence of alkali in a great deal of the soil makes it difficult for plant life to exist.

The natural vegetation resulting from this wide range of climate is correspondingly odd and various. From the desert plains to the lofty heights of the mountains, the character of the plant life is ever changing. A general impression prevails that Nevada is a desert entirely covered with sagebrush. Indeed, and perhaps rightfully so, it is called the "Sagebrush State." This plant, rarely occurring south of the Mount Diablo base line,[19] covers about two-thirds of the state. The *artemisia tridentata* (sagebrush) is now the state flower.[20]

Wherever the sagebrush grows, nutritious grasses, in such quantities as to furnish some feed for stock, are found. In the southern part, the creosote bush with glossy, sticky evergreen leaves and bright yellow roselike flowers, takes the place of the sagebrush. Numerous cacti of all shapes and sizes everywhere abound. The tree yucca, known also as the joshua tree, assumes considerable proportions on the southern Nevada desert. The century plant or agave, and the mesquite bush, are other plants in the same region. The juicy pulp of some species of cacti has often served as a substitute for water for the thirsty desert traveler.

19 The Mount Diablo base line crosses Nevada just south of Tonopah.

20 On March 20, 1917, the Nevada state legislature adopted it as the state flower.

A rare and unusual desert plant, known commonly as desert holly, is found in the region around Death Valley. Early in the spring this holly resembles the English variety, except that the leaves are much smaller and the color is a delicate olive green. In the fall the leaves turn a beautiful silvery white.[21]

When there is an abundance of spring rain no other region in the northern hemisphere can surpass the beauty of the wild flowers on the Nevada desert. More than two thousand species from one hundred separate families flourish in different parts. No word picture can paint the exquisite beauty of the carpets of purple, red, scarlet, blue, and white flowers which grow everywhere in profusion.[22] In addition to the desert flowers a large number of alpine plants growing above the timber line have all of the characteristics of the plants of the Arctic regions. The forest growth includes many species. John Muir, in a rambling mountaineering journey of eighteen hundred miles across the state, noted nine species of coniferous trees — four pines, two spruces, two junipers, and one fir.[23] The piñon produced the pine nut in great abundance and yielded the chief food for the Indian.

In this land of limited water and food, only small animals are found. They were, however, of great economic importance to the native. He used every device known to him to catch the rabbit, squirrel, gopher, and lizard. Even the insects were caught and dried to be made into a kind of paste and eaten during the winter months. Occasionally the coyote, badger, wild cat, deer, and antelope [24] were found in the mountains or along the streams. Beaver meadows were ex-

---

[21] Large quantities of this holly are picked before the holiday season and shipped to eastern markets, where it commands a high price.

[22] Statement of Mark W. Menke, Elko county extension agent and specialist for the state of Nevada in horticultural matters. For scientific treatises on desert plants peculiar to Nevada, consult Margaret Armstrong, *Field Book of Plants as a Source of Drinking Water;* and Ivar Tidestrom, *Flora of Utah and Nevada.*

[23] Muir, *op. cit.,* 166. At the present time, Nevada has 315,000 acres of forest under fire protection by the federal government.

[24] The federal government maintains an antelope sanctuary in northern Washoe county. It is six by eight miles in area. It is known as the "Charles Sheldon wild game refuge." This area was purchased by the National Association of Audubon Societies assisted by the Boone and Crockett Club. In 1929 these lands were deeded to the federal government.

tensive in the northern part of the state along the tributaries of the Humboldt and the Snake rivers. The streams and lakes were the homes of many kinds of fish. The Indian speared them, and invented weirs to catch them. Many of the tribal wars were fought for the privilege of fishing in the lakes and rivers. When the fish were caught in such quantities that all could not be eaten, the rest were dried for winter food.

The common game birds were numerous on the lakes and sinks. Eagles, owls, and hawks helped the coyote to keep down the objectionable animal life in the country, while the turkey buzzard and the magpie were the desert scavengers. The white pelican was the most interesting and peculiar bird to be found in Nevada. Ten thousand of these birds, the largest colony in the world, breed on Anaho Island in Pyramid Lake.[25] They remain on the island for about two hundred days from April to November, during which time they lay their eggs and hatch the young. It has been observed that the adult bird, weighing about twelve pounds, catches about four pounds of fish a day. If this observation be correct and the number of birds is multiplied with the pounds of fish consumed with the number of days the birds remain on the island, the staggering figure of eight million pounds is reached. The large trout are too wily for the pelican to catch, but it preys upon the smaller ones. The red sucker, lake minnow, chub, carp, perch, and cui-ui are the fish which are usually caught by the pelican. The pelicans have nested on Anaho Island from the time the white man first settled in the region to the present, and, according to Indian lore, for countless years before.[26]

[25] Anaho Island is three-fourths of a mile in diameter and four hundred feet high. It is nine miles north of the mouth of the Truckee river and one mile east from the shore of the lake. Pyramid Island is one mile north of Anaho Island. The federal government has declared Anaho Island a sanctuary for the pelicans. A number of scientific expeditions have observed the birds while they have been breeding on this island.

[26] There have been several scientific expeditions sent to Pyramid Lake to study the pelican. A very good account of one of them is found in a thesis written by E. Raymond Hall, "A Study of the Food Habits of the White Pelican at Pyramid Lake, Nevada, with special reference to its relation to the fishing industry," MS., M.A. thesis, University of California, 1925.

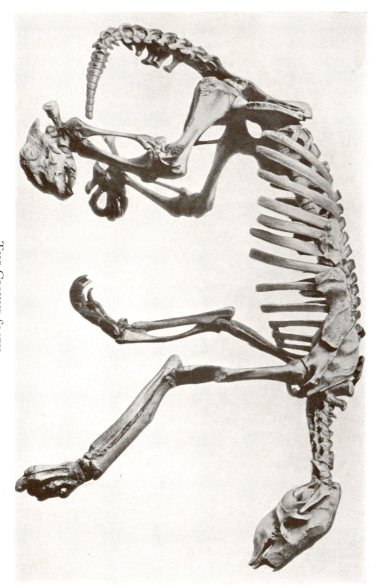

THE GROUND SLOTH
The ground sloth lived in Nevada many thousands of years ago.

Before 1924, although the fact that a prehistoric plant and animal life existed in the state many centuries ago had been on record for more than a hundred years, little was known of the antiquities of Nevada. From excavations and scientific study, it is known that giant animals once roamed throughout the state. It is now even believed that man was contemporaneous with the ground sloth and saber-toothed tigers of twenty thousand years ago. Excavations made in the Gypsum Cave near Las Vegas, Nevada, revealed fossil and human bones beneath a stratum bearing sloth refuse; nearby, was the evidence of a charcoal fire. These caves show three distinct periods of primitive culture. In the first one, a period of great dampness and rainfall, man and the camel-horse occupied the cave. A dry era followed the first period, and the ground sloth moved in with primitive man. A still drier and third period brought to an end the civilization of ancient man.[27] Footprints of the giant sloth, of large birds, and of other animals have been well preserved in ancient clay beds hardened by the long period of dessication.[28] Pre-historic bones of an elephant have recently been found near Fallon, Nevada. Scientists believe it roamed the country about the same period as the mastodon.[29] This same type of elephant is similar to the ones found in India today.

In a cave on the shore of old Lake Lahontan near Love-lock, Nevada, rich archaeological finds reveal a series of cultures of primitive man which date as recently as 1000 B.C. Each group of occupants left its refuse, until the mass came to average from four to five feet in depth, and in one spot, to fifteen feet. Innumerable interesting objects have been excavated. They range from human mummies and remark-ably natural duck decoys to crude household articles. Another civilization, recently uncovered in southern Nevada near the town of Moapa, has brought to light an interesting culture

[27] M. R. Harrington, "Archaeological Explorations in Southern Nevada," *Southwest Museum Papers,* no. 4, June, 1930.

[28] The best examples of these footprints thus far uncovered are in the yard of the Nevada State Prison at Carson City.

[29] This discovery was made by Laura Mills of Fallon, Nevada. She called it to the attention of the California Institute of Technology. F. D. Bode of that institution came to Fallon and shipped the skull and jaw bone to Pasadena, California. *Reno Evening Gazette,* August 10, 1931.

of many centuries ago, though more recent than in either the Gypsum or Lovelock caves.[30] In this later civilization, the "Pueblo Grande de Nevada," popularly called "The Lost City," "The Mesa House," and "The Paiute Cave," disclosed the culture of the pueblo and basket-maker Indians. On the floors of their dwellings, still well preserved, were found many woven articles, and around the skeletons in the shallow graves were bits of pottery revealing some of their ideas of a future life.[31] The inhabitants of these pueblos were undoubtedly the progenitors of the present Indian.

Petrified forests are found in several different places throughout the state. In northwestern Nevada, east of the Granite range of mountains, although there is not a living one within sixty miles, petrified trees are found. On one particular area in northern Washoe county, wonderful forests once existed. In this section there is an area of forty acres covered with the large stumps of petrified trees. The largest in this locality measures sixty feet in circumference; a petrified log lying nearby is fully ten feet in diameter. The wood, in its changes throughout the ages, has taken on a kaleidoscopic hue resembling opals. There is further evidence of timber growth once in this same region. The neighboring hills must have been covered with magnificent groves. This fact is borne out by the curious formations which can be found on Nut mountain. Plums, acorns, cherries, and other small fruits are reproduced in stone. So perfect are some of the specimens that by breaking open the pebbles even the pit and rind can be found.[32] Another petrified forest of great interest is found in Wilson cañon on the Walker river.

In this land, Nevada, with its varied climate, contrasting topography, scanty rainfall, and limited plant and animal life, there roamed a number of Indian tribes eking out a living from the resources which nature so scantily endowed.

[30] Irwin Hayden, "Nevada Cavemen," *Touring Topics*, February, 1930.

[31] M. R. Harrington, "A Primitive Pueblo City in Nevada," *American Anthropologist*, vol. 29, no. 3, July to September, 1927; Irwin Hayden, "Mesa House," Louis Shellbach 3rd, "An unusual burial in Mesa Ruin," M. R. Harrington, "Paiute Cave," *Southwest Museum Papers*, no. 4, June, 1930.

[32] William S. Brown, "Northwestern Nevada – Land of Enchantment," *The Sacramento Bee*, March 11, 1931.

# The Amerinds of Nevada

The Indians were the first of the historic people to live in Nevada. According to the commissioner of Indian affairs, twenty-seven different tribes have lived in this state at some time.[33] They have great diversity in their physical characteristics and cultures — each tribe having its own name, tongue, history, traditions, and customs. Even the location of the different tribes was involved in great confusion, for the very nature of this desert country forced them to be nomads. They were constantly on the move in search of food, generally traveling in bands numbering from ten to forty families. Owing to these facts, it was difficult for students of ethnology to trace the origin of the tribes living in the Nevada area of the Great Basin.[34] The Amerinds of Nevada are not autochthonous. They were undoubtedly of Asiatic origin. Their color, facial expressions, straight black hair, and stoic dispositions are strikingly similar to those of the Oriental. An early observer of the Nevada Indians gave the following description of them:

The bodies of the Wash-o were short and sturdy, with broad fat hips supported by bowed legs. Heavy cheeks smeared with red earth, dropped like dewlaps below the sensual mouth and short flat nose. In the pear-shaped face were small deep-set black eyes, sometimes twinkling and merry, sometimes somnolent and bleared. Coarse black hair grew low down on the narrow forehead and fell about the neck and cheeks in a thick mop. The hands and feet were small and shapely, but the form otherwise was clumsy and ungainly. Scanty coverings of patched and dirty skins were wound

[33] It was difficult to ascertain the number of Indians in Nevada. The first census of the Indians was taken in 1861, when 7,000 were counted; in 1865 there were 8,500. *The Report of the Commissioner of Indian Affairs*, 1861, 1865.

[34] Major John Wesley Powell made some interesting observations of the Indians of the Great Basin during the sixties. The original manuscripts of his reports are in the Smithsonian Institution. He organized also the Bureau of Ethnology. "Paiute Lore" in *Death Valley*, by Bourke Lee, is based on Powell's notes.

about the copper-colored bodies, but the natural layers of fat were the main protection against the winter winds.

The Nyumas (Paiutes), on the other hand, were taller and lighter colored than the Washoes, and their complexion had a peculiar ashen tint. The typical Nyumas of middle age had wide cheek bones and lean, long faces, with sunken cheeks and heavy superciliary ridges over large black eyes, which stared with keen, hungry looks, quite different from the tranquil and sensuous gaze of the Washoes.[35]

"Paiute" was the name given to the greater number of the Indians living in Nevada; however, this name was applied also at some time or another to most of the natives of western Utah, northern Arizona, southern Idaho, eastern and southern California. Major John Wesley Powell, probably the first student of the Great Basin Indian, maintained that those Indians living around Walker and Pyramid lakes were not Paiutes but Paviotsoes, a tribe closely related to the Bannock tribe. "Shoshone" was also loosely applied to the Indians who formerly occupied western Wyoming, central and southern Idaho, northeastern Nevada, and Utah west of the Great Salt Lake. In Nevada, they roamed along the Humboldt river from its source to the sink. In 1859 there were seven bands of them, each led by a separate chief.[36]

The Washoes, few in numbers, were confined to a small area in western Nevada. They lived chiefly in the vicinity of the upper rim basin lakes – from Honey Lake in the north to Lake Tahoe in the south; eastward along the Truckee river to the cañon below the Meadows, and on the Carson river to the first cañon below the present site of Carson City. They were different from the other tribes in the basin in every way.[37]

Three other well-defined groups or small tribes roved around in different sections of Nevada. The Bannocks, a tribe closely related to the Snakes of southern Idaho, lived on the streams north of the Humboldt river; the Goshutes,

[35] Stephen Powers, "The Indians of Western Nevada," MS., quoted in Eliot Lord, *Comstock Mining and Miners*, 5. Powers was the special agent of the Smithsonian Institution.

[36] Hodge, *Handbook of American Indians*, 555-558.

[37] A. L. Kroeber, "The Language of the Washo," *American Archaeology and Ethnology*, IV, no. 5, 1907.

a mixture of the Utes and Shoshones, wandered through Utah and Nevada south of the Great Salt Lake; and the Mono Indians, also unlike any other tribe in the basin area, lived in the region from Mono Lake, California to Fish Lake, Nevada.[38] Mention should also be made of the Mohave Indians, who lived on both sides of the Colorado river between the Needles in California, and the Black cañon in Nevada. (There are now 4,200 acres of Mohave Indian lands in the southernmost portion of the state.)[39]

The chief historical sources concerning the early culture and appearance of the Nevada Indian were the meager comments recorded by the trappers, the traders, and the first explorers. They were the first white people to come in contact with them, and from their reports are gained the conditions under which these aborigines lived. In the light of the limited resources of this state, it is not surprising to find these Indians low in the scale of humanity. A great deal of the land, barren in the extreme, in most parts, afforded them nothing more than a bare existence. However, as the nature of this land differed, so did the first inhabitants.

The fur-trappers were the first of the white peoples to come into Nevada. For a few baubles, the red man became his friend and his guide, and showed him the way to the best fur-bearing streams. Many of the trappers took squaws for mates, that is to say, bartered for them, thereby securing a wife, a servant, a beast of burden, and an expert skin dresser. "Mary," legendary wife of Peter Skene Ogden, probable discoverer of the Humboldt river, was the Nevada "Sacajewa." [40] This river bore the feminine appellation of Mary, Ogden's squaw wife, long after the trapping period was over, and St. Mary is still the name of an eastern tributary of the Humboldt.

The trappers came in small numbers; they did not settle

[38] Frank M. Parcher, a young ethnologist from the Southwestern Museum, is making a historic study of the eastern Monos. *Reno Evening Gazette,* July 14, 1931.

[39] The present Mohave reservation consists of fourteen thousand acres in Arizona, California and Nevada. *Ibid.,* March 19, 1931.

[40] The controversial evidence on this point belongs to another story. However, further readings on this subject may be found in Bancroft, *History of Nevada, Colorado, and Wyoming,* 36-37; T. D. Bonner, *Life and Adventures of James P. Beckwourth,* 432; Thwaites, *Early Western Travels,* XXVII.

in any place, nor did they remain for a great length of time. They tried to get along with the natives, and they succeeded in doing so, as long as their traps were not stolen, nor their animals driven off. The fur period in Nevada was short, extending from about 1827 to 1840. After the latter date, the large companies did not send out organized bands of trappers. However, many "free trappers" continued independently of company support. Some of them lived with the Indians; some were taken into the tribes. It was from these "freemen" that the red man learned many of the vices of civilization; it was believed these men, also, encouraged the Indian to prey upon the emigrant trains.

According to early written reports, the physical appearance and mode of living of these desert natives was anything but attractive. Their stature, their features, and their impoverished bodies seemed to be in keeping with their surroundings. In 1827, Jedediah Strong Smith, the fur-trapper, and first white man who left a record of crossing the state, described the Indians "as being hopelessly degraded, living on grasshoppers, lizards, and roots." [41] Zenas Leonard, the clerk of the Bonneville-Walker party, said in his report five years later, that the Indians were "generally small and weak and some of them very hairy." In 1844, Frémont gave a somewhat better picture of the Paiutes living around Pyramid Lake near the mouth of the Truckee river. He reported them to be "very fat and appeared to live an easy and happy life." [42] In 1859, when Captain James Simpson was making his exploration for a route across the Great Basin, he wrote in his report that the Goshute Indians were "talkative and lively," but those around Walker Lake were a low type. Near this lake he came "upon five old women hovering over a fire of a few twigs of six or eight inches in length . . . and thought if the personification of witches ever existed, these were they. Their withered bodies, almost entirely naked and emaciated, their faces smeared with dirt and tar, the dull, idiotic stare of their eyes, trembling from cold and dread of our intentions, rendered them to me the most pitiable objects I had ever seen." [43] Lorenzo Sawyer, the well-known Cali-

[41] Dale, *The Ashley-Smith Explorations*, 192.
[42] Frémont, *Exploring Expedition*, 132.
[43] Simpson, *Explorations across the Great Basin*, 71.

fornia jurist, crossed Nevada in 1850. He recorded in his diary that the Indians on the Carson river were an "ill-formed, mean, sneaking looking set, the most insignificant specimens of humanity I have ever seen. They are low in stature, with very little manifestation of intellect in the development of the head." [44]

John Muir has left a vivid description of a band of Mono Indians which he met during one of his jaunts through the Sierra Nevada mountains:

At length, as I entered the pass . . . a drove of gray, hairy beings came in sight, lumbering toward me with a kind of boneless wallowing motion like bears. I never turn back, though so often inclined, and in this particular instance amid such surroundings, everything seemed singularly unfavorable for the calm acceptance of so grim a company. Suppressing my fears, I soon discovered that although as hairy as bears and as crooked as summit pines, the strange creatures were sufficiently erect to belong to our own species. They proved to be nothing more formidable than Mono Indians, dressed in the skins of sage rabbits. . . Occasionally a good countenance may be seen among the Mono Indians, but these, the first specimens I had seen, were mostly ugly, and some of them altogether hideous. The dirt on their faces was fairly stratified, and seemed so ancient and so undisturbed it might almost possess a geological significance. The older faces were, moreover, strangely blurred and divided into sections suggesting exposure on the mountains in a castaway condition for ages. Somehow they seemed to have no right place in the landscape, and I was glad to see them fading out of sight down the pass.[45]

The native dwelling of the basin Indian was called a wickiup, a tipi, or a campoodie. It was usually a small rounded conical shaped hut made of tule or brush laid over a framework of poles with the ground for a floor. Sometimes the inside of the hut was covered with a layer of dried grass. A small fire was built in the depression in the center, the smoke from which was allowed to escape through the almost open top of the tipi. These primitive dwellings were almost bare of any kind of household articles except a few baskets of native weave, a stone mortar used for grinding the nuts and seeds, and sometimes a net used in the rabbit drives. Some of the early travelers came upon the Indians living in holes dug out of the ground in the side of the hills, while others noticed that the natives, when driven by the cold,

[44] Lorenzo Sawyer, *Way Sketches*, 93.

[45] Reprinted from John Muir, *The Mountains of California*, 106-108, by permission of the D. Appleton-Century Company.

found shelter in the thickets of low-lying branches of the trees.[46]

The arts and crafts of these Indians were limited to the resources at hand. They exhibited, however, considerable skill in fashioning them. Basket weaving was developed to a degree of remarkable beauty and perfection. Into their baskets they wove history, astronomy, legends, and religious beliefs. Since the basket was the most important household article, the skill of the housewife was reckoned by her ability as a weaver. The materials for the baskets were obtained from native plants, usually the willow. Every twig and fiber was selected at the proper season, and prepared for use by stripping off the outer bark, generally by pulling the twigs through the teeth. Some did it with their finger nails; others used a flint scraper. After being sorted the twigs were neatly tied into bundles and laid away to cure for a year or even longer. Because tribal law forbade them to copy in any way or to duplicate a former production, these primitive women planned, designed, and executed their baskets without a model. The result, therefore, of each effort was an unique and original contribution to their handicraft.[47]

The Paiutes wove an ingenious and graceful double-pyramidal shaped basket, or bottle, rendered water-tight by an outer smearing of pine pitch. The Shoshones were adept in weaving baskets for ceremonial purposes. But of all the basket weavers the Washoe was the best, and of all the Washoes Dat-so-la-lee was supreme.[48] She immortalized herself and her tribe in her baskets of wonderful workmanship, many of which are preserved in the leading museums of the United States.[49] This great basket maker, born about 1835 near the present site of Genoa, lived to be over ninety. As a young girl she remembered seeing the men in Frémont's expedition come into Carson Valley. These American soldiers

[46] Simpson, *op. cit.*, 478-480; J. M. Shively, *Route and Distances to Oregon and California*, 13.

[47] Mrs. C. Amy Cohn, "Arts and crafts of the Nevada Indians," *First Biennial Report Nevada Historical Society, 1907-1908.*

[48] The Washoe basket was very much in demand by other tribes; it was often used as a medium of exchange.

[49] The largest collection of Dat-so-la-lee's baskets is owned by Mr. Cohn of Carson City, Nevada.

stayed for several weeks among her people, made many friends among the natives, and gave them a number of small presents. Among the gifts she received were several brass buttons which she cherished to the time of her death.[50] The last thirty years of her life she spent weaving baskets for her friend and benefactor, Mr. Abe Cohn of Carson City. Her work has been pronounced perfect by leading students of Indian basket weaving. Her most beautiful basket took one year to weave and is now valued at $10,000. The symbols of this basket, done in three colors, denote that "Myriads of stars shine over the graves of our ancestors." [51] Dat-so-la-lee deserves to be ranked among the great American artists.

The desert Indians wore little or no clothing; they generally went most of the year as "naked as a worm." Zenas Leonard said that the Indians along the Humboldt were "totally naked – both male and female – with the exception of a shield of grass." It was not warm enough in this desert region for them to go without any clothing, but there was simply little or no material with which to make any.

In addition to weaving the robes, the buck busied himself fashioning his bow and arrow. The former was made generally from the juniper tree and reënforced with sinews glued to it. The arrowheads were made from flint and obsidian, an abundance of which was found all over the Great Basin.

In his nomadic life there was no way for the Indian to keep live coals, hence a device for making fire was invented. Near Middle Gate, Nevada, Captain Simpson observed an Indian making fire with a crude appliance, consisting of two pieces of greasewood, one about two feet long and the thickness of the little finger, the other a flat piece six inches long and one inch broad. In this latter piece, in which there were a number of semi-spherical cavities uppermost, he placed the other stick between the palms of his hands, and with the rounded end of the stick held in a cavity in a vertical position, rolled it rapidly forward and back, until the friction caused

[50] Peter Ruf, "Dat-so-la-lee," *The California Christian Advocate*, 3.

[51] Statement of Mr. Abe Cohn of Carson City to the writer, October 25, 1932. This wonderful basket weighs two pounds and four ounces. Its height is 14 inches; its orifice is 7½ inches, and its circumference is 47 inches. There are 28 stitches to the inch, or a total of 86,590 stitches.

the tinder, which he had placed against the foot of the stick, to ignite. In a few seconds fire was produced.[52]

In this land which nature had stinted, the Indians' chief occupation was assembling the food for the next meal. They ate everything – lizards, snakes, insects, desert plants, grass seeds, and pine nuts. In fact, everything alive, creeping, flying, or running was caught and eaten, generally without any preparation for cooking. The small animals were held over the fire by a stick and roasted – entrails and all were eaten and equally relished. Some of the Indians cooked in a pot made of stiff mud, but owing to the sandy nature of the soil the pot quickly fell to pieces and another one was made. The rabbit was by far the most abundant source of animal food in the basin area. The Paiutes had a very clever method of catching this animal. It is known that from five hundred to one thousand rabbits were secured in a single drive.[53]

The Indians in southern Nevada, along the Muddy and the Virgin rivers, were evidently in closer contact with some methods of agriculture. In 1849, it was noted by a traveler on the Los Angeles-Salt Lake Trail that they were raising corn, squash, and pumpkins; they had even developed a crude kind of irrigating system.[54]

The streams and lakes abounded in fish for those Indians who were fortunate enough to live near them, and who possessed the right to fish in them. The fish in the streams were generally caught by weirs or dams made of brush placed upright; in the shallower water on the border of the lakes or swamps, they were killed with flint spears or the sharpened fish bone. Zenas Leonard observed the Indians around Humboldt Lake catching fish with an eighteen inch leg-bone

[52] James H. Simpson, *The shortest route to California illustrated by a history of explorations of the Great Basin with its Topographical and geological character and some account of the Indian tribes,* 53. It is possible that this Indian learned to make his fire-making device from the fur-trappers.

[53] The description of the rabbit drive and many of the customs of the Paiutes was given to the writer by Edwin Newman, a very intelligent member of that tribe, who graduated from the Reno High School in 1930. He died in 1933.

[54] Walter Van Dyke, "Overland to Los Angeles by the Salt Lake route in 1849," *Annual Publications Historical Society of Southern California,* III. It is probable that these Indians obtained their rudimentary knowledge of agriculture from the Mexicans, who had been traveling along this trail since 1830.

of a sandhill crane fastened to a pole. In rafts made of rushes, the Indian floated on the surface to the deeper water, where he speared the larger fish. At this same place, the native was observed to be fishing also with a bone hook fastened to the end of a wild flax line. The hook was ground down with a piece of flint so as to have two beards cut into it. The line was fastened nearest to the bearded end of the hook, so that when the fish took hold of it, a quick pull caused the beard to catch, and a quick flip of the line, to turn the hook cross-wise in the mouth of the fish.[55]

In addition to fish and game, the Indian ate every form of vegetation available and known not to be poisonous. Roots formed an important part of his food, and because he seemed to be digging always for his food, Frémont in his report called him a "Digger." Seeds of almost every desert plant were carefully harvested by the squaws. An abundance of this kind of food was obtained from the sand grass, the seed of which was beaten out with a wicker paddle and the chaff winnowed off. The results of the harvest were then put into large burden baskets, and were taken home, later to be ground into flour. In the southern desert country, the Indian obtained a great deal of his vegetable food from the "devil's pincushion," the prickly pear, the mesquite, the screw bean, the agave, and the young buds of the joshua tree.

John Bidwell described a kind of food which his party obtained from the Indians around the Humboldt Sink. It consisted of a ball made from the dew which clung to the rushes growing in abundance on the edge of the marshes. The dew was covered with a pediculous-looking insect which fed upon it. The Indians gathered the dew in great quantities and pressed it into balls about the size of one's fist, having the appearance of wet bran. At first the party bought it and relished it, but after having seen that the insects were the chief ingredients, they lost their appetite for it.[56]

The pine nut, obtained from the piñon tree, was an important source of food when there was a crop. It took the place of the acorn and maize of the other tribes; it was the "bountiful orchard of the red man" in Nevada so long as

---

[55] Zenas Leonard, *Narrative*, 166.
[56] John Bidwell, *Echoes of the past about California*, 52.

the forests remained primeval. The gathering of this nut was the occasion for harvesting, feasting, and dancing. When the nut was about to ripen, the buck and his family repaired to the forest where, with long poles, they knocked the resinous burrs from the trees. The burrs were then rolled into a stone pit and covered with a light brush which was fired to burn off the resin. After this process, the nut was ready to be threshed, gathered into baskets, and taken home for use during the long winter. The nut was then ground and cooked into a porridge.[57]

The desert was threaded with trails, some narrow and others wide. They were food trails which indicated the way to either water or game. These trails were sacred to the tribe; they were followed year after year in search of a livelihood. When they were well-marked, they never failed to lead to an Indian camping ground or to a body of water, usually at the foot of a mountain or in a narrow ravine. The fur-trappers and early explorers learned quickly that these trails were to be relied upon; they were the means of saving the lives of many of them. Tribal wars were fought when the trails were trespassed upon.

In spite of the difficult time these Indians had in eking out a living in this inhospitable desert country, they had devised or had preserved in tradition some ideas of the supernatural. Behind his seemingly stolid and taciturn countenance the native concealed an intellectual power to remember, if not to reason out, a religion peculiar to the life he was forced to lead. He lived in a world of spirits who were everywhere — in the mountains, the springs, and the lakes. Every section was controlled by these active little beings, every mishap was attributed to their bad intentions, and every illness was due to the presence of evil spirits in their bodies. The Indian medicine man practised his art, chiefly in the pursuit of these spirits. The sick person endured great physical abuse from the hands of the doctor in his attempt to rid him of diseases. The patient, however, expected and demanded relief, and if it were not forthcoming, the doctor often followed his patient to the grave.

[57] It takes twenty-two months for the burr of the pine nut to mature. A. B. Dutcher, "Piñon gathering among the Panamint Indians," *American Anthropologist*, October, 1893.

Death was not of great consequence to this desert philosopher — to obtain a livelihood on this earth was such a problem, any relief from it was welcome. He also believed that the aged should not be allowed to become a burden to their families. Suicide was especially common among the squaws, starvation was considered a meritorious act on their part. The food they would eat was needed for the younger members of the tribe.

When Frémont was on his second exploring trip in central Nevada, one of his men, Sagundai, located a good spring for a camp. He noticed it had been cleaned out recently, and that nearby there were fresh tracks made in the sand by the bare feet of a woman. After dinner the men usually sat around the camp fire and smoked their pipes before turning in for the night. Kit Carson, one of Frémont's guides, who was lying on his back with his pipe in his mouth, his hands under his head and his feet to the fire, suddenly exclaimed, half rising and pointing to the other side of the fire, "Good God! Look there!" In the blaze of the fire, peering over her skinny, crooked hands which shaded her eyes from the glare, was stooping an old woman apparently eighty years of age, nearly naked, her grizzly hair hanging down over her shoulders. She had taken Frémont's camp for one of her own people, and, had even begun to talk and gesticulate before she realized they were not of her kind. She tried to run away, but the men preventing her from doing so, brought her back to the fire and gave her some food. When she was sure they meant no harm to her, she made them understand because she was too old to gather any more food, she had been abandoned by her people at the spring to die. The Frémont party departed the next morning, but before doing so, they left her some antelope meat and other food. She could keep up the fire, and she could seek shelter from the snow and cold in the low-lying branches of the cedars nearby; thus her life may have been prolonged through the winter.[58]

No written language was known to the Great Basin Indian. In fact, a babel of tongues confronted the white man when he came into this region. Each band or tribe spoke a different dialect. There had been, however, at some remote

[58] Frémont, *Memoirs*, I, 436-437.

period too far removed from the historical Indian for him
to have preserved it in his traditions, a race living all over
the basin area, which possessed a written language. Large
numbers of petroglyphs are found on rocks and cliffs, and,
although widely separated in location, all bear remarkably
similar characters. Some efforts have been made to reduce
to writing the spoken language of these Indians, but so far
no Rosetta stone has been found to yield a key to the meaning of these strange designs.[59] It has been suggested that
these writings recorded the migrations of the tribes into
this country. The deciphering of these pictographs is a fertile
field for some future anthropographist.

There is no limit to one's imagination in looking at these
prehistoric bulletin boards. In the first place, their striking
similarities make it reasonable to believe that the people
who carved these hieroglyphics spoke a common language.
All along the Indian trails from one water hole to another,
these picture writings occur. May they not define the hunting and fishing privileges of the different tribes in the vicinity?
The frequent repetition of the parts of the body in the petroglyphs may suggest tribal or family records. And then, these
writings may be the records of some peace council. It is known
that from time immemorial hostility existed among the basin
tribes; warfare among them was the normal status when the
white man arrived. Frémont noticed such hostility among
the Indians as to render it difficult to secure a guide who
would go beyond the limits of his territory. The Paiutes,
for instance, had defeated the Washoes in a contest for the
possession of Eagle Valley (Carson City), in which the
former were the victors. Henceforth, the vanquished could
never again possess or ride a horse. When Frémont put his
Washoe guide on a horse because his moccasins wore out, he
could neither guide nor ride it.[60]

The first English the Indians picked up was from the
bullwhackers or ox drivers. From them they learned to say

[59] Grace Melissa Dangberg, of Minden, Nevada, has translated some of the
myths of the Washoes. The language of the Washoes is practically unrecorded
except for a morphological sketch by Alfred L. Kroeber. Grace Dangberg,
"Washo Texts," *University of California Publications in American Archaeology and Ethnology,* vol. 22, no. 3, pp. 391-443.

[60] Frémont, *Memoirs,* 321.

A Prehistoric Bulletin Board

Ancient rock writings on a cliff in White Pine county.

to the emigrants: "How do you do — whoa!! haw! God damn
you!" These words were the usual greeting of the red
men to the white. On one occasion, a party was inquiring
from the Indians for a good camping ground on the Humboldt river. The natives assured them that there was plenty
of grass for the "whoa! haws! but no water for the God
damns!" [61]

The Spanish explorers did not make Nevada a missionary
field, so these Indians remained undisturbed and untouched
by the civilization of the early mission. The red man did not
learn of the superiority of the white race in that way. His
first knowledge of it came to him when his domains were
trespassed by the trappers, traders, and settlers. The result
was almost instantaneous hostility. The first record of a
fight between the two races in Nevada was occasioned by
the expedition of Joseph Walker in 1833, when he was
making his exploratory trip across this area for Captain
Bonneville. The Indians began to bother the Walker party
as soon as they started down the Humboldt river. So annoyed
were they by the theft of their traps that they had to abandon
trapping entirely. The more discontented members of the
party killed several Indians before Joe Walker found it out.
He immediately put a stop to it.

On September 4, the party arrived at the sink of the
Humboldt where there were a number of small bodies of
shallow water resembling lakes. The grass was good, and
since it was the first good grazing ground they had seen in
some time, they decided to camp for the night to permit their
animals to recuperate. A short time before sunset a view
of the surrounding waste was taken with a spy glass; smoke
was discovered rising from the high grass in every direction.
The whites were convinced they were in the midst of a band
of hostile Indians against which they must defend themselves
as best they could.

Preparation for the defense tactics began by securing
the horses so they could not be driven off. This was done by
fastening them together, and then hitching them to pickets.
Then the men began to prepare for their own defense. One
of the lakes was immediately in their rear, and so, by piling

---

[61] Delano, *Life on the Plains and at the diggings,* 159.

all of their baggage in front, they had quite a substantial breastwork. Before, however, they could complete their fortifications, the Indians, estimated to be between eight and nine hundred in number, rose from their hiding places in the grass, and made straight for the camp. When they were within one hundred and fifty yards of them, they all sat down on the ground, excepting five chiefs, who were dispatched to Walker and his party. They asked permission to come into camp, but the request was refused. They were told, however, they would be met half way. This suggestion did not suit them; they insisted they still wanted to come into camp. Whereupon they were made to understand that if they attempted to carry out their wishes, they would be fired upon. The chiefs only laughed at these threats and made signs they wanted some demonstration of the effectiveness of the white man's guns. So, ducks were shot at, and killed on the lake, a beaver skin was put on a stick and shot down. Night came on and the belligerents withdrew until the next morning. Early in the morning Walker and his party were up and gone before the Indians noticed their departure. They had not traveled very far, however, when the Indians began to follow, first in small numbers, but presently in large companies. Again they wanted to come up and smoke with them, but this advancement was interpreted as being only a means of delaying the party until all of the warriors could come up. Walker now began to be more stern than before, and gave them to understand that if they continued to trouble the party, they did so at their own risk. The Indians tantalized Walker's party until about one hundred, more bold than the others, came forward. This movement was sufficient to excite Walker, who was generally very calm. He gave orders, then, to charge upon the Indians. Thirty-two of his men selected the best horses; they closed in and fired on the red men, of whom thirty-nine were left dead. The remainder fled in every direction. Of this incident, Leonard said in his report: "The severity with which we dealt with these Indians may be revolting to the heart of the philanthropist; but the circumstances of the case altogether atone for the cruelty." [62]

[62] Leonard, *op. cit.*, 165.

For some time after this massacre, the small bodies of water in this vicinity were called "Battle Lakes."

Of all the pathfinders, none excelled Kit Carson in his ability to understand and get along with the Indian. Yet he had trouble with the Nevada Indians. He said:

At Muddy Creek, a tributary of the Virgin river, there were about three hundred Indians collected. They wanted to come into my camp. I would not permit them and I told them that the autumn before they had killed seven Americans, that they were of a treacherous character and could not be trusted, and that I would not allow myself to be deceived by them, that their object was to come to be friendly and then kill my party. I told them to retire; if not, I would fire upon them. I was compelled to fire. One Indian was killed and the balance went off. I had no more trouble on the road.[63]

Frémont took a howitzer with him to frighten the Indians. It had evidently the desired effect since he does not make note of any serious trouble with them while he had it with him. He felt nervous about their intentions when he was near Pyramid Lake, and he said he "kept strict vigilance" as "the Indians kept themselves armed." [64] On his second trip through Nevada, one of his most reliable men, Tableau, was murdered by Indians on the Virgin river, when he left the party to go back on the trail to recover a lost mule. In the search for him, his fellow travelers found the place where he had been killed, his body dragged to the river's edge, and thrown into the water.[65]

When the emigrant trains began to go through this desert country, the Indian began to prey upon the travelers' stock, to drive off a stray animal, or to stampede the herd so as to separate as many as possible from it. As early as 1846, warnings against the hostility on the Humboldt Route were published in the guide books. The travelers were advised "along this river to keep your guns in order, and sleep on your trail ropes, for the arrows of death are pointed at you from every gulch, and without the strictest care you will lose your animals, if not your lives." [66] When the gold rush of '49 was

[63] "Kit Carson's story as told by himself," MS., Bancroft Library, University of California.

[64] Frémont, *Memoirs*, 316.

[65] *Ibid.*, 380-381.

[66] Shively, *op. cit.*, 13.

taking thousands of people through this country, skirmishes
between the Indian and the emigrant increased, and there
were many lives lost before the federal government began to
police and protect the traveler through the hostile country.

There was some reason why the Indian in southern Nevada was hostile to all who came into his territory. For some
time, the New Mexicans had been making yearly expeditions
among the Utes to capture the children and take them back
to the Mexican settlements where they sold them into slavery.
So common was it to make a raid for these juvenile slaves
that it was considered no more objectionable than to go
on a buffalo or a mustang hunt. In August, 1853, when a
party was passing through southern Nevada, José Gallego,
a New Mexican, and an old hand at this kind of man-hunting,
related many stories, with much gusto, of the sport of such
a business. When the party reached the Muddy river, they
saw an Indian village in the distance. José, becoming very
excited at seeing the prospects of getting so many slaves,
rode ahead, and eagerly proposed to Mr. Beale, the leader,
to permit the party to "charge on it like hell, kill the mans
and may-be catch some of the little boys and gals." [67] In the
afternoon, the party reached the village. They went into the
Indians' huts, which presented a squalid scene of dirt and
wretchedness. When the women saw the party approaching,
they concealed their children, fearing that they might be
carried off. Noticing that something moved under a large
wicker basket, one of the party examined its contents which
were found to be a little naked fellow, his teeth chattering
with fear.[68]

Soon after the gold rush was over, stations sprang up
along the routes of travel; they were followed by permanent
settlers who reclaimed the more fertile spots; and finally the
silver rush to Washoe brought such large numbers as to
found cities. The control of the Great Basin slipped from
the Indian. This simple desert patriot resisted stubbornly
but vainly to prevent the civilization of the white man from
coming into his land. He stole from the emigrant trains; he

[67] Gwinn Harris Heap, *Central Route to the Pacific, from the valley of the
Mississippi to California,* 99-100.
[68] *Idem.*

drove off their stock, and he killed some of the travelers; but these acts seemed to be his only reprisals in the face of starvation. For was not his game killed with more effective weapons than his; were not his pine nut trees cut down for the homes of the settlers; and were not the best lands settled on, and fenced so that he could no longer roam at will over his hunting grounds?

In the red man's challenge to civilization, he was the loser. After this Great Basin area became a part of the United States, military forts were built at different places along the routes of travel, and soldiers policed the roads, accompanying the emigrant trains through the most hostile country. The Indian was taught finally that the virtues of peace were more to be desired than any attempt on his part to preserve his independence. In the place of his boundless realms, he was confined to small reservations; in lieu of his native food, he received scanty rations apportioned by the federal agents; and, instead of being a free man, he was the ward of the United States government.[69] After 1850, the Nevada Indian had many relations with the federal government, the discussion of which forms the theme of another chapter.

---

[69] Sarah Winnemucca Hopkins, *Life among the Paiutes*. This book discusses the reservation system and its effect on her people.

# Explorations in the "Unknown Land"

The Great Basin was the last portion of the United States to be explored; Nevada, the last area within this basin to be penetrated by the white man. Indeed, it was the "Northern Mystery" until well into the nineteenth century. As early as 1840, the maps of the United States were fairly correct for the territory between the Atlantic coast and the Rocky mountains; they were not wholly incorrect in tracing the Pacific coast line, but between the Rocky mountains and the Pacific coast as late as the date named there were only three features indicated, each delineated erroneously — the Colorado river flowed in a straight line from north to south; a wide stream, the Buenaventura river was shown to rise on the west slope of the Rocky mountains and flow south-westwardly across what is now Utah and Nevada into the Pacific ocean, halfway between the San Francisco Bay and the Santa Barbara Channel; and a third stream flowed out of "Youtaw" (Utah) Lake, across the northern part of Nevada into San Francisco Bay. The fur-traders were the only people who knew this to be untrue, but the fur-traders did not make maps.

The Spanish explored in the eastern and southern parts of the Great Basin. From 1540, when Coronado set out in pursuit of the Seven Cities of Cíbola, until the Spanish power declined in Mexico, the Spanish were carrying on explorations in the southwestern part of the United States. In 1609, they were successful in establishing their first outpost in Santa Fé, New Mexico; in 1769, the first one in California, San Diego. Other explorations were made and other settlements established, but in all of the wanderings of the Spanish explorers, there is no definite proof that a single one of them entered the boundaries of Nevada, unless it be Father Francisco Garcés. In 1774, he accompanied Captain Juan Bautista de Anza on his expedition to open an overland route from northern Mexico to San Francisco Bay. Captain Anza's route did not touch Nevada, probably, but it did prepare the way for Father Garcés to approach it. In 1776, Garcés received instructions from Antonio Bucareli, viceroy of New Spain, to continue his explorations in the vicinity of the Colorado river. His wanderings took him over the sandy stretches of the Mojave Desert and up the Colorado river for some distance. In the memoirs of his travels, he described his expeditions to the Jamajab and Yamaba Indians. When known to history, these Indians were the Mohaves who lived on the Colorado river between the Needles of California and the entrance to the Black cañon, Nevada.[70] So that Garcés, in his explorations up the Colorado river was probably either on or near the present boundary of southern Nevada.[71]

In 1776, the year Anza founded his colony on San Francisco Bay, the need was felt to open a direct route between Spain's most northern settlements – Santa Fé, New Mexico and Monterey, California. Besides their desire to explore a route between these two provinces, the missionaries of New Mexico wished to become acquainted with the Indians to the north and northwest of Santa Fé, with the idea of establishing missions among them. For this purpose, two Franciscan friars, Francisco Atanasio Domínguez and Silvestre Vélez de Escalante, led a company in a zigzag direction north-northwest from Santa Fé into what is now southern Utah. They did find out a great deal about the Indian tribes, but were unable to convert any of them to Christianity, nor were they successful in the main purpose for which they set out. Disagreements between the military and spiritual members of the party, the loss of their Laguna Indian guide, together with a heavy snowstorm, influenced the leaders to abandon the idea of going through to California at that time.

The party then turned south, and crossed the divide into

[70] Hodge, *op. cit.,* 919-921.

[71] For a detailed description of the routes of Anza and Garcés consult the following works: Bolton, *Anza's California expeditions,* and *Outpost of Empire;* and Coues, ed., *On the trail of a Spanish pioneer: the diary and itinerary of Francisco Garcés.*

the upper course of the Virgin river. From this point they turned northeast to the Colorado river, whence they found their way back to Santa Fé. When the Domínguez-Escalante party was on the Virgin river, it was on the eastern rim of the Great Basin, but at some distance from the Utah-Nevada line.[72] Nevada history, however, is interested in this expedition because through it trade between Santa Fé merchants and the Utah Indians was inaugurated, and later extended to the Indians in southeastern Nevada. The trail from Santa Fé to southern Utah was known as the Escalante Trail; its extension across southern Nevada to Los Angeles, made by the Mexicans a half century later, was called, erroneously, "The Old Spanish Trail."[73]

Nevada was approached by the Spaniards from still another direction — this time from the west. Lieutenant Gabriel Moraga, son of the first comandante of San Francisco, took part in forty-six expeditions against the Indians living in the interior valleys of California and in the foothills of the Sierra Nevada mountains. In 1819, while he was on an unsuccessful punitive expedition against the Mohave Indians, he was in the vicinity of the Nevada section of the Colorado river. A prominent historian thinks that he "got at, near, or over the Nevada line" at this time.[74]

The power of the Spaniards in the New World declined before this "Unknown Land" was explored or crossed by any of them. It was not their good fortune to "find a lake of gold, fabulous turquoise mines and the smoke hued Sierra Azul" which were supposed to be somewhere in the country north of Mexico. Nor did they discover "a north branch of the Colorado river, a second outlet, which, turning west across Nevada, merrily threaded its way through the high Sierra of California, and meandered to the ocean somewhere near the region . . . of San Francisco Bay."[75] It seemed a stroke

---

[72] Joseph J. Hill, "Spanish and Mexican explorations and trade northwest from New Mexico into the Great Basin," *Utah Historical Quarterly*, III, 3-23, January, 1930.

[73] *Infra*, 104-107.

[74] Reprinted from Charles E. Chapman, *A history of California; the Spanish period*, 433, by permission of The Macmillan Company.

[75] Reprinted from Bolton, *Outpost of Empire, the founding of San Francisco*, 12, by permission of Alfred A. Knopf, Inc.

of fate that the gold of California and the silver of Nevada were denied to the Spaniard in his lust for the precious metal. Spain's influence on Nevada was the place names – Las Vegas, Amargosa, and Esmeralda – applied, however, after the Spanish period.

Through the Spanish-American wars of independence, Spain lost control of Mexico. In 1821, the republic of Mexico took over the government of Alta California and New Mexico, parts of both of which are included in Nevada. The Mexican republic was incapable of organizing so vast a territory – [76] its government was a travesty, hence its great northern reaches were destined to fall into the hands of a more vigorous nation. However, from 1776 to Mormon days Spanish traders frequented the Great Basin.

Interest in the Nevada section of the Great Basin was manifested by more enterprising people than the Mexicans. American and British fur-trappers, each in search of untrapped beaver streams, were advancing toward the Great Basin. It was of little difference to the history of Nevada whether it was a Britisher or an American who first trapped on some stream in this state, but it was of prime importance that it was Americans who pushed the advancing line of the frontier settlements through the last bit of unexplored territory between the Atlantic and Pacific oceans. Since it was the operations of the fur companies which brought this to pass, a brief description of their activities in exploring Nevada is to the point.

The first white man known to have crossed the Great Basin was Jedediah Strong Smith. In 1826 Smith, twenty-eight years old, a native of New York, along with David E. Jackson and William Sublette, purchased the controlling interest in the Rocky Mountain Fur Company. Associated also with this firm was Thomas Fitzpatrick, "Broken Hand," about whom we shall hear more later. The trapping enterprises of this company centered around the Great Salt Lake and the region to the west – the Great Basin country. At this time the Nevada area was as much of a mystery to the trapper as it had been to the Spaniard.[77] To penetrate this unknown land to the west was the decision of the company. Smith, its

---

[76] Priestley, *The Mexican Nation,* chapters XII, XVIII.

[77] Dale, *The Ashley-Smith explorations,* 184.

chief executive and best educated member, as well as a man of imagination and experience, set out in the summer of 1826 to explore the country south and west of the lake. Experience had taught him that it would be folly to equip and send out a trapping expedition to an unknown land before explorations had been made in it.

Smith's journals have been found; the principal authentic information concerning his routes, however, is in letters he wrote, and in the records of the Mexican authorities in California. Late in August, 1826, he and his party of fifteen men set out in a south-southwest direction from the Great Salt Lake. Concerning this expedition, he wrote a letter to General William Clark, one of the leaders of the Lewis and Clark expedition and later superintendent of Indian affairs:

My situation in this country has enabled me to obtain information concerning a section which has hitherto been measurably veiled in obscurity to the citizens of the United States. I allude to the country S.W. of the Great Salt Lake west of the Rocky mountains.

I started about the 22nd of Aug., 1826 from the Great Salt Lake with a party of fifteen men for the purpose of exploring the country S.W. which was entirely unknown to me, and of which I could collect no satisfactory information from the Indians who inhabit this country on its N.E. borders.[78]

His course on leaving the lake took him south-southwest to Lake Sevier, then over the divide into Nevada, probably through the Meadow Valley Wash. This route would bring him into Nevada near the present town of Panaca, past which an old Indian trail led down the Muddy river to its junction with the Virgin. A short distance along the latter stream brought him to its confluence with the Colorado. While on the Muddy river he met a tribe of Indians which he called the Pa Ulches, who were undoubtedly the Paiutes. At the mouth of the Virgin he crossed to the east side of the Colorado, which he followed for four days. He found this country very barren, rocky, and mountainous, but farther down the river he came to a valley which opened out about five to fifteen miles in width.[79] Here he found a nation of Indians who called themselves Ammuchabas (Mohaves). He re-

---

[78] Reprinted herein by permission of the publishers, The Arthur H. Clark Company, from Dale's *Ashley-Smith Explorations*, 186-187.

[79] *Ibid.*, 189.

mained among them for a few days, during which time his
men and horses rested before they continued their journey
to California.

In December, he arrived at the San Gabriel Mission. A
Mexican law very definitely forbade the entrance of foreigners into California without proper passports. However, with
some difficulty, and aided by an American sea captain, W.
H. Cunningham, whose hide and tallow ship was then in
San Diego harbor, Smith and his men obtained the necessary
papers. These credentials were only to permit them to leave
the territory unmolested by the same route they entered it.
But the Smith party did not heed these instructions; instead,
they went into the valley east of the Coast range, where
there were no Mexican officials to question their movements.
Moving northward through the San Joaquin Valley, looking
for the San Buenaventura river as they went, they finally
arrived at the "Rancherías de Muquelemnes [Mokelumne]
y Cossines [Consumnes]." [80] Here, they trapped for a short
time before Smith thought he should report back to his
partners near Salt Lake. He tried to cross the Sierra Nevada
mountains in the early spring, but finding the snow too deep,
returned to the valley and remained with the Indians until
May.

There is nothing definitely known as to the exact route
Smith took across the mountains. It can be conjectured only
from the meager information to be gathered from the several sources bearing on the subject, the most important of
which were the letters concerning Smith's exact location
before setting out on his return journey. These data are
found in a letter written by Padre Durán to Comandante
Ygnacio Martínez on May 16, 1827, four days before Smith
set out. In this letter, Father Durán stated that for many
days the Americans had been camped at the "rancherías de
Muquelemnes y Cossines." In another letter from Martínez
to Governor Echeandia, he stated that he had been informed
by an Indian that the Americans were camped at the ranch-
ería of the "Muquelemnes." Here are two definite sources

80 Named for the two Indian tribes living between these two rivers. Hodge,
op. cit., 930.

for locating Smith and his party.[81] In addition to these letters, Smith wrote a letter to Padre Durán on May 19, 1827, in which he explained his motives for remaining in Mexican territory.[82]

On May 20, 1827, Smith and two companions, taking seven horses and two mules loaded with hay and provisions, started across the Sierra Nevada mountains. From the starting point fixed at the junction of the Mokelumne and the Consumnes rivers, his route eastward probably led up the ridge between these two streams to their sources in the mountains. (An old Indian trail and later an emigrant road led up to the mountains this way.) The snow on the top of the mountains was from four to eight feet deep, but its melting by day and freezing by night solidified the top so that the animals did not sink into it more than a foot.[83] The party crossed the mountains in eight days, having lost only two horses and one mule. The pass through which they went from the west to the east side of the Sierra can only be conjectured, but it is reasonable to believe it was through the Sonora Pass. The information for the crossing of the mountains at this point comes from two sources – the letter Smith wrote to Superintendent Clark, and the maps and the description of this country he sent to General William Henry Ashley of St. Louis, Smith's former employer. Ashley in turn sent this information to Albert Gallatin, who, in 1836, published his *Map of the Indian Tribes of America* – the most complete one of western America published up to that time.[84] These data, translated on paper by Gallatin, indicated two rivers flowing northward and parallel to each other; the map indicated that each river had two forks. There were no other identifying features. These rivers also ap-

[81] These letters may be found in the *Archivo del Arzobispado de San Francisco*, MS., V, part I, 27-33. In Bancroft Library.

[82] J. S. Smith to Durán, May 19, 1827, Department of State Papers, MS., II, 17-19. In Bancroft Library.

[83] Dale, *op. cit.*, 191-194.

[84] Albert Gallatin, "Synopsis of the Indian Tribes of North America," *Transactions and collections of the American Antiquarian Society*, II. A number of writers on this subject have advanced many different theories for Smith's route over the Sierra, but no two agree.

peared to disappear in the desert. To one who has a good knowledge of the terrain in this vicinity, the two streams may have been either forks of the Carson or of the Walker river, probably the latter, since it would have been crossed if Smith came through the Sonora Pass. If they had been the forks of the Carson, the journey homeward would not have been filled with the many difficulties which he described to Superintendent Clark:

> After travelling twenty days from the east side of Mount Joseph, I struck the S.W. corner of the Great Salt Lake, travelling over a country completely barren and destitute of game. We frequently travelled without water sometimes for two days over sandy deserts, where there was no sign of vegetation, and when we found water in some of the rocky hills, we most generally found some Indians who appeared the most miserable of the human race. . . When we arrived at the Salt Lake, we had but one horse and one mule remaining, which were so feeble and poor that they could scarce carry the little camp equipage which I had along; the balance of my horses I was compelled to eat as they gave out.[85]

Assuming that Smith crossed the two forks of the Walker river, he would have entered Nevada just south of Walker Lake, but he must not have seen that body of water, or it would seem reasonable that it would have been included on Gallatin's map. If he had crossed the Carson river, his route would have taken him north, and he would have returned to Salt Lake probably by the Humboldt river, information of which would undoubtedly have found its way to Gallatin. Along the Humboldt Route, especially in the spring of the year, he would have found good grass, plenty of game, and water most of the way.

The description of his crossing central Nevada south of Walker Lake checked with the difficulties one would have on such a journey even at the present time. There is very little water, practically no grass for livestock, no game, and the wretched condition of the Indians living in this region, all favor a route from the Sonora Pass across the two forks of the Walker river and northeastward through Mineral,

[85] There is no way to identify Mount Joseph. It may be one of the many peaks in the Sierra or it may refer to the entire chain. Reprinted herein by permission of the publishers, The Arthur H. Clark Company, from Dale's *Ashley-Smith Explorations*, 193.

Nye, and White Pine counties, Nevada, to the southwest corner of the Great Salt Lake.[86]

The reader may question the reason for so much discussion of Smith's route across the Sierra Nevada mountains and the state of Nevada. The answer lies in the facts that he was one of the first American pathfinders of the West; he was one of the first explorers of the unknown region west of the Great Salt Lake; he was the first white man to connect the East with the West; had he lived he probably would have established a fur business on the California coast similar to Astor's at the mouth of the Columbia; and, finally, no pioneer ever endured the hardships of western travel with greater heroism.[87] He is of particular interest to Nevada history because he was the first American to furnish information concerning the Nevada area of the Great Basin. Jedediah Strong Smith was the real pioneer of this state.

While still other American fur-traders were pushing westward into the heart of the Great Basin, the huge commercial empire of the Hudson's Bay Company, with headquarters at Fort Vancouver, was extending its trapping enterprises up the Columbia and its tributaries to the south and east. Fort Boisé and Fort Hall in southern Idaho were the factories for the trappers operating along the Snake river, several tributaries of which rise in northern Nevada. Peter Skene Ogden, the son of a Tory who had fled to Canada after the American Revolution, was the most prominent and earliest trapper in this field. He served his apprenticeship with the North West Company and then transferred to the Hudson's Bay Company.[88]

In 1824 Ogden, having been appointed chief trader to the Snake river country, set out on his first expedition to trap

---

[86] For further information on Smith's route over the Sierra and across to Salt Lake consult "First Crossing of the Sierra Nevada," *Sierra Club Bulletin,* XI (1923); "Eastward Route of Jedediah S. Smith, 1827," *California Historical Quarterly,* II (1923-1924), 344-349.

[87] Smith made a second trip to California. Dale, *op. cit.,* 229-230.

[88] Jessie Hughes Davies, "The expedition of Peter Skene Ogden in the Snake river region, with a brief survey of previous travel and exploration in that region," M.A. thesis, MS., University of California, 1925. A map of Ogden's journeys in northern Nevada and southern Idaho accompanies this thesis.

on the main stream and its tributaries. In the following years he made five expeditions at the head of the Snake brigade, during which time he blazed his way up and down and back and forth on three drainage systems in the northwest — of which one, the Humboldt River Basin, is in northern Nevada. He made familiar to the trapping fraternity the territory that had been heretofore shrouded in mystery; he led his trappers along practically every one of the numerous tributaries, both large and small, of the Snake river. The most important tributary to the Snake from the south is the Owyhee river, several branches of which rise in northeastern Nevada.[89] Farther south in the great desert he came upon the Humboldt river, which he named the "Unknown River." In 1825-1829, he trapped on it from its source to the "Big Bend." To the trapper, it was known as Ogden's river. Indeed, it was called by that name long after Frémont named it for the German explorer, Alexander von Humboldt, who, incidentally, never saw it. To Ogden's men, it was known as Paul's river, so named because Paul, one of their comrades, sickened, died, and was buried on its banks — probably the first white man to be buried in Nevada.[90]

The monetary return to the Hudson's Bay Company from the hitherto untrapped streams in Nevada was gratifying, but Ogden's permanent contribution to geography was even more so. The information which he gave Arrowsmith, the London map maker, concerning the topography of his trapping territory, resulted in making known probably for the first time that a stream did not wend its way through the Sierra Nevada mountains to the Pacific ocean.

When the bright red pennant of the British fur company with its magical "H. B. C." emblazoned in white upon it, flew from the bastions of Fort Hall and Fort Boisé, to signify that all of the territory explored by this company's trappers was British, there was no Mexican authority closer than San Francisco to challenge its claim to northern California, Nevada, and Utah. There were, however, American

---

[89] *Et supra,* 29.

[90] T. C. Elliott, "Peter Skene Ogden Journals," *Oregon Historical Society Quarterly,* vol. II.

trappers of the Rocky Mountain Fur Company competing with the British for the right to claim the territory.

Down in the southwest along the Colorado the story of the fur-trapping industry was quite another one. No one except Mexicans could legally obtain a license to trap on a stream within Mexican territory. Mexicans, however, would not trap, so the industry fell without competition into the hands of Americans. The clandestine nature of their business in this region makes it difficult to piece together the story of the Americans and their explorations in southern Nevada.[91] From what is now known about their activities, they carried on trapping operations along the Colorado river on the edge of Nevada between 1826 and 1832. During these years, the trappers followed up and down this river and crossed it to California by at least six different trails, several of which took them into southern Nevada.

Sylvester Pattie and his son, James Ohio Pattie, contributed largely to the opening of the region on both sides of the Colorado. The Patties, native Kentuckians, began trapping operations as early as 1824 in the Rocky mountains and in New Mexico. In 1826, a few months before Jedediah Smith went down the Colorado, the elder Pattie and some of his men made a trail up that stream from the Gila river to the Mohave Indian country. This tribe demanded tribute from them for the privilege of trapping in these waters, but Pattie refused to pay it. In the skirmishes which followed, two of Pattie's men and sixteen Indians were killed. Leaving the Mohave villages and proceeding on a northerly course, Pattie said the "Red river [Colorado] at this point bears a north course, and affords an abundance of the finest lands." He and his party continued up the stream until "they reached a point of the river where the mountains shut in so close upon the shores that . . . they were compelled to climb a mountain and travel along the acclivity, the river still in sight, and at an immense depth beneath." (Undoubtedly,

---

[91] Fur-traders belonging to companies had their headquarters at Taos and Santa Fé, New Mexico. Many of their papers and records were later scattered and lost. Joseph John Hill, "Ewing Young in the fur-trade of the far southwest, 1822-1834," *Oregon Historical Quarterly*, XXIV, no. 1, p. 19.

the party came to the series of cañons, Eldorado, Black, and Boulder, between Nevada and Arizona.) Following along the river on the ridges, they came to a point "where the river emerges from these horrid mountains which so cage it up." [92]

In 1829, another American party led by Ewing Young, a Tennesseean, for some years a trader and trapper in New Mexico, took a northwest course over the Old Spanish Trail or Escalante Trail into southern Utah, and then proceeded southwest over the route probably followed by Smith to California. In the following year, Young and William Wolfskill, a Kentucky trapper, formed a partnership the purpose of which was to trap the interior streams of California. The Young-Wolfskill expedition passed through southern Nevada to the Mohave villages and thence by way of the Cajon Pass, to Los Angeles.[93] By 1830 southern Nevada was fairly well known to the trapping fraternity; central Nevada had been crossed (though only from west to east); the extreme northern part had been more extensively covered by Ogden and his men, and the southern part of the state had seen the activities of the New Mexican traders and trappers.

In 1833, the northern section of the state was explored more thoroughly by a quasi-official expedition under the direction of Captain Benjamin Louis Eulalé de Bonneville, on leave from the United States army. He organized and elaborately outfitted a company to trap in the vicinity of the Great Salt Lake. In his company were some of the best American trappers to be found in the Rocky mountains. Among them was Joseph Reddeford Walker, formerly a Santa Fé trader, whom Bonneville selected as his chief lieutenant for the expedition, which he sent into the country west of the lake.

On July 24, 1833, Walker and his company of thirty-five or forty men started westward to explore the region immediately west of the lake and to have "all its secrets revealed . . . to keep a journal, and minutely to record the events of his journey, and everything curious or interesting, making maps or charts of his route, and of the surrounding country." [94] From the facts now known, although Captain Bonne-

---

[92] Hill, *op. cit.*, 16-17.

[93] Cleland, *A History of California: The American period*, 82-86.

[94] Reprinted from Leonard, *op. cit.*, ed. W. F. Wagner, 145, by permission of The Burrows Brothers Company.

ville did not give out this detail to his raconteur, Washington Irving, in *Bonneville's Adventures*,[95] the intended destination of the party was from the first, California. Everything points to the fact that Walker was directed to go there — the details of the expedition were very carefully planned, indicating a long journey; furthermore, several members of the party declared that they joined the expedition in order to go to California. Zenas Leonard, the clerk of the expedition, said the "division under the command of a Mr. Walker was ordered to steer through an unknown country toward the Pacific." [96] He further stated he was anxious to go to the coast of the Pacific, and for that purpose hired with Mr. Walker as clerk, for a certain sum per year.

No explanation can be given why Captain Bonneville withheld the real intention of the journey from Washington Irving, unless it had some bearing on his position in the army. The captain undoubtedly knew of the Mexican law forbidding the presence of foreigners in Mexican territory without a passport; [97] and the sending of an expedition into this region might compromise the United States government. And, then, too, Bonneville had overstayed his leave and had been dropped from the army; he was seeking readmittance when he was telling his story to Irving. Moreover, this part of his expedition had been very expensive. It resulted in a financial failure, information of which he may not have wanted to disclose to his business associates in New York. Whatever the hypothesis, the historical and geographical contributions of the expedition were highly important.

Walker led his party north to Bear river, where they encountered a band of Indians. From these natives they learned something of the hardships they would suffer in crossing the desert. Taking heed of this advice, they killed some buffalo and dried the meat. On August 13, 1833, they took a westerly course over "extensive and barren plains," — the Great Salt Desert. Water was very scarce so they followed the well-beaten trails of the Indians from water hole to water hole. At one of these springs on the edge of the

[95] Irving, *Bonneville's Adventures*, 345-349.

[96] Wagner, *op. cit.*, 147.

[97] Some of these trappers must have known of the difficulties that Smith and Pattie encountered with the Mexican authorities.

desert, an Indian chief described to them the southwest route
they were to follow so as to reach the headwaters of the
Humboldt river. Continuing westward for some distance,
the party came to the south fork of the Humboldt at the
foot of the Ruby range of mountains. It was easy traveling
northward to the main river. Noting the lack of trees along
its banks, Walker called it the "Barren river." Some trapping was done as they went down stream, but the Indians
were a constant annoyance. When the party reached the
Humboldt-Carson sinks, the attitude of the Indians was so
menacing that Walker gave orders to his men to fire upon
them. In the battle that followed thirty-nine Indians were
killed. To the number of shallow pools in this region, resembling small lakes, Walker gave the name of "Battle
Lakes." [98] After he crossed the Forty-mile Desert, he followed the Carson river to its source in the Sierra Nevada
mountains, the summit of which he reached on October 16,
twelve weeks after leaving the lake. Several days were spent
on the eastern ridges of the mountains before they found
a pass which led them down into the San Joaquin Valley and
thence to Monterey, California.[99] On February 14, of the
following year, Walker and most of the members of the
original party started on the return trip. A few days were
spent along the western base of the Sierra Nevada mountains, during which time they were looking for a suitable
pass to cross at that time of year. In their search they came
upon a band of Indians who led them through a pass south
of Owen's Lake. (A decade later, Frémont gave Walker's
name to this pass.) [100] They advanced eastward into the
desert region of western Nevada (southern Esmeralda
county) where they turned northward until they came to the
lake and river which later was also to bear Walker's name.
The Walker river was followed to the Big Bend, then a
short journey over some low ridges, and the party was on
the Carson. They followed its course to the sink, then,
crossed the Forty-mile Desert to the Barren river (the

---

[98] Reprinted from Wagner, *op. cit.*, 167; *et supra*, II, 53-55, by permission of
The Burrows Brothers Company.

[99] *Ibid.*, 191.

[100] *Ibid.*, 231.

Humboldt), the trail along which led them back to the Great Salt Lake.[101]

The Walker expedition is of prime importance to the history of the West, and especially to Nevada. In the first place, this Tennessee trapper deserves the distinction of being the first white man and first American to have made the round trip from the Great Salt Lake by the Humboldt river to the Pacific coast. His route was destined to be the one over which, a few years later, the thousands of gold seekers went to California; later, part of it became the route of the first transcontinental railroad. Walker's maps were turned over to the war department by Bonneville, thereby giving the federal government its first information of this territory.[102] Walker's journey across Nevada to California was the last of the great organized attempts to find un-trapped streams in the Great Basin.

Independent trappers continued their activities for a few more years, but the first great industry of the West was declining, and by 1840, the profits had almost vanished. However, the achievements of the American trappers were to endure and exceed in importance their monetary returns. One of the most important of the fur-trader's contributions to American history was the inauguration of a regular trade between the Mississippi river and the Pacific ocean; a second and a most significant effect of the fur industry on the West was the number of Americans who settled in the Mexican provinces; and a third result, probably the greatest, were the reports and stories brought back to the eastern states. Many of these tales found their way into the local newspapers. Illustrative is the one called the "Narrative of Zenas Leonard," which described the Walker-Bonneville expedition, and was published in the *Clearfield Republican* in Pennsylvania. [103]

While these trappers were engaged in their industry they were avidly though unscientifically exploring the great West,

[101] Wagner, *op. cit.*, 239.

[102] These maps were a great aid to Bonneville in seeking reinstatement to the army. President Jackson restored his rank in 1836.

[103] It was this story which W. F. Wagner edited in his book of the same name.

opening the different routes to the coast, familiarizing themselves with the resources of the far West, learning how to
get along in the rugged wastes without food and water, and
laying the foundation for the completion of Manifest Destiny. All of this information made them invaluable guides
for the later government exploring expeditions and the emigrant trains. "Thus, before government explorer, pioneer
settler, or gold seeker crossed the Sierra into California,
came the forerunner of all — the fur-hunter of the far
West." [104]

In 1840, close upon the heels of the last trappers, came
the first American emigrants. Indeed, it was one of these
trappers and traders, Antoine Roubidoux, who aroused sufficient enthusiasm in Platte county, Missouri, over California's climate and soil to bring about the organization of "The
Western Emigration Society." Roubidoux's enthusiasm was
supported by letters from Dr. John Marsh, an American
who in 1837 had bought a large ranch near Mt. Diablo,
California.[105] His letters were published in the Missouri
newspapers. Roubidoux gave assurance to one who inquired
about the chills and fevers in California, that, "There never
was but one man in California who had the chills. He was
from Missouri and carried the disease in his system. It was
such a curiosity to see a man shake with the chills that the
people of Monterey went eighteen miles into the country to
see him." [106] The purpose of the society was to unite people
who were going overland to California. The members wrote
letters to possible emigrants in the neighboring states and
collected data relating to routes, methods of travel, and information regarding the rights of foreigners in the Mexican
provinces. A pledge was circulated which bound the signers
to meet the following May at Sapling Grove on the Missouri
river in eastern Kansas, and to have the proper equipment
for travel to the Pacific coast. In a month's time, over five
hundred had signed the pledge to be ready the following
spring to start on the long journey.

However, before the coming of the spring of 1841, en-

104 Reprinted from Cleland, *op. cit.*, 89, by permission of The Macmillan
Company.
105 Cleland, *op. cit.*, 99.
106 Reprinted from *ibid.*, 100, by permission of The Macmillan Company.

thusiasm for California had waned. Instead of the five hundred setting out, not more than sixty-nine put in an appearance at the appointed rendezvous. Ugly rumors about the treatment of Americans in California went around to the members. The hazards of the different routes discouraged many of them. The only member of the party who had signed the original pledge was John Bidwell. He was a New Yorker, twenty years of age, who in 1839 had come to Missouri in search of health. John Bartleson, a settler in the neighborhood, was elected captain of the company. He had not been a member of the first group, and therefore, had not familiarized himself with the routes or the necessities for traveling in the West. Bidwell, on the other hand, had collected some maps and other data on the subject. Most of this material dealt with the country east of the Great Salt Lake. No member of the party knew anything of the region embracing the Great Basin. Of this lack of knowledge, John Bidwell wrote some years later:

We knew that California lay west, and that was the extent of our knowledge. Some of the maps consulted, supposed to be correct, showed a lake in the vicinity of where Salt Lake now is; it was represented as a long lake, three or four hundred miles in extent, narrow, and with two outlets, both running into the Pacific Ocean, either apparently larger than the Mississippi.[107]

So far as any member of this party was concerned, the Buenaventura river still flowed to the Pacific. So prevalent was this conception of a river flowing supposedly from Great Salt Lake across Nevada and through the Sierra Nevada mountains to the Pacific ocean, that Bidwell was advised to take tools with which to build canoes when he arrived at the lake. The party believed they could float from the Great Salt Lake to California.[108]

To this meager knowledge of the details of the route was added poor leadership in the election of Bartleson as captain. It is a question open to speculation what tragedies might

[107] John Bidwell, "California," MS., 32-33; *Echoes of the Past about California*, 6-13.

[108] No member of the Bidwell-Bartleson party could have seen a copy of Bonneville's map. It is the first American-made map to show the true course of the Humboldt river. Bancroft, *History of Utah*, 26.

have befallen this first emigrant party to California with all of its handicaps, had it not joined a missionary party bound for Oregon, piloted by the famous guide, Thomas Fitzpatrick. The superior knowledge of this well-known trapper concerning the West probably saved the party from complete disaster. He tried to persuade all of them to go on the known trail with him, but they had set California as their goal.

On May 19, 1841, fourteen wagons and eighty-one persons set out on the trapper's trail, later known as the Oregon Trail, which extended up the Platte river and over the South Pass to Soda Springs, about forty-five miles southeast of the present Pocatello, Idaho. At the springs, Fitzpatrick, the missionary party, and thirty-two of the Bartleson party separated from the rest of them and went on to Oregon. In this party went most of the married men with families. The rest turned southwest, and headed toward California. In this division there was one lone woman, Mrs. Benjamin Kelsey, who was with her husband and young daughter, America. (Other members of this party who became prominent later were Bidwell, Bartleson, and Joseph B. Chiles.) The route to California was unknown to anyone in the party. Even Fitzpatrick was able only to give them what information he had learned from the trappers. A guide was sought at Fort Hall to take them across the desert country, but none was available. They knew they were to keep as nearly due west as possible after leaving the Great Salt Lake. If they bore too far north, they would lose themselves in the labyrinth of broken and ill-defined mountain ranges north of the Humboldt river; if they went too far south, they would reach a desolate desert region, with strong possibilities of death by thirst. However, with these indefinite and disheartening instructions, they pressed on across the Great Salt Lake Desert where at times they traveled as long as twenty-four hours without a drop of water. After leaving this desert, upon which some of their wagons had to be abandoned, their objective was the head of Mary's or Ogden's river (Humboldt river), but no one in the party knew where it was. On September 9, Captain Bartleson and a companion rode ahead to find it. It took five days' travel to reach the headwaters of the river.[109]

It was now the middle of September. If greater progress were not made, winter would set in before they could reach the mountains. So, on September 15, they decided to leave the rest of the wagons, and "pack" through to California. Several days' travel brought them to the Ruby range and the South Fork of the Humboldt. Uncertain as to what this stream was, they decided to follow it to its mouth; it brought them finally to Mary's or Ogden's river. Descending the river to its sink, a portion of the company, which had the best animals, parted from the others and went on faster. They hoped to reach California before becoming completely exhausted. The rest of the party crossed the desert to Carson river and then turned south, in which direction after short travel, they came to Walker river, which they named the "Balm." While the party was camped on the Walker not far from Walker Lake, there was some difference of opinion among the members as to whether they should cross the mountains, or whether they should turn back and return to Fort Hall. The decision was to go on. On the morning of October 16, just when the party was about to start out, they saw dust rising on the trail over which they had traveled the preceding day. It proved to be the nine men who had left the party at the sink. They had gone too far south to Walker Lake, where the Indians had given them some pine nuts and fish. This fare had made them sick, so they were very happy to be back again with the rest of the party. The company, now reunited, worked its way up the west branch of Walker river with some difficulty. They reached the summit of the Sierra Nevada mountains, deeply covered with snow, on October 18. The descent into the San Joaquin Valley was made by the way of the Stanislaus river. On November 4, 1841, after having been six months on the way, they reached Dr. Marsh's ranch at the foot of Mt. Diablo.[110]

The paramount interest attached to the Bidwell-Bartleson party and its successful trip to California lay in the fact that

[109] Charles Kelly, *Salt Desert Trails,* 32.

[110] Bidwell, "California," 36-40; George D. Lyman, *John Marsh, Pioneer,* 243.

it was the first emigrant party to cross the Great Basin; Mrs. Kelsey was the first woman to cross the Nevada desert. Of such stuff was pioneer woman made! Several members of this party returned to the states and guided emigrant parties over their route. Among these was Chiles, who returned to the states the following year. In 1843, he organized a company bound for California which followed the same route, as did the Bidwell-Bartleson party, as far as Fort Hall. At that place, the party divided, Chiles and a few men took a new route to California by way of Fort Boise, the Malheur and Pit rivers, while the rest of the party in wagons, guided by Joseph Walker, took the Humboldt-Walker river route to Walker Pass, and thence went on to California. The wagons of this party were the first to cross Nevada.[111]

Three hundred years had elapsed between the time the Spanish first approached Nevada and the year the first emigrant train crossed the state. During these years, the Great Basin had been circled, and had been crossed many times by the trappers; the "Unknown Land" had become familiar as a long stretch of desert and sagebrush, almost devoid of water or food. Two routes, however, had been quite definitely marked out across the state – the northern one by way of the Humboldt river, and the southern one extending from southern Utah to the Muddy river and the Mohave villages.

Interest in the far West had been growing steadily in congress; it had been stimulated by the proponents of Manifest Destiny. To learn scientifically of the possibilities of this vast region, known as the Great American Desert, was one of the underlying reasons for the organization of the exploring parties which the federal government sent out to the Pacific coast.

---

[111] Bancroft, *History of Nevada, Colorado, and Wyoming*, 56.

# With Frémont in Nevada

The first official exploring expedition to the Great Basin was led by Captain John Charles Frémont. This undertaking was the result of the influence of the doctrine of Manifest Destiny advanced by that group of expansionists belonging to the generation of Henry Clay and Andrew Jackson. The extension of the United States to the Pacific ocean, the completion of continent-wide boundaries, the annexation of California, and the development of the enormous natural wealth in this vast area were part of the program of these avid expansionists. One of the most ardent proponents of this ultra-American viewpoint was Thomas Hart Benton, for thirty years United States senator from Missouri. In 1841, his independent and clever daughter, Jessie, married Captain Frémont, then a second lieutenant in the topographical engineers of the United States army. Through Senator Benton's influence with the federal government, Lieutenant Frémont was to accomplish the exploration of the territory between the Missouri river and the Pacific ocean.

In his first expedition Frémont did not enter Nevada territory, an account of which, accordingly, does not belong in a history of this state. But it was significant inasmuch as it was the beginning of his career as an explorer. From a geographic standpoint, the chief importance of this expedition was derived from the careful surveys he made of the South Pass, the natural gateway through the Rocky mountains to the West. From an historical viewpoint, it was outstanding; it stimulated greatly the emigration to the West.[112]

Frémont's second expedition was organized, like the first, under the authority and direction of Colonel J. J. Abert, chief of the topographical engineers of the United States army. It was by virtue of this fact an official expedition — the expenses were borne by the federal government, and the

[112] Cleland, *A history of California: The American period*, 131.

commander of the expedition was an army officer. The primary object of Frémont was to make a reconnaissance of the country as far as the Pacific ocean, and to connect his explorations with those made in 1841 by Lieutenant Charles Wilkes, commander of a United States naval squadron.[113]

The personnel of the first official exploration party to enter the boundaries of Nevada was interesting. There was gathered together a distinguished and well-known group of mountaineers, pathfinders, and guides. In it were Americans, Germans, Creoles, Canadian-Frenchmen, one free negro, and two Delaware Indians. Thomas Fitzpatrick, of whom Frémont said that "many years of hardship and exposure in the western territories had rendered him familiar with a portion of the country it was designed to explore," [114] was selected as his principal guide. He was to act also in the capacity of quartermaster, and for a part of the journey, commander of one of the divisions. Fitzpatrick's protégé and very good friend, Christopher ("Kit") Carson, joined the party at Bent's Fort, the present Pueblo, Colorado.[115] He had become famous through the prominent part he had taken in Frémont's first expedition. Frémont's assistant in topography was Charles Preuss, a well-trained German scientist who had also been on the first expedition; Louis Zindel, a Prussian artilleryman, assisted by two other members of the party, was placed in charge of the only piece of ordnance in the equipment; Theodore Talbot, whose unpublished diary in the Library of Congress gives us so much new, fresh information on the movements of the expedition, was in this company, as was Alexander Godey, companion and good friend of Kit Carson.[116]

The equipment of the expedition was carefully chosen. Every necessary instrument [117] for carrying on a scientific

[113] Ibid., 132.

[114] Frémont, Exploring Expedition, 426.

[115] Fitzpatrick had picked up Carson in Taos, New Mexico, in 1831, when he was a "short, stockily built youth with bandy legs, blue-gray eyes and light hair." Le Roy Hafen and W. G. Ghent, Broken Hand, 87.

[116] Ibid., 140.

[117] It is of interest to note here that his barometers were broken before he reached Nevada, so that his estimates as to altitude had to be determined from the boiling point of water. The instruments consisted of one refracting

expedition was furnished by the government. A light covered wagon mounted on good springs, carried the instruments, while twelve carts, each drawn by two mules, carried the camp equipage and provisions. As an innovation in a scientific expedition, Frémont obtained permission from Colonel (afterwards General) Stephen Watts Kearny, commander of the army at St. Louis, to take with him a twelve pound howitzer, designed probably to teach the Indians the virtues of peace. Since the cannon is the only permanent souvenir of the party left in Nevada, more will be heard about it later in the story.

Frémont, with every detail apparently settled, bade farewell to his young wife and set out from St. Louis. On May 17, 1843, he arrived at the junction of the Kansas and Missouri rivers (the present site of Kansas City, known then as Westport). This small community was the last town where one could get supplies for the long westward journey. While he was waiting for his party to assemble at this point, an official order from the war department, addressed to him at his home in St. Louis, was opened by his wife. The order commanded him to return to Washington at once, and to explain why a peaceful, scientific expedition should take along a cannon. His prudent wife, realizing an eventuality which might lead to difficulties, and possibly to the abandonment of the expedition if he received the order, sent a message forward by fast carrier in which she urged him to get under way without delay. Mrs. Frémont gave no reason for her ambiguous message. The courier returned to her in a few days carrying the brief reply, "Goodbye, I trust you and go." [118] The government order went forward by regular steamboat, but Frémont had started, and the howitzer was still a part of the camp equipage.

From the Kansas landing the general route of the expedition was along the Oregon Trail as far as South Pass, where it turned south to the Great Salt Lake. Frémont, after having spent some time exploring this body of water,

telescope, one reflecting circle, two sextants, one pocket chronometer no. 837, one pocket chronometer no. 739, one syphon barometer, one cistern barometer, six thermometers, and a number of small compasses. Frémont, *op. cit.*, 170.

[118] Nevins, *Frémont,* 142-146.

went back to the emigrant road to Oregon. From there he proceeded west to the Snake river, which he followed down to the Columbia. Once on that stream it was easy for the party to reach the Pacific ocean and to accomplish the object of the expedition. On November 5 Frémont, having gone forward more rapidly than the rest of the party, arrived at the Dalles. From there he sent word back to Fitzpatrick to abandon the carts at the mouth of the Walla Walla river, and come on with everything packed on the animals. Leaving Carson in charge of his division, Frémont and several of his men went down in canoes to Fort Vancouver. At this fort, the headquarters of the Hudson's Bay Company for the West, he was cordially received by the chief factor. From him, Frémont purchased a large quantity of supplies, with which he prepared for the homeward journey. His orders were now fully executed – he had made a reconnaissance as far as the Pacific, and he had connected his explorations with those of Commander Wilkes. There was nothing to prevent his choosing a different route home.[119]

For the journey back to the states, Frémont mapped out an entirely different route from that by which he had come west. He had three principal fields in mind for further exploration – the Klamath Lake region, from which the Sacramento river was supposed to flow, the Mary's Lake, lying somewhere between the Great Salt Lake and the Sierra Nevada mountains, and the Buenaventura river, which was so far as he knew still flowing to the Pacific ocean. This river was the same mythical stream which appeared on the early Spanish and later American maps. They indicated that it rose in the Rocky mountains, flowed into the Great Salt Lake, and then out of it across the northern part of Nevada and into the Pacific.[120]

On November 25, 1843, with one hundred and four mules and horses, provisions for not less than three months, some California cattle, the camp equipage packed on the animals,

[119] Frémont, *Exploring Expedition*, III.

[120] "Frémont's report shows that in his expeditions he had not seen, or did not care to give heed to, the previously published history and map of the explorations of Bonneville." Bancroft, *History of Nevada, Colorado, and Wyoming,* 5, fn. 59.

and the howitzer as the only wheeled carriage, the party set out toward southeastern Oregon. Lower Klamath Lake (the most northern lake of this group) was reached on December 10. The party spent two days here before it started out on the journey that was one of exploration and discovery all of the way, and "where the imaginary maps of the country, instead of assisting," Frémont said, "exposed us to suffering and defeat." [121] He expected fully to recruit the animals, and rest the party "on the banks of the Buenaventura, where, in the softer climate of a more southern latitude," they would be away from the "rigors of winter and from the inhospitable desert." [122] Little did anyone in the party realize the hardships that were in store for him before he would repose in the "softer climate" of California.

The course of the party from now on was to the east and south. It passed first a series of lakes, each named by Frémont. On Christmas eve they were camped on Christmas Lake (Warner Lake on some maps), where on the following morning the gun crew awakened the party by firing a salute in honor of the day. This was the last time the cannon was fired until many years later, when it was used in Virginia City, Nevada.[123] The day after Christmas the party camped on the Oregon-Nevada line, now the boundary of Washoe county, and about ten miles east of the California line. It may be noted that from the time Frémont left South Pass he was outside of the definite boundaries of the United States. The Oregon territory was then, however, being jointly occupied by Great Britain and the United States. When he crossed into Nevada, he was in Mexican territory.[124] Since this chapter is primarily concerned with Frémont's explorations in Nevada, officially commissioned to dispel the general ignorance of the characteristics of this part of the Great Basin, a more detailed description of his movements is given.

After crossing into Nevada, Frémont and his party con-

---

[121] Frémont, *Exploring Expedition*, 118.

[122] *Ibid.*, 123.

[123] *Infra*, 92-94.

[124] The 42nd parallel was the definitive boundary agreed upon between the United States and Spain in the Treaty of 1819. Thomas Maitland Marshall, *A History of the Western Boundary of the Louisiana Purchase, 1819-1841*, 46-70.

tinued up Twelve-mile Creek for a short distance, and then turned up a branch to the left, where an Indian trail led them to a pass in the mountains. At this point, coming upon some large cedars covered with frost, indicating, he thought, the nearness of water, Frémont began to look for Mary's (Humboldt) Lake. Descending the mountains, the party came into another basin, "on the flat bed of which," Frémont said, "we found no water" (Dry Lake or Alkali Lake), but on the edge of which camp was made because green grass was found (the upper extension of Long Valley). They continued down this valley "bordered by steep mountainous ridges rising very abruptly from the plain." This route led them "towards a range of hills in the southeast." The sky soon became so dark with snow that little could be seen of the surrounding country; they reached the summit of the hills in a heavy snowstorm.

Due to the cloudiness and the gradual ascent, the party was surprised to find themselves on the summit of a series of broken mountains, which declined very rapidly as far as they could see. A grassy hollow at the head of one of the hills was noticed, and Frémont decided to follow it. It led fortunately to a small stream (the headwaters of High Rock Creek) where a willow grove gave them a sheltered camp for the night. A few years later an old emigrant trail – the Applegate Cutoff to Oregon, followed through this way.[125]

On December 30, the party followed High Rock Creek in a southerly direction, where it entered a cañon they could not follow (High Rock cañon rises about eight hundred feet above the creek). They were determined not to leave the creek. Frémont said, "we searched a passage below, and entered a regular narrow valley. . . From our position, it was reasonable to conclude that this stream would find its outlet in Mary's Lake. . . We had descended rapidly. . . On both sides, the mountains showed often stupendous and curious-looking rocks. . . It was a singular place to travel through . . . a sort of chasm, the little strip of grass under

[125] Here in February, 1911, Harry Cambron, Peter Arramouspé, Bert Indiano, and J. B. Laxague were murdered by Shoshone Mike and his band of Indians. Their bodies were found near this willow grove.

our feet, the rough walls of bare rock on either hand, and the narrow strip of sky above." [126]

Instead of finding Mary's Lake, as they had expected, after an hour's ride, they came into a valley. Before them lay one of the dry basins, which after some search and a descent of several hundred feet, led into a long, broad basin through which another stream flowed. (This stream is Soldier Creek, which flows through Soldier Meadows.) On the edge of this stream, the party spent a gloomy New Year's eve. The going had so far been very hard on the animals.

New Year's day, 1844, was spent by the party continuing down the valley over a very rough road where the sand was covered with a "saline efflorescence." (They were on the western edge of the Black Rock Desert, where they saw the rocky, jagged, and broken, black cape that was to be a landmark to the early emigrants going over the Applegate or Lassen Cutoff.) The dense fog continued to blur the landscape so completely that Frémont's people could not see more than one hundred yards ahead. The men sent out for the horses became bewildered and were lost for several hours. This event delayed the party until late in the afternoon. Frémont now became worried; he had reached a position where, according to the best maps he had in his possession, he should have found Mary's Lake or river. (His maps were correct, for the Black Cape and the Mary's or Humboldt river directly east of it some sixty miles, were on the same latitude.) Frémont, however, thought he was on the verge of the desert against which he had been warned, so instead of going east toward the Mary's river, he bore toward the south, keeping close to the mountains in the full expectation of reaching the Buenaventura river. The animals were becoming so lame and fatigued from lack of water and good grass that he ordered every man to dismount. As they traveled some seven or eight miles along the ridge bordering the desert, they noticed that the rocks composing the mountains had changed to white (Granite range). A few miles further around the western point of the ridge, they came to a desert (Granite Creek Desert) where they camped for

---

[126] Frémont, *Exploring Expedition*, 129.

the night. The condition of the animals continued to worry Frémont.

On January 6, the fog blurred the horizon so completely that Frémont, Preuss, and Carson ascended the mountain so as to get a view of the surrounding country. When they reached the summit the fog had partially lifted and they saw in the distance, some sixteen miles, "a lofty column of smoke, indicating hot springs." Frémont determined to go toward them, at which place he thought there should be grass. After a hard day's travel over "ground of yielding mud and sand," (Granite Creek Desert merges into Mud Lake) they reached the boiling springs (Gerlach). They were of great interest to him; he made careful observations of the temperature and contents of the water.

The continued loss of animals from fatigue forced Frémont to take two precautionary measures – he explored the route fifteen or twenty miles in advance of the train, and he did not leave one encampment until another was found.[127] After a thorough exploration of the neighboring valleys was made, a good camping place with water and grass was finally located. While in search for this camp site, they came upon a plainly marked trail and some horse tracks (the Indian trail that led north from the southern end of Pyramid Lake). "On the western mountains of the valley, with which this of the boiling spring communicates" (Lake range), they saw scattered cedars which they thought indicated "the timbered region extending to the Pacific." Indians began to appear from all directions; they prowled around their camp like "wild animals." [128]

On January 10, Frémont and his companions continued to search out a good camping site, but the finding of the Indian trail relieved him from the further search for suitable places. Continuing south, they reached the end of a basin where good grass was found. "Leaving a signal for the rest of the party to encamp," they followed up the ravine to see what was over the mountain. The ravine, several miles in length, formed a good pass (Frémont's Pass).

[127] Fifteen animals had been lost from fatigue and Indian thefts after they left the Dalles. Frémont, *Exploring Expedition*, 130.
[128] *Idem*.

PYRAMID LAKE

This sketch was made by the artist with the Frémont expedition in 1844. Note the little howitzer to the left of the tent.

Beyond, a defile between the mountains descended rapidly about two thousand feet; and, filling up all the lower space, was a sheet of green water some twenty miles broad. It broke upon our eyes like the ocean. . . The waves were curling in the breeze, and their dark green color showed it to be a body of deep water. . . It was set like a gem in the mountains, which, from our position seemed to inclose it entirely.[129]

At first, Frémont thought it must be Mary's Lake, but the rugged character of the surrounding mountains did not tally with the description of the rushy shores and open country which he associated with that water. On the following day, they hurried down to the water's edge, where Frémont took note of the calcareous coating of the boulders.

On January 13, they followed the trail on the east shore of the lake southward where at times the mountains were so precipitous as to force them around the base of these precipices, "against which the water dashed, . . . five or six feet high." They could not get the howitzer into camp that evening. The next morning was spent in getting the little cannon around the cliffs so that only nine miles were made in going along the lake. That night they camped on the shore "opposite a very remarkable rock in the lake. . . It rose, according to our estimate, 600 feet above the water [Pyramid Island], and from the point we viewed it, presented a pretty exact outline of the great pyramid of Cheops. . . This striking feature suggested a name for the lake," and Frémont said, "I called it Pyramid Lake." The last of the cattle bought at the Dalles was killed here for food.[130]

A few miserable looking Indians were seen lurking about; they were successful in getting one of them into camp. He spoke a kind of Snake dialect, but no one was able to understand very much he told them. He was, however, able to make them understand something about the topography of the country by drawings in the sand. They learned that there was a river at the end of the lake, but whether it ran in or out of it, they were unable to determine. So there was still a chance that this lake (Pyramid) might be the Mary's Lake for which they were looking. As the party proceeded up the lake they could see a large grove of cottonwoods

129 *Ibid.,* 131.
130 *Loc. cit.*

near the mouth of a river, which proved on their coming
up, to be of considerable size. When the party reached the
grove they found the river was a large fresh-water stream
which flowed into the lake. At once, they were all satisfied
the river was neither Mary's nor the Sacramento, but the
feeder of a lake which they had discovered.[131]

Frémont selected a strong place for the encampment,
"nearly enclosed by the river." A short distance farther up
the river, the Indian village, consisting of a number of straw
huts, was located.[132] The natives brought in trout (salmon)
with which to trade. Frémont's men were delighted to have
such a feast. They boiled, fried, and baked them. Although
the Indians appeared friendly, Frémont took no chances —
one third of the men was placed on guard duty during the
night. Members of the party were not certain these Indians
had seen white men before despite the fact they possessed
some brass buttons and other manufactured articles.[133] A
guide was sought from among them but none would consent
to act in that capacity. However, with drawings on the
ground, they represented the river as flowing from a mountain west of south three days distant, beyond which they
indicated two more rivers.[134]

On January 16, they continued up the stream, which
Frémont appropriately named the "Salmon Trout River"
(Truckee), for eighteen miles (to Wadsworth). Because
Frémont was looking for the great Buenaventura river, and
was convinced that the Truckee was not it, the party left this
river and continued south for another twenty miles, where
they came upon another large stream, "timbered with cottonwoods, and flowing also out of the mountains, but running more directly to the eastward." They were now on the
Carson river near Buckland's Ranch [135] (Fort Churchill).

[131] Frémont said it was thirty-five miles long and from the mark of the
water line along the shores, the spring level was about twelve feet above its
level when he saw it. Frémont, *Exploring Expedition*, 132.

[132] The site of the village is now Nixon, and the surrounding area is a
reservation.

[133] These articles may have been obtained from the fur-traders or they
could have been bartered from tribes in California.

[134] Frémont, *Exploring Expedition*, 132-133.

[135] The ranch is now occupied by Frank Garaventa.

Again Captain Frémont was confused. Although there were no beaver cuttings, which Kit Carson maintained would indicate a fresh water stream, it "turned around to the right" (westward). Hoping it would prove to be their long looked for Buenaventura river, Frémont, Mr. Fitzpatrick, and Kit Carson reconnoitred the country which, much to their amazement, "joined with the open valley (Fallon) of another to the eastward (Humboldt river); but, which way the water ran it was impossible to tell." [136]

(The explanation for this peculiarity of the direction of the flow of the water is that before the water of the Humboldt and Carson rivers was diverted for irrigation purposes, the Carson and the Humboldt sinks were joined by the overflow of the two rivers. When the discharge from the Humboldt was in excess of that of the Carson the water flowed south, but when the Carson was higher than the Humboldt, the water flowed north.)

When Frémont and his scouts returned to the camp, they found the feet of their animals so cut by the rocks that they could not cross the desert to the Rocky mountains. Frémont therefore determined to abandon this plan, and "to cross the Sierra Nevada into the valley of the Sacramento, wherever a practicable pass could be found." [137] His men were overjoyed with the news. At daybreak on the nineteenth of January, 1844, there was a heavy snow, so after a short time spent in this vicinity, he decided to go further southward to cross the mountains. After having traveled twenty-four miles, they reached another large river (Walker river) flowing northward and eastward "to meet that we had left." (Frémont believed erroneously the Walker and Carson rivers met farther east.) [138] It ran through broad bottoms, with a fine meadow-land (Mason Valley). The party continued up the stream for about fourteen miles where they ascertained that one branch of the river (west fork of the Walker river) "issued in the southwest, the other flowing

[136] Frémont, *op. cit.,* 133.

[137] *Loc. cit.*

[138] According to Dr. J. C. Jones, the two rivers once met in Carson Sink. But due to a series of wet years a new channel was cut resulting in a change of the course to Walker Lake. He estimated it to have taken place 2,000 years ago.

s.s.e., (the east branch of the Walker river). Frémont decided then to travel up the west branch of the river; after some distance he saw "a circular valley [Smith Valley] about fifteen miles long through which the stream wound its way issuing from a gorge in the main mountains." [139] Although a pass was evident, the snow was still falling heavily in the mountains. The animals were so fatigued that Frémont kept them on the grass along the river's edge which he followed to the forks of the river.[140] When the party had ascended thus far, it was near the California-Nevada line, but was still in the Great Basin.

From January 23 to February 6, the party struggled up the steep cañons attempting to find a pass that would take them over the mountains and into the sunny valley of California. During these days the snow continued to fall, making travel much more difficult. Although Frémont was still looking for the illusive Buenaventura, he concluded, after having noted these several streams which he had just crossed flowed east, that since the time the party descended into the plain at Summer Lake (Oregon) it had been following the "great range of mountains which divided the Great Basin from the waters of the Pacific," and that the continued succession and almost connection of lakes and rivers were the drainage from that range of mountains.

It had been very difficult to transport the little cannon in this mountainous country. January 29 was the fatal day for the howitzer. While trying to ascend a very steep hill, the leader decided to abandon it. As far as can be ascertained, the cannon was left on the right or east side of the West Walker about ten miles up the river from the present site of Coleville, California. Frémont reluctantly gave orders to Preuss to leave it there for a time. The captain's comment on leaving behind the ordnance piece was a tribute to the protection it had given the party:

In anticipation of the snow-banks and snow-fields ahead, foreseeing the inevitable detention to which it would subject us, I reluctantly determined to leave it there for the time. It was of the kind invented by the French for the mountain part of their war in Algiers; and the distance it had come

---

[139] The present highway from Gardnerville to Yerington follows down this cañon. Frémont, *Exploring Expedition,* 134.

[140] Two forks of the West Walker.

with us proved how well it was adapted to its purpose. We left it, to the great sorrow of the whole party, who were grieved to part with a companion, which had made the whole distance from St. Louis, and commanded respect for us on some critical occasions, and which might be needed for the same purpose again.[141]

It is fitting that a pause in the story be made to relate what finally happened to the cannon which had caused so much concern to the war department, and which probably gave Frémont's wife no little comfort in knowing it protected her husband. It was never recovered either by Frémont or any of his men.[142] Instead, it lay at the foot of the cañon until 1861, when it was recovered by a man named Sheldon. He took it to Carson City, the newly made capital of Nevada territory, and offered it for sale at two hundred dollars. Failing to find a purchaser here, he took it up to Gold Hill, and tried to sell it at that place. While he was endeavoring to interest some enterprising citizen of the town, some men from Virginia City slipped down with the purchase price and bought it before sufficient enthusiasm and money could be raised in Gold Hill.[143] It was used to celebrate the fourth of July and other notable occasions in the famous silver camp. The cannon was later taken to Glenbrook, Nevada, by Captain Pray; it remained there until 1933.[144] And thus it turned out that this surplus piece of camp luggage was dragged over the Rockies, around the Great Salt Lake, over the Oregon Trail to the Dalles, down through Nevada deserts, and abandoned finally at the foot of the Sierra Nevada mountains. It is proper perhaps that is should remain

[141] Frémont, *Exploring Expedition,* 138.

[142] The Indians removed all the parts of the cannon they could carry away. It is believed by some that it may have been moved from the original place where it was abandoned. This point is discussed in the *Second Biennial Report, Nevada Historical Society, 1909-1910,* 135.

[143] *Daily Alta California,* July 6, 1861.

[144] For some time the cannon was kept in a corner of a dance hall in National Guard Hall in Virginia City where it had a place of honor. On special occasions it was decorated and that part of the hall was known as "Cannon Corner." The cannon passed through a number of hands and became finally the property of the proprietors of the hotel at Glenbrook, Nevada, where it was set in a cement base in the yard. In 1933, the cannon suddenly disappeared. So far as the writer has been able to ascertain, the cannon was put in hiding to prevent its loss.

forever in these mountains as a reminder to posterity of the great exploratory achievements of the party that had brought it so far.

Although Frémont was outside of the boundaries of Nevada when he was looking for a pass through the mountains, a brief account of the ascent belongs properly to this story. On January 31, with the "jagged saw-toothed Sierra" towering above, the party prepared for the final attempt to cross. From the Indians it was learned that it would be a very difficult thing to do, the natives warned him against it. The snow was from three to four feet deep, and several of the men were suffering from frost bites and exposure. Everyone was set to work to prepare for the ascent. Leggings, moccasins, and clothing were repaired. To keep the Washoe Indian guide with them, "a suit of green, blue, and scarlet" was given to him. Everything made ready, the order was given. They plunged forward to find a pass that would lead them across the divide. Frémont and Carson went ahead with the guide to point out to them the best trail. The snow was so deep that it was necessary to make a path for the animals by cutting foot holds and by beating down the snow with mauls. The mules were so weak from lack of food that they could no longer carry the packs. Sleds were therefore hurriedly made, the baggage was loaded on them, and they were pulled by the men up the steep slopes; the jaded animals were driven from behind. Many of the animals lost their footing, rolled down the steep cliffs, and were killed. Among these was the one carrying the pack of botanical specimens which Frémont collected on this two thousand mile journey. Food became very scarce, they had neither tallow, grease, nor salt; it became necessary to kill a fat dog for food and finally mules were killed and eaten.

On the night of February 2, Frémont and his scouting party camped without a tent under a low-branched pine tree. Here an old Indian came into their camp and made a long speech in his language, from which they gathered he was warning them against trying to cross the mountains. The Chinook Indian guide was so frightened that he hid his head under a blanket – he thought his time had come. Of this incident Frémont wrote: "Seated around the tree, the fire illuminating the rocks and the tall boles of the pines round about, and the old Indian haranguing, we presented a group of very serious faces." [145] That night, Melo, the Washoe Indian guide, disappeared and was never seen again. Frémont with Fitzpatrick and Carson tried again; the top was finally gained. From the summit of the Sierra, on what is now Kit Carson Pass, the party looked down into the valley of the Sacramento river. Carson recognized a peak in the distance which he had seen when he was in California with Ewing Young in 1830. It required eleven days, however, to bring the entire party up to the summit, an elevation of 9,338 feet. Kit Carson carved his name and the date on a tree at this point. (Years later, this part of the tree was cut out and it may be now seen at Sutter's Fort, Sacramento.) On March 8, Frémont and his party were down in the pleasant valley of the Sacramento. The crossing of the mountains at that time of year had been a heroic one. It had been very hard on the men and animals. When they arrived at Fort Sutter, every man on foot, each leading a horse or mule, as weak and as emaciated as he was, they were hospitably received by Captain Sutter. After remaining at the fort for two weeks, during which time they recuperated and purchased supplies and animals, they set out for the journey homeward.

Instead of returning through the mountains over the route which they had just taken, Frémont decided to turn southeast. He intended to try to cross the Sierra Nevada through the Walker Pass (a short distance northeast of the present city of Bakersfield) but the party was dissuaded from doing so by a Christian Indian from one of the California missions. He led them through the Tehachapi Pass, and when he left them he pointed eastward, and said: *"aqui es camino, no se perderá siempre."* [146] After the pass was gained the course of the party was southeast until it came to the Old Spanish Trail, which led northeast from Los Angeles to southern Utah. They comforted themselves that they were now on a well-traveled road. By following along

[145] Frémont, *Exploring Expedition*, 140.

[146] Frémont, *Exploring Expedition*, 159. "Here is a road where one will not always be getting lost."

the trail, stopping at the camping places of the Santa Fé caravan, they made their way eastward by a series of *jornadas* from one water hole to another, generally from fifty to sixty miles apart.

When the party was camped for the last time on the Mojave river, two Mexicans, a man and a boy, named Fuentes and Pablo Hernández respectively, came into camp. They were the only surviving members of a company of six, including the father and mother of the boy, who were on the trail early in the year, driving a band of horses ahead of the big Santa Fé caravan. Some eighty miles in advance of Frémont's camp the party had been attacked by Indians. Fuentes and Hernández, in charge of the horses at the time, succeeded in driving most of the horses back on the trail. In doing so they met the Frémont party, which they joined in the hope of recovering the lost horses.[147]

Frémont made camp at a spring where the Mexicans had left their horses, but they, too, had been driven off by the Indians.[148] Carson and Godey, volunteering to go with the two Mexicans in pursuit of the marauding Indians, traced the natives to a narrow ravine where they surprised them with an early morning attack. Shots were exchanged – an arrow pierced Godey's collar; two Indians were killed in the engagement. The horses were recovered, and the party returned to camp.

With the exception of this incident, the journey eastward across the southern part of Nevada was uneventful. Although it was in April the heat of the day made travel very hard, so the *jornada* was made at night. So far apart were the water holes that many animals had perished before water could be reached. On April 29, the spring (just across the Nevada-California line) where the massacre had taken place was reached. The dead bodies of Pablo's father and one other man were found. The young boy was inconsolable – he cried out many times in anguish for his parents. Frémont named the spring "Aqua de Hernández" (now Resting Springs) in memory of the sad event. A note was left in the

---

[147] *Ibid.*, 161-164.

[148] Frémont gave this spring the name of Aqua de Tomaso on his map. Frémont, *Memoirs*, 372.

cleft of a pole telling the oncoming caravan the news of the disaster.

On May 3, the party camped on a spring called Las Vegas de Quintana (now the city of Las Vegas, Nevada) where "Two narrow streams of clear water, four or five feet deep, gush suddenly, with a quick current, from two singularly large springs." [149] The journey to the northeast from this point was a long dry one. They came first to the Muddy river near the site of the present Moapa, Nevada, and then, about twenty miles farther to the banks of the Virgin river. The Indians along this route were very annoying. One of Frémont's men was killed when he became separated from the main party. After leaving Nevada, the route led northeast to Utah Lake, at which point it crossed the Wasatch mountains to the northeastern part of Utah. Frémont could now have returned home by the Oregon Trail, but he loved adventure, so he decided to turn south, and to go through the Colorado park country to Bent's Fort. Carson left them here and returned to Taos, New Mexico; the rest of the party went east to the Missouri where they disbanded.[150]

In writing up his report for the government, Frémont was ably assisted by his gifted wife. Over 100,000 copies were printed and circulated free throughout the states. They acquainted thousands of people with the wonders of the far West. This report had a profound influence upon later emigration. Although it contained the first official description of the Great Basin, Frémont had been only around the rim of it at this time. The report of the basin read as follows:

The existence of the Great Basin is therefore an established fact in my own mind; its extent and contents are yet to be better ascertained. It cannot be less than four or five hundred miles each way. . . Of its interior but little is known. It is called a desert, and, from what I saw of it, sterility may be its prominent characteristic, but where there is so much water there must be some oasis. The great river, and the great lake, reported, may not be equal to the report; but where there is so much snow, there must be streams, and where there is no outlet there must be lakes to hold the accumulated waters or sands to swallow them up. The contents of the Great Basin are yet to be examined.[151]

[149] Frémont, *Exploring Expedition*, 165.
[150] Frémont, *Exploring Expedition*, 165ff.
[151] Frémont, *Memoirs*, 391-392.

While Frémont was writing up this report, he was making preparations to examine "the contents of the Great Basin." At least, that was ostensibly the object of his second expedition into the far West. He wanted to discover a more feasible route to the Pacific coast from the Mississippi river. However, in addition to this general reason were coupled several specific ones – to explore the Colorado river country, to complete the examination of the Great Salt Lake, and to survey the country to the west and southwest of the lake as far as the Sierra and Cascade ranges. Incidentally, and uppermost perhaps in his mind, was the desire to keep apprised of the developments of the revolt of the Americans in California.[152]

Again he gathered together a group of well-chosen men. Among the sixty, who set out on this expedition, were Carson and Godey of the former expedition, Edward Kern, chief topographer, Thomas "Dick" Owens, Joe Walker, Lucien Maxwell, and Thomas Fitzpatrick.[153] On August 16, 1845, the party started west from the Missouri landing for the Arkansas, Colorado, White, and Green rivers country. Some time was spent in the exploration of the headwaters of the rivers rising in the Rockies of western Colorado.

The Great Salt Lake was reached on October 13, where two weeks were spent in explorations and the taking of astronomical observations. Finally, the long march west was begun. The party proceeded along the south shore of the lake, crossed Skull Valley, and continued out to the edge of the Great Salt Desert where a pause was made. A few days were spent here in speculation over the best direction to take for the journey across the desert and the Great Basin of Nevada. So far as is now known, no white man had crossed the desert westward at this point. (Smith had come from the west somewhere near here in 1827.) Frémont himself says that "of my own men none knew anything of it; neither Walker nor Carson. The Indians declared, too, that no one had ever been known to cross the plain, which was a desert; so far as any of them had ventured no water had been found." This formidable desert of salt extended about

---

[152] Frémont, *Memoirs,* 422-423.
[153] *Ibid.,* 426-427.

sixty miles west of the Great Salt Lake to the border of the Utah-Nevada line. It was completely devoid of water and vegetation.

In Frémont's observations of the surrounding country, he noticed on the other side of the desert and nearly on a line with his intended route of travel, a "pear-shaped mountain" about fifty to sixty miles away. It looked fertile to him, so he decided to make for it. "By some persuasion and the offer of a tempting reward," he induced one of the local Indians to act as a guide for Carson, Auguste Archambeau, and Maxwell to the mountain, Frémont to follow with the rest of the party and to make one camp out on the salt plain. "They [the scouting party] were to make a signal by smoke in case water should be found." (This route was known later as Hastings' Cutoff.)[154]

Frémont traveled out on the salt plains during the night. After a few hours away from camp, the Indian he had brought with him as a guide lost his courage at being so far from his own habitat. He became so frightened "that his knees really gave away under him and he wabbled about like a drunken man." He was released with his promised reward and so happy was he, "he bounded off like a hare through the sagebrush." Camp was made before morning and while the party was waiting for Carson's signal, Archambeau rode into camp and reported both water and grass had been found at the foot of the mountain. That afternoon the entire party camped near the mountain to which Frémont gave the name of "Pilot Peak." (It is just across the line in Nevada.)[155]

On November 1, Frémont and his large party continued their journey westward. He used precaution lest he tire his animals while in search of a good camping site. Just ahead of the advancing party he dispatched a number of his men, spread out over quite a distance to search for the best route and for a suitable camping place. The reward for finding such was the naming of the place for the man who found it. Continuing southwest from Pilot Peak, they went through the Silver Zone Pass to Whitton Springs, named for one of

[154] Frémont, *Memoirs*, 433.
[155] *Loc. cit.*

his men who discovered it. (Now called Flowery Springs, a short distance south of Shafter, Nevada.) Winter was coming on and the experiences of the preceding one were still vivid in his mind, so Frémont decided not to "linger long in the examination of the Great Basin." Near Whitton Springs, he divided his party, so as to run two lines across the basin. With Joe Walker as guide, Edward Kern as topographer, and Talbot as leader, he sent the larger party, known as the Humboldt party, northwest to the Humboldt river, to follow the route that Walker of the Walker-Bonneville expedition took in 1833. This party was to follow the river to its sink, to cross the Forty-mile Desert to the Carson river, to turn south and to go to the Walker river, and thence to follow up the main stream to the east side of Walker Lake, where it was to wait for Frémont and his party.[156] The Walker-Kern party had no unusual experiences in going down the Humboldt river except that travel was very slow. Frémont with his small party of ten men turned south and west to Franklin Lake. Passing south of this body of water, he traveled to the Ruby range, the source of the streams flowing into the Humboldt river from the south. These mountains are among the most rugged of the basin ranges, but Frémont crossed them with little difficulty. He camped on a small creek which he named Crane Creek for one of his Delaware Indians. (This creek flows into the south fork of the Humboldt.) It was at this time, he also gave the name of "Humboldt" to the mountains which he had just crossed, and to the "river stretching across the basin." After crossing the south fork of the Humboldt, he conducted his party over a "tortuous course rendered unavoidable by the necessity of using just such passes as the mountains gave, and in searching for grass and water." This route took him down into Diamond Valley, through Ruby Pass and to Connor Spring, named for one of his men (located north of Eureka). From this spring, he turned west "until he came to a stream which he called Basin Creek (at the head of Big Smoky Valley). Following along the east side of the Toyabe mountain range, he came to the boiling springs (Darrough's Hot Springs) south of the alkali lake where he camped on Novem-

---

[156] Frémont, *Memoirs*, 434-435.

ber 16. Continuing west-southwest for three days, he arrived on the east shore of Walker Lake. There he waited a week for the rendezvous with the Kern-Walker division. It was at this time that he honored Joe Walker, the famous trapper, scout, and guide, by naming the lake, river, and pass for him.[157]

As soon as the party was reunited, Frémont decided to divide it again – this time he sent Kern at the head of his division south through Owen's Valley to Walker Pass and thence to the headwaters of the Kern river. Frémont with fifteen of his best men, went north up the Walker river to the bend, where he proceeded due west to the Carson river (he had camped near this place on the river in 1844), and thence further north to "the river which flows into Pyramid Lake" (Truckee river). At the Big Bend of the Truckee, Frémont followed the river to the Sierra where on December 5, 1845, he and his small party camped on the divide (above Donner Lake) which separated California from the Great Basin. It was some weeks later before the two parties met at the crossing of the San Joaquin river north of Tulare Lake.[158] The following year Frémont took an active part in the Bear Flag Revolt.

Although almost a hundred years have passed since Frémont first entered Nevada, his report of what he saw here is still a fresh and vivid story. His observations were so accurate and his story so well told that today one can take his report in one hand and point out the geographic features he described with the other. Frémont contributed very little additional information to that supplied already by the furmen and the mountaineers, but these men did not write reports. He was the first white man to have flanked the eastern base of the Sierra Nevada mountains from southern Oregon to the source of the Walker river and, thereby, to have ascertained scientifically that there was no river that rose in the Rocky mountains and flowed through the Great Basin to the Pacific ocean; he added a very large number of names to topographical features in the far West and especially in Nevada, and in his voluminous and brilliant report he gave

---

[157] Frémont, *Memoirs,* 438.
[158] *Idem.*

the first official information of this region. In his second expedition into the West, he explored for the first time the central part of the state of Nevada.

Frémont Pass, between Pyramid and Winnemucca lakes, unfamiliar and little used except by sheep men and the Indians, is the only physical feature in Nevada named for the first government explorer to enter the state. However, with very few exceptions, the names he gave to the mountains, rivers, lakes, and valleys, remain today. His greatest contribution to the opening of the West was his reports. Hundreds of them were distributed in the eastern states; many of the emigrant parties had one of them when they started out on the long trek.

# Early Emigrant Trails and Cutoffs
## across Nevada

There is no more fascinating chapter in American history than the story of the opening of the trails to the far West. All trails have evolved slowly. Over the well-beaten path of the wild animals, which the Indian widened and shortened, came the trapper, trader, explorer, and settler. The path used only by a pack-horse at first, later became a wagon road. It was followed by the railroad, and still later, the airplane. The exploration of the trails and passes through Nevada was a thrilling episode in the progress of a westward expanding nation. It was well into the nineteenth century, however, before the Great American Desert, more recently referred to as the Great Basin, was approached from all directions; it was 1827 before it was even crossed by a white man. To the boldest adventurer it was a trackless waste of sagebrush and sand to be avoided. The advancing settlements of the frontiersmen, however, swept westward to the very edge of the desert, and a few pushed across it to the Pacific coast. There, national highways across this area had to be made to connect the East with the West. The several early emigrant parties bound for California sought out different approaches to the Great Basin; they tried out, also, the different passes through the mountains as they left it. In consequence, there developed, eventually, several highways across Nevada, the most important of which were Salt Lake-Los Angeles Trail through southern Nevada, the Humboldt Trail across northern Nevada, and the Egan or Simpson Trail through central Nevada. Each of these main trails was supplemented by several cutoffs on entering the state; and by a number of passes through the Sierra Nevada range on leaving it.[159]

The Salt Lake-Los Angeles Trail was, in fact, the first

[159] See "Map of the Early Emigrant Trails and Cutoffs across Northern Nevada," 105.

of the overland routes across Nevada to be discovered. It
has been known in different periods of history by several
names — "The Old Spanish Trail," "The Armijo Trail,"
"The Mexican Trail" (Mexican and Spanish were synony-
mous to Americans), "The Mormon Trail," and finally "The
Salt Lake-Los Angeles Trail." The beginning of this highway dates back to 1776, when the Domínguez-Escalante
expedition failed to explore a route from Santa Fé, New
Mexico, to Monterey, California by way of southern Utah
and Nevada. The object of the expedition was to find a land
route between New Mexico and California. Although this
party did not succeed in connecting the two most northern
outposts of the Spanish empire, it did open up a trail for
trade with the Indians in southern Utah, which a few years
later extended to the Indians in southeastern Nevada living
along the Muddy and Virgin rivers. The Salt Lake-Los
Angeles Trail was an extension of this trail from Utah across
southern Nevada to California.

Many of the trails which led out of Santa Fé were called
Spanish trails, so the one extending into Utah was only one
of the many which radiated from the New Mexican hub.
Over one of these trails, leading from St. Louis, Missouri,
to Santa Fé, New Mexico, and known particularly as the
Santa Fé trail, came the great caravan trade from the United
States.[160] The long journey, made in wagons heavily loaded
with merchandise, necessitated a sturdy animal to withstand
the *jornadas*. One of the main factors in the opening of this
first overland trail from New Mexico to California was this
Missouri trade demand for mules and horses from California — noted for its animals of large size and endurance.
So great was this demand that it led to the organization of
a number of expeditions to California for the purpose of
trading New Mexican articles for the California animals.

The first of these expeditions was organized in the fall
of 1829 by José Antonio Chávez, governor of New Mexico.
He selected Antonio Armijo for the leader of the expedition.[161] This party set out northward over the Escalante or

160 The best account of this trade is Gregg, *Commerce of the Prairies.*
161 "Itineraire du Nord-Mexico à la Haute Californie," in *Bulletin de la
Société de Géographie,* Paris, 1835, ser. 2, III, 316-323. Taken from the *Registro
Oficial del Gobierno de los Estados Unidos Mexicanos,* Mexico, 1830.

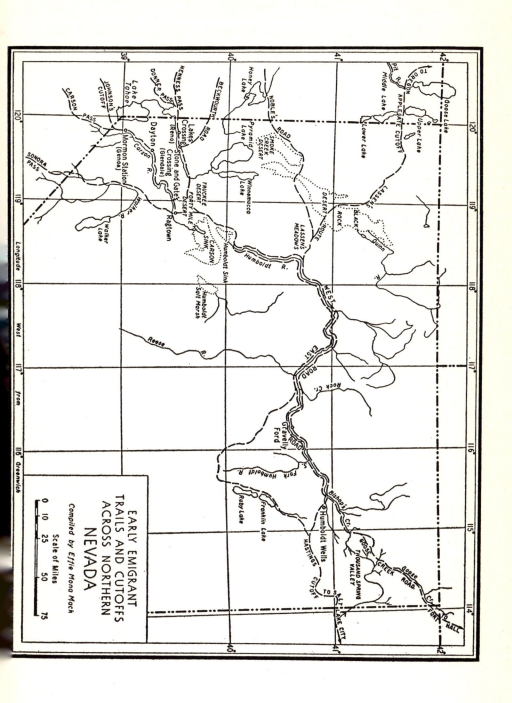

EARLY EMIGRANT
TRAILS AND CUTOFFS
ACROSS NORTHERN
NEVADA

Compiled by Effie Mona Mack

Scale of Miles

0  10  25   50   75

Longitude    West    from    Greenwich

CARSON PASS

JOHNSON'S CUTOFF

SONORA PASS

DONNER PASS

HENNESS PASS

BECKWOURTH ROAD

Lake Tahoe

Mormon Station (Genoa)

Dayton

Stone and Gates Crossing (Glendale)

Lakes Crossing (Reno)

Ragtown

Carson R.

Walker R.

Walker Lake

Honey Lake

Pyramid Lake

Winnemucca Lake

TRUCKEE DESERT

FORTY MILE DESERT

CARSON SINK

Humboldt Sink

Humboldt Salt Marsh

Reese R.

NOBLE'S ROAD

SMOKE CREEK DESERT

LASSEN'S ROUTE

DESERT ROUTE

LASSEN'S MEADOWS

Humboldt R.

WEST ROAD

EAST ROAD

Rock Cr.

Reese R.

Middle Lake

Lower Lake

Upper Lake

Goose Lake

Pit R.

OREGON

APPLEGATE CUTOFF

ROCK

BLACK R.

Quinn

Gravelly Ford

South Fork Humboldt R.

Franklin Lake

Ruby Lake

Bishop Cr.

Humboldt Wells

HASTINGS CUTOFF

TO SALT LAKE CITY

THOUSAND SPRING VALLEY

GOOSE CREEK ROAD

ROSE CREEK

FORT HALL

120°  119°  118°  117°  116°  115°  114°

39°  40°  41°  42°

Spanish Trail into southern Utah, where it turned southwest across southern Nevada, arriving finally at the San Gabriel Mission on January 1, 1830. So far as is now known this is the first time an extension of this road from Santa Fé to southern Utah was made across Nevada. After two months spent in trading Indian blankets for California stock, the party returned to Santa Fé by the same route. Thereafter, for a number of years one large caravan set out yearly for the same purpose over this route. These traders went always in one large company for protection. The size of the caravan often reached three hundred men on horseback and a number of pack animals, each laden with provisions and articles to be traded for California products. The trading party would return with as many as a thousand head of stock, chiefly jacks and jennets, and the Mexican jackass, progenitors, respectively, of the famous mule of the Ozark state, and the lowly western burro.[162] During the early history of the trail, mules were its *raison d' être* in every sense of the word, hence "Mule Trail" could rightfully be added to "Spanish," "Mexican" and "Armijo" as names for it. The springs at Las Vegas de Quintana (now Las Vegas, Nevada), Agua Escarbada, and Ojo de Archillete, all named by these Mexican traders, were regular camping places in southern Nevada.[163]

Mention in an earlier chapter has been made of the part the first Americans played in the opening of the southern part of Nevada during the era of the fur-trappers. They were followed a few years later by a small party of Mormons with ox-teams, who were sent in 1847 by the church authorities to Los Angeles for seeds and grain. They traveled in a south-southwesterly direction from Great Salt Lake until they came upon the Mexican or Old Spanish Trail, which they followed to California. In January, 1847, Miles Goodyear, who since 1845 had raised horses and cattle on the site of Ogden, Utah, took a pack train loaded with deer and elk hides to Los Angeles.[164] On April 10 of the following year,

---

[162] A good description of a New Mexican caravan on its way back from Los Angeles is in J. C. Tramp, *Prairie and Rocky Mountain Adventures.*

[163] Joseph J. Hill, "Old Spanish Trail," in *Hispanic American Historical Review*, IV, no. 3, 1921.

[164] Charles Kelly, *Salt Desert Trails*, fn. 67, p. 87.

H. G. Boyle and James Shaw, who had gone over the route the preceding year, guided twenty-five soldiers of the disbanded Mormon battalion from Los Angeles to Great Salt Lake. On June 5, 1848, one wagon drawn by oxen, and one hundred thirty-five pack mules laden with seeds arrived in the Mormon city. From this time on the Mormons and other Utah settlers used this trail for trade and emigration to California. Small Mormon settlements grew up along the way, a number of them being in southern Nevada. It is of interest to note here that there was recently found near Kane's Springs, Wahmonie, Nevada, the cornerstone of an old stone house, now in ruins, with the name "R. J. Byor, 1847," carved on it. This house may have been one of the stopping places for the Mormons.[165]

After the Mexican War ended in 1848, there was little or no travel over this route, except that which was carried on by the Mormons, until the Forty-niners used it. It was not the most direct route to the California mines, but it was the safest for those who were slow travelers, and for those who did not wish to take the risk of crossing the Sierra Nevada in winter, or did not care to remain with the Mormons in Utah until spring.

There was one man, named Williams, in Salt Lake City, who maintained that five hundred miles could be cut off from the trail. Although he had never been over the route, nor had apparently anyone else, he produced a map showing clearly the new cutoff which, he said, ran directly west to the gold regions. "Williams' Short Route" began to have its advocates, and at last a few emigrants tried to follow it, much to their regret. This cutoff was made from the regular trail at the eastern rim of the Great Basin, near the head of the Virgin river, by turning to the right and proceeding directly west across Nevada to the western rim, thence north of Death Valley, and on to California through Walker's Pass. This route proved very disastrous to the one and only party which took it during the gold rush; its story will be related later.[166]

---

[165] Wahmonie is a short distance northwest of Las Vegas, Nevada. The stone is now in the Mackay Museum, University of Nevada, Reno.

[166] Owen Cochran Coy, *The Great Trek*, 266-272.

The trail-blazing to the Pacific coast over the northern route, for the greater part, had been carried on by the trappers, traders, and explorers, and by a few Americans who had settled in California before the gold rush. The publication of the reports of the government explorations to the far West, thereby giving a quasi-official impetus to the western movement, encouraged large numbers to go west, many of whom settled in Oregon and California. However, the most far-reaching influence on the pre-'49 rush was the dissemination of the propaganda sent to the states by a group of enthusiastic settlers in California, such as John Bidwell, Captain John Sutter, Dr. John Marsh, [167] Lansford W. Hastings, and the Roubidoux brothers. A number of emigrants, thus attracted, had tested the different routes, the merits and short-comings of which had been partly known before the great rush came.

The first important company to blaze a trail to California across northern Nevada was known as the Stevens-Murphy party,[168] consisting of over fifty men and a number of women and children. It left Missouri in May, 1844, going over the Platte river, South Pass, and Fort Hall route.[169] At the fort named, about half of the party went on to Oregon, the remainder turned southwest to the Humboldt river. The trail followed up the Raft river, over the Goose Creek mountains, on to the Humboldt, downstream to its sink, across the desert to the Truckee river, thence up that river, and over the Truckee (Donner) Pass to Sutter's Fort. Over this untraveled route Caleb Greenwood and his two half-breed sons,

---

[167] Sutter and Marsh wrote letters which were published in many newspapers in the states. Sutter had agents at different places along the trail, especially at Fort Hall. Among some of the well-known books which influenced the early emigrants to come to California were John Bidwell's *Trip to California*, 1841; Edwin Bryant, *What I Saw in California;* and Lansford W. Hastings, *Emigrant's Guide to Oregon and California.*

[168] Various names have been given to this expedition – Stevens-Townsend, Stevens-Murphy, or Miller-Murphy, depending upon the importance attached to certain members of the company by the narrators of their adventures. Elijah or Elisha Stevens was the leader of the company. *San Francisco Call,* September 13, 1864.

[169] Fort Hall belonged to the Hudson's Bay Company, which, by the treaty of 1846 with England, remained in the possession of this company for nineteen years so as to enable it to close its affairs.

agents of Sutter stationed at Fort Hall to divert Oregon-bound emigrants to his settlement on the Sacramento river, guided the party. The taking of such a large company over a new route was no small task, and so weary were the animals when they reached the sink of the Humboldt that a month was spent in resting and feeding them. This wait delayed the crossing of the Sierra summit until December. A late winter saved this party from the tragedies which were to overcome the Donner party two years later because of an unusually early fall of snow.

The progress of the Stevens-Murphy party across Nevada was uneventful. It made, however, the first wagon trail from Fort Hall to and down the Humboldt river; and it was the first party to take wagons across the Donner summit – a feat accomplished by building a windlass and hoisting the dismantled wagons over the steepest places. One member of the party, Moses Schallenberger, was too ill to cross the summit with the party. A cabin was built for him on one of the creeks flowing out of Donner Lake, where he spent the winter, going on to Sutter's Fort the following spring. He kept a diary of the journey which contained the story of the naming of the Truckee river.[170] It is believed that the river, lake, and pass were named "Truckee" after a young Indian buck who guided the party up the river. It was said that his characteristics reminded a member of the party of a former acquaintance by the name of "Truckee" who bore oddly no resemblance to the Indian.[171]

Another version of the naming of the river came to the writer from a young Paiute. He said he had talked with a number of the oldest living members of his tribe, who had told him a different story, the main features of which were as follows: among the Paiutes living on the Truckee river near the Big Bend (Wadsworth) was a bright young buck who picked up quite readily a few words of English from the white men who had come through there. (Frémont had been with these Indians the previous winter.) Among the

---

[170] The name was spelled a number of different ways on the early maps and in the diaries: "Trucky," "Truckey," and "Truckie."

[171] Schallenberger's cabin was used by the Donner party in the following winter. His diary has been lost, having been burned in a fire in San Jose.

words he heard most frequently from the whites was "talk" to which the Indian added "ey." When the emigrant parties reached the river, the first thing they asked the Indians was for someone who could talk, whereupon, this young Indian came forward and "talkeyed" with them. Because of his ability to say a few words of English he was often engaged as a guide to the travelers up the river. To his fellow tribesmen he became "Talkey," from which the name "Truckee" has been derived. Even today, if one hears a Paiute pronounce "Truckee" and "talkey," little difference is noted.[172]

The cutoff from Fort Hall, located on Lewis Fork (now the Snake river) of the Columbia to the Humboldt river, extended southwest up the Raft river for some distance, thence over Granite Pass to Goose Creek [173] near Record Bluff — so called because of the large number of names carved by the emigrants in the soft stone. This bluff was near the junction of the three states: Idaho, Utah, and Nevada. The road continued up the east bank of Goose Creek to its head on the great divide that separated the Columbia river basin from the Great Basin, thence over another low rise into Thousand Springs Valley (Elko county), where numberless springs of hot and cold water were in some places so near each other that if a person should lie full length on the ground his feet could be bathed in a spring of hot water while at the same time his hands might be washed in cold water. The trail continued down Thousand Springs Valley about twelve miles to Cold Water Creek, a tributary of Thousand Springs Creek,[174] followed up this creek, passed a few miles over some low-lying hills; it then ascended the mountains through a ravine, and descended gradually into the valley five miles farther to the headwaters of the Humboldt, near the site of Wells, Nevada.

During the year 1845 a large number of persons went to California by this Fort Hall-Humboldt Route. The story of each of these parties across the desert stretch was one of

172 Statement of Edwin Newman to the writer, December 4, 1931.

173 Goose Creek rises in Goose Creek mountains in northeastern Elko county, Nevada.

174 Thousand Springs Creek is a basin river in Elko county. It flows northeast through Thousand Springs Valley, then turns to the right and flows southeast to its sink near Tecoma, Nevada.

trials and vicissitudes, epic and romance, adventure and mo-
notony. Several of them became prominent for various
reasons — such as the Swasey-Todd party, consisting of thirteen young men; the Sublette party, having rather unusually
large sums of money with them, and being very well equipped
with oxen and wagons; and the Grigsby-Ide party, the largest
of the year, having over one hundred persons in it.[175]

The Fort Hall-Raft River-Goose Creek Cutoff to the
Humboldt necessitated a long detour to the north so as to
avoid the Great Salt Lake and the Great Salt Desert west of
it. In order to shorten the route and attract Oregon-bound
emigrants to California, Lansford W. Hastings, one of California's first press agents,[176] sought to find a more direct
route. He was an ambitious young man who had gone to
Oregon in 1842, and to California in the following year. He
believed he could make himself president of the republic of
California if he could induce a sufficient number of Americans to settle in the Mexican province and assist him in oust-
ing the incompetent Mexican authorities. To accomplish this
scheme, he must explore a more direct route. So in 1845 he
joined an eastbound party of emigrants dissatisfied with
conditions in California, guided by James Clyman, the veteran trapper and explorer. The party consisted of nineteen
persons: Hastings, Clyman, three women, three children,
Hastings' Indian servant, and seven men, old Caleb Greenwood, Sutter's eighty-year-old agent, and his two sons — all
mounted on horses and mules. They crossed the Sierra over
the Donner summit, followed the Truckee to the Big Bend,
and crossed the desert to the Humboldt river, which they
followed as far as Bishop's Creek (near Halleck, Nevada).[177] The Fort Hall road turned northeast at this point,
but Hastings had heard of Frémont's exploration of a route
to the south of the Great Salt Lake which would greatly
shorten the distance. A long consultation was held, Hastings
advocated the new cutoff — Clyman and Greenwood opposed
it. Hastings won, so the party proceeded east and southeast-
ward until they stood on the summit of the Toano range

[175] Bancroft, *History of Nevada, Colorado, and Wyoming*, 60.
[176] Lansford W. Hastings, *Emigrant's Guide to Oregon and California*.
[177] Kelly, *op. cit.*, 43-46.

(Silver Zone Pass) – the most eastern one in Nevada, a few miles west of Wendover. The great salt plains extended eastward as far as the eye could reach. From this point they proceeded about twenty-two miles northeast to Pilot Peak, where they found their last good grass and water. On May 28 they set out across the Great Salt Desert, which they made in about twenty hours with no undue suffering. On the far side of the desert they camped for the night, and then proceeded to the Salt Lake Valley (now the site of Salt Lake City) and eastward to Fort Bridger. Clyman took his party on to St. Louis; Hastings, accompanying them as far eastward as Black's Fork on the Green river (southwestern Wyoming), there awaited the arrival of the first emigrant trains of the year bound for California or Oregon.

Hastings' theory was now a reality; he therefore decided to guide wagon trains over the newly discovered cutoff. While on Black's Fork he wrote letters in which he recommended his new route as being three hundred miles shorter than the more northern one, and being "perfectly safe for wagon trains." He gave these letters to a lone traveler on the trail, a Mr. Bonney, who had gone west in 1845 and was now returning east to bring out his family, instructing him to give them to any emigrant he chanced to meet.

The first party to come under the influence of one of the Hastings' letters was the Colonel William Russell party, which left Independence, Missouri, on May 5, 1846. It was joined a few days later by Edwin Bryant; and on May 19 nine wagons from Illinois led by George and Jacob Donner and James F. Reed were added, making forty-six wagons altogether in the party. At Fort Laramie, Wyoming, in order to make better time to California, the Russell-Bryant party traded their wagons and oxen for mules to ride. From that time on the wagon train was known as the Donner party, under the leadership of George Donner. The Bryant party progressed rapidly and soon camped with Hastings on Black's Fork, where  he gave them the description of his newly discovered route. Bryant was not favorably impressed. However, guided by James M. Hudspeth, an old mountaineer, he took the Hastings' Cutoff. Hudspeth went with the party to the eastern edge of the Great Salt Desert, where he told them to "ride like hell." They succeeded in crossing it to Pilot Peak, but not without considerable suffering from heat and thirst. After a day's rest, they traveled southwest to the Toano range, and then proceeded west over the Humboldt-Truckee river route to California. They reached Fort Sutter on September 1, the first party to arrive during that year.

Hastings also induced the Donner party, numbering eighty-seven, to take his cutoff; but their travel was so slow with the heavy ox-drawn wagons that it was September 9 before they reached the Great Salt Desert. Three days were spent in getting the first wagon across the desert to Pilot Peak, and several more days passed before it was decided to abandon some of the heavier wagons on the desert, among them the "Pioneer Palace Car" drawn by eight oxen and owned by James F. Reed.[178] On September 16 the Donner party crossed into what later became Nevada, and headed toward the Humboldt River Trail. It took, however, a roundabout way to get there. Instead of going in a more or less direct line toward the river, the party went south through Steptoe Valley, west over Flowery Lake Pass, across Clover Valley (called Valley of Fifty Springs by the Donner party), where it turned southwestward, traveled three days, and passed west of Ruby and Franklin lakes to the southern end of the Ruby range. Here they turned north and followed along the western base of the mountains to the Humboldt river, where they came upon the Fort Hall road. By this time their supplies, either consumed or left behind to lighten the loads, were so diminished that it was decided to send two volunteers ahead to Sutter's Fort for relief.

Misfortunes and tragedies dogged the footsteps of the party as it wended its way down the Humboldt. The first tragic event occurred at Gravelly Ford (near Beowawe, Nevada). James Reed killed John Snyder in a heated argument over the pulling of some of the wagons up a sandy hill. Reed was cast off from the party to shift for himself, leaving his grief-stricken wife and family behind with the rest of the party. The Indians hovered around constantly, and killed or drove off as many of the stock as they could stampede or

---

178 See photographs and maps in Kelly, *op. cit.,* 11, 85.

separate from the herd. An old man in the party by the name of Hardcoop was compelled to walk with the others over the desert between the Humboldt Sink and the Truckee river. He dropped by the wayside from fatigue, and was finally left to die alone. A short distance before they reached the Truckee river, a man by the name of Wolfinger disappeared entirely when his wagon lagged behind the rest. A search was made, but nothing was ever heard of him again. His frantic wife had to go on to California without him. He was believed later to have been murdered by the Indians or by some member of the party for his money. Near the Big Bend of the Truckee, the relief party from Sutter's Fort met them with seven mules, five of which were loaded with flour and dried beef, sufficient provisions, however, to last for but a brief period.

Had the party proceeded to California with all possible speed, the summit could have been gained before the storms came. But such was not the decision of the party – instead, on October 20 they stopped to rest and feed the cattle on the fine wild hay that grew in the Truckee Meadows (near Sparks, Nevada); it was decided to send another relief party to Sutter's Fort.

The loss of four days spent on the meadows was fatal to the party; storm clouds were gathering on the Sierra Nevada which presaged an early winter.[179] The harrowing details of the rest of the story do not properly belong in this volume, but it may be noted here that if the party had remained in the Truckee Meadows all winter they would have fared better. The snow rarely falls to any great depth; the sufferings or loss of the livestock would not have been very great; and they could have killed it as it became necessary; and then, too, some food could probably have been obtained from the Indians. The party continued, however, up the Truckee river as far as Donner Lake. The snow had now fallen to such a depth that the entire party could not make the summit. So again a relief party of the strongest and most stout-hearted men pressed over the pass to the fort to return as quickly as possible with food and help. The remaining number camped on Alder Creek a short distance from Don-

[179] C. F. McGlashan, *History of the Donner Party*, tells the story.

ner Lake, where they built rude cabins. The snow fell so deep that the relief party could not get back to their friends and families. Forty-five survived the winter; the remainder were either starved or frozen to death. It is needless to add that as news of the Donner tragedies was circulated throughout the states, travel across Nevada, especially by the Hastings' Cutoff and Truckee River Route, fell off during the next two years.

The Fort Hall-Goose Creek Trail and the Hastings' Cutoff were the first trails to lead to the Humboldt river. The road down the river was known as the Humboldt Trail. It began near what is now Wells, Nevada, and continued along the river to its sink, a few miles south of Lovelock, Nevada. The Humboldt is the largest river in Nevada, and the only one in it which flows from east to west.

In the progress of westward-marching empire few streams on the North American continent have played a more important part than the Humboldt river of Nevada. Among the water courses of the world, it can lay claim to neither great beauty nor to remarkable utility. Its great work was to open a way, first for the cattle train and then for the steam train, through a wilderness of mountains, through ranges which otherwise would run straight across its course.[180]

The Humboldt Trail varied from year to year and from season to season. If the river was low, the trail ran close to the waters' edge; if there was a heavy runoff, it skirted around the bluffs in order to avoid the swampy bottoms. The trail was often changed in order to avoid the smothering clouds of dust, churned to a fine powder by the large number of animals driven along it. "There were drifts of ashy earth in the flats in which the cattle sank to their bellies." [181] The earth was reduced to an impalpable powder, finer than flour — so fine that at every step a man was enveloped in a cloud; and so light that the least wind raised it, and yet so dense that the emigrants could not see the wagon ahead and so alkaline that it blotched and blistered the lips of nearly everyone.[182]

Not far from the present town of Carlin, the trail cut

---

[180] Bancroft, *History of Nevada, Colorado, and Wyoming*, 15.

[181] Bancroft, *History of California*, vi, 152.

[182] Delano, *Life on the plains and at the diggings*, 166; C. W. Smith, *Journal of a trip to California*, 71; David Leeper, *Argonauts of Forty-nine*, 16.

across one of the bends of the river to a point not far from Beowawe. At this section of the river there was a part about six miles in length that could easily be forded. Because of the hard and gravelly bottom of the river, it was called by the early emigrants Gravelly Ford.

Toward the end of the trail, near the present town of Rye, the bottom lands form a great natural meadow called "Lawson's [Lassen's] Meadows" (Rye Patch) for Peter Lassen, who had a trading post at this point. Excellent grass grew in great abundance in this valley. Many of the emigrants stopped here for a few days, cut the hay, and let it cure before feeding it to their animals, or kept it to feed them while they crossed the Forty-mile Desert between the sink of the Humboldt and the Carson river. Toward the western end of the Humboldt Trail several roads cut off to the different settlements in California — the most northern one was the Applegate Cutoff. This road was opened in 1846 by Levi Scott and Jesse and Lindsay Applegate for the purpose of finding a more accessible route from Fort Hall to the Willamette Valley, Oregon, than was afforded by the Old Oregon Trail up the Snake river.[183] The cutoff branched off from the Humboldt near the meadows, and extended northwest. It passed Rabbit Springs, crossed the Black Rock Desert, and went through High Rock cañon to the lava beds of northeastern California. Here the road passed around the southern end of Goose Lake and continued northward to Oregon.

During the gold rush, Peter Lassen founded a trading post at the meadows, and at this point the emigrants were induced to turn off, and take this supposedly shorter route to California. Lassen's trail was the same as the Applegate Cutoff as far as Goose Lake. Here Lassen's route turned south along the Pit river and continued to Lassen's Ranch, a trading post at the mouth of Deer Creek. Lassen's Cutoff from the Humboldt route was neither shorter nor easier than any of the other cutoffs to California. In fact, it was a longer route to the main diggings than the more southern trails, thereby earning the name of "Lassen's Horn Route," perhaps because it was as much of a cutoff as going around

---

[183] Bancroft, *History of Oregon*, 542-552.

Cape Horn. It was never used extensively; its chief advantage was to Peter Lassen, whose post was the first settlement to be reached after leaving Salt Lake.[184] The Indians were particularly hostile in the Black Rock Desert country on this route; so much so that guards had to be placed at either end of High Rock cañon in order to protect the emigrants while they were camping there. Many travelers carved their names and the dates of their passing through this country on the walls of the cañon; the inscriptions are visible today.

In 1851 a cutoff from the Lassen Trail was discovered by William H. Noble, who had migrated to California in 1849, and settled at Shasta. In the making of this road available for travel Noble was aided by Isaac Roop, W. Bonnefield, and several other enterprising citizens of Shasta. Altogether $2,000 was secured to build this road, which followed Lassen's Trail from the meadows on the Humboldt for about sixty miles, or about to the Hot Springs near Black Rock Peak. At this place, Noble's road turned southwest, went down Smoky Creek Desert country to the Susan river, passed north of Honey Lake to the Susan river, followed it to the site of the present town of Susanville, California, and thence proceeded due west to Shasta.

Near the sink of the Humboldt were two trails to California, the Truckee river and the Carson river routes. The former passed west of the Humboldt Lake, extended across the Truckee Desert in a southwest direction to the Big Bend of the Truckee river, and followed it to a point near the present town of Verdi, Nevada. In the short distance of forty miles from the Big Bend to the Truckee Meadows, the river was forded thirteen times. One of these fords was made on the Truckee Meadows near Glendale; the other one crossed at a point near the present bridge over the river on Virginia street in Reno, Nevada. At Verdi the road turned up Dog Valley Grade for some miles until it came upon the river again near the present town of Boca, California; thence it went along the river to the present site of Truckee, California. There it turned due west, followed along the north shore of Donner Lake, passed up and over the summit or Donner Pass. Over this route a very large part of the

---

[184] Fairfield, *Pioneer History of Lassen County,* 6.

travel went to the mines as well as to other California settlements.

The first cutoff on the Truckee route, known as Beckwourth's Road, was made at the first fording of the Truckee river in the meadows, later known as the Stone and Gates Crossing (Glendale, Nevada). A low pass over the Sierra Nevada (about 5,000 feet) was discovered by James P. Beckwourth, a half-breed negro trapper and miner.[185] This mountaineer was wont to tell fantastic tales of doubtful authenticity of hair-raising experiences which he had had in his checkered career with the Indian tribes of the Rocky mountain region. He thereby gained a reputation which rivaled Baron Munchausen himself. According to his own story, one day in 1849 when he was on a prospecting trip with several other miners, he saw this very low-lying pass over the mountains. He said nothing about the discovery to his companions, but thought to himself that it would be a good plan to build a road over it so as to gain some of the benefits from the emigrants whom he could turn off at a point on the Truckee river. Two years later he obtained encouragement and the promise of financial aid from a Mr. Turner, proprietor of the American Ranch, and from some of the residents of Marysville, California. The mayor of the latter place was very active in urging Beckwourth to prosecute his scheme. He believed his town would be greatly benefited by the diversion of the travelers from the Truckee-Donner Route to Beckwourth's Road. When it was completed in 1851 Beckwourth went to the Truckee river to await the arrival of the emigrant trains. While on this mission he was seized with a severe attack of erysipelas and, according to his own story, had "abandoned all hopes of recovery" when a passing train rescued him. The women of the party nursed him back to health. When he was able to travel, he guided the party over his road (Beckwourth Pass) to Marysville, California. On the night of the arrival of this company the mayor arranged for a big celebration. Later on the same evening, most of the town burned, so Mr. Beckwourth was never paid by the city for building his road. He was rewarded, however, when in 1852 he built a trading post at the lower end of Sierra Valley (now Beck-

[185] Bonner, *The life and adventures of James P. Beckwourth*, 426-432.

James P. Beckwourth

"Jim" Beckwourth's Trading Post

The old trading post building, located at the foot of Sierra Valley, is now the dairy on the Guido Ramelli Ranch. It is the oldest building in the valley. Reproduced for the first time from a rare photograph.

wourth, California).[186] This post was the first stopping place between Salt Lake and the mines in the vicinity of Marysville.

Beckwourth's Road turned northwest from the Truckee river, near Glendale, followed along the eastern part of the meadows, passed through the Spanish Springs Valley, the Red Rock country, and proceeded over Beckwourth's Pass, the lowest pass in the entire Sierra Nevada chain (known later as Chilcoot Pass) to the headwaters of the Middle Fork of the Feather river in Sierra Valley, thence west and southwest to the main Feather river, which it followed down to Marysville. There was not a great deal of travel over this route because the road down the Feather river cañon was very hazardous.

The second cutoff on the Truckee Route was the Henness Pass Road, which could be taken by turning due west on the Truckee River Route near the modern town of Verdi. It continued up the grade (later known as the Dog Valley Grade), crossed Sardine Valley to the Little Truckee river, which it followed up to the west side of Weber Lake, and thence through the Henness Pass to the rich diggings of the upper Yuba river country near Downieville, California. Chief interest in this road to Nevadans lies in the fact that a great many of the early miners who rushed to the Comstock discovery came over this route.[187] A short cut to the Henness Pass Road could be made near the present town of Boca, California, by following up Dry Creek and passing across Russell Valley to the Little Truckee river, where it connected with the main Henness Road.

All of the routes described thus far ran north of Lake Tahoe. There were, however, large numbers of emigrants who took routes south of the lake, influenced probably by Frémont's report of his explorations in the West. He had discovered Carson Pass, reached by the way of the West Fork of the Carson river. The first road over this pass was

---

[186] The spelling of the town and pass was "Beckwith" until July 1, 1932, when the United States post office department ordered the former to be changed to Beckwourth. The former spelling of the name was confused probably with Captain E. G. Beckwith, who headed a party of government explorers. He was looking for a suitable pass for a railroad in 1854.

[187] Statement of Robert Gracey to writer, August 27, 1927.

built by a group of Mormons, a number of whom had served in the Mormon battalion in the conquest of California. In the summer of 1848 a party of forty-five men and one woman (the wife of William Cory), seventeen wagons, one hundred horses, and about the same number of cattle, two brass cannons obtained from Captain Sutter, and every man armed with a musket, set out from Sutter's settlement to return to the Great Salt Lake. In order to take their wagons, they had to build a road over the mountains by hewing down trees, cutting away the underbrush, and rolling aside boulders.

Henry William Bigler, a member of the party and a co-discoverer of gold with James Wilson Marshall, kept a diary of his road-building enterprise. He recorded a very graphic picture as the road building advanced over the mountains. In it, he described the difficulties with the Indians and the features of the country at that early date. The road they built branched off at a point near Brighton, California, a short distance northeast of Sutter's Fort. It continued into the foothills to the site of Hangtown (Placerville), California. At this point it followed along the ridges to some springs where grew many leeks, hence the name Leek Springs.

It was the custom of the party to have several men go forward to find the best route to build the road, and a suitable camping place. On the morning of June 17, Bigler and four other men went on in advance of the party to work the road for ten miles. When they were returning to camp on the same evening, they came upon some ashes of a recent camp fire, near which was a fresh grave. Some of the men thought it might be an Indian grave since an old wickiup stood nearby. On their arrival at the main camp they found that three of the men, who had gone on still farther in search of a pass through the mountains, were missing. They then linked the missing men with the fresh grave and the Indians. In consequence, camp was called together and an organization for protection was perfected. Captains of tens were appointed and Lieutenant Thompson was selected to be the captain over the whole company in case of fighting. It was decided also that they would open the grave to see if by chance their missing companions had been murdered and buried by the Indians. Upon doing so, they were shocked at

the sight of their companions robbed of every stitch of clothing, and lying in one hole about two feet deep. There were
arrow heads lying plentifully on the ground, many of which
were bloody and broken. The gory battlefield showed that
the men had not died without a desperate struggle, even the
rocks were stained with blood, and one of the men's purses,
containing gold dust, was found about a rod from the grave.
Their riding animals and pack mules were gone as were all
of their clothes, guns, and provisions. The bodies were re-
buried, and the grave was sealed with a large granite rock
to prevent the wild animals from robbing it, and to stand
as a monument to the murdered men. An inscription on a
balsam fir tree was cut which bore the following words: "To
the memory of Daniel Browett, Ezrah E. Allen and Henderson Cox who was supposed to have been murdered by Indians
on the night of the 27th of June, A.D. 1848." To this place
was given the name "Tragedy Springs."

The party built the road over the Sierra Nevada range at
Carson Pass and descended then into Hope Valley to the
headwaters of the West Fork of the Carson river (named
Pilot river by them), which it followed to the main stream.
As they continued northeast down river into Carson Valley,
they stopped at some hot springs (Walley's Hot Springs).
The Washoe Indians began to be very troublesome; at night
a hundred fires could be seen in the mountains, signals made
by the red men that danger was approaching. The Indians
following closely behind the party, stole some of their stock.
The party continued down the Carson river for some distance
(just how far the diary does not say); however, five days
were spent camping along it.

On August 12 the party left Pilot river and set out on a
northwest course. After traveling for twenty-five miles they
reached the "Truckey" river near the Big Bend. They were
now on the Humboldt Trail, which they followed to Salt
Lake City. This road was the first one to be built from the
Sacramento river to the Carson Valley.[188] A few years later
Johnson's Cutoff (discovered by a mail carrier of that name)
through Hope Valley saved the traveler from going over
the steep Carson Pass. When settlements were made in

188 William Henry Bigler, "Diary of a Mormon," MS., 53ff., Bancroft Library.

Carson Valley in 1851, several other roads were built over the mountains — notably through Daggett's, Luther's and DeGroot's passes,[189] all of which connected with the Humboldt road by continuing down the Carson river to Ragtown (Leeteville). At this place either of the two routes — Carson or Walker river — could be taken. The Walker river route was the left hand road going southwest to the bend of the river, thence up this river to the West Fork which was followed to its headwaters and then over the Sonora Pass to the Stanislaus river and on to the mines near Columbia and Sonora, California. The Walker River Route and pass were very difficult to negotiate so they were not used as much as were some of the more northern ones.

Over the two main routes across Nevada — Humboldt and Mormon — with their many cutoffs, thousands of men, women, and children crossed our state in the "Great Trek" to the land of golden promises. There is no doubt that there were still other trails — every pass, valley, and river cañon around the rim of the Great Basin bore, probably, its quota of the incoming and outgoing travel.[190] Of many of these there is little or no printed record, and so for them, there can be proclaimed no fame except that which remained in family tradition or local lore. Each one, nevertheless, bore evidence of the grit, the energy, and the perseverance of the pioneers of the western empire. From animal path to Indian trail; from mule trail to wagon road; from steam engine to automobile highway, these routes have been substantially the same. On mountain tops along them where signal fires were once lighted by the red man to warn his tribesmen of the approach of trespassers, today beacon lights flash to guide the aviator on his flight. The federal government had no need to build a wagon road to the Pacific coast. That task was done by trapper, trader, emigrant, and miner.

[189] In 1859 a third road across Nevada was explored by Captain J. H. Simpson from Camp Floyd on Utah Lake across central Nevada to Genoa, Nevada. It was used by the pony express and the overland mail, and today is the Lincoln Highway.

[190] The passes through the Sierra Nevada north of Lake Tahoe were Lassen's, Madeline or Smoke Creek, Noble's or Fredonyer's, Nightingill's, Wasson's, Beckwourth's, Henness, Truckee or Donner; those south of the lake were Johnson's, Daggett's, Luther's, Carson, DeGroot's, Ebbett's, Mono (Tioga), Sonora, and Walker passes.

# Across Nevada with the Golden Army

The decade 1840-1850 was a momentous one, not merely for Nevada nor yet merely for the far West. Although the actual impressive pageant was enacted chiefly upon these stages, a nation partook and profited thereby, and the political face of a continent was altered. At the opening of this era the first emigrant party crossed the continent to the Pacific coast. Between 1843 and 1845 the first scientific explorations were made in the Great Basin by the federal government. And in 1846 the long-pending Oregon question was settled. In the latter half of the decade the Mormons sought out Zion on the shores of Great Salt Lake, then Mexican territory. On January 24, 1848, gold was discovered on the South Fork of the American river, forty-five miles northeast of Sutter's Fort, now Sacramento. Two weeks later the war between the United States and Mexico was terminated by the Treaty of Guadalupe Hidalgo, which ceded to the United States the territory embraced in the states of California, Nevada, and Utah, much of Arizona and parts of New Mexico, Colorado, and Wyoming. In 1849 thousands of gold seekers migrated from the eastern states and from European countries to California; one of these "Forty-niners" discovered gold in a cañon on the Carson river (Gold cañon). In 1851 the first permanent settlement in Nevada was made by the Mormons in Carson Valley.

In 1849 and the years following, eager adventurers streamed by all discoverable land and water routes to make their fortunes in the gold fields of California.[191] Many of these emigrants kept records of their experiences as they crossed the continent. Hundreds of journals, diaries, memoranda — some of them published — are extant. These daily recordings must have been made with difficulty — scrawled

[191] Thirty-one routes to California are given by Lieutenant Randolph B. Marcy, *The Prairie Traveler*, 179-251.

by the light of a camp fire during watch, hastily jotted early in the morning before others had awakened, or while the cook prepared the evening meal in camp; there could have been little time for writing on the trail. Most of the books which retell the stories of these manuscripts give only a general impression of Nevada as the emigrant saw it. It is worth while to give a more detailed story of this migration across our state, not only as the golden army experienced it, but as nearly as possible as they told it.[192]

Life was full and intense for every member of the golden army on its trek. Families were made smaller one day, and increased the next.[193] Romances of the trail ripened into marriages. Quarrels resulted either in expulsion from the party or in death. High was the reward the emigrant expected for courage and loyalty; just as high was the penalty suffered for unfitness or deceit.

Slow means of communication and John Sutter's efforts to keep the discovery of gold secret, delayed the news of that epochal find from the rest of the world for several months. Stories and letters about the discovery began to appear in the newspapers of the states in the summer of 1848, but it was not until President Polk officially announced it in his December message of that year that the infection spread into every town, village, and hamlet from the Missouri river to the Atlantic. Businesses were sold out, families were broken up, and officials resigned their positions — all in feverish preparation to go west singly or with one of the hundreds of companies organized to make the trip. The papers were full of advertisements of devices to detect gold, of treatises on mining, guidebooks, preserved foods, and patent medicines. One part of a nation was getting ready to go to California, and the other part was equipping and aiding it to get off.

The great army swept across the country

. . . for miles, to the extent of vision, an animated mass of beings. . . Long trains of wagons with their white covers were moving slowly along,

---

[192] Exceptions of accuracy are the works of Owen Cochran Coy, *The Great Trek,* and Archer Butler Hulbert, *The Forty-niners.* It is regrettable that the maps in the latter book are incorrect and misleading.

[193] Judging from the names of the "covered wagon babies," many were born in Nevada. From the list of officers for 1931, note the following: president, James Carson Needham; Elijah Carson Hart, one of the vice-presidents; and Kate Nevada Bassett Hunt, treasurer.

a multitude of horsemen were prancing on the road, companies of men were traveling on foot, and although the scene was not a gorgeous one, yet the display of banners from many wagons, and the multitude of armed men, looked as if a mighty army was on its march.[194]

Most of the emigrants followed the historic path of the fur-trader and the early western explorer — northwest from the Missouri river to the Platte, up the Platte to the Sweetwater, across the Rockies through the South Pass, and on to Bear river in northeastern Utah. Once over the divide into the Great Basin, there was a choice of two routes, each of which led into northeastern Nevada. The golden army first viewed Nevada from Goose Creek, in Elko county. To some of them it looked like "the breaking up of a world, a world no one wanted."

The beds of the streams in this vicinity were covered with mica, which many mistook for gold.[195]

The mountains enclosing one of the branches of Goose Creek were high and precipitous, the formation appeared to be of igneous origin and is often turret-shaped. . . The rock in many places is columnar in form and position, many columns standing together with seams and crevices running in a perpendicular form and position.[196]

Along this cañon there were many chalk ledges curiously hollowed into caverns. Because so many of the emigrants carved their names on the smooth walls, the name "Record Bluff" was given to them.[197]

Now the real hardships of the journey began. Since the hills were almost bare of grass, thousands of livestock starved to death. The necessity of lightening the loads forced many travelers to break up their outfits and "pack" through the remaining distance to California. Some made carts out of their wagons, and themselves pushed their few precious possessions. Some threw a few necessities onto mules and

[194] "During the first week of January, 1849, fifty vessels sailed from American ports for San Francisco, many others came from foreign countries, and before the end of the year, 230 American vessels reached California harbors. . . . Within three weeks during the spring of 1849, nearly 18,000 crossed the Missouri river for California. A single observer counted eleven hundred wagons on the prairies beyond Independence. . . Fully 35,000 took part in this great movement of 1849. . ." Cleland, op. cit., 232-233.

[195] Delano, Life on the plains and at the diggings, 153.

[196] Sawyer, Life on the Plains, 153.

[197] Hosea B. Horn, Overland Guide, 45; see above, 110.

horses and rushed on as fast as possible. Others had lost
everything and were compelled to walk. In 1850 one emigrant
noted in the Goose Creek country "an immense amount of
property strewn all along the road, such as wagons, har-
nesses, broken guns, trunks, clothing, abandoned by the
owners because their teams have failed." [198]

At length the great army was on the Humboldt river – the
stream of many names, about which they had heard so very
many tales. The trip down it took its appalling toll of animal
and human life and frayed the nerves of the strongest sur-
vivor.[199] One early passer described it as:

> . . . a veritable Dolorosa from the point where the trails from Fort Hall
> and Salt Lake united, to and beyond the base of the Sierra Nevada. From
> June until October it was crowded with men and women, and children,
> struggling as best they could through one vast cloud of blinding, smothering
> dust while their jaded teams were dragging their almost empty wagons
> over hills of crumbling shale, or loose sand and gravel; through deep
> trenches worn by other wheels, in beds of alkali earth or volcanic ash, or
> across broad stretches of desert in which there was no water, and not
> even a mouthful of bitter wormwood for horses or oxen. It was here that
> the heat of summer was greatest by day, and the cold severest by night;
> often when the temperature would be almost unbearable at midday, ice
> would form in their pails while they were asleep. It was here that the
> Indians were most troublesome, watching them from behind the hills or
> some other places of concealment during the day, haunting their camps
> by night, wounding their cattle with their arrows when they could not
> stampede them, and butchering any unarmed straggler who strayed beyond
> the protection of his fellows.[200]

Delos R. Ashley, the purser of a company which called
itself the "California Association," crossed Nevada in 1850.
Such staccato excerpts as these from his record are brief and
illuminating:

TUES. JULY 17. Very warm - sand roads. Toilsome as hell.
WED. J. 18. Sand!!! Grass parched and dry - P.M. 8ms [miles] of
R[iver]. Camp 8. P.M.
THURS. JULY 19. Camped 10 P.M. No grass (wheugh!)

---

[198] Sawyer, op. cit., 68.
[199] The alkali made the animals have cramps and spasms. An antidote in
the form of a sandwich of "a plug of tobacco bound between two slices of
bacon . . . was a kill or cure; sometimes it was one, sometimes it was another."
Alfred Lambourne, The Pioneer Trail, 66.
[200] Zöeth Skinner Eldredge, History of California, III, 245-46.

Fri. July 20. 10 o'c. Hot!!! No halt at noon - camped 6 o'c p.m.
Grass 3ms.
Sat. July 21. Staid at slough.
Sun. July 22. From slew to sink (O. Barrenness).

Mr. Ashley could scarcely have foreseen at the time that a
few years later he would be representing this very territory
in the congress of the United States.[201]

Kit Carson, too, contributed to the damning record.

Truly, the Humboldt is the burying ground of horses and oxen; we pass
daily large numbers dead by the roadsides and at every watering ground,
and in the river and sloughs . . . in fact the river water is nothing but
horse broth, and not fit for man or beast, but it is the only water we can
get, so we have to swallow it.[202]

If midsummer found the emigrant still on the Humboldt,
the water had evaporated to a few pools, "stagnant and their
edges invariably lined with dead cattle that had died while
trying to get a drink." Another traveler said that while:

. . . selecting a carcass that was solid enough to hold us up we would
walk out into the pool on it, taking a blanket with us, which we would
swash around and get full of water as it would hold, then holding each end,
would twist the filthy water out into a pan, which in turn would be
emptied into our canteens, to last until the next camping place.[203]

Great was the number of dead animals along the way. On
July 31, 1850, one emigrant counted "126 head of horses,
mules and oxen, and then got tired of the business and quit
it." Two days later, another man counted in a distance of
fifteen miles "350 dead horses, 280 oxen, and 120 mules
and hundreds of others left behind, unable to keep up. A
tanyard or slaughter house is a flower garden in comparison." [204] One traveler noted that the beaten trail was so
encumbered with dead animals that it had to take a new
course in some places.[205] Another of the same party observed

[201] Delos R. Ashley, "Documents for the History of California, 1827-1860,"
ms., Bancroft Library, University of California.

[202] *Infra,* 130.

[203] G. L. Cole, *In the early days along the Overland Trail,* 15.

[204] Eleaser Ingalls, *Journal of a trip to California.*

[205] Silas Newcomb, "Journal, kept during an overland journey to California
and Oregon, 1850-51," ms., Coe collection, Huntington Library. Quoted in
Sawyer, *op. cit.,* 85.

. . . a number of ox teams of five or six pairs each, lying down in their yokes - some of them dead, some of them with their swollen tongues lying extended out in the dust, and moaning and groaning as pitifully as one of our kind - unable to avoid the almost perpendicular rays of the sun now beating upon this spot with a fury almost indescribable. . . A myriad of buzzards hovered around, alighting now and then to pick out the eyes of the prostrate whether dead or alive.[206]

The toll of human lives was also great, but there is no way of telling the numbers of those who were killed by disease, thirst, or Indians. Cholera was very bad among the emigrants on the trail in 1849 and 1850. Many stricken with this disease died from lack of care or from drinking the stagnant water in the pools. Hubert Howe Bancroft, the historian, estimated that five thousand persons perished from disease.[207] At the bottom of a steep hill three miles east of the present town of Beowawe lies a cemetery which contains some very old graves. At this point — Gravelly Ford to the emigrant — was one of the best camping places along the Humboldt Trail. Undoubtedly many of the trains remained here until the sick in the party either were better or had died.[208]

Generally from two to three weeks were spent in traveling down the Humboldt river, a distance of three hundred miles, each of which invited curses upon its waters. One traveler inscribed the following lines to it:

> Meanest and muddiest, filthiest stream,
>     most cordially I hate you;
> Meaner and muddier still you seem since
>     the first day I met you.
>
> Your namesake better was no doubt, a
>     truth the inscriptions tell.
> Her seven devils were cast out, but
>     yours are in you still.
>
> What means these graves so fresh and
>     new along your banks on either side?
> They've all been dug and filled by you,
>     thou guilty wretch, thou homicide.

[206] Silas Newcomb, *op. cit.*, quoted in Sawyer, *op. cit.*, 85.
[207] Eldredge, *History of California*, v, describes the epidemic.
[208] "The Maiden's Grave" is in this cemetery.

Now fare thee well, we here shake hands
and part (I hope) to meet no more,
I'd rather lie in happier lands than
longer live upon your shore.[209]

The Humboldt may have been mean, muddy, and filthy, but what would the gold seekers have done in crossing this stretch of the Great Basin had there been no river at all?

When the emigrants reached the sink of the Humboldt near Lovelock, they might choose one of three routes to the Sierra Nevada range – the Truckee River Route passing north of Lake Tahoe, the Carson River Route going south of it, or the Walker Pass Route. To reach either of the first two they had to cross the Forty-mile Desert. To those of the golden army who were well-informed about the preparations necessary before crossing it, the hardships of the desert were not greater than others they had suffered; but to many not forewarned, the crossing of these few miles was the worst of the entire journey. Because there was neither water nor vegetation on this stretch, it had to be crossed without a halt. Consequently, a few days were spent at the sink of the Humboldt cutting all the grass that could be carried, and filling all receptacles with water. Even with such precautions, the loss of life and property was great.

The year 1849 was hot and dry, and this stretch of the trail was reached usually late in August, hottest month of the year. One record says that in this year:

There have been so many cattle and horses left here to die by starvation, that the road is filled, and you can hardly pass between them in such places; and there is such a stench you are nearly suffocated. There is probably one thousand wagons left teamless here within forty-three miles.[210]

Another reported nine days later that "bonfires were made all along the trail out of the wagons and vehicles left by the emigrants who had gone on before. The light of the fires lit up our pathway and revealed the awful loss of stock." [211]

---

[209] These lines were written by Dr. Horace Belknap when he crossed Nevada on his trip from Iowa to California in 1850. Quoted in Leander V. Loomis, *A Journal of the Birmingham Emigrating Company*, 94, fn. 1.

[210] John Udell, *Incidents of travel to California, across the Great Plains*, 30.

[211] G. W. Thissell, *Crossing the Plains in '49*, 133.

A count of the dead stock and the graves along the route was made in 1850, showing appalling numbers as follows: 1061 dead mules, 4960 dead horses, 3750 dead oxen and cows, and 963 graves; and the value of the abandoned property was placed at a million dollars! [212]

The mirage on the Carson Desert was particularly tantalizing to parched animals and travelers. In a trackless waste where there was not a spear of grass nor a trace of other vegetation or water, they could see through the rays of the broiling sun "a clear, beautiful lake with its rippling waves sparkling in the sun-beams but a short distance ahead, and to the left. . ." They discovered after traveling awhile that the water receded as fast as they advanced. "Sometimes the mules, a mile ahead, appeared to be ungainly, misshapen animals as large as elephants; sometimes they appeared very tall as though set up on poles." [213] The effect of this dreaded desert has been perhaps best recorded by the pen of an intelligent lady, Sarah Royce, mother of Josiah Royce the philosopher. In her diary, *A Frontier Lady,* a classic of western travel-journals, she wrote of the bitter crossing with her husband and her baby girl on October 9, 1849. Since the little family had set out on its great trek later than most of the golden army, they found themselves among the last to cross this desert in that year.

About noon on the day named, they set out upon the crossing. During most of the afternoon Mrs. Royce walked, but toward twilight her husband persuaded her to ride. She climbed into the wagon, and after an anxious hour or two, fell asleep beside her baby. But her rest was short. The wagon stopped suddenly, and she heard her husband say, "So you've given out, have you, Tom?" She got out of the wagon quickly, to see one of the four oxen prostrate on the ground, and his companion looking as if he were about to follow soon. The yoke was unfastened and Tom was left on the desert to die. When another cow had been put to the yoke, the party started on. Mrs. Royce walked the remaining distance to the Carson river. At first she trudged along beside the team, but they moved so slowly, struggling to pull against the deep sand,

[212] *Ohio Statesman,* December 2, 1850, quoted in Sawyer, *op. cit.,* 91, fn. 137.
[213] Sawyer, *op. cit.,* 88.

that they fell yards behind her. When she was so far ahead
that she could no longer hear the sound of the hoofsteps and
the grinding of the wheels in the sand, she paused to listen,
"dreading lest they had stopped" and another animal had
given out. She waited, then, for them to catch up with her,
and through the darkness tried to see if the heads and horns
of the oxen drooped lower.

Through the endless night the little Royce family crept
slowly on, past dead "bodies of cattle lying here and there
on both sides of the road." As they advanced, the number
of dead increased. "Some animals were lying in front of a
wagon, apparently just as they had dropped down, while loose
yokes and chains indicated that part of the teams had been
driven on . . . for the contents of the wagons were scattered in confusion . . . at still shortening intervals." Similar
scenes kept recurring, until it seemed to them that they were
"the last little, feeble struggling band at the rear of a routed
army." From midnight on through the early morning hours,
they had to stop and rest the animals more frequently. The
moon rose, "showing trunks, clothes, boxes from among
which they found several sides of well cured bacon." They
gave the oxen the last bit of hay, and let them drink the last
drop of water. How much longer could they hold out?

"But westward look the land is bright!" [214]

Soon dim morning approached. Surely there must be signs
of the Carson river soon! After a meager breakfast hurried
by anxiety, they pressed forward. From this point on, let the
courageous young pioneer wife tell the story:

For a long time not a word was spoken save occasionally to the cattle.
I had again, unconsciously, got in advance, my eyes scanning the horizon
to catch the first glimpse of any change, though I had no definite idea in
my mind what first to expect. But now there was surely something. . . It
was very low at first and I feared it. . . I paused, and stood until the
team came up. I asked my husband what he thought that low dark line
could be. "I think," he said, "it must be the timber on Carson river."
Again we were silent and for a while I watched anxiously the heads of
the two leading cattle. . . I observed how low their heads drooped as
they pressed their shoulders so resolutely and yet so wearily against the
bows. Another glance at the horizon. Surely there was now visible a little

[214] Arthur Hugh Clough, "Say not the struggle nought availeth," in John
Mathews Manly, *English Prose and Poetry.*

unevenness in the top of that dark line, as though it might indeed be trees. . . . At that moment the white faced leader raised his head, stretched forward his nose and uttered a low "Moo-o-oo." I was startled fearing it was the sign for him to fall, exhausted. "What is the matter with him," I said. "I think he smells water," was the answer.[215]

A little distance farther and the desert was behind, but it was noon before the family sat in the shade of "those longed-for trees, beside the Carson river." [216]

If there is one spot on the California Trail across Nevada worthy of being commemorated, it is this place on the Carson river (later Ragtown, now Leeteville) where the weary, footsore emigrant and his beasts rested for the first time in the shade of trees and drank the first pure water in hundreds of miles. Almost all the diaries of the trip comment on the actions of the animals when, still floundering through the last few miles of soft sand, they caught scent of the Carson river water. Completely unmanageable, they stampeded down the slope to check their mad rush only when up to their bellies in the stream. As for men, they were "seen to rush up, half crazed with thirst, and weep as children, and bless God for their deliverance." [217] One cried ecstatically "Trees — real trees, green trees, shade-giving trees!" and fell on his face and wept. So the emigrant, released from the rack of the desert, became a tree-worshipper.[218]

When the emigrant had reached the Carson, the most harrowing experiences of the journey were over. The trail up the river and over the mountains was slow and tedious, but there were grass, trees, and good water for the greater part of the way.

If the traveler elected the Truckee River Route he found the hardships of the trip about the same: the distances were about equal, the hazards as great, and the same good fortune awaited him at his goal. Although water was to be obtained about halfway between the sink of the Humboldt and the

[215] Reprinted from Sarah Royce, *A Frontier Lady*, 51-57, by permission of the Yale University Press.

[216] In 1850, a trading post was established at this point on the river. It was Ragtown, now the Morgan Ranch about ten miles west of Fallon, Nevada.

[217] Jasper Morris Hixson, "A gold hunter; the itinerary across the continent in 1849," MS., quoted in Coy, *op. cit.*, 202.

[218] G. L. Cole, *In the Early Days along the Overland Trail*, 111.

Big Bend of the Truckee, it was from hot springs. Usually some member of the party rode ahead to cool some water for the animals before the main party arrived. As the road left the sink, it passed over high undulations; but as it approached the river, the sand was even deeper than on the Carson River Route.[219]

This desert, too, produced strange optical illusions by day, and gave a distorted appearance to objects by night. The crossing of it was well described by a Forty-niner:

The impressions of that night ride were most extraordinary. As the sun sank and twilight shaded into night the atmosphere was filled with a hazy dimness. . . Only a tinge of moonlight from above softened the dull hue. . . . It was an impenetrable, opaque narrowing of the horizon, and closing in of the heavens above us; which, as we advanced constantly shifted its boundary, retaining us still in the center of the great amphitheater of half-night. We could see one another, but beyond or above the encompassing veil all was mystery . . . no moon nor stars visible. . .

As the night merged into morning the sunlight gradually dispelled the mantle of gloom from our immediate presence; but still we could not see out . . . on we went guided only by the tracks of those who had gone on before us. . .

In the after part of the night, the loose cattle, having been for two nights and a day without water, and instinctively expecting an opportunity to drink, quickened their pace . . . till the drove was strung out two or three miles in length along the sandy trail.

From midnight to daybreak, seemed a period amounting to entire days and nights; from dawn till sunrise, an epoch; and from sunrise to the time of reaching the river, as a period that would have no end. As the sun finally rose behind us the faintest adumbrations of the nearest ridges of the Sierras was discerned in a dim, blue scroll across the western horizon. On we labored, overcoming distance inch by inch; nodding in our saddles; occasionally dismounting to shake off the almost overpowering grasp of sleep.[220]

This party reached the Truckee river about nine o'clock in the morning, just ahead of the cattle. They tried to check the rush of the animals, but:

. . . Ten men on ten mules could not have stopped one cow from plunging into that river. . . [both man and beast washed off the] dust from the Black Hills, overlaid with alkali powder from the Humboldt, veneered with ashes of the desert; all ingrained by weeks of dermatic absorption,

[219] The sand was especially deep in the few miles between the present towns of Fernley and Wadsworth.

[220] Maxwell, *Crossing the Plains*, 145-164.

rubbed in by the wear of travel, [and] polished by the friction of the wind. . .[221]

Although the Humboldt River Trail was the route followed by most of the gold seekers, there was a trail from the Great Salt Lake to Los Angeles used by emigrants who did not want to remain among the Mormons for the winter, or who feared to cross the Sierra Nevada in the snow season. Although the Salt Lake-Los Angeles Trail had long been a well known road there was not much definite information to be obtained regarding it. There was, however, a general opinion in Salt Lake that a direct route to the mines could be made by taking the Williams' Cutoff, a description of which was given in the preceding chapter.

In the late fall of 1849 several parties of emigrants found themselves at Salt Lake City. Desiring not to remain with the Mormons all winter, nor yet to have the fate of the Donner party, they decided to take the Los Angeles Trail. One party set out on November 3, 1849, guided by a Mr. Jefferson Hunt, a Mormon leader desirous of founding a colony at San Bernardino. Their route was south-southwest through a series of fertile valleys to the southern rim of the great Utah Basin. Here they struck the Old Spanish Trail, which they followed to the Santa Clara river, a tributary of the Virgin. Although they found sufficient feed along these streams, the stock had been already so worn by the long journey westward that many were too weak to continue and had to be left behind. "Las Vegas, further on this way, is another famous camping ground. It is a large meadow with several springs at the head uniting which form a stream flowing through it. One of these springs is so large as to make a good bathing pool, and the water is warm and boils up with such force as to buoy the swimmer like a cork." [222] The weakened condition of the cattle delayed the party so much that their provisions were almost exhausted. Consequently several rode on ahead to get relief, which was obtained readily from the American settlers in southern

---

221 Maxwell, *op. cit.*, 166-168.

222 Walter Van Dyke, "Overland to Los Angeles by the Salt Lake Route in 1849," *Annual Publications of the Historical Society of Southern California,* III (1894), 76-83.

California. The entire party finally arrived, but they had consumed eight months in the journey.

No such good fortune fell to the party which essayed the Williams' Route, the cutoff on the Salt Lake-Los Angeles Trail. Once a number of late arrivals at the Mormon city united into one large group known as the Sand Walking Company, with Mr. J. Hunt as leader. There were one hundred and seven wagons and about five hundred head of live stock. Each wagon agreed to pay Mr. Hunt ten dollars for his service as pilot. The member of the party who was to become best known was William Lewis Manly, chiefly because he left a record of the experiences of the party in his *Death Valley in '49*.

This company proceeded southwest from the Great Salt Lake in October, 1849. When they reached the rim of the Great Basin near the head of Virgin river on November 1, they were overtaken by another train captained by a Mr. Smith. The Smith company had a map of Williams' Cutoff.

This map [says Manly] was quite frequently exhibited and the matter freely discussed in camp, indeed speeches were made in the interest of the cutoff route which was to be so much shorter. . . The more the matter was talked about, the more there were who were converted to the belief that the short road would be the best. The map showed every camp on the road and indicated where there was water and grass, and as to obstacles to the wagons it was thought they could be overcome. A general meeting was called for better consideration of the question.[223]

The opinion of their pilot, Captain Hunt, was sought as to the feasibility of the proposed new route. When he consented finally to discuss it, he said that:

. . . he really knew no more than the others about this particular route, but he very much doubted if a white man ever went over it, and that he did not consider it at all safe for those who had wives and children in their company to take the unknown road. Young men . . . could possibly get through. . . But he said, "If you decide to follow Smith, I will go with you, even if the road leads to Hell. . . ."[224]

That is exactly where the Williams' Cutoff led, to Death Valley, California.[225] When the time came for the party to

---

[223] Lewis Manly, *Death Valley*, 109-110.
[224] *Ibid.*, 110.
[225] *Ibid.*, 131.

divide on the Old Spanish Trail, Hunt kept with the larger group who took the longer but definite trail, and Manly assumed the rôle of leader and scout for the smaller group which took the cutoff.

It is impossible to ascertain just where the cutoff was made. It was probably near Mountain Meadows in southwestern Utah; the intention was to travel due west to the San Joaquin Valley. If the cutoff was made at this point, the party entered Nevada just north of Mesquite. In the record left by Manly, there are no features to identify the exact route followed. Some members of the party which took the cutoff, realizing before they had gone far into the desert that all was not right, turned back and rejoined the main party on the Los Angeles Trail. On account of the forbidding nature of the country, Manly became dissatisfied with the northwesterly route indicated on Smith's map of the Williams' Cutoff, and guided the party in a line more directly west, where he glimpsed across the barren landscape a snow-capped peak, probably in the Panamint range. Unable to find any of the springs and camping places indicated on the map, the party struggled through sand and mesquite bush. The oxen began to wear down under the heavy strain of pulling, and the lack of food; all unnecessary supplies and equipment were abandoned to lighten the load, and many of the party, as they pushed on toward the distant mountain, were often ready to give up the struggle.

They suffered intensely from thirst, going sometimes several days without water. After weeks of travel, they came to a dry river bed, the Amargosa river, near Beatty, Nevada. Turning west, they came to a low-lying and absolutely barren valley. One of the company described it as "the Creator's dumping place where he left the worthless dregs after making a world, and the devil had scraped these together a little." [226] As they proceeded down this sandy waste it became apparent that some of the party, if all were not to perish, must hasten ahead for help. Manly and another member went on to California to get succor.

The sufferings of this small relief party and of those who

[226] Manly, *Death Valley*, 141.

remained behind in the valley are not a part of this story. Fatigue, starvation, thirst, and death beset them. The party escaped finally from the valley, the lowest and hottest place in North America. It is related by Manly that when the party had climbed to the top of the mountains above this desolation, they took off their hats and "overlooking the scene of so much trial, suffering and death, spoke the thought uppermost, saying: 'Goodby, Death Valley.' " [227] And ever since the Manly party gave it that name, it has been called Death Valley. So far as is now known, none of the other gold seekers took the Williams' Cutoff.

Countless stories preserved only in local lore, or guarded only in the stilled echoes of the cañons in which they were enacted, remain to be told of the grim determination of the golden army as it crossed the continent to its coveted goal.

The earliest arrivals of the gold rush in California told of the hundreds of others who were still on the trail destitute, and who must perish without relief. Since California was still under military control, General Persifor H. Smith, in charge of the forces there, dispatched pack trains with army supplies across the mountains by all of the known emigrant routes. Major Rucker was placed in charge of the work. Through this splendid work his organization succeeded in bringing in safely from the desert the last of the emigrant trains of 1849 before the snows rendered the passes in the Sierra Nevada unsafe.[228]

Relief was also necessary for emigrants on the trail in 1850. Again parties were organized and supplies were sent out. Some of the emigrant bands were found without food for three days past. The early towns of California rose magnificently to their responsibility in aiding those who desired to make the golden state their home. These relief trains had everything that a family or a single man would need, food, clothing, or medicine. Everything was free to the emigrant. The California miners assessed themselves three dollars a man for this relief.

In 1852 there were so many emigrants ill that the relief

---

[227] *Ibid.,* 216.

[228] Bancroft, *History of California,* VI, 152.

party was forced to erect a temporary hospital in Carson Valley where three thousand were given treatment.[229] The outstanding good Samaritan was William Waldo, a member of the relief committee of Sacramento. When the supplies which he had personally conducted to the Humboldt river had been exhausted, he sent back a letter, an extract from which gives an idea of the need of such aid:

> Should your committee still be unable to collect funds, I then ask that the committee, city council, or some other body of men, advance to me the amount of eight or ten thousand dollars, and forward the amount in flour and little articles for the sick, to this point, and to the summit, for which I pledge my honor, if I live to return where it can be legally done, to set over all my right, title and interest to real estate in Sacramento City, that has cost me ten thousand dollars. This sum will send between twenty and twenty-five thousand pounds of flour to the summit. . . This in connection with the beef, horses, mules and dead stock that can be jerked before it putrifies, will save ten thousand human beings from starvation. . . Can you believe that the destitution is so general that during an absence of six days from this station, I found but two trains of which I could procure a piece of bread and a cup of coffee? I have known a cup of soup, containing not more than a spoonful of flour, to sell for one dollar, and the buyer considered himself fortunate to get it on those terms.[230]

Aid was also sent out on the Lassen Trail, where travel was slow and raids of Indians on the food supply frequent.

The federal government was also very helpful to the emigrants, especially in aiding late comers over the mountains before the snow came. An illustration of this splendid work was the aid given the little Royce family in 1849. After the dreaded Forty-mile Desert was passed, the steep Sierra Nevada mountains were still ahead of them. It was the middle of October. As the party was moving slowly up the Carson river, dust was seen to rise from the road at one of the turns a few miles off. Soon two horsemen appeared, each leading a mule. Mrs. Royce and her husband were at the heads of the cattle, little Mary in the wagon. When they were within speaking distance one of the men said:

"Well, sir, you are the man we are after!!" "How can that be?" said my husband, with surprise. "Yes, sir," continued the stranger, "you and

229 *California Senate Journal*, 1853, app. no. 8.
230 Bancroft, *History of California*, VI, 155, fn. 18.

your wife, and that little girl, are what brought us as far as this. You see we belong to the Relief Company sent out by order of the United States government to help the late emigrants over the mountains. We were ordered only as far as Truckee Pass. When we got there we met a little company that had just got in. They'd been in a snow storm at the summit; 'most got froze to death themselves, lost some of their cattle, and just managed to get to where some of our men had fixed a relief camp. There was a woman and some children with them; and that woman set right to work at us fellows to go on over the mountains after a family she said they'd met on the desert going back for grass and water 'cause they'd missed their way. She said there was only one wagon, and there was a woman and child in it; and she knew they could never get through them cañons and over them ridges without help. We told her we had no orders to go any farther than there. She said she didn't care for orders. She didn't believe anybody would blame us for doing what we were sent out to do, if we did have to go farther than ordered. And she kept at me so, I couldn't get rid of her. You see I've got a wife and little girl of my own; so I felt just how it was; and I got this man to come with me and here we are, to give you more to eat, if you want it, let you have these two mules, and tell you how to get right over the mountains the best and quickest way." [231]

The government relief men advised them to abandon their wagon, pack the necessary equipment on the mules, and hurry over the mountains as quickly as possible. They then assisted the Royces to prepare for the quick ascent. The two extra government mules were to be ridden by Mr. and Mrs. Royce. To the latter was given "this white one . . . a perfectly trained, mountain saddle mule." [232]

Thus, by the generosity of the California miners, by the chivalry of the volunteers who went out on the trails to meet the on-coming trains, and by the wise forethought of the federal government, thousands of the argonauts were brought in safety through the last gruelling miles to their El Dorado.

[231] Royce, *op. cit.*, 63-64.
[232] *Ibid.*, 66.

# Zealous Zionites Settle Nevada

From September 22, 1827, the traditional day on which
Moroni, angel of the Lord, delivered to Joseph Smith the
"Golden Plates" and the "Urim and Thummim" with which
to translate them, to July 24, 1847, when a revelation from
the same divine source directed Brigham Young, upon seeing
the pulsating panorama of the Great Salt Lake Valley, to
exclaim, "This is the place," calamity and persecution dogged
the footsteps of the Mormons. From their Holy Land in
western New York to Kirtland, Ohio; from Jackson and
Clay counties, Missouri, to Nauvoo, Illinois; repeated misfortunes beset the Zionites.[233] Where could they go to wor-
ship unmolested? Accounts of the great western country, still
under control of Mexico, were read and discussed by the
twelve Elders and their leader, Brigham Young.[234] They
learned that just over the eastern rim of the Great Basin
there was a fresh, unbounded, magnificent wilderness, inhabited only by the red man. This was "the place" for the
Mormons, where they could live their religion without interference. So in 1846, with their eyes fixed on the little known
and uninhabited West, all of which south of the 42nd parallel
was at that time a part of old Mexico, 15,000 Mormons
set out from Nauvoo, Illinois. Brigham Young and a company of one hundred forty-seven men hurried on ahead to
prepare "the place" for the Saints. The remaining number
arrived in the valley of the Great Salt Lake in the early
summer of 1847.

---

[233] "This is the place; here we will raise a temple to our God." Bancroft,
*History of Utah*, 45, 261-262.

[234] Brigham Young was believed to have talked with Jim Bridger, the
trapper, scout, and proprietor of Fort Bridger; Father De Smet, the French
missionary; and "Peg Leg" Smith, the trapper and explorer, concerning the
Great Basin area. Robert Morris Werner, *Brigham Young*, quoting Young's
*Journal of Discourses*, v, 230-231.

During this movement of the Mormons, the Mexican War was being fought; Alta California became a part of the United States. Almost simultaneously with the signing of the Treaty of Guadalupe Hidalgo in 1848, gold was discovered in the Sacramento Valley. Some of the brethren, members of the Mormon battalion,[235] were present at the discovery, and when a number of them returned to Great Salt Lake City in the spring of 1848, they brought some of the gold dust. They told many thrilling stories of the new El Dorado. Many of the Saints wanted to go to California, but President Young forbade. If they should go his plan to colonize the Great Basin would be dissipated. Indeed, it took all of the persuasive powers he could muster to keep many of his Saints from succumbing to the gold fever. With very few exceptions, they heeded the advice of their leader; they were seeking "Zion" and not gold [236] – a compliment to the Mormon institution.

The first year in the Great Salt Lake Valley was a hard one. Although they did not arrive until late in July, a small crop was harvested. However, thereafter, with their assiduity in tilling the soil, the desert soon yielded abundant harvests. The valley became the half-way resting place for the weary travelers to California – the Saints were glad for the opportunity to trade their food for the surplus baggage of the emigrants. The Utah settlers are said to have made the most of their opportunities and there are accounts of their receiving the big end of the bargain.

The business acumen of the Mormon, his missionary zeal and desire to set up a theocratic state in the Great Basin, led the enterprising leaders of the faith to organize the free and independent state of Deseret. It embraced an immense tract of land, extending from "latitude 33 to the border

---

[235] A battalion of about five hundred young Mormon men was recruited for General Kearny's army of the west while the Saints were camped at Council Bluffs, Iowa. They were sent to Ft. Leavenworth, thence to San Diego, California. They took part in some of the skirmishes near Los Angeles and then were discharged. Some returned to Utah over the Los Angeles-Salt Lake Trail; others went north, and found employment at Sutter's Fort during the winter of 1847-1848. Brigham H. Roberts, *The Mormon Battalion*, gives the account of its activities.

[236] "Utah Early Records," MS., 31, 69.

of Oregon, and from the Rocky mountains to the Sierra Nevada, together with a section of the territory now included in southern California, and the strip of coast lying between lower California and 18° 30′ of west longitude." [237] Most of the state of Nevada was included in this area. The capital of the state of Deseret was Salt Lake City; the constitution and the powers of government were similar to those of the states of the Union. It is believed that the Mormons did not intend, however, to remain an independent republic, as a memorial asking for a territorial government was dispatched to the congress of the United States. Almon W. Babbitt, chosen the delegate to present the memorial, met, however, with a cool reception in Washington, and after an unfavorable committee report and dissenting votes in both houses of the congress, the proposed state of Deseret was rejected by the federal government.[238]

While the Mormons were urging the congress to give them control of this vast western area, another political organization was proposing to incorporate it into another state — the first constitutional convention of California was debating over the geographical extent of their proposed state of California. There were two parties in the convention; one, the large state party, led by William M. Gwin, advocated the inclusion of the territory between the Pacific and the summit of the Rocky mountains; the other, the small state party, sought to confine the limits of the state to the land between the ocean and the Sierra Nevada mountains. The members behind the large state plan argued that their area approximated more nearly the historical limits of Alta California under Spanish control, and that a larger state could bear the financial burdens of a state government more easily than a smaller one. "There was, also, an immediate need for courts and the enforcement of law in the region beyond the Sierras through which the immigrants were coming to California." [239] The adherents of the small state plan contended that it would be impossible "for a state located on the Pacific coast to administer a government for the

---

[237] Bancroft, *History of Utah*, 440-441.
[238] *House Journal*, 31 Cong., 1 sess., 414.
[239] Cleland, *History of California*, 254.

vast semi-desert region across the Sierras. Nor did they believe that the people of California had any right to extend their boundaries to include the Mormon inhabitants of Utah, who were already seeking to establish their own state of Deseret." [240] Besides it was believed by them that the congress would look more favorably on a small state than a large one. After a prolonged debate, a compromise line was settled upon and adopted by an overwhelming vote; the boundary was fixed approximately as it exists today between California and Nevada, then the western boundary of the territory of Utah. By this action on the part of the California convention, the area which later became the state of Nevada was destined to become part of the organization of the remaining territory of the Mexican cession. If the large state plan had succeeded, there would probably never have been a state of Nevada.

Slavery was the all-absorbing subject of the thirty-first session of the congress. However, something had to be done to organize this newly acquired territory. On September 9, 1850, the date the celebrated "compromise of 1850" was adopted, purporting to settle forever the slavery question, a bill passed the senate admitting California as a free state; another one created the territories of Utah and New Mexico, with a proviso that "when admitted as states the said territories or any portion of the same, shall be received into the Union, with or without slavery, as their constitution may prescribe at the time of admission."

The territory of Utah was bounded on the south by the thirty-seventh parallel, on the north by Oregon territory, the summit of the Rocky mountains formed the eastern boundary, and California bordered it on the west. Brigham Young was appointed governor over the new territory. The remainder of the Mexican cession was incorporated into the territory of New Mexico lying between the thirty-seventh and thirty-third parallels. The present state of Nevada was then a part of both of these territories. [241]

---

[240] Cleland, *History of California*, 254.

[241] *United States Public Laws*, 31 Cong., 1 sess., 453-458; *United States Charters and Constitutions*, II, 1236-1240; and *United States Acts and Resolutions*, 31 Cong., 1 sess., 53-58.

The refusal on the part of the federal government to recognize the state of Deseret did not prevent the Mormons from sending out missionaries to found missions in this region, nor from planting colonies in it. One group of Saints even formed a company to visit the California gold mines without asking the sanction of the church. On April 18, 1849, this party set out for California over the Humboldt-Carson Route. It was led by a Captain DeMont; Mr. Hampden S. Beatie was the clerk of the company. The intention of all of the members when they started was to mine for a short time, and then return to Great Salt Lake City. When the party arrived early in June in the Carson Valley, Beatie and several of his companions were so impressed with its beauty and desirability for a trading post that they decided to stay there and sell their provisions to passing emigrants; the others went on to California.[242] At the time of their arrival in Carson Valley, there were no other white men in what is now Nevada, but during the summer months of 1849 many "gentile" traders from California came over, and went out on the trail to sell supplies to the oncoming caravans. They returned home, however, before the mountain passes were closed for the winter.

Beatie and his companions, probably because they had nothing else to do, erected a shell of a 20x60-foot log, two-compartment house at the base of the Sierra Nevada mountains near the site of the present town of Genoa on the California trail. They put neither floor nor roof on the house, but it was nevertheless the first attempt to build any kind of a structure in Nevada.[243] There was no effort on the part of these men to fence or plant anything during their stay in the valley. The earliest arrivals of the '49ers told the Beatie party about the thousands of people who were coming that way later in the year. Beatie knew his supplies would be exhausted soon, so he and one of his companions, a Mr. Blackburn, went over the mountains to the American river to secure more. They sold three yoke of cattle, and with the money derived therefrom made their purchases. Because

---

[242] H. S. Beatie, "First in Nevada," MS., 2. At the time Beatie came to Nevada he was not a Mormon, but he joined the church later.

[243] Beatie, op. cit., 3.

these provisions were sold so quickly, they made another trip to Sacramento, where Beatie had a friend from whom he secured still added stocks for their station. These were carried back on fifteen pack mules.

The principal trade at Beatie Station was in horses and mules. Prices were exorbitantly high; flour sold for two dollars, fresh beef for one dollar, and bacon for two dollars a pound. Beatie had a limited quantity of flour which he sold in small amounts only, in order to help more people. He told of one captain of a train who wanted to purchase five hundred pounds of flour at two dollars a pound, but he would not sell to him and let others starve. In 1849, not being fully equipped for the long journey, the emigrants endured a great deal of suffering. So exhausted were many of the travelers and so short of provisions, that a good horse could be obtained for a few loaves of bread.[244] In the fall, Beatie sold his roofless and floorless house to a Mr. Moore, and with his companions returned to Salt Lake City. They took with them over one hundred head of horses obtained from the emigrants. While on the Humboldt river, they were attacked by Indians who captured all their animals and supplies. They were even forced to get rations from a passing emigrant train. Thus the first Mormon post in Nevada was a temporary one.

In August, 1850, Amasa M. Lyman and about thirty others, who had spent some time at the mines in California, left the coast for Great Salt Lake. They passed through Carson Valley which they, too, found to be a desirable place. When they returned they gave a flattering report of it to President Young and other Mormons. No doubt this report had some influence on the founding of the Genoa settlement in the following year.[245]

Carson Valley, situated on the extreme western rim of the Great Basin and lying in a northerly and southerly direction at the eastern base of the Sierra Nevada, is one of the most beautiful, fertile, and productive regions in the western part of the United States. It is well watered by the Carson river which flows through the entire length of the valley, and by

[244] Beatie, op. cit., 3, 5; Bancroft, History of Nevada, Colorado, and Wyoming, 67.

[245] Daniel Tyler, The Mormon Battalion, 339-340.

innumerable rivulets from the mountains. A natural wild hay grows in the rich loamy soil, affording an ideal place for farming and grazing. In 1850, Lorenzo Sawyer, then a young attorney, later a well-known California jurist, was struck with the beauty of Carson Valley, and especially with this wild grass. In his diary, he described it as being "the best we have found. It is now nearly ripe enough for hay-making. I never saw a more luxuriant crop of grass in my life than we found in this valley. It is superior in quality to any wild grass I have ever seen . . . densely thick and nearly as high as one's shoulders." [246] It was not surprising, then, that the tales told about this valley by the members of the DeMont-Beatie party influenced John and Enoch Reese, merchants of Salt Lake City, to establish a branch of their business in it.[247]

John Reese, Stephen Kinsey, his nephew, and seventeen men in his employ started west in the spring of 1851 with ten wagons loaded with flour, butter, eggs, bacon, and seeds of all kinds. On the first day of June they arrived at Ragtown on the Carson river, but not being struck with this location, they went on up the trail. On July 4 they came upon the old site of the Beatie house which now belonged to a man by the name of Moore. Reese paid him fifteen or twenty dollars for it; to be sure that his ownership would not be disputed later on, he gave Captain Jim of the Washoe tribe two sacks of flour for the surrounding land.[248] There has been considerable disagreement among writers of Nevada history concerning this house. Some have contended that there was not a sign of a house when Reese arrived; but they could not have had access to the diaries written contemporaneously with Reese's arrival or before, because many of the accounts mentioned this house in 1849, and again in 1850. Sawyer said in his diary of 1850 that:

Here [Genoa] we found two trading establishments with provisions and liquors brought out from California for the supply of the emigrants. These enterprising traders had just arrived and set up a brush shade for

[246] Lorenzo Sawyer, *Way Sketches*, 94, 95.

[247] Beatie became a clerk in the Reese store in Salt Lake City after he returned from Carson Valley.

[248] Myron Angel, *History of Nevada*, 31; Bancroft, *History of Nevada, Colorado, and Wyoming*, 67; John Reese, "Mormon Station," MS., 5.

a house till they could finish a log house which was in progress in a grove of pines at the base of the mountain. They sold provisions at exorbitant prices. Nothing in the eating line such as flour, pork, fresh beef, etc., could be had at a less price than two dollars a pound.[249]

Reese took a land claim along the side of the California trail, thirty acres of which he fenced and plowed. Upon hearing that there was going to be a great rush of emigrants the coming summer, he planted a large field of turnips which he sold for one dollar a bunch. In his own words he said, "I never saw such things to make money on." Wheat, corn, barley, and watermelons were also planted. A combination two-story store and hotel was built of logs in an "L" shape with a front of thirty feet and a depth of fifty.[250] This elbow-shaped house formed two sides of a pentagon-shaped stockade built at a cost of $2,000. It was made especially strong by setting fifteen foot logs, each touching the other, three feet in the ground to resist Indian attacks and for protection against marauding white men with which the country was then infested.[251] His stock consisted chiefly of oxen; pigs were obtained from California; and he bought up or traded his supplies for the cattle and horses of the emigrants, which he fattened on the fine wild hay of the valley. The little settlement that grew up around Reese's or Mormon Station was the first in what is now the state of Nevada; his ranch was also the first land to be reclaimed in the state.

During the year 1851 many other people came into Carson Valley and took up claims near Reese's and farther up the valley. There were also a few placer miners in Gold cañon. To them the farmers sold their products in the fall and spring, and to the emigrant trains during the summer.

Although the general assembly of the "state of Deseret" during its first session in 1849-1850 extended the boundaries of the counties of Weber, Deseret, Tooele, Juab, Millard, Iron, and Washington to western Utah there was no county or township officer sent out to these settlements. Carson Valley and its surrounding settlements were in Juab and Millard counties. In the succeeding legislatures of Utah

249 Sawyer, *op. cit.*, 94-95.
250 *San Francisco Daily Evening Bulletin*, January 3, 1859.
251 Reese, "Mormon Station," MS., 5.

MORMON STATION

Built by John Reese in 1851, Mormon Station was the first house constructed in Nevada. The later settlement was named Genoa in 1855. From a rare contemporary photograph.

territory, judges, clerks, and constables for a number of precincts were added, but nothing was done to bring Carson Valley under an organized government.[252] Salt Lake City was five hundred miles from the Mormon settlements in western Utah. Thousands of people were passing through it every year, some few of them remaining, and a number of Californians came over the mountains during the emigrant season and established trading stations along the routes of travel. Bandits, horse thieves, and other desperadoes realized quickly that Carson Valley was a safe refuge, hence the lives and property of the permanent settlers were constantly endangered by them as well as by threatened Indian attacks. Some form of government had to be devised for self-protection.

On November 12, 1851, the Mormon settlers and a few gentiles formed a squatter's government. They desired especially to have some regulation concerning the amount of land each person could hold. Resolutions were passed providing for the circulation of a petition asking the federal government for a distinct territorial government for Carson Valley. Other actions taken by the meeting included provision for survey of land claims, the appointment of James H. Haynes as surveyor, and of other officers by a board of seven men.[253] At a second meeting in May, 1852, of the self-constituted pioneer government, John Reese presiding, land claimants were given the right to sell their holdings and take up new ones; at a third meeting in November it was provided that a justice of the peace, a clerk of the court, and a sheriff be elected. A kind of supreme court was devised in the form of a jury of twelve men, beyond the decision of which there was no appeal.

Many Mormons and a few gentile settlers came into the valleys of western Utah during the years following the establishment of Mormon Station. In 1851 Eagle Valley, now the site of the capital of Nevada, was taken up; in 1852, the first attempt to establish a community in Washoe Valley was made; in 1853, settlements were made in Jack's Valley, a

---

[252] Bancroft, *History of Nevada, Colorado, and Wyoming,* 72; Bancroft, *History of Utah,* 449-450.
[253] Bancroft, *History of Nevada, Colorado, and Wyoming,* 70.

few miles north of Carson Valley; "Mormon" Smith took up land in Pleasant Valley; in 1852 H. H. Jameson, a Mormon, established a trading post at the first crossing of the Truckee river in Truckee Meadows, which in 1857 became Stone and Gates Crossing, and still later, Glendale. Some of these men brought their families with them.[254]

The advent of family life increased the duties and responsibilities of the temporary squatters' government in Carson Valley. Because it lacked the authority to enforce its rules, a petition signed by forty-three citizens requested the legislature of California to annex this section for judicial purposes until the congress should provide otherwise. The committee to which the petition was referred recommended that jurisdiction be extended eastward to the 120th meridian, to the 42nd parallel northward, and south to the intersection of the 35th parallel with the Colorado river.[255] The petition was not accepted by the California legislature, but it is interesting to note that if they had extended their jurisdiction to these limits, Carson Valley and all the other settlements would have been outside of the present state of California.[256] On June 24, 1852, Thomas A. Williams wrote to Governor Young that some of the citizens of Carson Valley, notably gold miners, objected to Mormon rule from Salt Lake City, and desired to have Carson Valley annexed to California.[257]

When the territorial government of Utah learned of the action taken by the residents of Carson Valley, steps were taken to give these settlers a county government of their own. Consequently on January 17, 1854, the legislature created Carson county out of the western limits of Juab, Millard, and Iron counties. This area embraced what is now Washoe, Douglas, Ormsby, Storey, Lyon, and Mineral counties, and parts of Esmeralda, Churchill, and Humboldt counties, Ne-

---

[254] Bancroft, *History of Nevada, Colorado, and Wyoming*, 73-74; *Nevada Historical Society Papers, 1923-1924*, p. 60.

[255] *California Senate Journal*, 1853, pp. 10, 130, 131, app. 46.

[256] These are the present boundaries between California and Nevada.

[257] The writer is deeply indebted to Professor Thomas Cottam Romney of Brigham Young University, for considerable information on this period. Dr. Romney obtained this information from the *Journal History*, June 24, 1852.

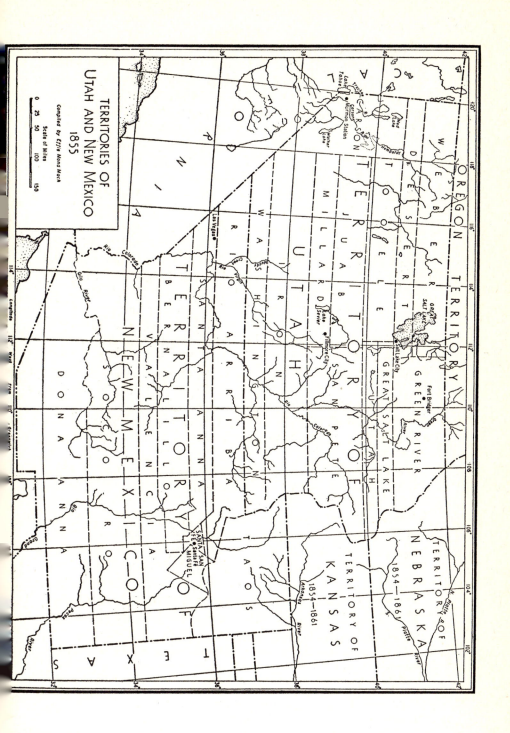

TERRITORIES OF
UTAH AND NEW MEXICO
1855

Compiled by Effie Mona Mack

Scale of Miles
0    25    50    100    150

vada.[258] Two days later the same legislature divided Utah into three judicial districts, Carson being the third. George P. Styles, United States district judge for the territory of Utah, was appointed to preside over it. Carson county was given one delegate in the territorial legislature.[259]

It was an important group of Mormon dignitaries that left Salt Lake for Carson Valley on May 17, 1855, to organize the first county government in what is now the state of Nevada. Orson Hyde, one of the twelve Apostles of the church, was appointed by Governor Young to carry out the mandates of the territorial legislature; he was also to remain in the county and be probate judge, as well as spiritual head of the community. Other prominent persons to come at this time were United States District Judge Styles, United States Marshal Joseph L. Hayward, and Enoch Reese, a leading merchant of Salt Lake City, brother and part owner of Reese's Station in Carson Valley. Among the thirty-five other Mormons mention should be made, for sentimental reasons chiefly, of Mr. and Mrs. Alexander Cowan. The latter was Alison "Eilley" or Ellen Orrum, once a Scottish lassie who, at the tender age of fifteen had been converted to the Mormon faith and married a Mormon bishop, Stephen Hunter, on mission in Scotland. In 1853 Hunter brought her to Salt Lake City. Because the bishop entered into plural marriage "Eilley" left him and married Alexander Cowan.[260] A short time after coming the Cowans took up a land claim in Washoe Valley. We shall hear more about this Scottish lassie later on.

Soon after the arrival of the Carson county officials, Elder Hyde wished to determine whether Carson Valley was in the territory of Utah or the state of California. He therefore requested Governor John Bigler of California to have the boundary line opposite Carson Valley surveyed. On August 3, 1855, Surveyor S. H. Marlette of California sent George H. Goddard to Carson Valley to run the line. By September

258 Bancroft, *History of Utah*, 591.

259 A delegate was taken from Salt Lake county and given to Carson county; Bancroft, *History of Nevada, Colorado, and Wyoming*, 38.

260 The revelation on polygamy was given to Joseph Smith. It was published July 12, 1843. Perhaps Eilley Orrum did not know about plural marriages until she reached Salt Lake. The life of Eilley Orrum has been written in popular style by Swift Paine, *Eilley Orrum*.

5 Goddard had made sufficient observations to know that the angle of the state boundary (that is the intersection made by the meeting of the oblique line run northwest from the point where the 35th parallel crosses the Colorado river and the 120th meridian) was in the southeastern part of Lake Bigler (Tahoe) rather than east of Carson Valley, as was being held by the dissatisfied "gentiles" who had asked the California legislature to set up a judicial jurisdiction over the valley. Hyde accompanied the surveying party and assisted them in every way possible.[261]

When Judge Hyde was satisfied that he was in the territory of Utah, he issued his proclamation calling for an election of county officers to be be held at Mormon Station on September 20. The result of the election was a victory for the Mormon candidates. Every Mormon who ran for office was elected; only one non-Mormon, Charles D. Daggett, prosecuting attorney, was elected.[262] The gentiles were more dissatisfied than ever. They maintained that the territorial laws were not being justly administered. There were other objections, too; among them to Judge Hyde's "spiritual wife." It made the non-Zionites "look with disgust upon the prospect of raising up their daughters among such associates, and they ardently desired that their homes in their pleasant valley shall not be 'defiled' by the horrible favoritism and deception of Mormonism." [263] So a second attempt on the part of the Gentile settlers to be annexed to the state of California was made in a petition submitted to the California legislature in January, 1856. This petition was incorporated in a resolution requesting the federal government to make the 118th meridian the eastern boundary of California.[264]

[261] Sherman Day, "Report of a survey of a portion of the eastern boundary of California and of a reconnaissance of the Old Carson-Johnson immigrant roads over the Sierra Nevada," Sacramento, 1855, 81-96, *Pamphlets on California*, vol. 26, no. 28. In Bancroft Library.

[262] The records of Carson county are preserved in the office of the secretary of state of Nevada in Carson City. This history does not touch upon local matters except where they have some relation with the federal government. A fuller account may be had in Angel, *History of Nevada*, and Bancroft, *History of Nevada, Colorado, and Wyoming*, 75-78.

[263] *Pamphlets on California*, vol. 26, no. 28.

[264] *Senate Misc. Doc.*, 34 Cong., 1 sess., 48; *House Com. Report*, 34 Cong., 3 sess., 264.

Congress did not act favorably upon the petition, but when the church authorities in Salt Lake City learned of this second attempt at separation from the territory of Utah, they took immediate steps to increase the number of Mormons in the western section. At this particular time there was a vigorous reformation and colonization movement going on in the church. Hundreds of new converts were being received. In the spring of 1856, a colony of between sixty and seventy families was ordered to Carson Valley, thereby giving the Mormons a considerable majority over the gentiles.[265] Most of the new arrivals settled in Carson, Eagle, Washoe, Jack, and Pleasant valleys. In the same year Hyde laid out streets and had lots surveyed at Mormon Station, dignifying the town by giving it the name "Genoa," in honor of the birthplace of Columbus.[266] A short time later, he laid out Franktown in Washoe Valley, which he intended to be a miniature Salt Lake City, with broad, regular streets, on either side of which small ditches, to carry water from Franktown Creek for the gardens and for household purposes, were dug. About one hundred Mormon families settled in Washoe Valley, chiefly on the west side of Washoe Lake. They built their houses and barns close to the base of the mountains; their fields extended down toward the lake. This was an ideal spot for working out the tenets of Zionism. Very little was cultivated for ornament, everything was thoroughly practical, their one-room houses were built of hewn logs or rough lumber and of adobe or undressed stone laid up with mud. A very few of them had glass windows. The architecture of their buildings was simple, and they dressed in keeping with the same idea. To work and to get the most out of life with the least self-indulgence was their law. These first hardy settlers were characterized as "brave, patient, ignorant, industrious, hardy, and frugal, knowing only to work and save."[267]

[265] Bancroft, *History of Nevada, Colorado, and Wyoming*, 78.

[266] The plot for the Genoa townsite is among the territorial records in the secretary of state's office in Carson City.

[267] This statement would not seem correct according to the tenets of Mormonism. There was only the one baptism; all others were performed for the dead in the temples. *San Jose Pioneer*, May 26, 1877; Bancroft, *History of Nevada, Colorado, and Wyoming*, 79.

Judge Hyde took up his home in Franktown where he erected a fine saw mill to cut timber from the luxuriant growth of pine trees that covered the mountains west of Washoe Valley. In 1856 an official mission of Zion was established in this part of western Utah, known as the Carson Valley Mission. Chester Loveland was appointed by the High Council of the church to be spiritual head over this region. Alexander Cowan and his independent wife "Eilley" acquired a land claim not far from Franktown. Upon it they built a little house near some hot springs which flowed from the base of the mountain. They lived there and cultivated their fields during the fall and winter of 1856-1857.

Education and Mormonism went hand in hand. The high motto of the Mormon church, "The glory of God is intelligence," was well observed in this remote settlement. Although in 1854 the first school, an informal one, was held in the home of Isaac Mott at Mottsville, a short distance south of Mormon Station, the first official organization of school districts in Carson county was ordered by Judge Hyde in 1856. The county was divided into four districts and the first school house was built in Franktown in 1857. The Mormon children did not attend school here very long because their families left that year. This building was later sold to William "Lucky Bill" Thorrington, who moved it to Genoa, where it was used as a stable.[268]

As the population of Carson Valley increased and the acreages that each settler took up and cultivated increased accordingly, the need for appropriation of the waters of the rivers became obvious. In order that the first settlers in the valleys be protected in their prior water rights, a special term of court was held on October 27, 1855, at the house of John Reese for the purpose of legalizing "the sole and exclusive right to take out any portion of the waters of Carson river which they may desire in a ditch or canal for mining and other purposes, in the vicinity of Gold cañon," to John Reese, Stephen Kinsey, Orson Hyde, John McMarlin, James McMarlin, and others.[269] The grant to these men of the sole right to use the waters of Carson river was an example of

[268] Bancroft, *History of Nevada, Colorado, and Wyoming*, 80.
[269] *Ibid.*, 77.

the exclusiveness of the Mormon system. These self-chosen owners of the water of Carson river began the construction of a ditch to divert the water from the river to the placer miners in Gold cañon. To construct it some fifty Chinese came over from California. The headquarters of these Orientals was at the foot of the cañon of the Carson river. The little settlement at this point had been started by Spafford Hall and was known as Hall's Station. In 1854, because Hall was seriously wounded, he sold his interests to James McMarlin, his clerk. From that time until the Chinese came to this station, it was known as McMarlin's Station. From the diary of a pioneer wife came the description of this station, ultimately to be named Dayton. She described it as

... a tavern and trading post, and being the first we reach after the long journey, everyone stops here, and pack trains, and thus we get the news of the outside world. . . This is a great rendezvous for gamblers. Cards are being played day and night. . . The Carson river is back of the log house. . . There are twenty boarders here, most of them mining for Mr. McMarlin up the canyon. Each night the pans containing the black sand and gold are brought to the store, and there washed in big tubs or half barrels. This is our first introduction to gold mining. There's a little creek of clear water across the road, and sometimes I go and pick up clear, pretty rocks, in some, gold is plainly seen. . .[270]

It was from this settlement that these placer miners worked the cañon and discovered the Gold Hill mines. A number of Mormons lived there, also, engaged chiefly in trading.

After the Chinese built the ditch they were permitted to remain near the mouth of the cañon and mine under certain restrictions. For this reason this station was known as Chinatown until the rush to the Comstock began; then, the white inhabitants named it Mineral Rapids; for a brief time it was known as Nevada City; and then in 1861 it received its final christening of Dayton, in honor of Mr. Day, who surveyed the townsite.

Many other colonies were founded by the Mormon church at the time the valleys of western Utah were being settled.

[270] Lucy Rutledge Cooke, *Crossing the Plains in 1852*, 68-69. Mrs. Cooke kept her diary day by day and wrote also a number of letters en route. They were kept by her relatives and later incorporated in this book. The little girl named "Cissy" in the diary became later Mrs. J. B. Lane, whose husband was the proprietor of Lane's woodyard in Reno, Nevada.

RUINS OF FORT CALLVILLE

The Mormons built this settlement at the head of navigation on the Colorado river for shipping supplies from Mazatlán, Mexico. Reproduced for the first time from a rare photograph.

Among the attempts to found settlements in southern Nevada was one at Las Vegas Springs, now Las Vegas, Nevada,[271] then a part of the territory of New Mexico. In 1855 William Brinkhurst was called to take thirty men and proceed to this point to establish a permanent settlement. It was planned originally as a station on the Los Angeles-Salt Lake Trail as well as a mission "to teach the Indians the arts of civilization, husbandry, etc." These missionaries, the first to be sent to Nevada to convert the Indians to Mormonism, started the first settlement in the southern part of the state.

These earliest settlers of Las Vegas built their crude dwellings within an adobe wall one hundred fifty feet on a side, the enclosure forming a defense against Indian raids. From this wall it became known as the Old Mormon Fort. A carefully guarded stock corral was built adjoining the fort. A dam for conserving the water from the springs, and four bridges across the little stream which flowed from them were built. A plot of land was taken up by each of the first settlers. The land claims were fenced with mesquite, "a bush with as many prickles on it as the locust tree." Crops were planted in the rich black soil.

When the Mormons were not busy reclaiming land they were preaching the gospel to the Indians. A few of them accepted the faith, were baptized, and were given Christian names. But the red man must have interpreted his new association in a different way from that in which the white man meant it. Repeated incidents of bad faith on the part of the Indians were recorded in the pitiful accounts of the attempts to civilize them. They stole everything – cattle, clothes, and other supplies. In 1857 the fatal blow to the mission occurred when the Indians swooped down on the ripe crops and carried them off entirely. The buildings, lands, and everything that could not be carried back to the Utah settlements were abandoned to the natives. (Probably the Mormons would have left this year in any event because of the approach of General Johnston's army.)

These early Zion settlers of southern Nevada were the first to discover minerals in that part. An extensive deposit

[271] *Supra,* 106.

of silver lead was found southeast of the mission. This metal was especially desirable at that time on account of the expected warfare with the United States army. However, it was too difficult to smelt easily; and when smelted was too hard for bullets, the reason being the rich silver galena in the ore.[272] Although the Las Vegas Mission was abandoned after two years of hard labor, and after the sad attempts to Christianize the Indians, it probably paved the way for the later Mormon settlements in southern Nevada. This area was embraced in the counties of Rio Arriba, Santa Anna, San Juan, and Bernalillo, New Mexico.

In 1857, the thriving Carson county communities were mentioned in the California newspapers. Articles appeared frequently which described the resources of the valleys. One San Francisco newspaper reported that the crops were in good condition and that business was excellent on account of the overland migration, but that mining was dull due to lack of water.[273] A few days later the same paper gave an interesting survey of the number of people in the different valleys in western Utah. This report stated that Wassau (Washoe) Valley had twenty-five families, or about one hundred fifty people, all Mormons, each with a good farm. There was a good sawmill (Orson Hyde's mill) in the community which furnished building material at a reasonable rate. Jack's Valley with agriculture and grazing as its chief industries, had nine Mormon families, whose supplies came from Genoa. Eagle Valley (Carson City) had ten Mormon and four gentile families, while Carson Valley, the most thickly settled of all, had twenty Mormon and seventeen gentile families. The survey continued that, "These are wonderful valleys, capable of supporting more people, which matter should be of interest to California merchants." [274] In addition to these settlements, there were many miners in Gold cañon, and a number of people living at Chinatown.

When the mail route was established between California and Salt Lake City, mail stations were placed at regular intervals across what is now the state of Nevada in fertile

---

[272] Hoffman Birney, *Zealots of Zion*, 80-86.
[273] *Daily Alta California*, July 4, 1857.
[274] *Daily Alta California*, July 9, 1857.

spots on the rivers and near the springs, and soon began to attract other settlers. The intervening desolation between the two limits of civilization was beginning to disappear. The establishment of another frontier, "the most American thing about America," was made.

Many gentiles from California came into western Utah in 1855 and 1856. They objected to any law administered by the Mormons, and often snapped their fingers at it. This refusal to obey the officials culminated in an order from them demanding that the newcomers leave the country. The "two weeks' war" that followed consisted only of the two opposing forces fortifying themselves within sight of each other. The menacing news reached the California mining camps where recruits were enlisted to go to the aid of their gentile friends. When the Mormons heard of this, "The Lord, ever watchful over his Saints, revealed to 'Brother Orson' that it was necessary to call off his brethren" and the war ended without bloodshed.[275] A *status quo* truce was proposed in which everyone was permitted to remain on his land. Elder Hyde had tried to offset the coming of these gentiles by writing to Brigham Young for one hundred more men, but Governor Young answered "No." He said he wished all of the Saints were back in Salt Lake City.[276]

To prevent the gentiles from getting political control of Carson county, as they were now beginning to outnumber the Mormons, the territorial legislature of Utah repealed the act creating Carson county, and ordered all of the records of the county moved to Salt Lake City. Judge Hyde himself was recalled in November, 1856; he never returned. Carson county was attached to Great Salt Lake county for election purposes; it also lost its delegate to the Utah legislature. On January 14, 1857, an act was passed permitting Carson county to retain its organization so far as a recorder, surveyor, and precinct officers were concerned. These officials were to be elected in accordance with the existing laws, "until further directed by Great Salt Lake county court of legislative enactment," and "the record books, papers, blanks, and seals, both of probate and county courts, shall be handed

[275] Thomas B. H. Stenhouse, *Rocky Mountain Saints*, 284.
[276] William Alexander Linn, *The Story of the Mormons*, 472.

over to the order of the probate court of Great Salt Lake county." This order meant that any person who lived in western Utah had to travel five hundred miles to transact any legal business, and, too, all of the officials would be Mormons.[277] This conflict between gentile and Mormon existed in most of the Utah settlements.

Before Judge Hyde, pioneer organizer of the first county government in which is now Nevada, went away, he hurriedly disposed of his interests in Washoe Valley. He rented his $10,000 sawmill to Jacob Rose, a former trader on the Carson river and an early settler. Hyde received at the time, two mules, some worn-out harness, two yoke of oxen, and an old wagon, but never received more than these few things for his investments. The subsequent Utah war, and the creation of the territory of Nevada clouded the titles of the abandoned Mormon property in Carson county. In 1862 Judge Hyde attempted to recover his sawmill, valued at $20,000, which had been acquired by R. D. Sides. Because Hyde received nothing but promises for the payment of his property, he pronounced a public curse. In an open letter, he hoped the people of Carson and Washoe valleys would be:

. . . visited of the Lord of Hosts and with thunder and with earthquakes and with floods, with pestilence and famine until your names are not known amongst men, for you have rejected the authority of God, trampled upon his laws and his ordinances and given yourself up to serve the god of this world; to rioting in debauchery, in abominations and drunkenness and corruption.[278]

The people took their chances with the Lord, but the mill of "the Mormon God" ground slowly. The curse pronounced in 1862 took effect in 1880, when a dam broke and the consequent flood wiped out the very site of the old mill town below it and ruined Sides' farm; in 1882, another flood swept away the adjoining town of Ophir; and a later one carried off the only remaining evidence of the Mormon settlements – the old Mormon meeting house, which floated farther than any other building, and was left in ruins on the shores of Washoe Lake.[279]

277 Bancroft, *History of Nevada, Colorado, and Wyoming*, 81.
278 The curse is given *verbatim* in Angel, *History of Nevada*, 40-41.
279 Angel, *History of Nevada*, 40-41.

Friction and hostility between the gentile and Mormon settlers existed wherever the two groups lived together, particularly in the vicinity of Salt Lake City, where the federal officials came into direct conflict with the church officers. In the early history of Mormonism, both before and after the Mormons had fled beyond the frontier of civilized communities, the worst feature of their faith – polygamy – was rather suspected than definitely known. This suspicion was at least prophetic; in 1853 polygamy was openly announced as the peculiar institution of the people of the Great Salt Lake Valley. It has been explained that the pronouncement of this doctrine was an economic necessity due to conversion to the Mormon faith of a preponderant number of women. Something had to be done to absorb them, hence divine sanction of the institution. To many of those outside the faith, an attempt to establish such a system in the United States as part of a social and religious scheme was abhorrent to the accepted morality of Christendom.

There were other reasons for a growing national hostility to the Saints. For example, at first the early emigrants to the Pacific coast rejoiced at the thought of a resting place at Salt Lake City; and, too, the peaceful relations which the Mormons had cultivated with the Indians made that route a far safer one than it would otherwise have been. But it was not long before the emigrants complained that in the Mormons themselves they found an enemy almost as dangerous as the savages. These overland travelers alleged that they were defrauded in trade, plundered of their goods, robbed of their cattle, and, in various ways, harassed on their toilsome journey. It was generally believed that the Saints were guilty of these practices. The following item in a San Francisco paper helped to crystallize these contentions:

It is said that the Mormons have the most complete system of espionage established. Not a single detachment of troops, nor a train, nor hardly a party of civilians travelling across the plains either on business or for pleasure, left the Missouri border during the last summer, without being accompanied by a Mormon spy in some subordinate capacity, such as teamster or cook. It is known that they have several spies in Sacramento, San Francisco, Carson Valley, and in fact all over the United States.[280]

[280] *San Francisco Evening Bulletin,* April 6, 1858.

The Zionites denied indignantly these charges. They affirmed that the emigrants were the aggressors.

> ... that they mocked at Mormonism, insulted Mormon wives, and outraged Mormon husbands; that they turned their cattle into Mormon fields, helped themselves, without pay, to Mormon produce, laughed at the Mormon judges before whom they were arraigned, escaped the penalty of their misdeeds by defiance or by flight; and in short conducted themselves always as if among a people toward whom they were under no obligation of observing any relation of fair dealing or good fellowship.[281]

In addition to these reasons for enmity, petty jealousies had been constantly arising, until at length the serious incrimination of the Mormons by Judge W. W. Drummond and other United States officials, who asserted that they were driven from the territory of Utah by Mormon outrages, and that Brigham Young and his followers were in open resistance to and defiance of the federal government, aroused national sentiment against them. Judge Drummond's most serious charge was that they had burned the library and records of the United States district court. In justice to the Mormons it should be stated that the alleged burning of the court records was without foundation. The records were later found intact. But true or false, these charges were made the pretext for sending a large division of the United States army against the Mormon institution.[282]

President Buchanan removed Governor Young, and the position of governor of the territory after having been refused by several persons, was finally accepted by Alfred Cumming, superintendent of Indian affairs on the upper Missouri river.[283] In September, 1857, ex-Governor Young, after issuing a proclamation forbidding entrance to the Great Salt Lake Valley of an armed force, proclaimed martial law in the territory. The Mormons had their backs to the wall. They would go no farther – the Lord would surely take care of His Saints. Everything was made ready to resist the siege of the United States army and defend "the place." Scouts were sent out to tear up the roads leading into Salt Lake City. A sufficient number of huge boulders were placed on cliffs and hills overlooking the roads in such positions that

[281] New York Tribune Almanac and Political Register, II, 37-38.
[282] Ibid., 38.
[283] Bancroft, History of Utah, 500.

they could be hurled down upon the soldiers. The state of rebellion and siege continued until the following June, when the army was permitted to enter the valley. A *modus vivendi* had been arranged, not by the officers of the United States army, nor by Governor Cumming, but by Colonel Thomas L. Kane, who in 1846 had befriended the Mormons in Nauvoo, Illinois. He was sent by President Buchanan as an ambassador of peace to the Mormons. A private interview was arranged between him and Brigham Young. This conversation has never been made public nor has it ever been known what credentials Colonel Kane had from the president. The world knew and was concerned only with the results of this visit. On April 6, 1858, President Buchanan issued a proclamation promising amnesty to all who would swear allegiance to the United States; the army was indeed permitted to enter the valley,[284] but what it failed to do one man of straightforward and sound judgment accomplished in a brief conversation.

In this impending war, President Young called upon all faithful Zionites, regardless of their location or circumstances, to return with all possible speed. It was a tribute to the spiritual head of the Mormon church that most of the Saints in the missions and colonies returned to Salt Lake City. The Mormons in Carson county unhesitatingly sacrificed their years of labor; they left their unharvested crops standing in the fields and obeyed. Property was abandoned or sold at a tremendous sacrifice for what could be obtained at short notice. Aside from the apostates and the Josephites (followers of Joseph Smith's family) none hesitated. Judge Loveland, head of the church in Carson county, aided in the organization of the exodus. A correspondent to the *New York Tribune* described it:

He [Brigham Young] ordered the Mormons in Carson Valley to move to Salt Lake and they went. Many had been established there five or six years in that valley and they had become wealthy; they had made farms which furnished them with all the comforts of life and many luxuries, in so far as they were obtainable in a new country, remote from the great centers of commerce. They had fine houses, fences, barns, orchards, gardens and fields; and, at the word all these were sacrificed by men who had nothing to fear from refusal. Gentile neighbors were abundant and friendly, and willing to protect any Mormon who should refuse to obey Brigham's

[284] *House Ex. Doc.,* 35 Cong., 2 sess., 69-72.

request; but nine hundred and sixty-eight persons sold their property for such prices as could be obtained at a few days' notice from gentiles in the valley, and started joyfully to obey the word of Brigham. According to *Exodus,* the ancient Jews paid far less respect to Moses, and scarcely so much to the Almighty himself.[285]

A description of the exodus was given in a San Francisco paper:

The company consists of nine hundred and eighty-five souls, three hundred and fifty men, the balance women and children, having in their possession seven hundred and ten head of stock, consisting principally of horses, mules and oxen, and one hundred and forty-eight wagons, the estimated value of which, together with goods and money, amounts to one hundred and ninety-three thousand dollars, twenty-five thousand of which is cash in the hands of individuals. The train is divided into three divisions of fifties, commanded by Judge Loveland, Captain Lytle and Captain —, which divisions are sub-divided into tens, both having commanders. It is the intention to travel in separate divisions to afford sufficient feed for stock until they reach the seat of Indian difficulties, on the Humboldt, when they will move en masse, to insure protection from attacks by the hostile Indians, who have been so troublesome to the emigration during the present season.[286]

The progress of the Mormons as they left the valleys of western Utah was watched and described in the papers:

A few miles below the mouth of Gold cañon orders were given by the leaders not to move until satisfactory settlements were made between the Mormons leaving and the Gentiles with whom they had dealings; and it is a fact worthy of especial notice, that, with the exception of one or two instances, the Mormons paid their debts and fulfilled their contracts with credit to themselves, individually and fraternally. Much is due to Judge Loveland and other gentlemanly conductors of the train, in bringing about this result, by their known integrity, impartiality and firmness. The adjudging of accounts, where differences arose, in the absence of law, was left to arbiters and satisfactorily settled.

Their leaving so suddenly has been sensibly felt by the traders in the valleys, but their places are being filled up by honest industrious emigrants who are settling here to make it their future home. Many of the Mormon homesteads have been purchased at a low rate by speculators and in our opinion there never will be a better opportunity afforded those who wish

---

[285] Copied in the *Millenial Star,* vol. 20, no. 6, p. 92.

[286] *Daily Alta California,* October 8, 1857; William Jennings said he sold his ranch in Franktown for a trifle, "Carson Valley," MS., 4; Samuel A. Nevers said that John Mankin bought a great deal of the Mormon land in Eagle Valley paying for it in wheat. "Nevada Pioneers," MS., 1, 2.

to procure good stock and agricultural farms in this region of the country than at present.[287]

The Mormons took all the arms and ammunition which they could purchase or obtain by trade. In fact there was such a lack of arms after the exodus that the remaining citizens of Carson Valley applied to California for means with which to protect themselves from the Indians.[288] Among the Saints who refused to obey Brigham's command was "Eilley" Or-rum-Hunter-Cowan, soon to become the wife of Lemuel S. "Sandy" Bowers. Truckee Meadows was almost without a settler when the Mormons left; and Johntown was without a store to supply the miners in Gold cañon. The property left by the Mormons was worth many times the amount for which they sold it; indeed, in a couple of years, due to the discovery of the Comstock, it was worth a hundred-fold more.

Western Utah, soon to become the territory of Nevada, would have fared better had she kept her Mormon colonists. Their zeal and ability to develop virgin territory was ably demonstrated by what they did in Utah. Admiration for the excellent qualities of the Mormon settler was expressed by Frederick Dellenbaugh, great explorer of the Colorado river, when he said:

It must be acknowledged that the Mormons were wilderness breakers of high quality. They not only broke it, but they kept it broken. . . They planted orchards, gardens, farms, school-houses, and peaceful homes. . . A people who have accomplished so much that is good, who have endured large privation and suffering . . . deserve admiration.[289]

Oliver La Farge saw beauty in the Mormon settlements: "Oh, the Mormon roses and the Mormon poplars! Wherever the Mormons went they planted; wherever they have been, there roses bloom." [290]

Today as the people of western Nevada skim over the smooth Reno-Carson Highway and around the base of the mountains to Genoa, Carson Valley, and visit other parts of Nevada where the Mormons settled, few of them realize

[287] *Daily Alta California,* October 10, 1857.

[288] *Loc. cit.*

[289] Dellenbaugh, *Breaking the Wilderness,* 307-308.

[290] Hoffman Birney, *Zealots of Zion,* quoted Oliver La Farge, 292.

that the tall stately poplars were planted by these first wilderness breakers. In the autumn when the leaves of the poplar
are gilded a deeper gold by the setting sun, they resemble
tongues of flame, silently proclaiming that they were planted
by "Zealots of Zion."

By the foolish and hasty actions of the federal government, the organized communities of western Utah were
disrupted. It was four years more before order succeeded
the chaotic condition occasioned by the departure of the
Mormons.

# Anarchy and Confusion, 1857-1861

After all the loyal Mormons had returned to the Great Salt Lake Valley there was only a handful of gentiles and apostates left in western Utah. Most of the remaining settlers were either hostile to the Mormon officials or not in accord with Brigham Young and his administration of the law half-admitted and half-denied, which was really no law at all. It was pointed out in the preceding chapter that control by the territory of Utah over a region as distant as Carson county was never satisfactory; this was more true when the county became disorganized. Efforts by the settlers in Carson Valley to be attached to the state of California had failed; the federal government had been indifferent to their pleas. There was nothing left for them to do but evolve some system of autonomous government. For four years, from the summer of 1857 and exodus of the Mormons to July, 1861, date of the arrival of James W. Nye, first territorial governor of Nevada, there was little government; a hopelessly confused state of affairs existed in the western part of the territory of Utah. Nevertheless in these few years the law-abiding citizens took matters in their hands, as any group of Anglo-saxon people would do, and set up a factitious government. This squatter's government was followed by a provisional territorial one. While the Carson Valley people were trying to work out their political problems, officials in Utah tried to recreate Carson county; and the federal government tried to reëstablish the United States district court for this section. Once there were three governments trying to function at the same time. Complications were multiplied by the discovery of the Comstock Lode. The situation was not saved until 1861 when the congress organized the territory of Nevada. The story of the conflict between law and disorder was the same through which most frontier societies passed, but the particular situation was unique, probably, in the history of the United States.

On August 8, 1857, before the Mormons left Carson county, even, the people intending to remain seized the opportunity to call a mass meeting in Genoa, the purpose of which was to petition the congress for a separate territorial organization for western Utah.[291] This petition made the Goose Creek mountains (eastern Elko county) the eastern boundary; the Colorado river the southern (to include a part of the territory of New Mexico); and the Sierra Nevada the western boundary of the proposed territory. The most prominent mover in this matter was Major William Ormsby, formerly of Sacramento, later agent in Genoa for the Pioneer Stage Company. In a series of resolutions it was declared by the inhabitants that the life and property of emigrants passing through western Utah were not secure; their safety depended upon the organization of a territorial government. No complaints against the Mormon rule were set forth in the resolutions, but in the memorial accompanying them, it was alleged that no law existed there except theocratic rule exercised by the Mormon church without reference to statutory regulations.[292] These memorialists were no more abashed in their exaggerated figures as to the number of inhabitants in their proposed territory than they were in asking that it include approximately what is now the state of Nevada. They estimated that there were between seven and eight thousand white people and from seventy-five to one hundred thousand Indians in the region.[293] In order further to impress the congress to grant their petition, they promised to assume the obligation of guarding all of the routes across the territory.

At this same meeting a committee was appointed to obtain signatures to the resolutions and to the memorial. Other committees were appointed, also, in the different settlements to "manage and superintend all matters necessary and proper

---

[291] The communities represented at this mass meeting were Honey Lake Valley (Susanville), Eagle Valley (Carson City), Carson Valley (Genoa), Willow Town (on Carson river), Ragtown, Twenty-six mile Desert, sink of Humboldt, Walker river and Hope Valley.

[292] Bancroft, *History of Nevada, Colorado, and Wyoming*, 82.

[293] *Sen. Misc. Doc.*, 35 Cong., 1 sess., 181.

in the premises." [294] Genoa was selected as the capital; it was thought appropriate, also, to name the new territory "Columbus." [295] The world was to know what was done at this mass meeting – a copy of the proceedings of this convention was sent to the newspapers of California, Utah, and New Mexico, as well as the leading eastern newspapers.[296]

James M. Crane, a native Virginian, late from California, where he had been an active Whig politician and journalist, happened to be in the territory collecting material for a series of geological lectures at the time the convention was in session. He was requested to address the convention because his superior experience and skill as a politician were recognized by the members. He was selected, moreover, as the delegate to Washington to present the resolutions and memorial to congress, and to represent the new "territory of Columbus," when it should be organized.[297]

Crane could seemingly not have gone to the capital at a more propitious time to present the memorial in which the people of western Utah set forth their grievancees against the Mormons. It was just when the United States army under the command of General Albert Sidney Johnston had entered the Great Salt Lake Valley. The newly appointed governor, Cumming, had just declared the Mormons in a state of rebellion; he had warned any member of the church that proceedings would be instituted against the ringleaders of the insurrection; and he had issued, also, an order for the Mormon militia to disband. But as time went on the military expedition began to be unpopular throughout the United States. The president had virtually made war upon the territory of Utah without any declaration of war; he had ordered an army sent there before the causes of offense had been fairly and fully investigated; furthermore, at this critical period in the history of the nation he was isolating in a distant and almost inaccessible region more than one-third of the nation's war material and nearly all of its best troops. It was becoming known as President Buchanan's blunder.

[294] Bancroft, op. cit., 83; Angel, op. cit., 42-46.
[295] San Francisco Daily Evening Bulletin, July 17, 1861.
[296] J. Wells Kelly, Nevada Directory, 1862, pp. 29-30.
[297] San Francisco Daily Evening Bulletin, July 17, 1861.

Throughout the United States and Europe the question was being asked, "What has become of the army of Utah?" Although peace was made with very little bloodshed, the Utah war was an ill-advised measure.[298]

Upon his arrival in Washington, Delegate Crane placed his bill in the hands of a fellow Virginian, Representative William Smith; in the senate he intrusted the same to William M. Gwin of California.[299] By February, 1858, Crane had received so much encouragement for his bill that he wrote a long letter to his constituents in Carson Valley in which he predicted that it was going to be successful; the sponsors of the bill would urge the committee on territories to advance it as a war measure to restrict the boundaries of the Mormons, and defeat their efforts to corrupt and confederate with the Indian tribes.[300] He advised the farmers in the valleys to plant extensive crops, which he thought they would be able to sell for good cash prices to the federal government to supply the army, and the Indian reservations.[301] The committee to which the bill was referred changed the name "Columbus" to Nevada, otherwise the bill was the same. Through strenuous efforts on the part of Mr. Smith the bill passed the lower house. In the senate, when it reached its third reading Senator Gwin dropped it, because, he said, it interfered with his Arizona bill which had precedence on the list. Although Crane waited patiently until the close of the first session of the thirty-fifth congress, hoping he might "omnibus" his bill through the last minute, his efforts were futile, and he returned to Carson Valley.[302]

While Crane was in Washington urging the passage of the Nevada territory bill, and Governor Cumming was directing affairs in Salt Lake City, the residents of Carson Valley were virtually without any law at all. In 1857, after the departure of the Mormons, many of whom were office-holders, some of the remaining settlers and others who

298 Bancroft, *History of Utah*, 512-542.

299 Bancroft, *History of Nevada, Colorado, and Wyoming*, 83-84.

300 Angel, *History of Nevada*, 46.

301 *House Journal*, 35 Cong., 1 sess., 789-1221; *House Committee Report*, 35 Cong., 1 sess., 375; *Sen. Misc. Doc.*, 35 Cong., 1 sess., 181.

302 *San Francisco Daily Evening Bulletin*, July 17, 1861.

came in after the Mormons left thought they had license to do as they pleased. Something had to be done to preserve peace and prevent crime. In March, 1858, the citizens of Carson Valley held a mass meeting at the home of James McMarlin for the purpose of correcting and amending the old laws of Carson county.[303] The law-abiding citizens of the community took into their hands the administration of justice in the form of frontier law and a vigilance committee was formed. In June, 1858, a man named Olds was arrested on a complaint of grand larceny and tried by a jury of eighteen men; he was found guilty, sentenced to pay a fine of $800, and banished from the valleys east of the Sierra Nevada mountains. About November 1 of the same year, when he returned to Carson Valley, an assemblage of the citizens again sentenced him to banishment. They gave him five months to settle up his business, and at the same time warned him that if he returned, he would be dealt with summarily and hanged.[304]

The most notorious acts of this popular tribunal were the hanging of William "Lucky Bill" Thorrington and the sentencing of William "Bill" Edwards to death for murder. The details of the guilt or innocence of these parties do not have a place here. Suffice it to say that although Thorrington's guilt as an accomplice and his protection of the suspected murderer were never established, he was loaded in a wagon, driven to the Clear Creek Ranch, and hanged to a tree. Edwards was turned over to a posse of men from Honey Lake Valley. The same sentence was to be carried out for him, but it was believed subsequently that he bought off the posse and was allowed to go free on the condition he would leave the country.[305] The aftermath of the unfortunate affair was to divide the community into two factions; the few who sympathized with Thorrington and believed him to

[303] McMarlin lived on the site of the present town of Dayton.

[304] *Territorial Enterprise,* June 16, 1859. Quoted in Angel, *op. cit.*

[305] Conflicting stories concerning the crime committed by these two men were circulated. One version of it is given in Bancroft, *History of Nevada, Colorado, and Wyoming,* 84; and others are found in William Cradlebaugh, "Nevada biography," MS., 1, and Henry Van Sickle, "Utah Desperadoes," MS., 3.

be innocent were called "Mormons," [306] and those who condemned him were referred to as anti-Mormon.

After Governor Cumming had recomposed matters in eastern Utah, he reorganized Carson county. John S. Childs, who was appointed probate judge, issued a call for an election for the other officers of the county to be held on October 30, 1858. In the intense rivalry of the election the votes of four out of the six precincts were thrown out because of alleged illegal voting, and because a majority of the "Mormon party" candidates was successful. The anti-Mormons were determined to control the territory at cost of whatever method might be necessary to throw off the rule of the territory of Utah.

From the founding of Mormon Station in 1851 to the fall of 1858, Genoa had been the leading town and political headquarters for western Utah. But it was not always to be such. In September, 1858, a town was laid out in Eagle Valley to which was to be shifted the *mise en scene* of this contest between the two parties. In the above year, Abraham V. Z. Curry [307] laid out Carson City and erected a stone house near some hot springs not far from the site. In a short time several other houses were built. Soon there were more people in Carson City than in Genoa, so the county seat of Carson county was moved to the latter place.

The beginning of the future capital of the state of Nevada was interesting. In November, 1851, a group of men came over from California to look for gold in Carson Valley, but not finding it in paying quantities, they took up the land where Carson City now stands. One day one of these men, Frank Hall, shot an eagle and stretched its skin on the front of their cabin. From this circumstance the overland travelers called this place "Eagle Station;" later it was known as Eagle Ranch, and finally the name was extended to the entire valley from the mouth of King's cañon to the hot springs.[308] A number of Mormons came to the valley and took up land.

---

[306] Thorrington was supposed to have condoned some of the acts of the Mormons.

[307] Curry had a station at the hot springs not far from Carson City. He developed the stone quarry adjoining them from which these first houses were built.

[308] Samuel A. Nevers, "Nevada Pioneers," MS., 1.

When they left they sold most of their property to John Mankin, who gave them wheat instead of money for their holdings. Curry obtained a part of the land from Mankin. One of the most enthusiastic men in promoting Carson City was Major Ormsby, who named it, and for whom the county in which it was located was named.

During the winter months of 1858, due to the news of increased profits in placer mining in the cañons leading to Sun Peak (Mount Davidson), there was a considerable rush of miners to the scene of the new strike. After the Mormons left many other people settled in the abandoned valleys. This new influx of people gave the anti-Mormon party and the politically ambitious citizens a justification for a second attempt to create a territory. Acting on the advice of former delegate Crane, a mass meeting of the citizens of the several valleys was held in Carson City on June 6, 1859. It was decided that fifty delegates should be elected on July 14 to a territorial convention, and that they should convene in Genoa four days later. It was further decided these delegates should choose a representative to be sent to Washington and to complete the efforts begun by Judge Crane to create the territory of Nevada.

The convention was held pursuant to the election of delegates. It is interesting to note here that the original Carson county was the nucleus of this organization. Delegates were included from all of the former precincts. Two factions developed early in the meeting – one, the majority, contended that they were elected to frame a constitution for a provisional government which congress would be asked to recognize; the minority group argued that they were elected for the purpose of providing for a constitutional convention to be held in the future for which delegates were to be elected precisely for that purpose. The majority group prevailed, and a constitution was framed, modelled closely after that of the state of California.[309]

Aversion to Mormon rule was again employed in the movement for separation from the territory of Utah. In

---

[309] A verbatim copy of the proceedings of this convention is reproduced from the *Territorial Enterprise*, Saturday, July 30, 1859, in Angel, *History of Nevada*, 69-72.

the constitution the usurpation and abuse of power and the danger to life and property on the routes leading to the Mormon capital were two principal evils dwelt upon.[310] After the enumeration of the reasons why they were declaring themselves free to separate from the territory of Utah, a summary of the steps taken thus far to relieve themselves from the control of Utah was given:

> We have for the last two years invoked congress to erect for us a territorial government, and that body has been deaf to our appeals.
>
> Therefore, believing in the rectitude of our intentions and believing the time has arrived, we make known and declare our entire and unconditional separation from eastern Utah.
>
> To provide for and secure our future protection, we pledge to each other our sacred obligations, to erect for ourselves a territorial government, founded upon the republican principles of the constitution of the United States and that we will maintain and defend it to the best of our ability. And we look to the support and protection of the federal government, and our fellow-citizens in every part of the Union.[311]

The convention provided further for the submission of the constitution of the territory of Nevada to the people at a time when the offices created by it were to be filled by election. The minority group protested that "the framing of the constitution was an unwarranted assumption of power;" the canvass of the returns for the delegate to congress was not carried out as specified in the call for the convention; and the guilty parties responsible for the election frauds were not brought to account.[312]

In the election for the delegate to congress James Crane, the former delegate, was opposed by Major Frederick Dodge, United States Indian agent on the Humboldt river. Major Dodge was very well liked. Although he had many friends, he did not seem to be the man decided upon by the "slate makers." Secrecy surrounded the canvass of the votes, and fraud was charged in the election. Anyone passing

---

[310] The Mountain Meadows massacre in which one hundred twenty men, women and children were brutally murdered on September 11, 1857, on the Salt Lake-Los Angeles Trail near the Nevada-Utah line. Hoffman Birney, *Zealots of Zion*, 134-198; Bancroft, *History of Utah*, 543-571.

[311] Bancroft, *History of Nevada, Colorado, and Wyoming*, 82; Angel, *op. cit.*, 70.

[312] *Ibid.*, 87.

through the territory was allowed to vote. A correspondent to the *San Francisco Herald* described the situation as follows:

> Convention canvassed votes for congress believed by many that Major Dodge would receive a majority of 150 votes. . . Crane's friends kept the polls open two weeks on the Humboldt for the accommodation of the travelling public - although 122 votes were brought in from the Humboldt, where nobody lives except the few employees of the Mail Company. Notwithstanding all these facts, Crane was declared duly elected, and would have been if Dodge had received a majority of 5,000.[313]

The constitution for the territory of Nevada submitted to the people was overwhelmingly adopted. The roster of state officers provided for in the constitution was voted for at the same time. There was no contest or interest in the election of any of the offices except that of governor. Isaac Roop of Honey Lake Valley (Susanville) was opposed by Dr. J. A. Slater. John J. Musser, president of the constitutional convention, certified that the constitution was adopted by a "large majority" and that Mr. Roop was elected in the same manner. Secrecy surrounded this election; the ballots were not preserved, and although the election was held on September 7, Musser did not issue his certificate until December 12, and then not one of the four territorial officers elected, except the governor, was ever called upon to serve.

The discovery of the Comstock Lode was an evil star to the functioning of this government. Indeed, it was the influx of a heterogeneous horde of transient irresponsibles that swept away the fabric of this half-completed government. It was a singular coincidence that the mass meeting was called in Carson City on June 6, 1859; the lode was discovered about a week later, on June 12, 1859; the first public announcement of the discovery was made in a California newspaper on July 1; the first session of the constitutional con-

---

[313] A correspondent from Genoa to the *San Francisco Herald* who signed his name "Tennessee." The first letter appeared in November, 1857. The above statement was quoted from letter no. 43, dated August 5, 1859, and appeared in the *Herald* on August 14, 1859. No one has been able to identify the writer. Samuel P. Davis says in his *History of Nevada* that W. G. Atkinson was known as "Old Tennessee." He does not, however, connect him with the above letter.

vention was held on July 19; and the first crowd to rush to Washoe came early in August.[314]

Having discussed an attempt to institute a government unauthorized by any law, let us turn to another effort made in the fall of 1859 to revive the government of Carson county under existing laws. It will be remembered that Governor Cumming had appointed John S. Childs probate judge of Carson county in 1858 but, due to the fact that his appointment had come from Utah, the orders of his court had been practically ignored. However, when the population began to increase very rapidly in the fall of 1859, Judge Childs attempted to reëstablish the authority of the probate court by issuing a proclamation calling for an election on October 8. After dividing the county into ten precincts, he ordered an election for the various county and precinct officers. The citizens were not interested in voting for officers to serve under the laws of Utah; of the ten precincts, only three opened their polls, Carson City, Gold Hill and Walker river. However, when Governor Cumming received the result of the election, he forwarded the commissions for the newly elected officials. The following comment expressed his opinion of the election in which "he presumed the matter would eventually have to submit to legal investigation, as there was no authority for calling the election; but as he was anxious to aid in organizing, he had forwarded the commissions." [315] The officers elected were not very much interested in assuming their duties, and eight months after the election, on June 4, 1860, Judge Childs addressed a communication to two of the electives as follows: "I urge upon you the necessity of appearing immediately and taking the oath of office, from the fact that with the population now within the limits of Carson county it is indispensably necessary that we should have some law." [316] None of the elected men accepted the positions they were chosen to fill, consequently the only legal county officers in Carson county were those who had received their offices by appointment from Utah. They could, however, keep up only a shadow of government. The confusion was more confounded.

[314] *Infra*, 209.
[315] Angel, *History of Nevada*, 64.
[316] *Idem*.

pleading with the congress to separate them from the territory of Utah, the placer miners in the vicinity of Gold Hill
felt the necessity of having some well-defined and recognized
rules of action. Because of the rapidly increasing population
in the vicinity of Virginia City, some form of protection
against lawlessness and "for meting out justice between man
and man had to be made." Consequently, on June 11, 1859,
a day or two before the Comstock Lode was discovered, a
few rules and regulations were adopted by the miners. This
code of laws was observed but for a short time, for the rush
from California in the fall swept it away with the other
attempts at self-government. An example, however, of how
this group of men agreeing to live under a code of their own
making acted when an injustice was committed may be given
in the case of the punishment of two men who stole a yoke
of oxen. When the thieves were finally apprehended in
Washoe Valley, the jury of citizens who tried them ordered
each to have an ear cut off, after which they were told to
"travel west for their health." [321]

In retrospect the winter of 1859-1860 was probably the
most momentous in the history of what is now the state of
Nevada. In the first place, it was one of the most severe thus
far experienced by the settlers in the valleys. Most of the
passes were closed with deep snow drifts until late in the
spring. The news of the rich silver discovery had proved to
be genuine. Many of the California and eastern newspapers
had published accounts of it. A number of prominent Californians and many prospectors came over the mountains in
the late summer and fall to verify these accounts, and many
of them planned to settle permanently in the vicinity of the
new discovery of the following year. The hard winter delayed an early spring rush, but a great army was gathering
on the western side of the Sierra Nevada. They were preparing to join the great "rush to Washoe" (named Washoe
because the discovery was made in the Washoe mountains,
the single spur which the Sierra sends into Nevada). Some
few even braved the rigors of winter to be the first at the
new "diggings."

The second reason for the importance of this winter was

---

[321] Angel, *History of Nevada*, 61-62.

the transition through which western Utah was passing. The scene was shifting from the town of Genoa to Carson City, Virginia City, Gold Hill, and Nevada City (Dayton). And lastly, all the efforts that had been made for some form of government were being swept into the discard. Western Utah was shaking off her ten year era of small agricultural life and taking on the new habiliments of a roistering, boisterous frontier mining society. The territory of Nevada was being born.

Thomas Carlyle said, "the history of a country is largely the history of the great men and the influential men who have lived there." Every once in a while nature, for her own recondite purposes, produces a man with something fatal and compelling about him, a man who has a faculty of making other men obey him, who knows instinctively how to make others help carry out his ideas. Such a man was William Morris Stewart. Upon a few of the men trained in law and politics who came into western Utah with the great rush, rested the responsibility of whipping this restless, lawless, excited mass of humanity into some form of government.[322] When Stewart came to Carson county in 1860 to set up a law office in Genoa he was in the prime of his life, thirty-three years of age, a giant in physique and a tower in intellect. Ten years of his life spent in the practice of law and active participation in politics in California had prepared him for the part he was to take in Nevada. Into this confused state of affairs in western Utah where the law was being made according to the circumstances, and administered in a rough and ready fashion, he plunged with all the force he possessed. Brains had to be accompanied with brawn to hold respect. That "Bill" Stewart, as he was familiarly known among the miners, was capable of holding his own may be imagined from a description of him at that time: "He was six feet two inches in height, weighing about 200 pounds. He had light red hair, clear blue eyes and a ruddy complexion." [323] Although Stewart married Annie Elizabeth Foote, daughter of United States Senator Henry Stuart Foote of Mississippi, he was an ardent and devoted Unionist; he was a New Yorker by birth,

[322] Effie Mona Mack, "William Morris Stewart, Empire Builder," in *Proceedings, Pacific Coast Branch American Historical Association*, 1930, 185-192.
[323] Oscar T. Shuck, *Representative and leading men of the Pacific*, 636.

a graduate of Yale College, lawyer by profession, and empire builder by force of circumstance. After living a short time in Genoa he moved to Carson City, where he built a home. A few years later he built a very palatial house in Virginia City. To the end of his life he was closely connected with the history not only of Nevada but the entire West.

Stewart's reputation as a mining lawyer followed him. He was employed as counsel as soon as he arrived in the mining community by a number of corporations which owned feet along the lode. Many companies had been incorporated under the laws of California, a code with which he was entirely familiar. Stewart's influence was felt in the summer of 1860 when the first litigation arose over the rightful ownership of mining properties along the lode. Affairs seemed hopelessly confused in the absence of established mining laws, and in view of the fact that there were three different governments feebly trying to function. In most of the mining cases, Stewart was opposed by Judge David S. Terry of Calaveras county, California, a southerner by birth who had gone to California in the gold rush days. He had become in due time chief justice of California, the position from which he had resigned to fight a duel with David C. Broderick. Terry, among the first lawyers to come to Nevada, arrived two days before Stewart. It was said that Terry went to the Comstock at the request of Jefferson Davis, from whom he was believed to have received a commission to be the territorial governor of Nevada in the event it became sympathetic with the southern cause.[324] Terry declared even at that date, one year before the Civil War, that there was going to be a division of the Union, that the proposed territory of Nevada would be a part of the Southern Confederacy, and that whoever was in possession of the mines would be allowed to hold them. He selected, therefore, three prominent places in the Comstock region, and caused forts to be erected thereon. Terry, too, was a giant of great physical strength and agility; he weighed two hundred and fifty pounds, "his jaw was firm, and cold steel-gray eyes looked out from beneath heavy dark brows." [325]

On account of the confusion concerning the jurisdiction of

[324] Charles Rothwell Brown, *Reminiscences of Wm. M. Stewart*, 129-134.
[325] Carl Brent Swisher, *Stephen J. Field, Craftsman of the Law*, 129-134.

the courts, these two leading lawyers met in June, 1860, and
agreed to try their cases before United States Judge Cradlebaugh. What a picture these two Herculean lawyers, each
backed with about a hundred armed men to assist him if
necessary, must have made in the court room![326] The court
at its first session was held in the upper story of a one and
one-half story building in Genoa, access to which was had by
means of a ladder from the street.[327]

In October, 1860, President Buchanan, who was believed
to have southern proclivities, removed Judge Cradlebaugh
and in his place appointed R. P. Fleniken, a judge in the eastern district of Utah territory. Judge Cradlebaugh maintained that he was the legal judge on the ground that the
president did not have the right to remove a territorial judge.
Stewart supported Judge Cradlebaugh in his contentions;
Terry announced that he was going to support Fleniken. To
test the validity of Cradlebaugh's authority, Stewart appealed a criminal case to the supreme court of Utah in Salt
Lake City. An interesting comment on the removal of Judge
Cradlebaugh appeared in the San Francisco newspaper:

> It is stated that Judge Cradlebaugh, whose heroic conduct in exposing
> the iniquities of Mormondom has won him the respect of all good men
> who have looked into the conditions of affairs in Utah, has been removed!
> It is also announced that the vacancy will not be filled for some time.
> Mr. Buchanan doubtless sees that any judge equally honest and firm will
> pursue practically the course adopted by the patriot; it is convenient,
> therefore, to leave the place vacant.[328]

Judge Fleniken arrived late in the fall of 1860. Terry told
Stewart that he was going to discontinue their agreement to
recognize Cradlebaugh as the judge of western Utah and
henceforth would try cases in Judge Fleniken's court. The
county seat had now been removed to Carson City. At the
time Fleniken arrived in the territory, Cradlebaugh agreed
to resign if the supreme court of the territory of Utah held
against him in the case brought before it by Stewart, or, if,
when the Lincoln administration was inaugurated, it refused

---

[326] Brown, *op. cit.*, 135.

[327] Bancroft, *History of Nevada, Colorado, and Wyoming*, 90, fn. 65.

[328] *San Francisco Evening Bulletin*, May 31, 1859.

to pay him his salary and paid it to Judge Fleniken. The arrangement seemed to be agreeable to both parties. There were now two federal judges in the territory. The next suit of any importance, called in February, 1861, involved the issuance of an injunction against Terry's clients to prevent them from holding a valuable mining claim near Silver City, which they were defending by force of arms. Stewart brought suit in Cradlebaugh's court, which issued an injunction in favor of Stewart's clients. That there might be no doubt about the legality of the injunction, Stewart called on Judge Fleniken the same day to hear the testimony and give his decision. If he was in accord with Judge Cradlebaugh's opinion, the marshals of the two courts were to be asked to carry out the mandates of the courts. To avoid any bloodshed Fleniken agreed to grant an injunction also, but when called upon to issue his injunction along with Judge Cradlebaugh's, he refused to do so. He denied publicly, even, that he had made such an agreement. Later in the day, when Stewart was studying his next move, the pony express brought in from Salt Lake City the decision of the supreme court of Utah in favor of Judge Cradlebaugh. When Fleniken heard of the decision, he said he would abide by it, and assured Stewart that he would. Resting on this assurance, Stewart got out an order for the arrest of the men holding the fort, then retired for the night. Early the next morning, Stewart's associates in the case called at his house. They told him Judge Fleniken was out on the street asserting that he was the legal judge, and denying Judge Cradlebaugh's right to sit. Whereupon, Stewart belted on his pistols and started out to find Fleniken. He met him on the square where the Nevada state capitol now stands and told him that he, the judge, was being slandered. He stated further that it was reported that he was defying the authority of Judge Cradlebaugh. Stewart told him also that he had had the marshal deputize him so that he could summon a *posse comitatus* to assist in carrying out Cradlebaugh's injunction and he was now summoning him to carry a musket. Fleniken, surprised by this order, stepped back, whereupon Stewart, grabbing him by the coat collar, and throwing him to his knees, at the same time drawing his pistol, ordered him to carry a musket in front of him. Fleniken begged to be let off, and his pleas were granted on condition that he dictate four or five telegrams to the officers of the court declaring that not he but Cradlebaugh was the legal judge. When the telegrams reached the officers who were in Silver City ready to carry out the orders of the court, consultation between the opposing parties was held. The forces at the fort surrendered to Judge Cradlebaugh's marshal, who brought them to Carson City. When the prisoners were arraigned before the judge, Stewart moved their discharge on the ground that they had been misled by a usurper by the name of Fleniken, who falsely pretended to be judge. The motion was granted. Judge Cradlebaugh continued to sit as judge until the formation of the territory of Nevada in the summer of 1861. Judge Terry left when the Civil War broke out, and never returned.[329] Stewart took an important part in the affairs of the territory and state of Nevada for fifty years. He left an indelible imprint on the history of the state. A great deal more will be heard about him later.

It was interesting to note the attitude of the Utah authorities toward this confused state of affairs in the western part of the territory. The only expression found by the writer concerning their attitude toward the formation of a provisional government by the dissatisfied colonists was uttered by the editor of the Salt Lake *Mountaineer,* a prominent member of the Mormon church, who said that "Since the first organization of the territory, Carson county has been a most unremunerative burden upon Utah. What is she now? A worthless unaccountable scab, which cannot find a place in any class of an honest vocabulary. So let her remain, dried up, buried, and forgotten!" [330]

During this confusion in the jurisdiction of the United States district judgeship, events were moving very rapidly toward the organization of the territory. Petitions were being circulated in which a separate form of government was sought. The California legislature was petitioned to persuade the congress to create a new territory, national repre-

[329] Brown, *op. cit.,* 129-139.
[330] Copied in *Sacramento Union,* December 22, 1860.

sentatives of California being asked to use their best influence to attain it.[331] "Tennessee" wrote:

Although we are cut off from all participation in the presidential contest, there are some good and loyal men in this country who deserve a better fate than to be placed beyond the light and warmth of Uncle Samuel's smiles. We need the care of the federal government more than any other people within the limits of Uncle Sam's domain. We have the Mormons only to legislate for us, truly, we are in the hands of the Philistines; we have no postal facilities, no Indian appropriations and no competent tribunal, except Judge Cradlebaugh's, and nothing has been done by that, so far.[332]

Senators Gwin and Latham of California presented a bill to create the territory of Nevada.[333] The latter senator presented three petitions from the citizens of western Utah which asked for separation. Senator Green of Missouri was the author of the bill which finally passed the senate on February 26, 1861; the house of representatives passed the same bill on March 2. Buchanan signed the act as one of the last important bills of his administration.[334] The state of anarchy and confusion was over for the citizens of western Utah; congressional interposition had brought order out of chaos. It was left, however, for President Lincoln to organize the new territory. But before the difficulties of this federating process can be fully appreciated, the reader must know more about the great silver discovery.

---

[331] *California Statutes*, 1860, 409.

[332] *San Francisco Herald*, July 28, 1860, "letter no. 8."

[333] *Cong. Globe*, 36 Cong., 1 sess., 317, 374, 2668.

[334] *Senate Journal*, 36 Cong., 1 sess., 228, 317, 372; *House Ex. Doc.*, 36 Cong., 2 sess., XXVI, 1084.

# The Silver Rush to Washoe

The territory and state of Nevada came into being through the discovery and development of the precious metals. Indeed, the history of Nevada was in large measure the early history of the Comstock Lode. It is unique in the annals of the history of the United States that a state was created out of a desert wilderness through the ever-changing vagaries of the mineral veins. The discovery of the Comstock led to that of many other silver ledges. Around each of these a community sprang up, some of them permanent, others too transient even to exist in name. In the short space of two years there were so many people in western Utah that congress was compelled to create a territory out of it, and four years later, to elevate it to statehood. This nationalizing process came about through the discovery of the "American Potosí." The story of its discovery is the prologue of the epic of Virginia City, one of the most thrilling episodes in the settlement of the West. To understand more fully this extraordinary situation, the story of the discovery must be known.

The Sierra Nevada, one of the ranges of the great mineral bearing cordillera of western North America, sends a single spur, the Washoe mountains located between the Truckee and Carson rivers, into the Great Basin. This short range is joined to the main chain by a series of parallel ridges, between each of which is a valley – Truckee Meadows, Pleasant Valley, Washoe Valley, and Eagle Valley. The lower ridges converge on the eastern side of the valleys into the Washoe mountains, which reach their highest point in Sun Peak, later called Mount Davidson.[335] From this mountain the range gradually slopes eastward until it merges with the plains of Carson Sink.

---

[335] This mountain was called Sun Peak by the early settlers, but was named later for Donald Davidson, one of the first ore buyers to appear on the Comstock.

The Washoe mountains, outcroppings of which occur in many places, are highly mineralized. Across the southeastern face of Mount Davidson extend a series of parallel veins. The atmospheric changes brecciated the ledges into minute particles, which in turn were washed into the ravines to the north and south of the mountain. Down the southeast side of Sun mountain ran a five mile lateral ravine to the Carson river. Because gold was found in the bed of this ravine the early emigrants called the stream Gold Creek and its cañon Gold cañon. Coming from the northeast side of the same mountain was another large ravine, Six Mile cañon, the head of which was about a mile from the head of Gold cañon. It, too, opened on the Carson river a few miles north of the mouth of Gold cañon. About 2,000 feet from the summit of Mount Davidson and around the mountain, the outcropping of the Comstock Lode was visible for several miles. It took, however, about ten years for the silver discovery to be made even after it was known that gold was found in the creek beds below the lode.

The honor of the discovery of gold in Gold cañon is, at this late date, a moot point. Through many years of research, the writer concludes through deduced evidence that gold was discovered by members of the Mormon battalion who were traveling along the Carson river in the early part of August, 1848. Because this view of the discovery has never been vigorously advanced, it is necessary to give the reader some of the reasons for the contention. In 1847 the men in the Mormon battalion, after having served a year in the Mexican War in New Mexico and California, were discharged. The soldiers wished to return to their families and friends in Salt Lake City. A few of these men returned at once to the Mormon city over the Los Angeles-Salt Lake Road; most of them, however, desired to return by the northern or Humboldt River Route. At that time the only community of any size in northern California was Sutter's Fort, New Helvetia. When they arrived there, Captain Sutter wanted them to remain and work for him, but they were so anxious to get back to their desert Zion that they hurried on over the Truckee Pass. When they reached the other end of Truckee (Donner) Lake, they came upon "Cannibal Camp," the site of the gruesome remains of the tragic winter, 1846-1847, spent by the Donner party. After spending several days in burying the dead, they continued down the Truckee river for some distance, where they met the Mormon missionary, Samuel Brannan,[336] who was returning to San Francisco. He advised all of the battalion who did not have families to support in the Mormon city, or who did not have plenty of provisions, to return to California with him. Many took his advice and returned to work for Sutter for the winter of 1847-1848. A number of them were sent up to Coloma on the South Fork of the American river to help build a flour mill. Among them was William Henry Bigler, whose vivid diary, a copy of which is still extant, described not only what he saw of the tragedy at Donner Lake but also the first discovery of gold. In fact, Bigler claimed that he was present at the discovery when James Marshall picked up the gold particles in the tail race of the mill on January 24, 1848. Bigler and many of his Mormon companions placered in the surrounding ravines and obtained a good quantity of the dust. Some of these Mormons became apostates and settled in California; others desired to return to the parent colony in Utah. The latter group, consisting of forty-five men and one woman, set out for Salt Lake on June 17, 1848. It was this party that built the road from Brighton, California, by the way of Placerville to Carson Valley, the detailed story of which has been told in a preceding chapter.[337]

The men in this group were among those who had placered in California. Proof of this comes from an entry in the "Bigler Diary" relating the tragedy that befell three of the party at Tragedy Springs. He wrote that when

. . . we came to examine around about the ground we found. . . Mr. Allen's purse of gold dust lieing about a rod from the grave, the gold was still in the sack - it was known by several of the boys who had seen him make it - he attached a buck-skin string of sufficient length so as to put

---

[336] Sam Brannan brought a group of Mormon converts on the ship "Brooklyn" from New York to San Francisco in 1846. Some of them remained in California while others went to Salt Lake City. When Brannan found the Mormons in Utah to be short of provisions, he advised the battalion men to remain in California for the winter. Bancroft, *History of Utah*, 593.

[337] Henry William Bigler, "Diary of a Mormon," MS., 53-83, *et supra*, 121-122.

it over his head and around his neck and letting the purse hang in his bosom inside of his clothes.[338]

The party continued across the summit, descended into Carson Valley, and proceeded eastward, camping along the Carson river as they went. Although there was no mention made in the Bigler diary of any member of the party finding gold in the streams that flowed into Carson river, there is strong possibility that some member of this party or a later Mormon party found gold in Gold cañon. When the party returned to the Great Salt Lake, they told their brethren of the discovery of gold in California, and in western Utah.[339]

Early in the spring of the following year a number of the Zionites succumbed to the gold fever. On April 18, 1849, eighty men, many of them former members of the battalion, set out for California to mine for a short time. The company was captained by a Mr. DeMont; Hampden S. Beatie acted as the clerk. They traveled over the Humboldt-Carson rivers route, followed the previous year by the Bigler party. Most of the company went on to the mines. Beatie and six others remained in Carson Valley where they set up a trading station near the site of the present town of Genoa. According to Beatie, "There was no other white man in the region." [340] In July Beatie and a Mr. Blackburn went over to California for more supplies. While they were gone, Abner Blackburn went prospecting in the lateral ravines along the Carson river, and discovered gold in the little stream flowing out of the south side of Sun Peak. Of this discovery Beatie said:

He made the discovery in July while I was gone over the mountains - it seems he had an idea that gold was in the vicinity of what is now Virginia City, and while his brother and myself had gone over the mountains it appears that he went prospecting and discovered gold but got only a small quantity. No other mining was done by our party at that time.[341]

The site of Beatie's trading post was approximately forty miles from Gold cañon. There are innumerable cañons opening into Carson river between these two points. To have prospected all of them would have taken a long time. If

338 Bigler, "Diary of a Mormon," MS., 63.
339 *Ibid.*, 83ff.
340 H. S. Beatie, "The first in Nevada," MS., 3.
341 *Idem.*

Blackburn had not known that there were indications of gold at the mouth of this particular cañon, it does not seem reasonable that he would have gone so far from the trading post to look for it. At that time he may have done some placering as he camped along the Carson river.[342] It was but natural for these men to expect to find gold on the east side of the Sierra Nevada as well as on the west side. There is no doubt that gold was discovered in the summer of 1848, but as Mark Twain would say, it did not stay discovered.

From still another source came the claim that William Prouse, a member of the Thomas Orr party which entered Carson Valley in the spring of 1849, first discovered gold in Gold cañon. This party left Great Salt Lake later in the month of April than did the DeMont-Beatie party. They traveled over the same route, however, and on May 15 camped for a few hours beside a little creek which flowed down from the range to the east of it. During the short halt, Prouse, also a former member of the Mormon battalion, took a milk pan to the edge of the stream to wash some of the surface dirt. After a few minutes, he returned to his companions and showed them a few specks of gold on the bottom of the pan. Because these tiny particles were worth but a few cents they were carelessly thrown aside. Nevertheless, this party named the little stream Gold Creek and the cañon Gold cañon.[343] Prouse declared he had made a still earlier discovery of gold dust in the same creek bed in the autumn of 1848 on his return to the Great Salt Lake from California. He said of this discovery that he lingered behind his party in order to prospect, and on coming up with the train told its members that he would show them the place where they could find gold if they ever traveled that way again.[344]

The Orr party continued on its way. As it approached the Sierra Nevada range, they learned that the mountains were impassable, so they camped three weeks in Carson Valley. During this period, John Orr, the son of the leader of the

[342] Joseph Fielding Smith, Historian, Church of Jesus Christ of Latter Day Saints, to writer, June 30, 1931.

[343] Diary of William Prouse, quoted in Eliot Lord, *Comstock Mining and Miners*, 11.

[344] Letter of William Prouse, December 14, 1880, quoted in *ibid.*, 11.

party, and several other men, returned to Gold cañon to prospect farther up the stream. Orr, with one of his companions, Nicholas Kelly, worked up the cañon rapidly until on June 1 they reached a point where the banks of the rocky ravine approached so near each other that a narrow passage only was left (Devil's Gate, just above American Flat ravine, undoubtedly). The water in the little stream flowed swiftly at this point. Into a crevice at the edge of one of the falls, Orr thrust a butcher's knife, and pried off a loose fragment of rock. The rapidly flowing water washed off the dirt, revealing a small nugget of gold. They obtained at the same time other bits of quartz from the nearby outcroppings, but owing to lack of proper tools, limited supplies, and their intention to go to California, they left Gold cañon and hastened on to their destination.[345] So the honor of the first discovery of gold dust goes to Abner Blackburn and William Prouse, and for the first discovery of gold bearing quartz, to John Orr and Nicholas Kelly. Other emigrants passing that way soon learned of the discovery. The world began to know that gold could be found on the east side of the Sierra Nevada.

When the news of the gold discovery in Gold cañon became known in the mining camps of California, many prospectors came over to take a look at the new find. Reports were that there were rich surface diggings on the Humboldt, Walker, and Truckee rivers, but the miners found upon investigation that the returns from their work in Gold cañon were the highest.

Although there were placer miners in Gold cañon in 1850, there is no record of the number. However, in the following year it was estimated there were one hundred and twenty miners working about one hundred days [346] averaging about $5 a day, and extracting about $60,000 for the yield of the year. For the next seven years, placer mining continued to be good in Gold cañon and the smaller cañons opening into it. From 1851 to 1857 there were probably not more than one hundred and eighty miners in western Utah; the highest annual returns of any year in this period were probably not

[345] Lord, *op. cit.*, 12.

[346] There are about three months in the spring of the year when there is water running down Gold cañon.

greater than $118,000.[347] After 1857, as the miners neared the heads of the cañon and the gulches, their returns began to dwindle, for reasons not known to them. A bothersome kind of black, heavy dirt was the chief trouble. We shall hear more about this dirt later on.

The first trading post to come into existence near the first discovery of gold was made by Spafford Hall at a point on the Carson river about one and one-half miles from the mouth of Gold cañon. For the four years he kept the post, it was known as Spafford Hall's Station. In 1854, he sold out to his clerk, James McMarlin, and the name of the station changed with its new owner. In 1855, about fifty Chinese were brought over from California for the purpose of digging a thirty mile ditch to divert the water of Carson river to the placer miners in Gold cañon.[348] After the ditch was completed and the water turned into it, the end of it was found to be higher than the source. The Chinese were permitted, however, to remain on the river to placer over the ground after the white men had abandoned it. At first the Chinese lived on the river near McMarlin's store, thereby giving the station a new name, Chinatown.[349] This settlement was the nucleus of the later town of Dayton. When the miners advanced up the cañon with their placer operations, the supply venders went, too, and so did the Chinese. A newer settlement sprang up several miles up the cañon where the Chinese lived. On account of the universal custom of referring to the oriental as "John," this newer community became known as Johntown.

The Chinese were not the only foreigners who found placer mining profitable in Gold cañon. About 1850 a group of Mexicans from California came into this region to mine. They were led by Don Ignacio Paredes, who in turn had

[347] Lord, *op. cit.*, 24.

[348] The *Nevada Journal*, September 28, 1855; Bancroft, *History of Nevada, Colorado, and Wyoming*, 77-78.

[349] In June, 1859, Chinatown was described as a mining town of twelve houses, fifty Chinese, and about one hundred and fifty other people in the vicinity engaged in mining. Miners were clearing from $5 to $8 a day per man. They were using a "rocker" or a "cradle" to wash the gold from the dirt. Gold was selling at $13 an ounce. There were two stores in Chinatown: E. Sam, a Chinese, kept one and the other was owned by Keller and Cohen. J. H. Simpson, *op. cit.*, 13.

been guided to these "diggings" by two native California prospectors. These peon miners prospected in the neighboring hills, and found abundant traces of silver, but owing to the lack of necessary equipment did not remain long in the country.[350] Other Mexicans came later, and were to play an important part in the discovery of silver in Nevada. With the possible exception of these Mexicans, who were familiar with silver mining in old Mexico, the great body of placer miners in Gold and Six Mile cañons were not only not interested, but were thoroughly disgusted with this heavy black dirt which increasingly cut down the returns in their toms and rockers. If any one of them had thought that there were high values of silver in it, he did not know how to find this out, or how to reduce it to the pure metal.[351]

Just how long the ignorance of the existence of the great veins leading up to Mount Davidson would have continued, is doubtful, had not two young men, Ethan Allen Grosh and Hosea Ballou Grosh, sons of a Pennsylvania Universalist clergyman, come into Gold cañon. These young fellows seemed to have been ill-starred from the very beginning of their mining adventure. The raging storm at sea, the shivering of a mast of their vessel by a bolt of lightning, a perilous journey across Mexico from Tampico to San Blas, and the subsequent illness of Hosea from the tedious trip, were a few of the ominous signs which presaged a disastrous end to their western career. After they had recovered from the effects of their journey from New York to California, they went to Mud Springs, now El Dorado, California, where they engaged in placer mining. In 1851 they visited western Utah to prospect in several different places. On this latter trip they collected many specimens of ore which they took back to California to test. "Old Frank," a Mexican in Gold cañon, was instrumental in helping them to find the silver ledges. It was he, undoubtedly, who first called their attention to the probability of silver ledges in that region. That the boys recognized their indebtedness to him is beyond doubt; they named their first company after him.[352]

---

350 Lord, *op. cit.,* 13.

351 The proportions of gold and silver in the Washoe district were one-third and two-thirds respectively.

352 Angel, *op. cit.,* 52.

The Grosh boys corresponded frequently with their father in Pennsylvania. A number of years after the unfortunate death of both of them, he made a summary of their mining operations from these letters, which in turn was published. Excerpts from the letters form a diary of their discovery of silver in Nevada:

MARCH 31, 1856. Ever since our return from Utah we have been trying to get a couple of hundred dollars together for the purpose of making a careful examination of a silver lead in Gold cañon. . . Native silver is found in Gold cañon; it resembles thin sheet-lead broken very fine, and lead the miners to suppose it to be. . . We found silver ore at the forks of the cañon. A large vein shows itself in this situation.

NOVEMBER 3, 1856. We found two veins of silver at the forks of Gold cañon. . . One of these is a perfect monster.

NOVEMBER 22, 1856. We have hopes almost amounting to certainty of veins crossing the cañon at two other points.[353]

The boys returned to California for the winter of 1857-1858, during which time they prospected for quartz veins without success. The following spring they returned to Gold cañon. Allen wrote to his father:

JUNE 8, 1857. We struck the vein without difficulty but find some in tracing it. We have followed two shoots down the hill, have a third traced positively, and feel pretty sure that there is a fourth. The two shoots we have traced give strong evidence of big surface veins.

A diagram of the set of veins was enclosed in the letter with an explanation of their location:

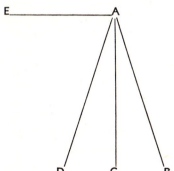

A seems to be the center from which all seem to radiate; B we have traced by boulders; C we have struck the end of; D the same; E is uncertain, though the evidence of its existence is tolerably strong; B A C may be the true vein and the shoots D A E may be superficial spurs. We have pounded up some of each variety of rock and set it to work by the Mexican process. . . The rock of the vein looks beautiful, is very soft, and will work remarkably easy. The show of metallic silver produced by exploding it in damp gunpowder is very promising. . . It differs very much from the Frank vein, the vein we discovered last fall.[354]

[353] Angel, *op. cit.,* 53; Lord, *op. cit.,* 27.
[354] *Idem.*

AUGUST 16, 1857. Our first assay was one-half ounce of rock; the result was $3500 of silver to the ton, by hurried assay, which was altogether too much of a good thing. . . We assayed a small quantity of rock by cupellation from another vein. The result was $200 per ton. We have several other veins which are yet untouched. We are very sanguine of success.[355]

While they were prospecting for veins of silver ore, they supported themselves by placering, which was just profitable enough to keep them in food and clothes. George Brown, a cattle trader of Carson Valley, promised them, however, a substantial sum of money to develop one of the rich ore-bearing ledges when they had determined the existence and course of it. Brown acted also as one of the mail agents at a station on the Humboldt river during the emigrant season. Fortune seemed about to enter the little stone cabin of the Grosh boys. Allen wrote again: "September 11, 1857. The black rock presented so many difficulties that we lost our patience, and, relying on Brown we dropped everything, determined to master it. The very day we had determined it we heard the first news of the murder." [356]

For the moment it seemed as though capricious fortune had deserted them, but they were undaunted. A fairy godmother in the person of Mrs. L. M. Dettenrieder promised to help them with money which she had saved from her boarding house enterprises along the California trail. They thought, too, they might be able to secure some capital in California.

Whether they would have succeeded with their expected aid, coupled with their persistency, in the face of their ill-omened beginnings, can never be known. The most serious misfortune befell them on August 19, when Hosea accidentally struck his pick into his foot just below the ankle. It made a deep and painful wound. There was no physician or drug store in the vicinity, but the devoted brother and the kindly miners did the best they could to prevent blood poisoning. Gangrene set in, and he died on September 2. Allen was grief stricken at the loss of his brother, yet he bore up nobly under his sorrow. Of Hosea's accident, illness,

---

[355] Lord, *op. cit.*, 28.

[356] Brown was murdered by Indians in his Humboldt mail station. Bancroft, *History of Nevada, Colorado, and Wyoming*, 97.

death, and burial so many miles from their home and relatives, Allen wrote philosophically to his father:

In the first burst of my sorrow I complained bitterly of the dispensation
which deprived me of what I held most dear of all the world, and I thought
it most hard that he should be called away just as we had fair hopes of
realizing what we had labored for so many years. But when I reflected
how well an upright life prepared him for the next, and what a debt of
gratitude I owed to God in blessing me for so many years with so dear a
companion, I became calm and bowed my head in resignation.[357]

It took some time for him to compose himself, and longer
to pay off the debts of his brother's illness and burial.[358] All
of this delayed his departure for California until November.
Before he left Gold cañon, he boxed up most of his papers,
books, and mining apparatus, and either cached them in the
hills, or left them in their cabin in American Flat ravine.
He took with him, however, a number of specimens to test.
On November 20, 1857, Allen Grosh and a young prospector friend from Canada, Richard M. Bucke, who also
had been placering in Gold cañon, started out for California
by the Donner Summit Route. Young Bucke kept a daily
record of their tragic experiences in the Sierra Nevada.
Most of the time they trudged along waist-deep in snow,
climbing from point to point, pulling themselves up by bushes
and jutting rocks. When they were near the summit, the
snow was so deep that it was impossible to follow the trail.
They killed the little burro that was carrying their baggage,
took as much of the meat as they could carry, threw away
the ore specimens, their papers, and excessive luggage, and
set out to cross the range as best they could.

The harrowing details of the remaining portion of their
trip cannot be related here. However, suffice it to say, it
took all the will power these men could muster, either to
drag themselves or to crawl down the western slope of the
mountain range, where by chance they came upon a Mexican
miners' camp. Their legs were frozen to their knees. The

[357] Lord, op. cit., 30.

[358] At first Hosea was buried near the little mining settlement at the forks
of the cañon. Later his remains were removed to the little cemetery in Silver
City. The elder Grosh had a memorial stone placed over it. The severe winters
broke the small slab in two. A generous Carson City undertaker had it pieced
together and laid flat in cement.

Mexicans put them on sleds and took them to the Last Chance Mining Camp. Richard Bucke had one foot and a part of the other one amputated, from the effects of which he finally recovered. Allen Grosh, having refused to submit to amputation, lingered for twelve days, and died on December 19. He was buried at Last Chance, where his friend and companion some years later marked the grave with a suitable headstone.[359]

With the death of the Grosh boys, the exact location of the silver ledges was lost for the time being; the discovery of the Comstock Lode was delayed. George Brown, the only man who had any accurate knowledge of the location of them, had been murdered; Bucke had seen the course of the veins, and a button of silver from one of the assays, but he knew little of the definite course of their discoveries; and Mrs. Dettenrieder said that Allen Grosh had pointed out to her in a general way the location of the ledges, but she could not give a definite description of the location.

With what fortune had tantalized the Grosh boys for seven years, she tossed carelessly into the lap of an undeserving, shiftless, and boasting fellow in a short time. Henry Tompkins Paige Comstock, a Canadian who had hunted and traded most of his life, came into Carson Valley in the fall of 1856, driving a herd of sheep. He was almost destitute, and had to get relief.[360] From Carson Valley he went to Gold cañon to placer. With the aid of two Indians, only a little less lazy than himself, he managed to earn a livelihood. To the miners he was known as "Old Pancake" because he was too lazy to make bread. Just how Comstock came into possession of the Grosh cabin and its effects will probably never be known. He told so many different stories, some of them under oath, that one is unable to judge which one was correct. Among the stories was one in which he said that the Grosh boys had left him in charge of the cabin, and that he was to receive one-third or one-fourth of their interests for his services. At another time he declared that

---

[359] Bucke went back to Canada to study medicine. He became subsequently the superintendent of the asylum for the insane in London, Canada. Lord, *op. cit.*, 32.

[360] "Wm. Jennings, Carson Valley," MS., 3.

he was their partner, which Bucke denied emphatically. At still another time he said he was on the spot at the time of the discovery and therefore was nearer than any of the Grosh heirs. There was one thing certain – he took possession of their cabin; the probability is that he learned of the location of their silver ledges from the papers and effects which Allen had boxed up before he left for California. "The total disappearance of their books and papers with all the evidence of their company and individual rights is strong, presumptive evidence against Comstock, as the person in charge." [361] The knowledge he gained from going through the papers he kept to himself. He did keep, nevertheless, a silent watch on the progress of mining in Gold cañon and the vicinity, ready to claim any rich ledge which was discovered by any of the other miners.

Unmindful of the tragic end of the first act in the drama of the discovery of the Comstock Lode, the other miners in Gold cañon went about their placer operations. In the summer of 1857, a number of men went prospecting in Six Mile cañon to look for better diggings. They found there a good quantity of gold mixed with a stiff blue clay, which had to be thoroughly dissolved to free the metal from it. By doing so they were able to earn from $5 to $13.50 a day. The news of the discovery spread quickly; many more miners came into the ravine. Among the late comers was a bibulous fellow known as "Old Virginia," whose real name was James Fennimore, or "Finney," for short. In company with Finney were Peter O'Riley, Patrick McLaughlin, Joseph Kirby, and Nicholas Ambrose. The last named was a saloon and boarding-house keeper for the miners.[362] In Six Mile cañon, the dirt became richer as they advanced up the ravine.

In January, 1859, during a warm spell, the snow melted sufficiently to permit prospecting. John Bishop, Comstock, and Finney placered in the vicinity of the head of Gold cañon with rich results. They marked off some claims, named the place Gold Hill, and built several log houses. This settlement

---

[361] Bancroft, *History of Nevada, Colorado, and Wyoming*, 98.

[362] "Dutch Nick" had lived in Carson Valley before he went to Gold cañon. Later he started a station on the bend of the Carson river. The town of Empire was built on the site of his trading post. Bancroft, *op. cit.*, 79.

became the rendezvous of the miners in both Six Mile and Gold cañons.

The placer miners had now worked up the north and south ravines leading to Sun Peak (Mount Davidson). Between the head of these two ravines about a mile apart extended the ledges of the great Comstock Lode. It was inevitable that some one of the miners would soon discover the source of their gold and silver.

When all of the snow on the mountain tops had melted, and the water no longer flowed in the ravines, the miners had to dig a small reservoir in Spanish ravine, a short distance above their claims in Six Mile cañon, in which to collect the water from a spring still higher up the mountain. On June 10, 1859, having excavated four feet of earth for their placering, they came upon an odd-looking stratum which they did not understand. O'Riley and McLaughlin were working on the reservoir when the discovery was made. They decided to test it; the result they found to be as rich as it was queer. Comstock, upon hearing of its richness, came to the claim, and informed the discoverers that the spring from which their water was coming belonged to him, Emanuel ("Manny") Penrod, and "Old Virginia." He informed them, also, that the ground belonged to other persons than themselves, whom he said he could buy off. Since the claim was a valuable one, and since it could not be worked without the water which Comstock claimed, the original discoverers agreed to the proposal. To these other owners, Comstock paid $50, and to "Old Virginia" he paid $40 and threw in an old blind horse. Joseph D. Winters, one of the claimants to the water, refused to sell out; he was admitted as a partner of the claim. The rotted surface ledge matter yielded about $300 to the rocker in gold.

So far this new discovery was a gold mine. On June 11, they came upon the solid ledge matter, which, Penrod said was a quartz vein. Comstock denied it at first, then, admitted it. After the ledge was traced for some distance, each man in the company was allowed to stake off three hundred feet, while the discoverers, according to the California law, were allowed an additional three hundred feet. Comstock and Penrod, having been the original owners, were allowed another one hundred feet to be segregated from the company's claim. This separate claim later became the Mexican mine from which millions were extracted.[363] Soon many other claims were located along the line of the lode, among them those belonging to Alison "Eilley" "Ellen" Orrum Cowan and to Lemuel S. Bowers. Their holdings were soon to be merged into one by their marriage.[364]

Comstock had used intimidating methods with O'Riley and McLaughlin without ever having himself discovered a thing; but because he could talk more familiarly about the various veins and their courses, the miners began to speak of the "Comstock Lode." The name was passed on until it became fast. Of all of the men connected with the discovery – Blackburn, Orr, Prouse, Fennimore, O'Riley, or McLaughlin – none deserved less to have his name immortalized than Comstock.

Penrod, Comstock and Company called their mine the Ophir, which was the first claim located on the lode. For a time the little community, consisting of a few houses quickly built up around the Ophir claim, was called "Ophir Diggings." On June 22, James Fennimore located a claim lying west of the Comstock which came to be called the "Virginia Lead" after the nickname of the locator. The legend that Fennimore had christened the ground near his claim "Virginia" may be true; however, it received the name Virginia Town officially at a meeting held in September, 1859.[365]

These first prospectors on the Comstock Lode worked the decomposed quartz near the surface of the ground in their toms and rockers. As they dug deeper into the decomposed stratum of earth, the quartz became harder. At first they tried to crush these harder masses with their picks and sledge hammers, but this was too laborious. On June 24, John D. Winters, Jr., and Joseph A. Osburn were given a one-third interest in 1400 feet of the Comstock claim, in return for which they agreed to supply two arrastras and two horses or mules for the use of Comstock and his partners. These old Mexican crushers satisfactorily pulverized the rock, and

[363] Bancroft, *History of Nevada, Colorado, and Wyoming*, 102.
[364] *Ibid.*, 171.
[365] Lord, *op. cit.*, 63.

the owners now began to make large profits. As yet, however, they had not taken cognizance of the black wedge in
the center of their claim, except as a hindrance to their work.
Gold was still the source of their sudden wealth.[366]

The news of the rich diggings along the veins extending
between the heads of the two ravines across Sun Peak attracted the attention of all of the miners in the vicinity, as
well as of the ranchers in the neighboring valleys, who sold
their produce to the miners. Among the ranchers who visited
the new strike was one from the Truckee Meadows, B. A.
Harrison. Mexicans had pointed out to the placer miners
the richness of the black rock. On one of Harrison's visits
to the discovery, he obtained a bag full of the black rock
specimens which he took back to J. F. Stone, member of
the firm of Stone and Gates, who owned the trading post
on the Truckee near the present site of Glendale, Nevada.
Mr. Stone had formerly lived at Alpha, Nevada county,
California, to which community he made frequent trips.
Late in June of 1859, he took one of these trips, and with
him the bag full of specimens, and left them with E. G.
Waite, editor of the *Nevada Journal* of Nevada City, California. He, in turn, took part of them to J. J. Ott of Nevada
City, and the rest of them to Melville Atwood in Grass
Valley, to be assayed. The assays were made at once, and
each gave the same results. On July 1, the *Nevada Journal*
published the first account of the strike and the result of the
assays. Because this announcement in a California paper
started the "rush to Washoe," the exact account is given
in part:

J. F. Stone . . . reports the discovery of a vein of ore of extraordinary
richness at the head of Six Mile cañon, about ten miles from the Truckee
Meadows. . . The vein is four feet in thickness and has already been
traced a distance of six miles, and prospected three miles and a half. The
ore is decomposed and easily worked. An assay of the ore by J. J. Ott, of
this city, gives a result warranting $840 to the ton worked in an ordinary
mill, leaving $130 in the tailings to be collected by other processes. The
metal obtained is composed of one-third silver and $12.40 gold per ounce.
There is a large quantity of antimony also collected besides about $40 in
copper to the ton. The ore is like that from which silver is sometimes obtained and not like decomposed quartz, though assuming more the appearance of the latter after being crushed and washed. . .

[366] *Ibid.,* 54.

The discovery was made by a man working in Six Mile cañon, who found as he worked up his claims the richer they became, till he struck the vein, when with a small and very muddy head of water he took out in half a day three hundred dollars, with two hands. . . Stone has furnished us with a quantity of the ore in which the mineral is plainly visible.

The news of the discovery has created quite an excitement in our hitherto quiet burg. Three men left for the diggings Wednesday night. Several other parties were making up yesterday. . .

Judge James Walsh and Joseph Woodworth of Nevada City left for Washoe two days before the foregoing account appeared in the paper. Being the first to arrive, they were able to obtain an interest in one of the best claims. They were followed by a large number of other miners from Nevada county and neighboring mining camps on the west side of the Sierra Nevada. Many of them came only to look over the strike and determine the possibilities of its extent and permanency. When Walsh and Woodworth returned to Nevada City, after having spent two weeks at the Ophir diggings, they confirmed the richness of the strike. A summary of their observations was published in the *Nevada Journal* on July 9, in which they reported:

. . . the diggings as being fabulously rich, both in silver and gold, and that a number of miners who had a small supply of water from springs, were making from $100 to $400 per day with the old fashioned rocker . . . only a few miners were there when they left, but they met on their return, many adventurers on their way to the diggings. . . They saw dirt prospected which paid $40 a pan, and heard it stated that as high as $107 had been obtained. . .

The scarcity of wood and water are the great drawbacks to the sudden development of that wonderfully rich country. It will take years of labor and immense sums of money to overcome the natural obstacles. To the single-handed miner, or men with small capital this country offers no inducements. That it contains an abundance of the precious metals, however, is a matter of no doubt. Time, and money, are necessary to open its unknown treasures to the hardy adventurer. . .

Both of these men were old, experienced miners, and their statements could be relied upon. And so the great rush to Washoe began in the summer of 1859. It continued until late in the fall, when the heavy snow closed the passes. Early the following spring, hundreds of miners, professional men, gamblers, swindlers, and other flotsam and jetsam of humanity, came over from California. The silver rush to the Nevada mines in 1859-1860 was truly the backwash of the gold rush to California. It has been said that the finest of the young men in the country went to California in the gold rush; and the best of the Californians came to Nevada in the silver rush. "Old Tennessee," a character in Genoa, wrote letters frequently to the California newspapers. In several of them he described the crowds on their way to Virginia City as they passed the window of his cabin situated near the road:

Genoa, Carson Valley
April 18, 1860

My humble habitation is built at the eastern base of the Snow range not far from the road which leads the fortune seeker to the promised land. This road is thronged day and night by persons plodding each way. I can sit at my window and scrutinize the features of the passers-by; here comes a fellow in a two horse buggy, going at a 2.40 rate, leaning back in his seat and casting his eyes toward heaven, as if in thankfulness; he expects soon to be a millionaire and upon the strength of his glorious hopes has managed to get over that offensive notice posted over the livery stable door, "Positively no Credit."

Hundreds of footmen go by every day, mostly loaded down with their "plunder," as if they were beasts of burden; but

"Primeval hope! thy glittering wings explore,
Earth's loneliest bounds and ocean's wildest shore!"

So upon the visages of these wayfarers, which were else a blank, a waste, a trackless desert, is depicted in most unmistakable colors the bright images of hope and anxious expectation.

He also observed those who had been to the scene of the strike and were returning to California. He commented that:

Yonder comes a crowd from the other direction; these "have seen the elephant" and from their rueful countenances we are led to the conclusion that they are no admirers of that sagacious but unwieldy animal. However, they possess one advantage over those who have not yet paid the door-keeper; their backs are relieved of that ponderous load with which they arrived in this country three or four weeks ago.[367]

In 1865, Samuel Bowles, editor of the *Springfield Republican,* who in company with Schuyler Colfax, speaker of the house of representatives, went to the Pacific coast by way of Salt Lake City and Virginia City, observed the large number of Californians in Nevada. He said: "California,

---

[367] "The Emigration," Tennessee, letter no. 69, *San Francisco Herald,* April 18, 1860.

mature at eleven, plants a colony in 1859-60 which ripens into a new state in 1864. Nevada is the first child of California." [368]

John Ross Browne, a "Forty-niner," who came to Nevada in 1859 to set up a mining agency in Carson City, wrote very entertainingly of his own experiences in Nevada. He was the first writer to describe the "rush to Washoe." When he arrived at Placerville, he found the town crowded with miners who were unable to find transportation for themselves or their goods. The road over the Johnson Cutoff, which had been partly graded as far as Strawberry Flat, had been cut so badly by the melting snows and early rains that it was impassable for wheeled vehicles; saddle horses and pack animals could hardly pick their way over it in places. All of the stores and warehouses and even the streets were piled with goods bound for Washoe. Horses and mules were bespoken for days in advance. There were men on foot and on horseback. Some of them were pushing wheelbarrows with their outfits in them; there were men in light and heavy carriages of their own; and there were farmers with their produce. Droves of sheep, hogs, and cattle were being driven over to be sold to the crowds who were pushing by.

Browne, too, set out with the crowd bound for Washoe. All along the way he found loaded wagons with broken wheels, poles, or axles half-buried in the mud. Most of them had been abandoned. Trains of pack animals picked their way from one dry spot to another, or floundered in the mud. From the other direction came trains of horses and mules carrying bags of ore from the Washoe mines. When the meeting occurred on a narrow place in the trail, some of the animals were crowded to the edge where they rolled over into the cañon below. [369]

A large number who came from California to Nevada were from Nevada county. Within two years it was estimated that one-third of the male population of that county had gone to the silver regions of Nevada. Some of them

---

[368] Samuel Bowles, *Across the Continent,* 139.

[369] J. Ross Browne wrote several other articles on Nevada and her resources. "A peep at Washoe" was published in the December, 1860, issue of *Harper's Monthly.* Other articles appeared in the *Overland Monthly.*

came to locate and make their fortunes; others to visit the scene of excitement. In fact, it was said that the Washoe rush carried away more people and capital than any other mining rush in the history of Nevada county.

Some small silver deposits had been discovered in California, and the Mexican miners in the country after a rude fashion crushed and amalgamated these ores. From these first silver miners the Americans learned all they knew or practised of silver reduction previous to the Washoe discoveries. Contemporary with the discovery of silver in the Washoe district there was sympathetic enthusiasm for silver in California.[370]

Prospectors began to flock to the new camp from every California town as soon as the news of the discovery was announced. These men were largely gold miners who knew very little about silver mining. Barren rock was equally as valuable to their untrained eyes as quartz-bearing ledges. As a result, the slopes of Sun Peak were literally covered with location stakes; notices crudely scrawled were posted, and the mountains for miles around were claimed by a constantly increasing swarm of fortune seekers.

The little Johntown colony was soon merged into the continuous line of huts and dugouts which extended the entire distance up the cañon to the base of the mountain near Gold Hill. The two largest communities that sprang up from the rush were Gold Hill and Virginia Town, the latter located directly below the peak of the mountain. Across the face of the mountain ran a single street which was laid out in October, 1859, by Herman Camp and Dr. Henry De-Groot. It extended along the supposed line of the Comstock ledge, running nearly north and south.[371]

On the line of this street two houses of roughly cemented stone had been built, surrounded by straggling lines of flimsy huts. Tents of dirty, ragged canvas pieced out with tattered clothes coated with grime - hovels of pine boards roughly nailed together and pierced by bent and rusty stovepipes - heaps of broken rocks with shapeless crevices into which men crawled like

[370] Edwin F. Bean, *History and Directory of Nevada county, California.* "Historical sketch of Nevada county [California]," written by E. G. Waite, 1855-1861. Waite was the editor of the *Nevada Journal;* Bancroft, *History of California,* VI, 650.

[371] This street later became "A" street.

lizards - shallow pits partly covered with boards and earth and embryo adits, dark slimy holes into which the melting snow dripped with a monotonous splash, these were the winter homes "of the miners in the Washoe mining region in 1859." The sacred thirst of gold had made them insensible to the cold, hunger, and fatigue.[372]

On the other side of the Sierra Nevada, men waited in their cheerful homes, impatient for the mountain barrier to be melted away so that they might participate in the drama of the silver rush. Rushes to different mining districts were common, but since the mighty migration by land and by sea toward California in 1849, there had been no excitement equal to this one.

Sam Brannan's dramatic parade up Market Street in 1848, with his bottle of gold held high for the excited crowds to see, was repeated in no less a dramatic manner when several bars of gleaming white silver bullion, extracted by the Joseph Mosheimer furnaces from the first ore shipped to San Francisco from the Comstock Lode, were carried through the streets of San Francisco, followed by a throng of excited people.[373] Later they were exhibited in a bank window where great crowds shoved and pushed to get a glimpse. This must have called to mind visions of the treasures of old Potosí, the ransom of a Montezuma, or the heavily laden galleons of Manila.

The rush to Washoe mining district continued unabated during 1860 to 1861. All of the would-be millionaires went to Virginia City first. When they found everything had been staked off for miles, they set out to look for other potential Ophirs. Their visit to the Comstock Lode trained their eyes for recognizing silver ledges in other ranges.

In the summer of 1860 the Esmeralda mines were discovered by J. M. Corey, James M. Braley, and E. R. Hicks. These men had come to Nevada for the purpose of prospecting on the east side of the mountains, but the Indian disturbances of that year prevented them from setting out on their quest until late in July. They prospected first in the vicinity of Pyramid Lake, and then in the Sullivan district to the east of the Carson river. Finding no values of such magnitude

[372] Lord, op. cit., 65.
[373] Loc. cit.

as to reward them for staying they started to go south along the eastern base of the mountains south of Walker Lake. After having prospected in these hills without any success, they decided to go farther south to the Coso region, and if this territory were not satisfactory, to continue still farther south to Arizona and Old Mexico. In order to ascertain the most feasible route southward, they climbed a high peak in the Wassuck range. From this elevated position they mapped out a route which would lead them over one of the most desolate sections of the desert country. They had not gone very far when lack of water compelled them to go toward the Sierra range, where there was water in the springs most of the year. On August 25, 1860, a fine spring of water was found in a small cañon surrounded by very steep mountains where they decided to camp for the night. Early the following morning, Hicks started out with his rifle to hunt for game. When he passed over the hill west of their camp, he noticed the peculiar appearance of a number of quartz ledges. He broke off a number of pieces from the ledges to take back to camp with him. His companions, being better miners than he was, recognized them as sulpherets of silver. A test was made of the rock, which revealed it to be very rich in silver. All intentions now of going south were abandoned, for a more thorough search of the surrounding hills. They were found to be literally seamed with quartz veins, all of which were more or less rich in silver and gold. In consequence of their find, the three men staked out seven claims for themselves before they told the outside world of their discovery. They then went to Monoville, a small community twenty-five miles southwest, to tell of their discovery. On August 30 twenty men returning with the original discoverers organized a mining district ten miles square. At the suggestion of Corey the district around the original discovery was named "Aurora," and the two mountain peaks that overlooked it were named Mount Braley and Mount Hicks after the discoverers. Reports of the new discovery, with samples of the rock, were taken to Virginia City. Before the winter, always severe, was over, there was a great rush of people to the Esmeralda mining district.[374]

374 Angel, op. cit., 415.

Two years later another rich silver discovery was made on the pony express-overland mail road by William M. Talcott, a former pony express rider. The road crossed Reese river at Jacobs Station, and passed eastward through the Toyabe mountain range. Almost directly east of the station there was another pass known as Pony cañon, so called because the riders often took it instead of the regular pass, thereby shortening their route. On May 2, 1862, while Talcott was gathering wood in this cañon for the mail station, he discovered a rich vein of quartz. Samples were taken to Virginia City for assay, which proved them rich. The Reese river mining district was organized immediately, and the town that grew up was named Austin.[375]

In 1860 the Humboldt district located on the western slope of the Star range of mountains was the first district organized in the vicinity of what later became Unionville, Humboldt county. There was a great rush of people to this district; other veins were found in the vicinity and other mining districts were organized.

Each of these mining districts organized in the early sixties in turn became the axis from which the prospectors set out in all directions. Many of them were successful in their search. Other mining districts were organized, and many other small mining communities sprang up. Each of these lesser communities was a suigenetic mining camp. This process continued until most of the western part of the territory of Utah was organized into mining districts. Small communities, too numerous to mention, grew up, some of which were permanent enough to become county seats, others too ephemeral to take part in the political process.

Nevertheless, the effect of this silver rush impelled congress to look favorably upon the demands of these people for a separate territory. Silver had brought recognition to this inhospitable desert region; silver mining was the chief industry. It was a difficult task that confronted the officers appointed by the federal government to organize this shifting mining society.

---

[375] Bancroft, *History of Nevada, Colorado, and Wyoming*, 264-265.

# From Carson County to Nevada Territory

The transformation of western Utah from a sparsely populated agricultural community to a heterogeneous mining one was kaleidoscopic, made in the space of a few months, and so rapidly that it swept away everything belonging to the older order. It was effected by a vigorous, bold, and self-assertive mass, composed chiefly of the more audacious members of the California gold rush. The feeble efforts of the earlier settlers in the valleys at the eastern base of the Sierra Nevada to establish an independent government were completely destroyed. What these first revolters against Mormon domination tried to do in four years was brought about in a few short weeks by this domineering new society. First, for the federal government to pass an organic act to create the territory of Nevada out of the territory of Utah was little short of a political miracle, as there was not a single stable, well-organized community in the entire area embraced in the region seeking the Nevada territorial status. The negative authority of the officers of Carson county of the territory of Utah had ceased, however, long before the territory of Nevada was set up by the federal government. The story of this metamorphosis is unique in our national history.

The organic act was the framework of the political organization as laid down by the federal government for the territory of Nevada; its chief provisions explained the necessary procedure whereby the important change was effected.[376] In addition to the organic act, the secretary of the territory, Orion Clemens, was given a set of instructions which his humorous brother Samuel (Mark Twain) said were so numerous that the two of them "had to read a chapter for breakfast every morning."

[376] A. J. Marsh, *Official Reports of Nevada Constitutional Convention,* v-ix.

Although the organic act creating the territory of Nevada was signed by President Buchanan on March 2, 1861, it was four months before the representatives of the federal government arrived in Carson county to put it into effect. The delay occasioned a great deal of concern among the more conservative citizens, who bemoaned the absence of authority, the recklessness of the lawless element which always followed a mining rush, and feared lest the southern sympathizers, who were not few, might seize the territory for the Confederacy. A correspondent to a San Francisco newspaper declared:

The non-arrival of Governor Nye is placing everything in a very awkward fix. Without law, we are in a state of confusion most confounded. A meeting is to be held for the purpose of organizing a temporary government; for the protection of life and property. At the present moment it is not an agreeable or enviable position of a newly-elected governor, however patriotic he may be. His proper place is in Nevada territory, not in New York. This state might secede, and what then? Not an official, not a man in power to advise and act. A pretty state of things, truly. Although Union men are numerous and strong and love the stars and stripes, as the banner of freedom, still there are a few who would see it trampled in the dust of Southern secession and rebellion.[377]

The reason for the delay was that when Governor Nye left New York, in the haste of his departure, the baggage containing his commission and other papers necessary for the organization of the territory was left on the wharf. The official territorial party sailed on the steamship "Ariel" by way of Panama, where they took the steamer "St. Louis" for San Francisco, arriving on June 26. During their ten day wait for the next steamer they were guests at the International Hotel. Governor Nye accepted an invitation to deliver the fourth of July oration, in connection with which a San Francisco paper referred to him as "one of the jolliest orators that ever stumped a state. When he was a Democrat all of the Whigs went to hear him and when he was a Republican, you couldn't hire the Democrats to stay away." [378]

The personnel of the federal group of officers sent to organize the territory of Nevada was selected, not for their fitness, but to reward them for party services. James W. Nye,

[377] *Daily Alta California,* May 20, 1861.
[378] *Daily Evening Bulletin,* June 26, July 5, 1861.

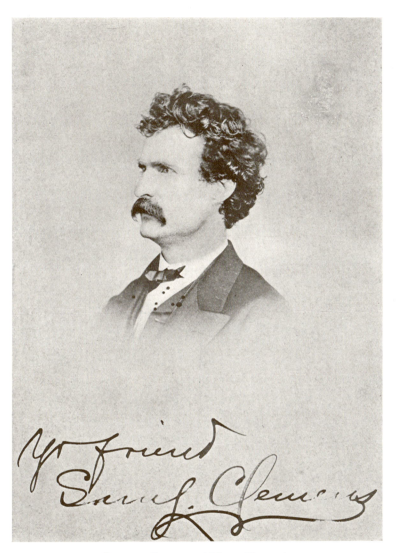

SAMUEL CLEMENS (MARK TWAIN)
This photograph was taken when Mark Twain was a reporter on western newspapers. It was given to his fellow reporter, Frank W. Gross, whose daughter kindly loaned it to the writer. Reproduced from an exceedingly rare and hitherto unpublished photograph.

forty-six years old at the time of his appointment, was a lawyer by profession and a Whig Democrat by political conviction. From youth he had taken an active part in politics. In 1857, he was appointed commissioner of police of New York City, where he was known as "an active, energetic, and talented man." [379] He had occupied a prominent position in the politics of New York City for ten or fifteen years, where he made for himself an enviable reputation as a "capital stump speaker with a fund of humor which never failed to tell upon an audience." When the metropolitan police was created, Nye was made a member of the commission; later, he was president of it during the troubles that preceded the establishment of the police force on an efficient basis. After several years in this position, he resigned to resume his law practice, but continued to take a very active part in state and national politics.

Mr. Nye was one of the delegates from New York state to the famous convention in Chicago in June, 1860, where he tried very hard to secure the nomination for the presidency of his very good friend, William H. Seward. Failing to do so did not deter him from giving his voice and influence to the election of Abraham Lincoln. Seward and Nye toured the West, and spoke in many places for Lincoln. It was for this work, and for his friendship with Seward that Nye was appointed territorial governor of Nevada.[380] Not only was he given this position, but was granted the privilege of appointing other New York politicians to Nevada positions of lesser importance. A glance at the list of men who accompanied him to Nevada, and at the appointment each was given, is revealing. J. C. Gallagher, once connected with the business management of the *New York Daily News,* was among those who came with Nye; he acted as secretary of the territory until the arrival of Orion Clemens, and later became the governor's private secretary. W. M. Gillespie, of Albany, New York, was appointed secretary of the territorial convention; John F. Kidder, chief clerk to the surveyor-general, and Julius E. Garrett, assistant clerk, were from Syracuse, former home of Governor Nye. Other New York

[379] *Daily Alta California,* June 18, 1861.
[380] *Loc. cit.*

men in the party were Dr. John Ives, surgeon to the metropolitan police department of New York City at the time Nye
was president of it. Butler Ives, of Detroit, received the
position of deputy United States surveyor-general for Nevada; and J. S. Lawton, of New York City, assistant United
States deputy surveyor-general. The remaining members of
the official party were Benjamin B. Bunker of Thornton,
New Hampshire, United States attorney; Gordon N. Mott
of California, associate justice; George Turner of Ohio,
chief justice; Horatio M. Jones of Missouri, associate justice; and John W. North of Minnesota, surveyor-general.

One other member of Nevada's first official family arrived
even later; it was August before Samuel [381] and Orion Clemens came. The latter had been appointed secretary of the
new territory through his friendship with Edward Bates,
in whose St. Louis law office he had studied. Bates, being
influential in national politics, became attorney-general in
President Lincoln's cabinet. When Orion Clemens [382] was
given the appointment he was so poor that he did not have
the means to pay his overland stagecoach fare to Nevada.
Samuel Clemens, ten years younger than Orion, agreed to
pay the fares if he could be the secretary to the governor's
secretary.[383] Sam had saved some money from his earnings
of $250 a month as a Mississippi river pilot. It was agree-
able to everyone that he should have the position, but when

---

[381] Samuel Clemens was born November 30, 1835, in Florida, Missouri. He
was only twenty-six years old when he came to Nevada. His father died
when Sam was twelve years old. His mother apprenticed him to a printer
under whom he learned the trade. After working on papers in Keokuk and
Cincinnati, he learned to be a river pilot. He followed that trade until the
Civil War suspended river traffic. He saved $800 which he brought with him
to Nevada. He mined for a short time in Aurora, Nevada. In 1862, he became
a reporter on the *Territorial Enterprise*. In 1864, he went to California and
then to the East where he spent the remainder of his life.

[382] Orion Clemens was born in Jamestown, Tennessee, in 1825. He, too,
learned the printer's trade, but he wanted to be a lawyer. He practiced for
a short time in Keokuk but was never successful in the profession. He left
Nevada in 1864 and went to New York City where he worked on the *New
York Evening Post*.

[383] Statement of Cyril Clemens, cousin of Samuel and Orion Clemens and
president of the Mark Twain Society of America, in *Nevada State Journal*,
June 15, 1929.

he and Orion looked into the book of "instructions," they found that there was no salary for it.

On Wednesday, July 6, 1861, Governor Nye left San Francisco for Nevada and arrived in Carson City on the following Thursday evening. His welcome to the territory over which he was to preside as its first chief executive was a royal one. He was met at Clear Creek, about five miles from the city, by a cavalcade of horsemen and several carriages, all decorated with the stars and stripes. The booming of a cannon (Frémont's twelve pounder) announced his approach. Everyone rushed to the main street, along which the governor and his escort passed, to cheer him. After a short rest at the home of William M. Stewart, he delivered a brief speech to the people, for which he was again cheered enthusiastically. Governor Nye's first address to the people of Nevada won their hearts as he had won many political audiences when he said:

With the most heartfelt emotion I greet you. I come among you with a full appreciation of the important duties devolving upon me as the chief executive of the new territory. . . As we progress in the labors before us, I shall at all times expect good order and observance not only of the laws of the federal government, but of the laws which shall be enacted by your legislature, that we may realize a certain protection to our property and our persons. . . Allow me to assure you that not one star shall be permitted to be removed from the old [34]. (Vociferous applause.) Twenty-five million freemen will not permit it. And I have come here to this distant country with the hope of adding one more - a bright and glorious star - Nevada![384]

Several days later Governor Nye went to Gold Hill and Virginia City. The latter, only two years old, greeted him with "pomp and ceremony." [385] The five trustees [386] of the city, escorted by the brass band and the Virginia Union Guards, met him at the head of Gold cañon, where the Gold Hill Guards joined the procession. A military atmosphere pervaded the scene; the band played "Hail to the Chief," the guards presented arms, the trustees rose in their carriage

[384] *Daily Alta California*, July 22, 1861.

[385] *Sacramento Daily Union*, July 16, 1861.

[386] The five trustees of Virginia City were J. C. Bateman, N. W. Winston, G. H. Shaw, L. Fensier, and J. H. Scates. They were elected in March, 1861. *Daily Evening Bulletin*, March 15, 1861.

with uncovered heads, and the crowds cheered their new leader in true western style. The procession passed through the principal streets, and under a floral arch prepared by the women of the city. "The frog was almost as big as a bull."

At Union Square the governor was welcomed officially by the city trustees and responded to their greetings amidst continued cheering. The day was fittingly closed with a banquet at which many toasts were drunk to the new chief and the new territory.[387]

On July 12, the day following, Governor Nye issued his first executive proclamation in which he announced that the federal appointees to the territory of Nevada had assumed their respective offices according to the law, and that therefore the government was established. He admonished all persons to obey the laws of the United States as enumerated in the organic act. In addition to his duties as governor, Nye was made commander-in-chief of the territorial militia, and superintendent of Indian affairs.[388] The wheels of government had begun to move again; the territory of Nevada was launched.

Now the most urgent need was the establishment of a judiciary. On July 17 the governor issued his second proclamation, establishing a supreme court, district and probate courts, and justices of the peace. The three members of the supreme court had original and appellate jurisdiction collectively; each was assigned to one of the three district courts individually. The governor appointed the judges to the lower courts until an election could be held.[389]

The third gubernatorial proclamation was issued on July 24, providing for taking a census of the territory, the election of a delegate to congress, for the arrangement of districts, and for the selection of members of the territorial legislature. Dr. Henry DeGroot, formerly of California but then a resident of Carson City, was appointed to take the census, for which congress had appropriated $2500. Since the surveyor-general had not yet arrived to take up

---

[387] Eliot Lord, *Comstock Mining and Miners*, 110.

[388] *Laws of Nevada Territory*, 1861, 17.

[389] A. J. Marsh, *Official Reports of Nevada Constitutional Convention*, VIII; Angel, *op. cit.*, 77-78. See DeGroot's map of Nevada territory, 225.

his duties, Dr. DeGroot was appointed to arrange the electoral districts also.

Although United States Marshal J. T. Waters of the territory of Utah had taken an invoice of the business firms in Carson county, and a census of the inhabitants in 1860, another one was made in the following year. A brief comparison of the two censuses is interesting. In 1860 the total white and colored population of Carson county was 6,857 not including Indians; in 1861 the number had grown to 16,374 exclusive of Indians and transients (teamsters, travelers and emigrants). In 1860 Carson City had 701 people; in 1861, 1,466; in 1860 Virginia City had 2,437; in 1861, 12,704; while in 1860 Washoe Valley had 270, and in 1861, 1,005. It is of interest to note that there were only 190 people in the Truckee Meadows in 1861, whereas now there are over one hundred times as many. There were many settlements having several hundred people where at the present time there are none. At Fort Churchill 203 people inclusive of the officers, their families, and the soldiers, lived; [390] today the fort is in ruins. It was impossible to get an accurate census during the first few years. Hundreds were coming every day but there were also many who were leaving. By October of 1861 it was estimated that there were 20,000 people, or twenty per cent more than Dr. DeGroot counted in July.[391]

The election for the territorial legislature was held on August 31. Pursuant to the instructions in section IV of the organic act, the council (upper house) was to consist of not less than nine nor more than thirteen members, elected for four years; and the house of representatives of not less than thirteen nor more than twenty-six, elected for one year. The governor fixed the minimum of councilmen at nine, and of representatives at fifteen.[392] Several interesting facts came to light in consequence of this election — first, it revealed the number of Unionists and pro-slavery voters to be 4,306 and 985 respectively; second, it brought out a most important issue, the location of the capital of the territory.

[390] Marsh, *op. cit.*, VII; Angel, *op. cit.*, 78; *Daily Evening Bulletin*, August 26, 28, 1861.

[391] *Daily Evening Bulletin*, October 3, 1861.

[392] Marsh, *op. cit.*, VI.

The most hotly contested election was that for the delegate to congress. Judge John Cradlebaugh was opposed by
C. E. Olney. The former received 1,540 votes and the latter
1,138. According to an account in a San Francisco paper,

> There was a great deal of illegal voting. At Carson City, the law which
> allowed only those who were residents of the territory at the time of the
> passage of the organic act, was entirely disregarded, and all were per-
> mitted to vote. At Fort Churchill the soldiers, about whose suffrage much
> doubt is entertained, voted to a man. In another precinct - Esmeralda, the
> location of which is doubtful - quite a large vote was polled. The citizens
> there opened polls, voted on Wednesday last in California. The people of
> Honey Lake, whose location is also considered doubtful, voted at our terri-
> torial election. So we may safely predict that under any circumstance, the
> election for delegate to congress will be contested.[393]

In several places the election was exciting. At the Antelope
Ranch the ballot box was destroyed and all of the ballots
were lost; at Buckland's Station, there were fights between
the soldiers and thirteen citizens, fists and sundry missiles
being used. George Stead, a citizen, had a fractured head,
and was taken to Fort Churchill for treatment, where he
died in a short time.[394]

The election over, the governor issued another proclamation on October 1, 1861, in which he directed the recently
elected legislators to meet in Carson City.[395] What pressure
was brought to bear upon Governor Nye to call the legislature together in Carson City, thereby giving it the advantage over the other cities as state capital, may never be
known. The location of the seat of the government was the
most important issue discussed before the convening of
the legislature. Just how the decision was brought about
was veiled in secrecy. These facts are known: there was
strategy, diplomacy, and bargaining for its present location,
the results of which accounted for some of the peculiar size
and shape of some of Nevada's counties. So far as can be
ascertained from extensive research, the plan to have Carson
City the capital started two years before the organic act
was passed. Abraham V. Z. Curry, founder of the later

[393] *Daily Evening Bulletin,* September 11, 1861.
[394] *Carson City Silver Age,* August 6, 1861.
[395] *Laws of Nevada Territory,* 1861, 268; *Cong. Globe,* 37 Cong., 2 sess.,
2291.

capital, and Major William M. Ormsby were the most enthusiastic supporters of the proposal. As early as August 19, 1859, a news item appeared in the *San Francisco Evening Bulletin* stating that Major Ormsby was erecting a two story brick or adobe house, which would be completed in about six weeks. The lower story was to be used for a hotel and the upper rooms for the senate and assembly of the territorial legislature.[396] The county seat of Carson county was changed from Genoa to Carson City on January 18, 1861. In "section XII" of the organic act it was stipulated that the legislative assembly was to hold its first session when and where the governor required. Carson City must have had some advance agents to meet Governor Nye at the boat in San Francisco, since he announced when he left that city that he was going to make Carson City his headquarters.[397] However, this announcement did not prevent a vast amount of log-rolling for the capital, in which Carson City, Silver City, and Virginia City were the chief contenders.

Just before the legislature was to convene it was also announced that it would meet at Curry's Hot Springs Hotel, the upper floor of which was divided into four compartments by canvas partitions. The eastern end of the building was assigned to the territorial council, the western end to the assembly, while the central part was divided into two small rooms for the use of committees and for the sergeant at arms. Not only did Curry give the upper story of his hotel rent free to the territorial legislature, but he offered to transport the legislators to and from Carson City, a distance of two miles. His seeming generosity was turned into cash a few years later when the state of Nevada paid $75,000 for his hotel for a state prison.

The governor considered it very important that the territorial government should start well. In consequence, he went to Sacramento to get the benefit of the California state library in drafting his first message to the Nevada legislature.[398] The chief interest of California was similar to that

[396] This hotel was known as the Ormsby House.

[397] *Daily Alta California*, July 8, 1861.

[398] *Letter Book, Territorial Records*, August 21, 1861. The letter stating this fact was written by Secretary of the Territory Orion Clemens, to Elisha Whittlesey, first comptroller of the treasury, Washington, D. C.

of Nevada – mining – a subject upon which California had been legislating for some time. Her laws had not only been tested and found practicable, but they had received a number of adjudications by the supreme court of California. In addition, the code of California had been modeled after that of New York, from which state many of the Nevada legislators had come. Thus the laws of the territory, if assimilated with those of California, would have the benefit of New York judicial interpretations as well as of those of California. The governor also desired to confer with the officers-elect of California on the questions of boundary, which were at that time a very disturbing matter to California and Nevada settlers.

At noon, on October 1, 1861, the secretary of the territory, Orion Clemens, called the legislative assembly together. The two houses proceeded to organize. J. L. Van Bokelen of Virginia City was honored with the presidency of the council,[399] Miles Mitchell, also of Virginia City, was selected as the speaker of the house.[400] After the organization was perfected, addresses by the president and speaker of their respective houses were given.

On the following day Governor Nye read his first message before a joint session of the two houses. In it he glorified the Union and referred to the affection the "home government had for her children everywhere." He discussed the present condition of affairs in the East, and recommended that the legislature express immediately the loyalty of Nevada to the Union, enlarging on the advantages of the constitution of the United States. He recommended the enactment of laws calculated to develop the mineral resources of the country, and whenever applicable the adoption of the California code. He thought that the Utah statutes should be entirely superceded, suggested the taxing of the gross proceeds of the mines; he referred to the duty of the legislature to district the territory into three judicial districts, and assign the justices appointed by the president to each of the districts; he urged the early establishment of a common school system, recommended the division of the territory into coun-

[399] *Nevada Council Journal*, 1861, 1.
[400] *Idem.*

ties, and admonished the legislators to fix a capital for the
territory. He suggested the passage of a law making it a
penal offense to carry concealed or deadly weapons, of a
law regulating the sale of intoxicating liquors, of a Sunday
law, of stringent enactments to prevent gambling, and of a
law giving a lien for labor done; and he urged especially
that Nevada territory raise and herself collect her share
of the national war tax amounting to $4,591.

This first legislature found the people with few laws suited
to their needs, and most of them passed by a distant hier-
archy. It was necessary, therefore, for them to organize almost every department of the government, to provide for
the wants of a considerable population, and to draft new bills
for these purposes. The first act of importance was the adoption of resolutions declaring the fealty of the territory to the
Union.[401] It had been said there were many secessionists in
Nevada. These resolutions were an official pledge from the
loyal men, who were in the majority, that they would maintain the supremacy of the federal constitution. Every vestige
of Carson county was eliminated, and its records were ordered delivered to the secretary of the territory for safe
keeping.[402]

The common law of England, in so far as it could be applied to Nevada, was adopted;[403] a territorial seal designed
by Secretary Clemens was adopted; a formula for the enacting clause of all laws was established; acts were passed regulating proceedings in civil and criminal cases, and limiting the
time within which actions must be brought; crimes were defined and punishments were prescribed; it was provided that
mulattoes and persons having a certain amount of colored
blood should not be permitted to appear as witnesses in
cases where white men were parties;[404] marriage between a
white person and an Indian, a negro, or a Chinese was made
a crime.[405]

[401] *Sen. Ex. Doc.* no. 36, 37 Cong., 2 sess., v, 2 (ser. no. 1122).

[402] *Nevada Council Journal,* 1861, pp. 14-25. All of these records are in the
office of the secretary of Nevada in Carson City. The writer has gone over
all of them. They are in a very fine state of preservation.

[403] *Laws of Nevada Territory,* 1861, 1.

[404] Angel, *op. cit.,* 76-79.

[405] Bancroft, *History of Nevada, Colorado, and Wyoming,* 160.

It is interesting to note the laws passed concerning divorce: the grounds were habitual drunkenness, extreme cruelty, and desertion. California newspapers commended Nevada for passing more stringent laws concerning divorce than those "that have outraged Christian sentiment and disgraced the statutes of California." [406] How times and laws have changed!

The blue laws of this first Nevada law-making body deserve mention. The Sunday law prohibited any "person from keeping open any play house or theater, race ground, cock-pit, or play at any game of chance or gain, or engaging in any noisy amusement on the first day of the week, commonly called the Lord's Day." [407] There were acts relating to the support of the poor, and to the protection of the telegraphs and to the acquisition of a prison and an asylum.[408]

All the acts passed under the laws of Utah territory prior to the organization of Nevada territory were legalized. When they came up for consideration the house went into the committee of the whole. The section of one of these acts, to which there was the most objection, was the provision to legalize the official acts of Stephen A. Kinsey and Edward C. Morse, who had acted as recorders of Carson county during 1860 and 1861. The bill provided for the validity of the decrees of the Mormon probate court, by which some of the best land in the territory had been given away to various individuals. Besides, Kinsey was declared by some not to be the legal recorder, because his books had been taken out of the territory while he was professing to act. William J. Osborn, a member of the assembly from the Steamboat Creek and Truckee Valley district, said that he was the man who had taken the records to Salt Lake City; and that since at that time Carson county was a part of Utah territory they had never been out of the territory. He said he had acted in accordance with the wishes of a majority of the people of Carson county, who were alarmed at the mob law which then reigned there. He delivered the books to Governor Cumming of Utah territory, and took his receipt for them. The books, he asserted, were afterwards un-

[406] *Daily Evening Bulletin,* October 11, 1861.
[407] Bancroft, *op. cit.,* 162.
[408] *Laws of Nevada Territory,* 1861, 269.

touched. J. H. Sturtevant of Washoe Valley denied that the books had been taken away in accordance with the wishes of the people, but declared they were spirited away by Kinsey and the Mormons. Sturtevant said the locations of most of the valuable stock ranches in the territory were recorded in Kinsey's books, and he hoped nothing would be done to invalidate those records.[409]

Another bill, ostensibly intended to provide for the formation of incorporated companies, but really designed to break up all the companies incorporated in California engaged in mining in the Washoe district, was defeated after it had passed the house, and after, if the report be true, half the council had declared in favor of it. This bill attempted to recognize only mining companies whose books, papers, evidences, and ownership were kept within the precincts of the territory; and whose directors, majority of trustees, and managing officers should be positively residents of the territory. California mine owners protested vigorously. In fact, there was great consternation among them. The papers of that state published many editorials against the bill. It was claimed by them that California capital had developed the Washoe mines. They stated that such a law was without a parallel in American legislation, and was contrary to the customs of the country, and the liberal principles of the commercial and financial relations prevailing among the other states and territories of the Union.[410] It was claimed that when it passed the house, many of the members did not understand the bill. They had supposed that it differed in no important point from the law of California, and that its main principles agreed with the corporation laws of all of the states.[411] The defeat of the bill called for the comment that California "send up a few more money bags and manage them as you like." [412]

[409] *Daily Alta California,* November 29, 1861; *Sacramento Daily Union,* November 21, 1861. When the Mormons left very suddenly in 1857, their lands, improvements and stock were sold, leased or abandoned. They were acquired later by settlers. The titles in many instances were not clear until the first territorial legislature legalized them.

[410] The greatest number of the mining companies had organized under the laws of California.

[411] *Daily Evening Bulletin,* December 9, 1861.

[412] *Ibid.,* December 7, 1861.

The question of the location of the capital stirred the legislators to a very high pitch of excitement. It will be remembered that it was an issue when the election was being held. Let the master politician of the legislature, William M. Stewart, tell the way it came about:

Knowing that I had been elected for the purpose of locating the capital at Carson, I remained at home during the time the members of the legislature were coming in from different parts of the territory. I inquired how he wanted his county bounded and where he wanted the county seat. . . Each one told me and I framed a bill dividing the territory into counties and making Carson the capital. Virginia City lacked a few votes of half the legislature. . . The four counties of Ormsby, Storey, Lyon, and Douglas are so near together that a horse and buggy can be driven to each of the four county seats in half a day. . .[413]

Curry, who loaned his hotel to the territorial legislature, and Councilman William Morris Stewart were very good friends. The political perspicacity of the latter and the business acumem of the former undoubtedly had a good deal to do with the location of the capital in Carson City. The world may never know how it all came about, but this friendship took the shape of a memorial a short time after the legislature decided the capital question. From the stone quarry at Curry's place, a stepping stone was cut and placed in front of Stewart's residence in Virginia City. On one side of the stone there was carved "A. Curry to W. M. Stewart;" on the other side, "May our friendship be as lasting as this stone." [414]

Stewart in later years expressed regret for the part he took in creating so many small counties, but he felt he was justified at the time. Carson City, he believed, was a better place for the capital since it had fertile soil, sufficient clear level ground, plenty of wood for fuel, good water, and good building stone. It was in every way a better place than a mining town.[415]

---

[413] Charles R. Brown, *Reminiscences of Wm. M. Stewart,* 141. The county seats of these counties were Carson City, Virginia City, Dayton, and Genoa respectively.

[414] This stone was acquired by the Nevada Historical Society. It was brought to Reno and now stands at the right of the steps to the Washoe county building in Reno.

[415] *Daily Alta California,* October 24, 1861.

The capital question cropped up intermittently during the entire session until it was definitely settled by the vote of 15 to 9 in favor of Carson City over Virginia City. It was settled in another way also in the form of a fight in the barroom of the Ormsby House (headquarters for most of the legislators), between J. L. Van Bokelen, councilman from Virginia City and John D. Winters, representative from Carson City. A large crowd was in the room awaiting the arrival of the California stage when President Van Bokelen was giving utterance to indignation in regard to the action of the council on the corporation bill and the location of the capital. He declared that the Carson representatives had sold themselves or sold their county, and the sale was at a very cheap rate. When Winters overheard the remark, he demanded a retraction, which Van Bokelen granted. He said he referred to the action of the council and not to him personally. Winters, satisfied apparently with the explanation, turned away, whereupon Van Bokelen repeated his remark. Winters again demanded retraction; at the same time he stripped off his overcoat. Van Bokelen reiterated that he had not referred to Winters, but, he declared, he would fight him anyway, if he desired it. The council president told him to go and get his pistols. Other hot words followed, when the bystanders began to interfere. In the melée, Winters was pushed into a corner where there was a pile of firewood. He suddenly seized a large stick of it, swung it around his head and swore he would strike the best friend he had, if he stood in the way. He approached Van Bokelen, who was then leaning against the counter, and struck him such a blow that he fell to the ground. Other legislators seized Winters and dragged him away, but not until he had given the prostrate Van Bokelen several kicks with his heavy boots. The wounded man was carried to his room, where two doctors worked over him for some time to restore animation. Although he was badly bruised and swollen, in a few days he was able to be about.[416] Such was the manner in which frontier honor was defended.

To provide for revenue for the maintenance of the territorial government and for county purposes, an *ad valorem*

[416] *Daily Alta California,* October 24, 1861.

tax of forty cents and sixty cents respectively, per one hundred dollars of taxable property, was levied. All assessments were subject to the final decision of a board of equalization.[417] Upon all males between the ages of twenty-one and fifty years was imposed a poll tax of two dollars, to be paid by the first Monday in August. If tardily paid, the tax was three dollars.[418]

The territorial legislature provided for a common school system to be established under the direction of a state superintendent of schools assisted by the territorial auditor and the territorial treasurer.[419] The county superintendent, however, was in direct charge of schools. The maintenance of the schools was provided for by the sale of public lands (the usual sixteenth and thirty-sixth sections of each township) by ten per cent of the county taxes, and by seventy-five cents of the extra dollar collected on the delinquent poll tax.[420]

Other sources of revenue for the territory were licenses. Theatres paid five dollars a day, pawnbrokers one hundred dollars a quarter, "intelligence" offices fifteen dollars a quarter, circuses twenty dollars a day, bowling alleys twenty dollars a quarter, and agents one hundred dollars a quarter.[421]

The character of the population of the first rush of people to the territory necessitated the establishment of a state prison at once. The board of prison commissioners – Governor Nye, Secretary of State Clemens, and Supreme Judge North – contracted with Abraham Curry for $500 a month to keep all territorial prisoners during the year 1862 in a stone building, to construct substantial cells so as to prevent escapes, to feed and to clothe them. Mr. Curry was to perform all of the duties of a warden. From those who were sentenced to labor, he was to exact a reasonable amount of work. The prison board was instructed to purchase or to build a prison costing not to exceed $10,000. Federal prisoners were kept in the county jails upon the payment by the

---

[417] *Laws of Nevada Territory*, 1861, 152-154.
[418] *Ibid.*, 165.
[419] *Ibid.*, 273-275.
[420] *Laws of Nevada Territory*, 1861, 131-162.
[421] *Ibid.*, 152-154.

national government of five dollars a month to the county, which was in no case to be liable for an escape.[422]

The social conditions of the new community demanded that crimes and their punishments be carefully enumerated and defined [423] in order to keep down the lawlessness bred in the brothels, saloons, and hasty quarrels over the ownership of mining claims. The jurisdictions of the various courts, both probate and justice, were described in detail.[424]

In spite of the fact that Mark Twain said that "the legislature passed private toll-road franchises all the time . . .," and that "it was estimated that every citizen owned about three franchises . . . so many in fact that ends of them were hanging over the boundary line everywhere like a fringe," [425] only six road franchises were granted during the entire session.[426]

Secretary Clemens designed the territorial seal. The chief industry of the territory could easily be determined from it. In the background of the circle there were depicted mountains out of which a stream of water flowed and fell on the overshot wheel of a quartz mill at their base. On the left side of the circle, a five stamp mill was in operation. The central figure in the foreground was a miner with his pick in one hand, and the American flag in the other. On the scroll at the bottom of the circle were the words, *"Volens et potens."* [427] The engraving for the first seal to stamp the laws of the first territorial legislature was done on hard wood at a cost of $30.

On November 25, the territorial legislature divided the territory into nine counties; four days later it fixed the county seat of each one. Five of these nine counties bordered California on the west, and the boundary lines of the border counties were uncertain until a joint California and Nevada

[422] *Territorial Records,* Report of Prison Commissioners, 1862.

[423] Governor Nye did not approve of the civil and criminal code. He expressed his disapproval but it was too near the end of the session for correction. *Laws of Nevada Territory,* 1861, 56-60.

[424] *Ibid.,* 234-236; *Cong. Globe,* 37 Cong., 2 sess., 1022.

[425] Angel, *op. cit.,* 80.

[426] *Nevada Council Journal,* 1861, 46; *Nevada House Journal,* 1861, 43; *Laws of Nevada Territory,* 1861, 295.

[427] *Laws of Nevada Territory,* 1861, 51-52.

survey was made. Three of the counties on the east, Humboldt, Churchill, and Esmeralda, extending from the Oregon
state line to the northern boundary of New Mexico, included
about four-fifths of the total area of the state. The remaining six, Lake, Storey, Ormsby, Douglas, Lyon, and Washoe
counties, contained the greatest population. In organizing
them the government township plan was used.[428]

The most northern county on the west was Lake. It extended from the Oregon line to the southern end of Pyramid
Lake. Because of the dispute between the territory of Nevada
and California its western boundary was undetermined.
Susanville was intended to be the county seat, but the matter
was left unsettled, pending the boundary settlement of the
two states. On December 5, 1862, it was quite definitely
known that Susanville was in California. The area left of
Lake county was then renamed Roop county. It was attached
to Washoe county for judicial and revenue purposes.[429]
Washoe county, south of Roop county, extended from the
mouth of the Truckee river to the big bend (Wadsworth),
west along that river to the Washoe mountains which border
the Truckee Meadows on the east, south along these mountains to the low ridge (Lakeview Hill) which separates
Washoe Valley from Eagle Valley, and thence to the California line. From the earliest days of the Mormon settlers,
agriculture had thrived in the valleys in this county. Stone
and Gates Crossing on the lower meadows (now Glendale),
and Fuller's Crossing [430] (later Lake's Crossing of the
Truckee, and now the site of Reno), were the first and most
important places on the Truckee river during the territorial
period. Farms had been taken up in Steamboat Valley, Pleasant Valley, and Washoe Valley by the Mormons. Because
the latter valley was nearest to the mines in the vicinity of
Virginia City, it was the first to benefit from the rush of
people to them. The farms flourished from the sale of their
produce. From the luxurious growth of timber on the mountains bordering the valley on the west there were cut thou-

[428] Bancroft, *History of Nevada, Wyoming, and Colorado,* 262.
[429] *Ibid.,* 256.
[430] Emigrant parties had been fording the Truckee river at this point for
a number of years before Mr. Fuller built his bridge.

WASHOE CITY, ABOUT 1865

sands of feet of lumber for building and for mine timbers. The several small streams flowing from the Sierra Nevada mountains to the Washoe Lake were utilized for the first quartz mills. A considerable town which grew up at the northern end of the valley, Washoe City, was designated the county seat.[431] Ophir and Franktown were two other good sized communities in this valley during the territorial period.

Located between Washoe county on the north and Douglas county on the south, Ormsby county, the smallest in the entire state, was only one sixtieth the size of Esmeralda county.[432] It was named for Major William M. Ormsby, one of the founders of Carson City, who in 1860 was killed in a battle between the whites and the Indians on the lower Truckee river. This county embraced all of Eagle Valley. Although the smallest in area, the leading town, Carson City, received the state capital [433] and the county seat.

South of Ormsby county and north of Esmeralda county another small county, Douglas, was created. Besides containing the very rich Carson Valley, it had the oldest settlement in the territory, Genoa, which was made the county seat. Located on the overland road to California, it had benefited from the stage lines that plied between California and Nevada. This county, too, was rich in vast timber lands. Saw mills sprang into existence along the southeastern shore of Lake Tahoe, the most important settlement of which was Glenbrook.

Esmeralda, meaning "emerald," was the largest county created by the territorial legislature. The county seat was fixed at Aurora,[434] the only town of any size in this extensive area. It was on the extreme western side of the county. Of the 600,000 acres in this county, over one-half were highly mineralized.[435]

---

[431] The county seat was moved to Reno by a vote of the people in 1870 and by an act of the state legislature in 1871. Bancroft, *op. cit.*, 255.

[432] In 1861, Ormsby contained 10,000 acres, Esmeralda 600,000 acres. Ormsby remains the same size. Esmeralda has been considerably reduced in size.

[433] When the town was laid out a large plaza was reserved in the center of the city. This plaza was given to the state for the capitol.

[434] The location was in doubt until the California-Nevada survey located it definitely in Nevada.

[435] Mineral and Nye counties have been created out of Esmeralda county.

The eastern tier of counties, Humboldt, Churchill, Storey, Lyon, and Lander [436] comprised the divisions of the rest of the territory. Humboldt county, named for the river that coursed through it, was second only to Esmeralda in size. This political subdivision came into existence in the summer of 1861 through a mining rush to a silver strike in Star cañon, a few miles east of what is now Rye Patch. Owing to the fact that many of the first settlers in this section were Confederates, the settlement was called Dixie, but as the Union men became more prominent, it was changed to Unionville, and made the county seat. In addition to the mining community, there were a number of mail stations along the Humboldt river for the convenience of the emigrants and the overland stage.[437]

Churchill county, named after Fort Churchill, was created a county with Buckland,[438] a ranching community on the Carson river, the county seat. Before it was fully organized, a large portion of the eastern part of it was cut off and included in Lander county; so Churchill county was attached to Lyon county for judicial purposes. Although there were some farms along the Carson river in Churchill, the most of the county was desert, marsh land, and alkaline lakes.[439]

Lyon county, lying south of Churchill and east of Ormsby and Storey counties, was named for an army officer. The most important town, Dayton,[440] located on the Carson river at the foot of Gold cañon, was made the county seat. Silver City and Como were important towns during the early mining days.

Storey county, named for Edward Faris Storey, who also was killed in the attack on the Paiutes in 1860, was one of the small counties created as a result of the trade for the location of the capital in Carson City. Virginia City, the

[436] Lander was a very large county. Several other counties were made out of it. It was called the mother of counties.

[437] Among the settlements on this route of travel were French's Ford (now Winnemucca) and Stone House.

[438] La Plata was the first county seat after Churchill county was organized. It was moved to Stillwater in 1866. Fallon is now the county seat.

[439] These marsh and alkaline lands have been reclaimed by the irrigation from the Carson and Truckee rivers.

[440] In 1861 Chinatown was named for John Day who surveyed the townsite.

largest city in the territory, was made the county seat. Other towns of importance in this county during the silver rush were Gold Hill and American City.[441] Because this county was the most important one during Nevada's age of silver, a more detailed story of its history is given in a later chapter.[442]

The county governments were organized temporarily by the territorial legislature, and when the legislature nominated the three commissioners, the governor confirmed their nominations. It was their duty to apportion their counties into election precincts, and to prepare for a general election on January 14, 1862, for the purpose of choosing the other county officers. The officers elected on the above date were to hold office until the regular election on the following September 3. This procedure gave some of the counties three sets of officers in less than a year.[443] The various county and township officers created by law, and to be elected, were boards of county commissioners, sheriffs, three qualified electors, justices of the peace to act also as coroners, surveyors, auditors, assessors, tax collectors, treasurers, superintendents of common schools, recorders, road supervisors, and constables.[444] When these officers were chosen at the regular election held on January 14, 1862, the territory of Nevada may properly be said to have been fully organized.

The first territorial legislature of Nevada was in session forty-nine legislative days, from October 1 to November 29, during which time it organized every department of government. It provided for the wants of a considerable population, and it compiled a comprehensive and commendable body of laws. The members did not draft many original bills for these purposes. Nearly every act of the session, one hundred and seven in all, and many of the resolutions, were copied from the statutes of California, some of them without any alteration.[445] The expenses of this first session were

---

[441] An attempt was made to have the capital of the state located on the flat south of Gold Hill known as American Flat.

[442] Chapter xx.

[443] Angel, *History of Nevada*, 313.

[444] Angel, *History of Nevada*, 103-106, 125-129, 129-130, 147, 163, 170, 267-268, 295.

[445] *Supra*, 229-230.

estimated at \$35,000; congress had appropriated \$20,000 in depreciated currency. The salaries of the federal officers were wholly inadequate for their living expenses in a frontier community where everything had to be brought in.[446] Although the instructions to the secretary allowed expenditures for their offices, there were no funds for them. Most of them had to use their bedrooms for carrying on the territorial business. Perhaps Mark Twain was right when he said in his inimitable way that the organization of Nevada territory was a "political menagerie."

The outstanding member, perhaps, of the first territorial legislature was William Morris Stewart, councilman from Carson City. At least, he was the only member to attain any degree of prominence in later life. His influence prevailed throughout the entire session. Besides being the author of the most important bills introduced during the session, he wrote the act which adopted the common law. This bill was the most extensive one of the entire session; there were seven hundred and fourteen articles, under seventeen titles, in it. He also wrote the laws which regulated the proceedings in civil cases in the courts of justice, arranged the judicial districts, fixed the terms of the district and supreme courts, and established the county divisions and their county seats.[447]

An account in a San Francisco newspaper of the territorial legislature of Nevada, signed "X.Y.Z.," read suspiciously like Nevada's first humorist:

> The territorial legislature of Nevada has just expired in a blaze of glory. Every ferry, every sidewalk, every road, every inch of public thoroughfare has been granted to incorporated companies and tollgates erected. No legislature will be able to give away a monopoly in Washoe for the next ten years, because this one has granted to monopolists every valuable privilege in the territory. If two men sit down here to play cards, they incorporate the game. Everything is transacted by incorporation. If a man buys a horse he incorporates him and then applies to the legislature for certain privileges on the trade.[448]

[446] "Report of Governor Nye to Secretary Seward," *Sen. Ex. Doc.* no. 36, 37 Cong., 2 sess.

[447] *Nevada Council Journal,* 1861, 171; *Nevada House Journal,* 1861, 251. The laws passed by the first territorial legislature were forwarded to Washington, D. C., where they were approved by the committee on territories.

[448] *Daily Alta California,* December 1, 1861.

In such a manner did the federal government organize the territory of Nevada.[449] It was governed by these laws under the guidance of the federal government for three years.

---

[449] *House Journal,* 37 Cong., 2 sess., 38 (ser. no. 1126); *Senate Journal,* 37 Cong., 2 sess., 323 (ser. no. 1116).

# From Territory to Statehood

The territorial government and its inadequate laws were soon found unequal to the needs of a large and restless mining community. Conditions issuing from the rapid increase of population, the confusion resulting from the inability of the federal officials to handle the lawless element, and undetermined titles arising from an insufficient mining code, were responsible for the inauguration of a movement for a state government almost simultaneously with the inception of the territorial one. Nevada, similar to other newly organized governments, wanted the federal government to adopt a paternalistic attitude toward her. In Governor Nye's first report, he besought the national government to give more attention to the chaotic conditions in the territory.[450] Neither the territorial nor the local officials were capable of coping with the problems of the heterogeneous society in western Nevada; but the government at Washington was too absorbed in the war to consider the governor's appeal. So long as Nevada was loyal to the Union no attention was paid to these requests beyond the usual territorial routine.

President Lincoln commented, however, on the Nevada territory in his *First and Second Annual Messages to Congress.* He praised the administration of government in a region where the "leaven of treason" existed; he urged the congress to encourage immigrants to settle in Nevada by making known her natural resources; and he suggested that there might be an early possibility of organizing three states from the western territories – Nevada, Colorado, and Dakota.[451]

Although he alluded to the early possibility of admitting

[450] *House Journal,* 37 Cong., 2 sess., 486 (ser. no. 1126) ; *Sen. Ex. Doc.* no. 36, 37 Cong., 2 sess., 28 (ser. no. 1122).

[451] Richardson, *Messages and Papers of the Presidents,* vol. 6, 53, 129; the territory of Colorado voted against statehood.

Nevada to the Union, the immediate motive for early action toward statehood was furnished by the unsettled mining policy of the United States, and by the corruption of the territorial judiciary. Millions of dollars were ready to be spent in developing the silver industry as soon as the mine owners could be sure that their titles were valid. Ownership of the precious metals on the public domain was being actively discussed in congress, and it was imperative for the future of the mining industry that Nevada be made a state, so that her representatives could protect her chief industry by votes in congress.

The absence of a national mining code resulted in countless law suits.[452] Innumerable technical questions had to be submitted to judges who were incapable of deciding them. The meager salaries of these judges, called upon in almost every case to decide questions involving millions of dollars, made them susceptible to outside influences. The mine owners and their lawyers were helpless under a territorial form of government in which the judiciary held office on good behavior. The only correction, therefore, of these evils was statehood. Judges would then be responsible to the electorate of Nevada, and not to a far-off indifferent government. The very fact that several of the most prominent lawyers on the lode became very active in working for a state government was proof that they wanted a settled judicial condition for their clients.

The opportunity to become a state with such a sparse population was provided by the exigency of the Civil War. Countless books have been written about Abraham Lincoln and his policies. Almost all the writers of these books have ignored the political advantages which he obtained by the hasty admission of a new loyal state. Perhaps a lack of evidence precluded discussion of its significance. Nevertheless, the story of Nevada's admission was interesting – one chapter of it was written in Washington, the other one in the turbulent mining camps of western Nevada.

There the citizens, acting as all frontier communities did

452 At one time the Ophir mine was a party to thirty-seven suits; the Yellow Jacket, thirty-two; the Savage, twenty-nine; the Gould and Curry, twenty; and many of the other mines from seventeen to nine.

when the necessity arose, initiated the movement for statehood, and this but one year after the territory was organized. In 1862, at the session of the first territorial legislature, an act was passed which authorized the submission to the electorate of the question of statehood, and the choice of delegates to frame a state constitution at the general election on the first Wednesday in September, 1863. Each question was to have a separate ballot box. Every white male inhabitant twenty-one years of age was to be permitted to vote, and every man who had been a resident of the territory for six months and in the county forty days, provided he had not been convicted of a crime, was eligible to be elected a delegate to the constitutional convention. The thirty-nine delegates elected were to meet in Carson City on the first Tuesday in November to frame a constitution for the state of Nevada.[453] The result of the election was overwhelmingly affirmative. Out of 8,162 votes cast, 6,660 were in favor of statehood.[454]

Pursuant to the decision of Nevada territory to ask for statehood, a bill was introduced in the United States senate to enable Nevada, Colorado, Montana, and Nebraska to frame constitutions. Due to her small population, there were some objections raised against Nevada's becoming a state. Although the census of 1860 showed that there were only 6,857 people in Nevada (at that time, 127,381 were required for one representative in congress) the number of people in the territory had more than tripled by 1863. Was it not possible that the population might increase to the required number in a few years? At least California's senator believed that Nevada would grow. William Latham, United States senator from California, spoke in behalf of Nevada's request. By statistics he proved that the annual wealth of the young territory of Nevada was $24,000,000, and argued that this sum would increase to $36,000,000 if life and property were made more secure by a state government,[455] which of itself would induce many more settlers to come into the region. The discussion on the Nevada bill was led by Senator

[453] *Laws of Nevada Territory*, 1862, 126.

[454] Angel, *op. cit.*, 81.

[455] Bancroft, *History of Nevada, Colorado, and Wyoming*, 430.

Wade of Ohio, who outlined the contents of the bill – the proposed boundaries, the qualifications for voting, and the representation to the constitutional convention. He assured the members of congress that Nevada would frame a constitution, in which there would be a provision against slavery and a declaration for the support of the federal government. Arguments to the contrary having been overcome, the congress passed the *Enabling Act for the State of Nevada* on March 3, 1863.[456]

The constitutional convention convened on November 2, 1863. The personnel of the first convention was interesting. The delegates came from seven counties – Storey, Ormsby, Douglas, Washoe, Lyon, Humboldt, Lander, and Esmeralda.[457] More of them had been born in New York state than in any other, and all but four had come from California. There were eight lawyers, five merchants, one hotel keeper, one physician, one banker, one notary public, one coachmaker, one sign painter, and two farmers, while all the remainder came from the mining industry.[458] Their average age was about thirty-nine years – the youngest member was twenty-four and the oldest one fifty-six years of age. About one-half of the men were single; over seventy-five per cent of them had been in the territory less than three years. It was truly a young, vigorous, and courageous group of men who sat in Nevada's first constitutional convention.

The convention was in session from November 2 to December 11, 1863, during which time the delegates framed a constitution of eighteen articles. Several provisions were bitterly opposed by the secessionists and copperheads, particularly the provision denouncing the theory of state's rights and denial of the suffrage to anyone who had borne arms in defense of the Confederacy. Objections were raised, also, to the provisions which fixed the salaries of the state, judicial, and county officers.

The outstanding member of the convention was William

---

[456] *Cong. Globe,* 37 Cong., 3 sess., 166, 905; *Sen. Journal,* 37 Cong., 3 sess., 246, 293, 415 (ser. no. 1148).

[457] Roop county had been attached to Washoe county, and Churchill county to Lyon county.

[458] Angel, *op. cit.,* 81.

M. Stewart, councilman from Virginia City. It has been said, "He had as much to do in framing the state's organic law as did any other half dozen members." [459] His greatest contribution was his work as chairman of the judiciary committee in framing the judicial organization and the administration of the new state. He was responsible for the assertion in the declaration of rights that "no power exists in the people of this state or any other state of the federal Union to dissolve their connection therewith or perform an act tending to impair, subvert, or resist the supreme authority of the government of the United States." [460]

The question of taxation caused the bitterest debate of the entire session. Since it was this section which defeated the adoption of the 1863 constitution, it is given in full:

The legislature shall provide by law for a uniform and equal rate of assessment and taxation and shall prescribe such regulations as shall secure a just valuation for taxation of all property, both real and personal including mines, and mining property; excepting such only as may be exempted by law for municipal, educational, literary, scientific, religious or charitable purposes.[461]

When the convention went into the committee of the whole to discuss this section, Mr. Stewart proposed the following amendment to it: "In the state, corporations shall be taxed the same as individuals, and when so taxed no tax shall be levied upon the stock of such corporations. Unproductive mining claims shall not be subject to taxation, and productive claims shall only be taxed upon the net proceeds of the same." In proposing this amendment, Councilman Stewart pointed out that if his amendment were not adopted it would "impose a burden upon the miners which would be heavier than they could bear. It would mean a tax on the shafts, drifts, and bed-rock tunnels of the mines whether they were productive or not." In his opinion, "It would mean the death of the mining industry. A tax could not be paid before the mine was productive." Hence the greatest hardship would fall on the "poor miners" who had expended their

[459] *Second Biennial Report, Nevada Historical Society*, 1909-1910, 74.

[460] *Constitution of Nevada*, 1863, comp. by the secretary of state, 2.

[461] Section 1, reported from the "Standing Committee" on taxation, November 18, 1863.

energies in digging for the precious metal. In spite of his arguments against the measure, and his pleas for the adoption of his amendment, the vote stood six for and seventeen against it.[462] From that time on, Stewart bent every effort to defeat the constitution.

It has been alleged, however, that this taxation measure was an excuse rather than a reason. The politically ambitious citizens were more disappointed in another provision of the constitution than they were in the taxation measure. The constitution, as it was framed, contained a clause which provided that the various offices created by it should be filled at the same time the vote was taken on the instrument itself. Accordingly, those individuals who wished to be nominated and were not among the candidates became hostile to its adoption. Elections were held in the different counties for the purpose of selecting delegates to the state nominating convention to be held in Carson City on December 31. Due to the "unfairness and slate action of the assemblage," there was a split in the Union party in Storey county; eight of the delegates bolted the county convention, and held primary meetings in Virginia City to choose their own delegates. The persons so selected went to the state convention and presented their credentials, but they were not seated.

The split in the party was a serious one. Before the convention had made its nominations, a wing of the Union party led by William M. Stewart, assisted by his young law partner Alexander W. Baldwin, became violently hostile to the adoption of the newly made constitution. The secessionists in the state opposed it also, as did four of the nine newspapers. When the constitution and the one state ticket – the Unionist – were submitted to the people on January 19, 1864, they both went down to defeat. Stewart closed his law offices in Virginia City and went out into the important mining communities to talk against adoption of the constitution. He recognized that the voting power of the territory lay with the miners; it would be they to whom he would have to appeal for its defeat. Consequently he exploited the provision in the constitution which taxed the "poor miners' shafts, drifts, and

---

[462] *Proceedings of the Constitutional Convention,* November 25, 1863.

bed-rock tunnels."[463] Stewart's political astuteness was successful; aided by an aggressive press which exposed the motives of the different factions of disappointed office seekers,
he brought about the overwhelming defeat of the constitution. There were 8,851 votes cast against it, 2,157 votes
cast for it.[464]

Within twenty days after the 1863 constitution was defeated, the machinery was set in motion to give the territory
of Nevada another opportunity to become a state. There
were too many reasons why it should be admitted to keep
it in the territorial status very long. The politically ambitious
persons furnished one reason, the corrupt judiciary another;
the Civil War made the emergency, and the financial backing
of the largest mining companies on the lode provided funds
needed to hold the election. It will be remembered that the
federal government still owned the land upon which the
mines were located. The sale of these mines might be a way
to liquidate the fast-accumulating Civil War debt.

The national crisis, however, was more important than
any of the reasons which arose in the territory. There was
no doubt that the president was looking forward to the three
votes from Nevada to aid him in placing his proclamation of
emancipation in the federal constitution as the thirteenth
amendment, in which form it would be beyond repeal. In his
*Annual Message to Congress* on December 8, 1863, he urged
the congress again to provide means for fostering immigra-
tion to Nevada territory in order that it might more closely
approximate the requisite number for a congressional representative.[465]

The mine owners were particularly anxious for statehood
or a settled mining policy. By 1863, the potential wealth of

---

[463] A copy of the 1863 constitution with the proposed amendments is in
the territorial records in the office of the secretary of state in Carson City,
Nevada. A copy of the constitution submitted to the people was published in
full in all of the territorial papers at the time. *The Humboldt Register* issued
a supplement December 26, 1863, which contained a full text of the proposed
constitution.

[464] Bancroft, *History of Nevada, Colorado, and Wyoming,* 179, fn. 6; Angel,
*op. cit.,* 84-85.

[465] Richardson, *Messages and Papers of the Presidents,* vol. 6, 181; *supra,*
249.

the Comstock Lode, and of the many other mining districts in Nevada, was becoming known throughout the world. These mines were on the public domain; there was some agitation in the congress for the sale of, or the securing of, the proceeds from the lease of the mines.[466] The secretary of the interior recommended to the congress that some action be taken for obtaining a revenue from the mines. George W. Julian of Indiana ran twice for a seat in the house of representatives, and was elected both times on a platform promising to sell the mineral lands on the public domain at auction in order to pay the expenses of the Civil War. When he was seated he sought and was given the chairmanship of the committee on public lands.[467] As chairman of this committee he introduced several bills to suit his end. The Nevada mine owners were so alarmed over the discussion occasioned by this bill that they circulated a petition among the mine operators protesting against anything being done until Nevada's representatives could reach Washington.[468] All possible haste was necessary to stop the impending legislation until they could do so.

On February 9, 1864, Senator Doolittle of Wisconsin introduced a bill to enable the territory of Nevada to form a state government. By the terms of the bill, every person qualified to vote for the territorial assemblyman, including the soldiers stationed at the various forts and camps in the territory, was permitted to vote for the delegates for a convention to frame another state constitution. The congress laid down the following terms under which Nevada might draw up her constitution: "It must be republican and not repugnant to the constitution of the United States and the principles of the Declaration of Independence." The delegates elected to the convention must enact by an irrevocable provision: "First, that there shall be neither slavery nor involuntary servitude in the said state, otherwise than in the punishment of crimes, whereof the party shall have been duly convicted." Other stipulations concerned religious free-

[466] *House Ex. Doc.* no. 2, 38 Cong., 2 sess., 1220.
[467] *Cong. Globe,* 38 Cong., 2 sess., 562, 587, 595, 687; George W. Julian, *Political Recollection,* 256.
[468] *Infra,* chapter XIX.

dom and the relinquishment of all of the unappropriated lands lying within the territory.[469] Representative Ashley of Ohio sponsored Nevada's enabling act in the house of representatives; the California senators favored it in the senate.

There was opposition to the Nevada bill in both houses of the congress, and the possibility of its defeat worried President Lincoln. He discussed the question with his assistant secretary of war, Charles A. Dana,[470] who has told the inside story of how the vote was carried. Secretary Dana said that President Lincoln reasoned that to free the slaves would have a moral effect upon the states in rebellion, but added that it would have to be accomplished by a constitutional amendment. Another state must be created in order to secure the constitutional two-thirds majority. As a military necessity, the thirteenth amendment "would be equivalent to raising another army of a million men and fighting, no one knows how long." [471] The opposition to the admission of Nevada in the house was based generally upon the sparsity of population; a few members were dubious about its being admitted without the "fraudulent use of the power to admit new states by the military power of the federal government in the seceded states." [472] In the senate the Nevada bill was urged as an "effectual way of ridding the country of slavery so that it cannot be resuscitated." [473]

The opposition in both houses came chiefly from the New York and New Jersey delegations, who seized the opportunity to drive a hard bargain. Let Secretary Dana report the conversation on this situation between him and the president:

"Dana," he said, "I am very anxious about this vote. It has to be taken next week. The time is very short. It is going to be a great deal closer than

---

[469] *Cong. Globe,* 38 Cong., 1 sess., 521, 693, 787-788.

[470] Secretary Charles A. Dana was assistant secretary of war from 1863-1865. Prior to that time he was managing editor of the *New York Tribune,* the newspaper most powerful in solidifying the northern sentiment. After the war was over, he returned to his newspaper work again and became editor of the *New York Sun* for thirty years. Shortly after the war was over, he wrote his *Recollections of the Civil War.*

[471] Dana, *op. cit.,* 176.

[472] *Cong. Globe,* 38 Cong., 1 sess., 1313.

[473] Dana, *op. cit.,* 176.

I wish it was. . ." "What will they - New York and New Jersey - be
likely to want," asked Dana. "I don't know," said the president. "It makes
no difference, though, what they want. Here is the alternative: that we
carry this vote, or be compelled to raise another million, and I don't know
how many more men, and fight no one knows how long. It is a question
of three votes or new armies." "Well, sir," said Dana, "what shall I say
to these gentlemen?" "I don't know, but whatever promise you make to
them, I will perform." [474]

President Lincoln, superb politician that he was, allowed
the leader of the New York delegation to name the collector
of customs at the port of New York, a $20,000 a year po-
sition; the New Jersey opposition was overcome by the promise that they would be allowed to control the appointment of
two internal revenue collectors for their state. As federal
patronage goes, the support of the Nevada bill by these
two states was probably secured very reasonably, if we
consider that the three votes in congress gained by the admission of the state would give the president the required
two-thirds of the votes needed to pass the amendment. The
bill was passed, and the president signed it on March 21,
1864.[475]

In accordance with the act, Governor Nye issued a proclamation which fixed June 6 as the date to choose a new group
of delegates to frame another state constitution.[476]

The forty delegates elected to this second constitutional
convention were very similar to the first group. Ten men who
had sat in the first convention were returned to the second.
Again New York claimed the birthplace of the largest number; and again lawyers predominated. There were only two
farmers among them; all the delegates had come to the
Pacific coast during or after the gold rush; all but one had
come to Nevada from California; and all but one professed
to belong to the Union party. Yet less than half said they
had voted for Lincoln in 1860.[477] It took these constitution
makers but twenty-three days, from July 4 to July 27, 1864,

---

[474] Loc. cit.

[475] Cong. Globe, 38 Cong., 1 sess., 1228; Statutes at Large, 1864.

[476] A. J. Marsh, Nevada Constitutional Debates and Proceedings, XIII.

[477] Homographic charts of the members of the two constitutional conventions are given in Angel, op. cit., 81-86.

to frame the second constitution for Nevada, which was similar in many respects to the first one. However, in this draft the obnoxious provision regarding the taxation of the "miner's shafts, drifts, and bed-rock tunnels" was omitted.[478] This time there were no state officers to be voted upon at the time the constitution was submitted to the people,[479] nor was there a division in the Union party, then dominant in the territory.[480]

The fifth section of the enabling act had named the second Tuesday in October as the date for ratification. Because this date fell too late to permit Nevada to organize her election districts so as to participate in the presidential election of that year, Governor Nye sent a memorial to Washington in which he suggested an amendment setting the ratification date on the first Wednesday in September — the date of the general territorial election of county and territorial officers.[481] This was agreed to. On this date the constitution was overwhelmingly adopted. Stewart worked as hard to have this instrument adopted as he had worked to have the former one defeated. It is interesting to note that the constitution registered a majority in every district but one;[482] the greatest majorities, however, were attained in the more strictly mining centers. On August 12 the territorial Republican convention convened at Carson City, at which time John Cradlebaugh was nominated as the delegate to congress.

Nevada's second constitution brought forth a favorable comment from a California newspaper:

Considering the constitution as a whole we believe it to be better than any other in the United States. In its pledge of national allegiance, in its prohibition of special legislation, in its small number of legislators, in its

---

[478] *Constitution of Nevada,* article x.

[479] The constitution was submitted at the regular election of the territory. At this time the territorial delegate to congress had to be elected. Because Nevada was made a state before congress convened he never served.

[480] An exception should be made of Storey county. The split in the Union party over county officers in that county resulted in the defeat of the Republican nominees. Angel, *op. cit.,* 85.

[481] *Senate Journal,* 38 Cong., 1 sess., 392 (serial no. 1175) ; *Cong. Globe,* 38 Cong., 1 sess., 1673, 2119, 2139.

[482] Humboldt county rejected it by a vote of 320 to 544 votes.

brief limitation of the legislative sessions, and in its provisions relative to
jury trials, it appears to have very decided advantages.[483]

An added reason for the desire of Nevada's citizens to become a state was the stimulus of voting for President Lincoln.
Moreover, the corrupt condition of the territorial judiciary
had become so intolerable as to influence many people to
favor statehood who otherwise would have opposed it. This
latter issue was undoubtedly responsible for the heavy vote
cast on the Comstock in favor of the constitution. The mining industry had suffered immeasurably from the unsettled
legality of the titles to the mines. Because it was probably
unique in the history of the federal relations of a territory
for the legal profession in it to have removed the presidential
appointees, and to have refused to recognize any judiciary
except the judges the people had themselves elected, the
circumstances surrounding these conditions must be known
in order to appreciate the full significance of the situation.

Probably no tribunals of a new community have ever been
subjected to such temptations as were the courts of the territory during the first five years of their existence. It has been
related in a former chapter that the origin and settlement of
the territory was the direct result of the discovery of the rich
silver deposits located on the public domain in the western
part of the territory of Utah. In an area five miles in length
and one mile in width there was brought into existence within
a brief space of time, property worth millions of dollars.
This vast treasure house was, by the passive attitude of the
federal government, preëmpted and divided among the first
few hundred people who arrived on the spot after the discovery. But the title to this wealth had been no better than
that to derelict goods – possession was the best evidence,
and "quick on the draw" its surest protection. A man might
have located rightfully on the lode; yet his title rested only
in the memory or the virtue of witnesses. As may be readily
imagined every title on the Comstock was forced to submit
its legality to the territorial courts as soon as they were organized. The testimony of a witness could not be disputed very
well in a region so disorganized. For instance, to prove
ownership a witness had to testify that he had seen the loca-

[483] *Daily Alta California*, August 25, 1864.

tion monument at a certain place at such and such a time. At that early date a location corner consisted of a pile of rocks under which was placed a container holding the name of the locator of the mining claim. No survey of any kind had been made in this region.

Amid this confusion to determine the legal ownership of so many feet along the lode, there were certain unscrupulous men who found it profitable to testify for certain mining companies. They became, as it were, professional witnesses whose price was in some cases very high. Even Henry Tompkins Paige Comstock, living in Montana, whither he had gone after he had sold out for a comparative pittance, returned to testify to certain locations. He told many conflicting stories.

As for the judges, they were as incapable as the witnesses. In the first place, the salaries of the three territorial judges were fixed at the paltry sum of $1500, paid out of the federal treasury in currency worth, at times, only one-half its nominal value. Living in these isolated communities was extraordinarily high. "It is not too much to say that the entire annual salary allowed by the government to a Washoe judge would not at the place of his required residence have provided him with the bare necessities of life for a single month; and it was a matter of public notoriety that some of them lived in a style requiring an outlay of at least ten times as much as the compensation allowed them by congress." [484]

The consequence was soon to manifest itself too plainly to be mistaken. It came to be understood that certain lawyers were more successful in one court than in another; they must be employed, if possible, to win the case for the company concerned. The successful lawyers began to be known as "brokers" to the judges whom they handled at a certain price. At length it was discovered also that the decision of a case rested not entirely with the judges, but rather with the juries. They, too, had to be "professionalized." Nor did the story end with them; there were the sheriffs and the sheriff's deputies, and even the prothonotaries. That such a state of things could exist very long was obviously impossible.

To the confusion of determining the extent of land to

[484] John Franklin Swift, *Robert Greathouse*, 249.

which each mining company was entitled on the surface of the ground, there was added the perplexing question of the rights of each company to ledges beneath the surface. In the great upheaval of nature on the face of Mount Davidson, the rich ore on the surface presented the appearance of several parallel ledges. If these came together under ground and formed one, the judges had to decide which company was the rightful owner of the feet it claimed on the lode; if there were many ledges, the judges had to determine how many feet each company held legally on each. There was no law or precedent, either federal or territorial, by which the judges could be guided. There were, however, the simple rules and regulations of the miners, and the application of the common law, neither of which seemed to influence the judiciary to any great extent.

The corruption of the territorial judiciary became so flagrant in 1864 as to cause the newspapers of the district to wage a campaign against it. The uncertain and unjudicial behavior of the Nevada bench in its decision in the Chollar-Potosí case so embittered the public that they called a mass meeting, at which the judges were confronted with accusations of bribery. Simultaneously with the mass meeting, a petition asking for the resignation of the judges was circulated in Virginia City to which almost four thousand names were signed. The petition was published in a Virginia City paper in four columns. The result of the agitation against the judges was their resignation. William M. Stewart, perhaps the most prominent member of the Washoe bar at that time, was the most vigorous protestor.

On August 22, 1864, John W. North, former surveyor-general of the territory, who had been elevated to the bench because he was known to hold opinions beneficial to a certain mining company, resigned to avoid further scandal. On the same evening Chief Justice P. B. Locke and Judge G. Turner, under pressure of the Washoe bar, telegraphed their resignations to President Lincoln.[485] There is a story still told among the old residents to the effect that Stewart took Judge North by the coat collar and marched him down

[485] Bancroft, *History of Nevada, Colorado, and Wyoming*, 174.

to the telegraph office, and stood over him until he had written out his resignation to the president.[486]

On the morning after this unconventional procedure in suspending three federal judges, the entire bar of Storey county met to select, and to recommend to President Lincoln, a successor to Judge North. A number of resolutions were adopted, after which the members proceeded to ballot, each one having his name recorded as he voted. A committee consisting of William M. Stewart as chairman and Caleb Burbank and Joseph M. Noques as members was appointed to frame and to dispatch a telegram to President Lincoln to inform him of the action of the Storey county bar. The telegram read as follows:

> Virginia City, N.T., August 23, '64
> To His Excellency, Abraham Lincoln, President of the United States:
> At a meeting of the bar of Storey county, at which forty-nine attorneys were present, it was unanimously resolved to recommend R. S. Mesick, Esq. of this place, for appointment to fill the vacancy occasioned by the resignation of Judge North. And the attorneys earnestly request the appointment be made immediately and the undersigned informed by telegram.[487]

Two days after the resignation of the entire territorial judiciary, the same lawyers drew up the following resolution: "We the undersigned members of the bar of Storey county are in favor of a state government and will use all honorable means in our power to favor the same." [488] It is needless to add that the bar of Nevada vigorously supported the adoption of the constitution.

The vigorous action of the Washoe bar was not ended with these measures. As soon as it was learned in California that the territory of Nevada was without a judiciary, Supreme Judge Stephen J. Field, United States Senator John Conness, and Governor Frederick F. Low recommended John Franklin Swift, a prominent lawyer of San Francisco, for the position. President Lincoln nominated him and sent his name to the senate for ratification. The Nevada bar protested to President Lincoln, informing him that Nevada

---

[486] The story is told with dignity in Lord, *op. cit.*, 155.
[487] *Gold Hill Evening News,* August 24, 1864.
[488] *Loc. cit.*

By the President of the United States of America

A Proclamation.

Whereas the Congress of the United States passed an Act which was approved on the 21st day of March, last, entitled, "An Act to enable the people of Nevada to form a Constitution and State Government, and for the admission of such State into the Union on an equal Footing with the original States";

And Whereas, the said Constitution and State Government have been formed pursuant to the conditions prescribed by the fifth section of the Act of Congress aforesaid, and the certificate required by the said act, and also a copy of the Constitution and ordinances have been submitted to the President of the United States;

Now, therefore, be it known that I, Abraham Lincoln, President of the United States, in accordance with the duty imposed upon me by the Act of Congress aforesaid, do hereby, declare and proclaim that the said State of Nevada is admitted into the Union on an equal footing with the original States.

In witness whereof, I have hereunto set my hand, and caused the seal of the United States to be affixed.

Done at the City of Washington this Thirty first day of October, in the year of our Lord one thousand eight hundred and sixty four, and of the Independence of the United States the Eighty ninth.

Abraham Lincoln

By the President:

William H. Seward
Secretary of State.

did not want any judge who was not a resident. The president, under the circumstances, acquiesced and withdrew Swift's nomination. To Swift, a telegram was also sent informing him that he was *persona non grata* to the state. Nevada was without a judiciary from August 24 until the newly elected state officers were chosen in November.[489] Such was the character of the early society of Nevada; such was the "rugged individualism" of frontier society.

It was also provided by the fifth section of the enabling act that if the constitution were adopted the president was to proclaim Nevada a state without any further action from the congress. In order that the constitution might reach Washington and be approved in time to permit the people to participate in the national, as well as in a state election, the entire constitution was telegraphed to President Lincoln. The cost of the telegram, the longest on record up to that time, was $3,416.77.[490] The stagecoach moved too slowly when a nation's life was in the balance. President Lincoln was just as anxious for Nevada's admission as the people were to be admitted. Upon the receipt of the document in full, the president proclaimed Nevada a state on October 31, 1864.[491] There was great rejoicing in the new state when the news of the proclamation was received. This was true particularly on the Comstock where a torchlight parade, headed by the several bands in the city, was held.

Although Nevada was admitted on October 31, 1864, it was three months (February 1, 1865) before the representatives of that state were actually in Washington and participating in the national government. At that time of the year they had to go from Carson City over the mountains by stagecoach, from Sacramento to San Francisco by river boat, from San Francisco to the Isthmus by ocean steamer, across the Isthmus on mule or horseback or in some kind of crude conveyance, to New York City by another steamship, and thence to Washington by train. The national state elec-

---

[489] Lord, *op. cit.*, 151-155.

[490] Mr. Frank Bell was the telephone operator in Carson City who sent the telegram. Mr. Bell was lieutenant-governor of Nevada, 1887-1890; and acting governor September 21, 1890, to January 1, 1891. See appendix.

[491] Marsh, *op. cit.*, xv.

tion was held on November 8, 1864, at which time a full state ticket was chosen — the Republican and Democratic parties placed full tickets in the field. The result of the election was overwhelmingly Republican; only two members of the state legislature were elected by the Democrats. The Honorable Henry G. Worthington,[492] Republican, was elected to serve during the unexpired session of congress.[493]

The first Nevada state legislature convened on December 12, 1864. Besides framing a set of state laws and attending to other business of organizing a state, it chose its first United States senators. There were five candidates for the two offices. The first ballot was taken on December 15, at which time William M. Stewart was successful; for the second senator there were three candidates, none of whom had the twenty-seven votes necessary. James W. Nye and Charles DeLong were tied with twenty-three votes. Seven more ballots were taken, with but one vote changed. Just as an unbreakable deadlock seemed to have been reached the vote of the legislature was changed by some kind of bargaining which was not recorded as official business. It was said that Stewart, who seemed to have control of the majority of the votes in the legislature, sent word to Cradlebaugh that if he would yield all of the federal patronage to him, his election as the other senator would be assured. Judge Cradlebaugh replied to this offer: "Tell Stewart that I had rather be a dog and bay the moon than be such a senator." When the vote was taken the next day, Nye was chosen.[494] That Stewart [495] exerted influence for his election there can be no doubt.[496]

Senators Stewart and Nye drew lots for the two year and

---

[492] Mr. Worthington was one of the active pallbearers at President Lincoln's funeral. He was not reëlected in 1865, so he removed to the Atlantic coast. Angel, *op. cit.*, 87.

[493] *Senate Journal*, 38 Cong., 2 sess., 11 (serial no. 1208); *Statutes at Large*, 1864, 749.

[494] Angel, *op. cit.*, 87-88.

[495] Nye was reëlected for a full term in 1867; Stewart was reëlected in 1869. At the end of the second term, he retired from public life for twelve years. In 1887, he was elected to the United States senate again, where he represented Nevada until 1905. See appendix.

[496] Bancroft, *History of Nevada, Colorado, and Wyoming*, 187.

the four year terms. Stewart drew the four year term, Nye the shorter term. Soon after Stewart arrived in Washington he called on President Lincoln, who said to him:

> I am glad to see you here. We need as many loyal states as we can get, and in addition to that, the gold and silver in the region you represent has made it possible for the government to maintain sufficient credit to continue this terrible war for the Union. I have observed such manifestations of the patriotism of your people as to assure me that the government can rely on your state for such support as is in your power.[497]

On the same day that Nevada's representatives took their seats in congress the thirteenth amendment was passed. The legislature of Nevada ratified it sixteen days later.[498]

Of the admission of Nevada Charles A. Dana said: "I have sometimes heard people complain of Nevada as superfluous and petty, not big enough to be a state; but when I hear that complaint, I always hear Abraham Lincoln saying, 'It is easier to admit Nevada than to raise another million soldiers.' " [499]

Since Nevada was admitted into the Union with such a sparse population, there has been considerable criticism that the state should have the same representation in the senate as, for instance, New York, with more than one hundred times as many. To this Woodrow Wilson has replied:

> These critics are entirely wrong in assuming . . . that the newer, weaker, or more sparsely settled parts of the country have less of an economic stake in its general policy and development than the older states and those which have had a great industrial development. Their stake may not be equal in dollars and cents - that, of course - but it is probably greater in all that concerns opportunity and the chances of life. There is a sense in which the interest of the poor man in the prosperity of the country is greater than that of the rich man; he has no reserve, and his very life may depend upon it. The very life of an undeveloped community may depend upon what will cause a rich community mere temporary inconvenience or negligible distress.[500]

A nation as vast as the United States with such a diversity in its social, economic, and political aspects, could not have

---

[497] Charles Rothwell Brown, *Reminiscences of William M. Stewart,* 168.

[498] *Nevada Assembly Journal,* 1865, 25.

[499] Dana, *Recollections of the Civil War,* 174.

[500] Reprinted from Woodrow Wilson, *Constitutional Government in the United States,* 111, with the permission of the Columbia University Press.

held together had there not been equal representation of the states in the senate.

And thus Nevada, the thirty-sixth state to be admitted to the Union, aided greatly in preserving national unity in a crisis. From the standpoint of the state's preparedness the federal government may have acted too hastily in admitting Nevada; but from a national viewpoint, it was imperative to gain the votes necessary to legalize President Lincoln's emancipation proclamation. To the leading industry in Nevada, mining, the step was a great stabilizing force. It meant the adoption of a national mining code.[501]

---

[501] *Infra,* chapter XIX.

# Nevada and the Civil War

Nevada was truly "battle-born." From the creation of the territory in 1861, to the formation of the state in 1864, the nation was engaged in fighting the Civil War. During these four years of territorial status, every effort was made toward keeping Nevada loyal. By the suppression of secession sentiment, through the raising and the maintenance of troops in the territory without federal aid; through the generous contributions of money to the sanitary commission from the production of the mines, and the early assumption of statehood, Nevada had many relations with the federal government.

In 1860 secession sentiment was very strong on the Pacific coast. During the gold rush period and the following decade a large number of prominent southern politicians moved to the Pacific coast.[502] From the early days of Mexican rule in California, there had been a group of citizens who had advocated a far western republic. California at that time embraced the territory from the Pacific coast east to the Rocky mountains, and from the 42nd degree north latitude south to the northern boundary of New Mexico, or the 37th degree north latitude. Most of the territory that later became the state of Nevada was included in this region. In 1850, when California was admitted to the Union and the remaining area was divided between the territories of New Mexico and Utah, the idea of a republic was dropped.

The scheme, however, was revived with the approach of the Civil War. In 1860 the southern sympathizers in Cali-

---

[502] Among those southerners who came to California first and later to Nevada were Henry Stuart Foote, formerly governor and United States senator from Mississippi (the father of Annie Elizabeth Foote, wife of William M. Stewart), Colonel Daniel Hungerford (father-in-law of John W. Mackay), and David S. Terry, John R. McConnel, and Charles DeLong, prominent lawyers.

fornia were estimated to be thirty per cent of the total population. Since the greater part of the people who took part in the "rush to Washoe" were Californians, it is reasonable to say that at least the same percentage of southerners came to Nevada. The secessionists in California and Nevada did not want particularly to join the Richmond Confederacy, but they did hope to revive the old plan of a Pacific republic and thereby weaken the northern cause. They expected the new republic to furnish supplies for the Confederate states as well as to divert the silver and gold bullion from the California and Nevada mines to the southern states.[503] In 1861 a Sacramento judge, through open letters in the newspapers, advocated vigorously the formation of a Pacific republic to consist of California, Oregon, New Mexico, Washington, and Utah.[504] The *Carson Silver Age,* a Nevada newspaper, favored a Pacific republic.[505]

Even the military department of the Pacific was prosouthern. After General Albert Sidney Johnston, a prominent southerner, had arranged matters between the federal government and the authorities of Utah following the "Mormon War," he was placed in command of the western military department with headquarters at the Presidio in San Francisco. However, in 1861, through a letter written by James McClatchey and dispatched over the pony express to the war department, General Edwin Vose Sumner [506] was sent to San Francisco to relieve General Johnston of his command.[507] From that time on, secession was doomed on the Pacific coast. However, it was largely through the loyalty and earnestness of the Union men that public opinion was aroused against secession and the idea of a far western republic was precluded. In 1861, due to the efforts of the many patriotic citizens, and aided by a loyal press, Leland Stanford, an ardent Unionist, was elected governor of California; and, through the election of President Lincoln, the appoint-

[503] Cleland, *op. cit.,* 356.

[504] *San Francisco Herald,* January 3, 1861.

[505] Quoted in the *Nevada Democrat,* February 5, 1861.

[506] Angel, *op. cit.,* 265.

[507] General Johnston joined the Confederate forces. In 1862 he was killed in the battle of Shiloh.

ment of James W. Nye, equally as loyal to the Union, Nevada was kept loyal to the Union cause.

As a part of the compromise of 1850, California was admitted as a free state; but the same bill which created the territories of New Mexico and Utah (out of which the territory and later state of Nevada was formed), provided that "when admitted as states the said territories or any portion of the same, shall be received into the Union with or without slavery as their constitutions may prescribe at the time of admission." In other words the principle of squatters' sovereignty was to be applied to them.

If there had been a majority of southern sympathizers in western Utah at the time of the creation of the territory of Nevada, it would have been difficult to have held it for the Union. Sentiment was divided between the North and the South before Governor Nye arrived to take up his duties. In the spring of 1861, so demonstrative were the secessionists in Carson City and Virginia City that reports of their activities reached army headquarters in San Francisco. In consequence General Sumner wrote to the war department that he was trying to organize Nevada territory for the Union by sending reinforcements to Fort Churchill to put down secession sentiment. He wrote that:

. . . the leaders of this party [Secesh] claim to be acting by authority from the Montgomery government, which gives them some weight in the country. . . I would respectfully and earnestly represent the great importance of organizing the civil government in Nevada territory immediately. I believe if the governor and other officials had been there this difficulty would not have arisen. There is no law or government there at all, and the territory is a place of refuge for disorganizers and other unruly spirits.[508]

On June 6, 1861, Captain Moore and twenty dragoons were sent to Carson City to take possession of all such public arms as might be held by citizens of that place or in the vicinity. He reported there was a rumor of a secession organization in Virginia City, and that it had intended to secure by surprise all of the arms of the place. The captain found the reports had some basis – the day before he ar-

____

[508] Brigadier-general Richard H. Orton, *Records of California men in the War of the Rebellion, 1861 to 1867*, 18.

rived in the territory, the Confederate flag was raised over a building in Virginia City, the purpose of the action being to ascertain the strength of the secession feeling in the territory. He recommended that arms and munitions be forwarded to that city for the use of the Unionist citizens.

When Captain Moore arrived in Carson City, he called on United States Marshal John Blackburn to turn over to him all of the public arms in his possession. In Silver City, he obtained a stand of twenty-one. Several citizens reported to him that they knew of a number of muskets in private hands. Upon investigation he found that they had been turned over to the quartermaster of Fort Churchill. Another rumor which he hastened to run down came to the captain that the Confederate flag was to be flown again over a building in Virginia City on June 7. A thorough examination of all buildings was made. The one over which the rebel flag was to float contained no arms – the proprietor assured him it was done as a joke, and to create some excitement. The captain was not convinced that the affair was to be taken lightly. However, the secession organization was so quiet in its movements that he could not find out much about it. All of the arms he found he turned over to a company of volunteers enrolled in Virginia City. The arms were to be used by them in the defense of the Union. He formed two companies of fifty men each, and the oath of allegiance to the president and the laws of the federal government to suppress rebellion was taken by them. This was the first move toward placing Nevada territory under martial law.[509]

The rumors of secession sentiment in Nevada spread to California. In a newspaper under the title of "Civil War in Nevada territory," the following statement was made:

General Sumner has given orders for the removal of a company of United States troops from Benicia to Fort Churchill, N.T. They go over ostensibly to protect the mail route, although it is supposed that certain secession demonstration in the territory may have something to do with the movement. It was rumored yesterday afternoon that a fight had occurred at one of the towns on the eastern slope on the secession question, and that several lives had been lost. (Rumor without foundation.) It is certain, however, that a secession flag has been afloat at Virginia City for several days.[510]

[509] Orton, *op. cit.*, 19.
[510] *San Francisco Daily Evening Bulletin,* June 10, 1861.

From the time Governor Nye arrived in San Francisco, he began his work toward keeping the Pacific coast loyal to the Union. In his first address after his arrival delivered in San Francisco on July 4, 1861, and in his first message to the territorial legislature of Nevada, he made it very plain that no utterance against the Union would be tolerated, and that being neutral in the issue was not possible. The president of the territorial council, J. L. Van Bokelen, gave assurance as strong as the governor's of his own allegiance to the Union. As presiding officer of the upper house he had a great deal to do with the adoption of a set of resolutions which expressed the loyal sentiment of the first law makers of Nevada.[511]

The legislature forwarded instructions to John Cradlebaugh, territorial delegate to congress, to pledge the loyalty of Nevada to the Union cause and to express the desire of the new territory to do its part in perpetuating the Union.[512] Cradlebaugh, himself a Mexican War veteran, spoke on every opportunity given to him, to declare the indisputable loyalty of his constituents.[513]

On October 23, 1861, the transcontinental telegraph made its last connection. The privilege of sending the first telegram over the wire was given to the Nevada territorial legislature. A committee from each of the houses drafted the following telegraphic message which was sent to President Lincoln:

RESOLVED BY THE COUNCIL, THE HOUSE CONCURRING, that:
Whereas, the privilege of forwarding the first telegraphic message across the continent, has been given to the legislature of Nevada territory, therefore be it,
RESOLVED, THAT THE SAID COMMUNICATION SHALL CONSIST OF THE FOLLOWING LANGUAGE, viz:
Nevada territory, through her first legislative assembly, to the president and people of the United States—
Greeting:
Nevada for the Union, ever true and loyal! The last born of the nation

---

[511] *Nevada Council Journal*, 1861, 82-83, 102-103.

[512] *House Misc. Doc.* no. 70, 37 Cong., 2 sess., 1 (ser. no. 1141).

[513] In 1863, after the expiration of his term in congress, Judge Cradlebaugh entered the Union army, in which he was given command of a regiment. He was wounded and forced to retire, and returned to Nevada to spend his last days there. He is buried in the Genoa cemetery.

will be last to desert the flag! Our aid, to the extent of our ability, can be relied upon to crush the rebellion.

Signed, Thos. Hannah, William M. Stewart (chairman), committee from the council.

Signed, W. P. Harrington, Samuel D. Youngs, committee from the house.[514]

Soon after the war for southern independence broke out most of the regular troops stationed on the Pacific coast were called to join the Union forces in the East. This left the overland trails, the government property, and the settlers unprotected from Indian attacks. Because of this, the federal government made demands on the territory of Nevada to raise and equip soldiers for duty in the West. John Mason, acting assistant provost marshal general of California and Nevada, advised the federal authorities not to extend the draft to these states. He gave as his reason the inaccessibility of the region and the nature of the population. It would require a large force of men to pursue and to bring in deserters, and the high wages paid to the miners and the possibility of discovering a rich mine would make it very difficult to enforce the draft law.[515]

The loyal young men of Nevada territory, however, began the volunteer organization of local military units. A recruiting office was opened in Virginia City in the spring of 1862 by Lieutenant Soaper. In order to arouse enthusiasm, he obtained two drummer boys and J. H. Mathewson, later a lieutenant in the army, to carry a flag through the main streets of the city. When the triumphant march began, a southern sympathizer, springing from the crowd, destroyed one of the drums. He was in the act of destroying the other when young Mathewson knocked him down. The march continued to the city hall where an enthusiastic Union meeting was held — seventy-five volunteers enlisted.[516]

In the summer of 1862, the Third Regiment of California Volunteers, under command of Colonel P. Edward Connor, was sent to take possession of the United States forts in Nevada. "Order no. 1" issued on August 6, 1862, from Fort Churchill, military headquarters for Nevada, called upon

[514] *Nevada Council Journal*, 1861, 87.
[515] *Records of the Rebellion*, ser. 1, vol. 1, part 2, pp. 966-967.
[516] Angel, *op. cit.*, 266.

the disbursing officers to use economy and purchase only from loyal citizens, and to arrest and confine all persons who uttered any statements against the government of the United States.[517]

By 1862, the Panama and Cape Horn routes to California were closed because all Union vessels were needed to carry out effectually the southern blockade; the southern overland route through Texas, New Mexico, and Arizona to California was in the hands of the Confederacy. There was one remaining route to the Pacific coast — the Overland Trail which passed through Nevada. There had been left but one regiment of infantry and three batteries of artillery to guard what was practically the entire southwestern part of the United States. The closing of this route was threatened daily by the increase of Indian hostilities. Northern and southern deserters with government property (mules and wagons) were making their way west over this route. Some provision must be made to arrest and hold these men. The gold and silver from the California and Nevada mines were necessary to maintain the northern credit, hence the road must be policed to insure its safety for federal operations. Three different demands were made on the territory of Nevada to raise, equip, mount, subsist, and pay soldiers to police this highway, and keep Nevada in the Union. Under these calls, the territory of Nevada recruited 1,180 men for a three-year enlistment period.[518]

When the call for troops was made, Governor Nye issued a proclamation calling for volunteers, and the territorial assembly voted a bond issue of $100,000 for this purpose. To care for the bond issue, a tax of twenty cents per hundred was added. A bounty of ten dollars was given to the commanding officer of the company for each new recruit; and five dollars a month additional pay was granted to each volunteer soldier.[519]

By April, 1864, six volunteer companies of cavalry and

[517] Loc. cit. Colonel Connor was transferred later to the headquarters at Camp Douglas, Utah.

[518] Senate Report no. 154, 54 Cong., 1 sess., 70-72.

[519] Laws of Nevada Territory, 1864, 81-85. Nevada was not reimbursed for the money expended during the Civil War until 1929 when by an act of congress, $462,497 was paid to that state.

six companies of infantry were stationed at various forts in Utah and Nevada.[520] None of the companies of cavalry or infantry was ordered to the actual front in spite of the promises that were given to the contrary when the men enlisted. Many of the soldiers were keenly disappointed, but they were none the less patriotic in their duty in quelling Indian uprisings, suppressing secession activities, and policing the routes of travel for the safety of emigrants and express and mail coaches.

The Overland Route through southern Nevada was kept open for safe travel by four companies — three of cavalry and one of infantry, all stationed near the Potosí mines. A military post was established at the old Mormon fort in Las Vegas, Nevada, which was named Fort Baker.[521]

In addition to the regular troops stationed in Nevada, there were many men who served in home guard duty. Governor Nye, as commander-in-chief of the state militia, issued a proclamation calling upon the able-bodied young men to serve in this capacity. As a result of the governor's order, in practically every town in the territory, militia organizations were perfected. When the governor first assumed his office, he appointed to his executive staff an adjutant-general, five aides-de-camp with rank of lieutenant-colonel, one chief engineer, one paymaster-general, one judge-advocate-general, and one surgeon-general, with the rank of colonel. The chief duty of the adjutant was to coöperate with the county commissioners in establishing armories and ordnance store houses. Volunteer enlistment in the militia companies was open to all men between the ages of fifteen and forty-five. Each company was allowed one hundred dollars a month to be collected from an annual assessment levied in each county. The territorial auditor not only took charge of all the arms and military equipment belonging to the territory, but he was, also, the chief disbursing officer.[522] There was keen rivalry between the several larger towns in the formation of militia companies. Virginia City had the largest number with four companies — Dayton, Silver City, Carson

---

[520] Bancroft, *History of Nevada, Colorado, and Wyoming,* 182.

[521] Orton, *op. cit.,* 21.

[522] *Laws of Nevada Territory,* 1861, 196-225; 1864, 150.

City, and Aurora each had one.[523] The service of the Nevada state militia was a very valuable one in the support of the northern cause. It relieved the federal government of a large responsibility in keeping Nevada loyal.

Nevada was of assistance to the government in many other ways. The local incidents of patriotism were too numerous to mention. They were of varying nature such as handling individuals who were too demonstrative in their sympathies for the seceded states, flying a mammoth flag from a one hundred foot staff in Silver City, and the changing of the name of "Dixie," a mining community in Humboldt county, to "Unionville." [524]

Union clubs of a political nature were formed in the more populous districts. When the 1864 election approached they became very prominent in their endorsement of President Lincoln. Members of the clubs usually had charge of celebrations of the national holidays. Union leaders headed the parades, gave the oration of the day, and were favored for all of the political offices. Whenever the news of a Union victory arrived, it was celebrated by dinners, balls, the firing of salutes, and the singing of patriotic songs. The parades, usually at night, were particularly colorful. The miners with their torches furnished the light for the line of march, and election banners expressed the Union sentiment. The transparencies were especially expressive. One of them depicted a Union quartz mill crushing the copperheads. Expressions such as "those poor, despised, degraded, sneaking copperheads," were noted on other banners. Virginia City, with Frémont's twelve pounder, was always a little more military than the other towns. When the flagpole was erected near the top of Mount Davidson, the cannon was taken along to proclaim to the world that western Nevada was loyal.[525] Fitting exercises always marked the celebration of the fourth of July and Washington's birthday. Preparations were made weeks ahead of time – a huge platform was built and decorated with bunting; flags were flown from every

---

[523] *Daily Alta California*, June 21, 1861.

[524] Angel, *op. cit.*, 452.

[525] *Como Sentinel*, May 21, 1864; *Daily Alta California*, July 9, 1863, June 14, 1864; *Lyon County Sentinel*, September 17, 24, November 5, 1864.

mine and mill. The day was greeted by a cannon salute; a dress parade of troops from Fort Churchill preceded the exercises; brass bands played the national airs; and the best orator in the city read the Declaration of Independence and Washington's farewell address. The territorial militia and the regular army officers from the nearby forts gave the occasion a very military air. The crowning event of the day was the grand military ball which was always followed by an elaborate banquet — tickets for which sold as high as eight dollars.[526] There was no doubt as to the loyalty of the territory of Nevada to the Union cause.

There were secessionists in the territory, too, but they were not very loud in expressions of their sentiment after the arrival of Governor Nye and the organization of the militia. There was established in Nevada, secretly, however, a branch of the Golden Circle, a secret secessionist society which had originated in López's piratical attempt to seize Cuba. So active were the secessionists in the early part of the war that it was generally believed that an entire list of territorial officers had been appointed and their commissions delivered to them. Judge David S. Terry was supposed to have a commission appointing him governor of Nevada territory, in his pocket, signed by that "hell begotten, heaven forsaken, unmitigated traitor, Jeff Davis." [527] After the arrest of a few of the secessionists and the confiscation of their property, and after such punishment as being made to carry a sack of sand on their backs around the quadrangle at Fort Churchill, they were *sotto voce* in their expressions. So bold were they in Austin, Lander county, as to cause acting-Governor Orion Clemens to request Brigadier-general George Wright, commander of the Pacific, to station a company of troops at that place to suppress them. Governor Nye had been unwittingly responsible for this condition; he had appointed a secession judge, sheriff, and a number of notary publics in Lander county.[528]

In no other activity during the Civil War did the citizens of Nevada exhibit their patriotic spirit to the federal gov-

---

[526] *San Francisco Daily Evening Bulletin*, July 15, 1864.
[527] *San Francisco Daily Evening Bulletin*, May 13, 1861.
[528] *Daily Alta California*, September 5, 1863.

ernment more than in their lavish contributions of money for support of the government and relief of wounded soldiers. Although the small sum of $4,592.66 was levied on Nevada as her portion of the $20,000,000 direct tax on the states and territories, the first territorial legislature ordered it paid promptly so as to get a fifteen per cent deduction for doing so.[529] Of all of the volunteer services rendered to the federal government during the war, the citizens of Nevada point with the most pride to the magnificent contributions to the Sanitary Commission. The efficiency of the Nevada secretary, Almarin B. Paul, and his very enthusiastic committees in each of the counties, resulted in raising the largest per capita amount of any state or territory in the Union. Although the committee was not organized at the beginning of the war, $163,581.07 in currency was raised between 1862 and 1865.[530]

To the above amount there was added also the sum of $275,000 through the unique device of a clever citizen of Austin. During the Civil War there was no Red Cross nor other organizations to give aid and comfort to wounded and sick soldiers, but there was originated a Sanitary Fund administered by volunteer commissioners, the money for the support of which was raised by subscriptions or by any other possible means. Numerous devices were used to create an interest, and to offer opportunity for the people to contribute to this fund. Among those unique in origin and remarkable in its result was the sale of the "Sanitary Sack of Flour," the story of which has more than local interest.

On April 19, 1864, there was an election for city officials in Austin, a flourishing silver mining town on the Overland Mail Road. The candidates for mayor were Charles Holbrook, a Republican and prosperous hardware merchant, and Colonel David E. Buel, a Democrat and one of the owners of the townsite of Austin. Great interest was taken in the election; the excitement ran high, for Austin was a

---

[529] *House Misc. Doc.* no. 26, 37 Cong., 3 sess., 7 (ser. no. 1171) ; *Cong. Globe,* 37 Cong., 1 sess., app. 35; *Sen. Ex. Doc.* no. 36, 37 Cong., 2 sess., 1-5 (ser. no. 1122) ; *Nevada Council Journal,* 1861, 24, 218.

[530] This sum did not include the amounts raised in Humboldt, Nye, and Churchill counties which increased the amount to $10,000 more. Bancroft, *History of Nevada, Colorado, and Wyoming,* 182.

hotbed of secessionism. This mayoralty race resulted in the making of a number of wagers between the Republicans and Democrats as to its outcome, the most original of which was made between Reuel Colt Gridley, part owner of a grocery store and an avowed Democrat from Missouri, and Dr. H. S. Herrick, a Republican, and a collector of internal revenue in Nevada. Gridley challenged Herrick to carry a fifty pound sack of flour from Clifton, the western portion of Austin, to upper Austin, a mile distant, if Buel were elected; Herrick was to carry the same object from upper Austin to Clifton if Holbrook were elected. Subsequent and additional provisions to the wager required the loser to donate the flour to the Sanitary Fund, and, if the loser were Republican, he must march to the tune of "Dixie;" if he were a Democrat, he must march to the tune of "John Brown's Body." The Republican candidate, Mr. Holbrook, was elected.

On the following day the election bet was paid by Gridley. Dr. Herrick with the Austin brass band appeared before Gridley's place of business, where he demanded payment of the wager. Because Dr. Herrick was a federal employee, it was viewed at first as means of humiliating the southern sympathizers. But the doctor, being a popular and genial character and having no enemies, relieved the tenseness of the situation with his jocularity. Soon, Gridley appeared with the sack of flour which Dr. Herrick, in turn, decorated with a number of small American flags and red, white, and blue ribbons. By this time a large crowd had gathered to witness the unusual sight of a secessionist carrying the federal emblem. The line of march was arranged with the band in front, then the newly elected city officials on horseback, next Dr. Herrick carrying Gridley's coat and cane, and directly behind him Gridley with the sack of flour on his shoulder and his ten-year-old son by his side carrying a Union flag. Behind the loser was a man with a broom (the insignia of Democracy) draped in mourning, another marched by his side with a long pole on the end of which was a large sponge. The assembled citizenry brought up the rear; all marched through the main street with the flags flying, the

mine and the mill whistles blowing, the band playing, and
the people cheering, to the Bank Exchange Saloon, where
the ceremony of the delivering of the sack of flour to the
winner was held. The sponge was thrown up as a token of
surrender, and the broom was put away as a pledge of submission. The whole affair was concluded with appropriate
speeches by important participants.

The wager now having been fulfilled, Herrick returned
to the central part of the city, where in a public announcement, he donated the sack of flour to the Sanitary Commission. At the same time, he proposed that it be auctioned
and the proceeds go to the Sanitary Fund. In order to make
a big affair of it, a stand was erected in the front of the
newly elected mayor's place of business. Mr. Thomas B.
Wade, formerly mayor of Placerville, California, acted as
the auctioneer. Mr. Gridley was the first bidder of $200;
many other bids followed, Republicans vieing with Democrats to make the largest contributions to the fund. Everything was offered in payment — mining stock, town lots, cer-
tificates of indebtedness — but nothing was accepted but gold.
The flour was finally knocked down to M. J. Noyes, newly-
elected alderman, who returned it promptly to be reauc-
tioned. Again and again the flour was sold and returned.
When the memorable day ended, $4,549 in gold or $6,000
in currency had been collected. The Austin paper, the *Reese
River Reveille,* published a vivid account of the "Gridley-
Herrick" sack of flour.[531] Pictures were taken to be sold for
the fund; and a representation of the sack of flour was
adopted as the seal and coat of arms of the city of Austin.[532]

So great was his success that Gridley, now a thoroughly
converted Unionist, volunteered to travel with the sack of
flour from place to place, to pay his own expenses, and to
conduct the auction as Dr. Herrick had. In compliance with
a telegram sent by citizens of Virginia City, he went there
first, where Mark Twain, Gridley's old friend in Missouri,
Thomas Fitch, and others popularized the affair. On Sunday, May 15, $580 was contributed at an impromptu gath-

[531] *Reese River Reveille,* April 20, 1864.
[532] Angel, *op. cit.,* 268-269.

ering. On the following day, the real auction took place. An account of the affair was recorded in the Como paper as follows:

At eleven A.M., the Austin flour sack was placed in an open barouche, and accompanied by a line of carriages that were preceded by a band of music, started for Gold Hill from Virginia City. It was placed at auction in front of Maynard and Flood's Bank, where it sold for $5,822.50 to which add $240 paid for it by Gold Hill people in Virginia yesterday, makes a total of $6,062.50 paid by Gold Hill. Mark Twain accompanied the expedition, and Tom Fitch made a speech. The news had just arrived of the great victory by Grant. From Gold Hill the procession moved to Silver City, where an aggregate of $895 was bid. Thence to Dayton, where $1200 was added to the amount. Then returning through Gold Hill where about $1200 more was bid. In the evening the auction proceeded in Virginia, and the bidding continued until $12,025 flowed into the fund in addition to the $580 of the previous Sunday. Subsequent subscriptions resulted in the following totals:

| | |
|---|---|
| Virginia City | $13,990 |
| Gold Hill | 7,052 |
| Silver City | 2,000 |
| Dayton | 2,000 |
| Total | $25,042[533] |

The principal cities in California were visited and the sum was raised to $175,000, after which the triumphal march was continued to the east. The grand total of sales of the Sanitary Sack of Flour finally amounted to $275,000. Gridley, after having spent a year on his pilgrimage, and having ruined his health, returned to Austin, to find business very much depressed and himself hopelessly in debt. He left soon afterward and went to Stockton, California, where he died in 1871.[534] Not only did the sack of flour bring a large sum to the Sanitary Fund, but it helped to focus the attention of the nation on the generosity of the people of Nevada, which was then about to take its place as the thirty-sixth state in the Union.

[533] *Como Sentinel,* May 31, 1864; Angel, *op. cit.,* 270.

[534] For some time not a stick nor a stone marked the last resting place of Nevada's Civil War hero. However, some time after his death, through popular subscription sufficient money was raised to erect a large statue of Gridley over his grave in the Rural Cemetery in Stockton, California. The sack of flour ultimately became the possession of the Nevada Historical Society, and what is left of it can now be seen preserved in a glass case in the Washoe county building in Reno, Nevada.

Nevada also gave hearty support to the Grand Sanitary Exposition in St. Louis in the summer of 1864. Most of the communities of the nation sent needlework, silverware, books, relics, and similar contributions, but Nevada sent $70,000 in silver bullion from her own mines which the Wells Fargo Express Company carried free of charge to the exhibition.[535]

Although the citizens of Nevada gave money in a prodigal manner, the Civil War had sorely depressed business, largely by withdrawal of specie. On December 30, 1861, the banks of the nation suspended specie payment, compelling the government to do the same. Something had to be done quickly or the war could not go on. On February 25, 1862, congress passed a law, generally known as the Legal Tender Act. The resulting scarcity of money in the Nevada mining camps was particularly disastrous. In 1861 there were no banking facilities whatever in the territory. The Wells Fargo Company handled the purchase of bullion and paid the mining companies coin for it.[536] Early in May, 1861, the agent of the express company in Virginia City received instructions from the firm headquarters to purchase no more bullion for the present. Soon the universal cry went up from the miners —

Money! Property will not command coin - bullion is ignored. We must have a circulating medium. Let the several mining districts assemble, by chosen representatives, at some convenient place, and enact laws for the protection of mining claims until a law is passed authorizing the emission of coin for our own benefit. If this latter expedient is properly provided for - like the octagonal fifty-dollar coin of California [537] - those who have supplies for market will gladly receive it in exchange. . . Our people are starving, or leaving as rapidly as they have come.[538]

When specie began to disappear and greenbacks took its place there was serious objection by the miners. They did not want to be paid in currency which was worth at one time during the Civil War only twenty cents on the dollar. The Virginia City stock brokers on the other hand were in favor

[535] Bancroft, *History of Nevada, Colorado, and Wyoming,* 183.
[536] *Idem.*
[537] Fifty dollar slugs were issued by the assay office in San Francisco.
[538] *Territorial Enterprise,* May 4, 1861; *Daily Evening Bulletin,* May 11, 1861.

of an unstable currency. Inasmuch as it was profitable to them in their manipulations of the different stocks, the brokers started an educational campaign in Nevada and the Pacific coast to induce the people to accept greenbacks in payment of all debts. Their arguments that every business depression had been due to the antiquated standard of "hard metal;" and that currency would be good for Nevada as eastern and foreign investments in currency would be greater than in specie, did not convince the miners.

Anti-greenback mass meetings were held in the mining towns. Before the meetings, long parades of miners marched through the streets bearing banners which expressed antagonism to currency. On May 14, 1864, the banners carried before one of these meetings bore the following inscription:

WE WANT GOLD AND SILVER ONLY

One group of miners followed a banner that proclaimed:

WE ARE SATISFIED TO TAKE OUR PAY IN THE ORE WE PRODUCE

The teamsters declared that:

NOT A TEAM STIRS FOR OTHER THAN GOLD OR SILVER

The mechanics' banner said that:

GREENBACKS AND REDUCED WAGES WE OPPOSE [539]

Neither the federal law nor the arguments of the stock brokers could change the predisposition of the miners for gold and silver. So insistent were the miners and merchants in Virginia City in their demand for specie that they elected a majority of the members to the state legislature pledged to pass a law rejecting the national currency. On January 4, 1865, the legislature incorporated a provision in the Practice Act of 1863 which was substantially the same as the California act of the same nature. The provision stated that only gold could be paid where the contract read "payable in gold coin of the United States." Governor Nye, being opposed, vetoed the act on the ground that it was in direct conflict with the federal law.[540] A test was made of the law in the suit of Milliken versus Sloat. In a two-to-one opinion the court held against the law.[541] It stated that "all

---

[539] *Territorial Enterprise,* quoted in the *Daily Alta California,* June 1, 1864.

[540] Bancroft, *History of Nevada, Colorado, and Wyoming,* 183.

[541] Joseph Ellison, "California and the Nation," *University of California Publications in History,* Berkeley, 1927, 226, 1-2 Nevada, 481-511.

such laws stand in direct and brazen antagonism to the policy of the nation." The decision created a notable stir in financial circles in Nevada and California. In Virginia City a resolution was adopted unanimously at a banker's meeting to the effect that no credit would be extended to any person who paid his debt contracted under the Specific Contract Act.[542] On the other hand the leading merchants of the same city were disappointed with the court's decision. They issued an announcement that they would black-list anyone who paid his debts with greenbacks. The merchants and miners carried the affair so far as to suggest an increase in the number of Nevada judges for the purpose of overruling the decision. Nothing, however, beyond making these informal protests was done about the matter. As the tide of victory turned for the Union cause, the greenbacks began to be worth more, so that there was no longer any argument against the use of currency.

In discussions over the premature admission of Nevada to the Union, importance has been attached to the statement that Nevada's silver won the war. That the production of the Nevada mines helped to strengthen the northern credit, there is no doubt. President Lincoln recognized this fact when he signed the bill which authorized the building of the western railroads. He said: "The western mines will prove to be the treasury of the nation. The time will come when the United States will need the output of those mines."

The president appointed J. L. Van Bokelen provost marshal of Virginia City. It was his duty to see that the bullion from the mines was consigned to the northern mints so as to secure the bonds and to strengthen the credit of the nation. Although the Comstock mines had not produced in excess of $45,000,000 [543] by the end of the war, their potential production was many times that amount.[544] Nevada was justly proud of her services to the nation when an attack on its integrity was being made.

---

[542] *Laws, Nevada Territory*, 1865, 287.

[543] Bancroft, *History of Nevada, Colorado, and Wyoming*, 126.

[544] So important a factor in 1863 were the western mines that Emperor Louis Napoleon sent an expedition to California and Nevada to make a report on them. *Infra*, chapter XX.

During the Civil War period the Indian hostilities in
Nevada increased. To suppress the atrocities of the red
men, the federal government had to build a number of forts
and maintain a number of soldiers in Nevada.[545]

---

[545] *Infra*, chapter XIII.

# Federal Relations with the Nevada Indians, 1850-1860

The anthropologist and the ethnologist have made an extended study of the cultural past of the first inhabitants of the Great Basin, but the interest in the red man seems to have stopped at that point. The history of how these Indians became wards of the federal government and of its development of a settled policy in handling their problems which arose after this area became a part of the national domain, has not so far been written. It is, therefore, useful to trace the federal relations with the Nevada Indian from 1850 to 1860, the latter being the date when a more definite and settled policy was adopted.

There have been conflicting opinions concerning the attitude of the national government toward the western Indian. There were critics who condemned the policy entirely, characterizing it as full of promises, blunders, and crimes. Then there were those individuals who professed to have a more or less intimate knowledge of affairs at Washington; they thought that the government was apathetic and negligent in all western problems, Indians included. However, in the light of the following events, it will be seen that neither of the above criticisms was entirely correct. A combination of both is nearer the truth. The federal government seemed bewildered; it could not keep sufficiently in touch with the rapid occurrence of events to have a settled policy.

Previous to the acquisition of the Mexican cession, the United States government had adopted the policy of making treaties with the red man; he was settled on extensive areas outside of the asserted boundaries of the United States. But this region, designated Indian territory, was constantly invaded by white settlers. When the Indian resented the trespass on his domains and killed the white man, burned

his homes, and drove off his stock, the federal government
sent troops; the red man was pushed farther westward.
Several thousands of white men and their families moved
into the Indian's realms before the gold seekers broke
through the frontier and rushed through his hunting grounds
to California. The rapid migration of people completely
disarranged the national Indian policy of having an Indian
territory set entirely apart from the United States.

By the middle of the nineteenth century the federal government had broken or disregarded most of the treaties
with the Indians, even creating territories and admitting
states out of the Indian territory. A new Indian policy, therefore, had to be adopted. Although the Indian question was
only one of hundreds perplexing congress at this period the
members seemed not to realize its immensity nor seriousness.

A general policy, applicable to all Indians in a large area,
was attempted. But a policy which might be right for the
Indians in one part of the country was not right for those
in another. A policy for Oregon or California could not
be applied to Nevada or Utah. Nevada, like other frontier
states, had her peculiar Indian problems. They were, however, ever so much more troublesome and very much more
acute than in most states, both for the federal and state
authorities, because of the very rapid influx of people to
the territory, and because of the sterility of the soil. The
land did not provide sufficient food for the red man – how
could it support an additional white population? Driven by
starvation, and often provoked or urged by low, white men,
the Indians stole and robbed the emigrants and frontier
settlements in Nevada.

In order to understand more fully the federal relations
with the Nevada Indian, a brief review of the national administration of Indian affairs must be made. On July 9, 1832,
the congress passed an act which provided for the appointment of a commissioner of Indian affairs under control of
the secretary of war.[546] Two years later another act created
a department of Indian affairs for all Indian territory not
within the bounds of any state or territory west of the Mississippi; the superintendent of the new department was

---

[546] *United States Statutes at Large,* IV, 1832, 564.

stationed at St. Louis,[547] but the administration was still under the war department. In 1849, the congress transferred the administration of Indian affairs to the department of the interior. A commissioner was appointed to direct the work from Washington. The areas in which there were many Indians were divided into districts, and a superintendent was placed over each. He generally lived in the largest city in his district. Each district was further divided into sections, over which an agent was placed. Such an agent generally had supervision of the affairs of several tribes. He was assisted by many sub-agents, who actually came in contact with questions concerning Indians' welfare. The war department continued, however, to coöperate very closely with the interior department in helping to control hostile tribes. In Nevada, the two departments worked very closely together to administer the Indians during the formative period, when a number of forts and camps were built at strategic points.[548] A large number of troops were stationed in the state, their chief duty being to accompany the emigrant trains and protect the stage and mail coaches, as well as to give the Indians rations during the severest part of the winter.

The Indian question in the Great Basin was complicated by a rapid series of events during the middle of the nineteenth century. The acquisition of Oregon territory in 1846, and the addition of the Mexican cession in 1848 brought thousands of Indians under the control of the United States. These red men were entirely different from those with which the federal government had previously dealt; the conditions under which they lived were wholly unknown to the officials at the national capital. Before the government had had time to become acquainted with their needs came the great rush of people into their territory. In 1847, hundreds of Mormons passed through and settled beyond the Indian frontier; in 1849 and the years directly following, the trails through the Indian lands were crowded with the thousands of gold seekers unmindful of Indian rights. Many of the

[547] *United States Statutes at Large,* IV, 1834, 735-739.

[548] After the Indians were subdued, some of these forts were made into Indian reservations.

emigrants had heard Indian stories from their parents and grandparents, so that to them a killer of an Indian was a hero. To pioneering Americans, the Indians' legal rights were mythical. The white man squatted on the fertile spots; he killed the Indians' game; he cut down the pine nut tree. The Indians looked upon these invasions of their territory as a violation of their inalienable rights, and when the federal government repudiated the stipulations in the treaties made with them, they took up their own defense. Under the circumstances, the government became confused – it had to adjust its policy to each new situation.

The first recognition which the government took of the Indians in the Great Basin area was on April 7, 1849, when John Wilson was appointed Indian agent with his headquarters in Salt Lake City. His field of work extended from the Rockies to the Sierra Nevada mountains, the latter being under the California department. For looking after the Indians in this extensive territory, he received a salary of $1500 a year, $500 for interpreters, and $1500 for contingent expenses (purchase of small gifts and trinkets), two horses, house rent, and other incidentals.[549] The first report of Agent Wilson described the many difficulties of the Indian problem in his territory, foremost of which was the rapidly diminishing supply of Indians' food caused by the California migration.[550]

The first change in policy came when in September, 1850, the territory of Utah was created. The affairs of the Great Basin Indians were separated from those of California; a separate division was made. On January 3 of the following year, Brigham Young was appointed governor of Utah territory and ex-officio superintendent of Indian affairs in it for four years. It was over six months, however, before Governor Young did anything toward organizing the Indian administration for his district. On July 21, 1851, he established three agencies, one general and two sub-agencies. The part of Utah territory which later became Nevada was placed under the Parvan agency assigned to sub-Agent John H. Holeman of Fort Laramie.[551] Governor Young per-

[549] *Sen. Ex. Doc.* no. 18, 31 Cong., 1 sess., IX, 97-98.
[550] *Idem.*
[551] Bancroft, *History of Utah,* 455.

sonally directed the affairs of the Indians south and west of
Great Salt Lake; he took the attitude that it was cheaper
to feed the Indian than to fight him.[552] Hence the relations
between the Mormon and the Indian were peaceful until
the great tide of gentile emigrants began to move through
the Mormon and the Indian territory. The Mormon and
the Indian had something in common – the hundreds of
head of stock accompanying the emigrant trains broke down
the fences of the Mormon farms and ate their crops, and
this same live stock ate the grass in the Indian's lands. If
the Mormon had no food neither had the Indian. Friendli-
ness toward the emigrants was replaced by hostility. Indian
outbreaks began to be very frequent. Superintendent Young
advised his agents to teach the Indian agriculture, so that
he could raise his own food, but with the small sums of
money appropriated by the congress for Indian affairs it
was impossible to do anything of this kind.

When the Indian became desperate for food, he stole
from the emigrant trains. The agents found it difficult to
handle these cases of theft. To complicate matters further,
a number of white men were living with the Indians. Some
of them had been independent fur-trappers, "freemen," of
varied nationalities, who after the decline of the fur industry
settled among the savages. Many of them, having formed
marriage alliances, had set up domestic establishments. In
this later period they were known as "squaw men." [553] Their
influence on the Indian was almost wholly harmful. Being
too lazy to work, they inflamed the Indian to attack the
emigrant trains, drive off their stock, and then force the
emigrants to buy back their chattels at exorbitant prices.

By 1852, theft and murder became so prevalent along
the Humboldt route that Agent Holeman was sent out to
the western part of Utah to stop the depredations. He declared that only United States troops could protect the trail
through Carson Valley.[554] The Indians claimed that the
white people killed them without provocation, even luring

---

[552] *Ibid.*, 471.

[553] *Et supra*, 42.

[554] *Sen. Ex. Doc.* no. 1, 32 Cong., 2 sess., 152, 153, 440, 445 (ser. no. 658);
*H. Ex. Doc.* no. 3, pt. 3, 32 Cong., 1 sess., 153, 444; Bancroft, *History of Nevada,
Colorado, and Wyoming*, 205-209; Angel, *op. cit.*, 145.

them into their camps to do so. Holeman found that in many
cases the Indian was right. The Indian admitted, however,
that he killed as many whites as the white people killed of
his tribesmen; he stole as much from the whites as the white
man stole from him. The agent went to the chiefs of the
tribes and advised them to lead their tribes into the hills
and to stay away from the trails during the travel season.

When Holeman returned to Salt Lake from his trip
among the Indians along the Humboldt Trail, he vigorously
urged the establishment of several military posts along the
emigrant routes to subdue the Indians and check the "bad
whites." His report to the commissioner of Indian affairs,
George W. Mannypenny, said in part: "Our relations with
the Indians of Utah . . . remain in a very unsettled and
precarious condition, arising out of the constant and unavoidable encroachment upon their territory by the whites
and no provision being made for indemnifying and placing
them beyond the reach of the injuries inflicted." [555] The federal government had at last begun to take cognizance of
the Indian situation in the Great Basin.

Still another disturbing element in the administration of
Indian affairs in Utah was the mutual distrust between the
Mormon and the non-Mormon Indian agents. This was a
great handicap in bringing about harmonious relations between the Indian and the federal government. The red man
was bewildered by the opposing tactics of the two factions.
So annoying were the activities of the Mormon spies, that
the non-Mormon agents had to mail their letters and reports outside the territory. Holeman, a non-Mormon agent,
found it very difficult to continue in office under these circumstances. He said: "I have no idea with Governor Young
at the head of the Indian department that I shall be able
to do anything that can be of service to the government or
to the Indians or creditable to myself." [556]

In spite of his recommendations, no aid came to him from
Washington, consequently he acted largely upon his own
judgment and initiative. Early in the summer of 1852 he,
with the approval of Superintendent Young, went on the

---

[555] *Sen. Ex. Doc.* no. 1, 33 Cong., 1 sess., 259-260.
[556] *H. Ex. Doc.* no. 2, 33 Cong., 1 sess., X, 137, 152, 171.

expedition to the different tribes in western Utah. His object was to distribute gifts among the Indians before the emigrant trains began to come through. The effort was more or less successful; he reported very few murders or robberies for that year.[557] On September 26 of the same year and after the emigration season was over, he reported that:

> The Indians in this section of the territory Humboldt Valley although they appear to be in a savage and wild state, seem to have a very correct idea of the power and importance of our government. . . I think it important that the government should establish posts on this route; one on the Humboldt and one at the Mormon Station in Carson Valley. . . There are white men who are more desperate and commit more depredations, it is thought, than the Indians, and who keep the Indian in a state of excitement.
>
> I therefore recommend that a treaty should be held with the Indians in this territory. . . I earnestly repeat the recommendation . . . if something is not done . . . in the course of a few years the Indians will be compelled to give up their present locations to an emigrating population, and to be driven forth to perish in the plains. The Indians seem friendly disposed, and will at no time be better prepared for friendly negotiations than the present.[558]

In the spring of 1853 Holeman went again to the Humboldt and Carson rivers. He reported that the Indians were friendly, but that a new and more serious situation had arisen — California traders, whose chief stock was whisky, had come out on the trail and had set up temporary "grog shops." These white men were having a bad effect on the Indian; they "steal and commit more depredations than the Indian. I feel satisfied that until the government throws protection over this route and places means within the reach of the officers to enforce their authority and the laws, there can be no safety to travel." [559]

In spite of these reports to the federal government and Holeman's recommendations for Indian colonization, for training in the methods of agriculture and other industries, and for the stocking of farms for the Indians, nothing was done. Because Holeman continued to have trouble with Superintendent Young and the other Mormon agents, he

[557] *Ibid.*, no. 1, pt. 1, 32 Cong., 1 sess., 300.
[558] *Sen. Ex. Doc.* no. 1, 33 Cong., 1 sess., 447.
[559] *Loc. cit.*

resigned. From his reports there is little doubt of his sincerity in trying to achieve results. Although he refrained studiously from interfering in any religious, political, or economic affair of the Mormon state, he could accomplish very little for the Indian. The federal government did not comprehend the situation; the agents were too far removed from Washington to present the case in person.

In the next two years there were two agents appointed for western Utah: S. B. Rose succeeded Holeman, and Rose was followed shortly by Dr. Garland Hurt. In 1855 so many reports of Indian attacks came into Salt Lake City from the Humboldt Trail that Young sent Agent Hurt out to investigate them. He took with him a large quantity of gifts for the Indians, consisting of bright pieces of cloth, beads, rings, hair combs, needles, knives, bells, balls, razors, buttons, and awls. When Hurt reached the Humboldt river he was met by a number of Shoshone chiefs, and after talking a while he made a treaty with them, but in doing so he exceeded his authority. The treaty was held up in Washington because of the consideration at that time of several other treaties, with New Mexican Indians; the government wanted to have all treaties with the western Indians uniform. Nothing was done, however, about the Shoshone treaty,[560] a regrettable fact to Hurt, who thought that the treaty was more to be desired than gift-giving; the former was permanent, the latter bought only temporary peace.

The Indians' problem was equally perplexing to the settlers in western Utah. At that time it generally took six weeks to reach the territorial capital; and almost that many months to go to Washington. On account of the infrequent visits of the Indian agents to western Utah, and the inability of the citizens to cope with the situation, the settlers of Carson Valley addressed a number of communications to John M. Bernhisel, delegate for the territory of Utah in congress. Letters were sent also to Commissioner Mannypenny recommending to him that agencies be created at strategic points between Carson Valley and Salt Lake City — in Ruby, Humboldt, and Carson valleys. The commissioner replied favorably but the government took no action.

560 *H. Ex. Doc.* no. 37, 37 Cong., 3 sess., V, 142-143.

In 1856, when Hurt was returning to Salt Lake City from a tour of inspection of Carson Valley, he took a different route. From Carson Valley he went to Washoe Valley, then to the Truckee Meadows, thence down the Truckee to Pyramid Lake. In this circuit, he was the first federal agent to meet the main groups of the Washoes and Paiutes; his report on their condition was the first official one made.[561] Thereafter this route was taken when the agents visited western Utah.

In 1856 George Armstrong, sub-agent in southern Utah, visited the Indians on the Muddy and Virgin rivers. He found them, assisted by the Mormon settlers, engaged in farming. The white man had to choose between helping the Indian to be self-supporting, and supporting him. For this reason, the Indian was not as troublesome on the Salt Lake-Los Angeles route as he was on the northern trails.

The impending Utah war of 1857 entirely changed the Indian situation. In Young's last report he complained of the insufficient funds for the successful administration of the work, and dwelt at some length on the necessity of keeping soldiers out of the territory. Young said hostilities had increased owing to the rumor that troops were going to be sent in. In the summer of that year Young was removed from his governorship of the territory of Utah, and automatically ceased to be superintendent of Indian affairs for Utah.[562]

J. W. Denver, the newly appointed commissioner of Indian affairs to succeed Mannypenny, censored Young severely in a reply to his report. He stated that Young had sent Dr. Hurt to Carson Valley when there were no funds; that he had permitted his sub-agents to spend money in excess of the appropriation; that it was reported that he was the instigator of a planned rebellion in Utah; and, as for the soldiers, that the president of the United States would send them wherever he chose.[563] Young's salary was refused, and the entire affair was forgotten in Washington.

Jacob Forney, having been appointed to succeed Young as superintendent of Indian affairs in the territory of Utah,

---

[561] *Report of the Interior Department,* 1856, 16.
[562] *United States Statutes at Large,* 1855-1857.
[563] *Sen. Ex. Doc.* no. 2, 35 Cong., 1 sess., 698.

hastened to Salt Lake City to take charge of his work. He visited the Goshutes, Indians who roamed in what is now eastern Nevada, and made arrangements for them to be placed on land suitable for farming. At the same time, he held a council with the neighboring Bannock tribes.[564] Forney was not able to cope with the situation in western Utah. There were many murders, robberies, and attacks on emigrants reported to President Buchanan, who ordered General A. S. Johnston, in charge of the army in Utah, to send some of his troops to protect the emigrants along the trails. Major Isaac Lynde of the Seventh Infantry was ordered immediately to patrol the routes of travel west of the Salt Lake. In his report he stated that many of the emigrant trains were poorly armed, and that the Indians in many of the attacks were spurred on by unscrupulous white men.[565]

In 1859 Robert B. Jarvis succeeded Agent Forney for the western part of Utah territory. He was directed to collect the Goshutes and Shoshones on farms. When he went to their territory, he had a council with seventy-three of their warriors, at which a chief and sub-chiefs were elected. He found that in their previous efforts to farm in Deep Creek Valley, the Indians had dug up the ground with sticks. They had planted about fifty acres of wheat, but grasshoppers had descended upon the fields and destroyed them. Agent Jarvis became so discouraged after a few months in office that he resigned. In June, 1859, Frederick Dodge was appointed in his place.

In Dodge, the government had a real Indian agent. He went about his work in a very systematic way; he visited and numbered each tribe; he investigated their living conditions and the sources of their food. In his first report, he recommended the setting aside of the Truckee Meadows for an Indian reservation.

At the time he was making his first visit among the Indians, the Comstock silver strike was made public.[566] The entire situation was changed again — hundreds of white people began to rush into the western part of Utah. The federal

564 *Ibid.*, no. 1, 35 Cong., 2 sess., 561-565.

565 *Sen. Ex. Doc.* no. 1, 36 Cong., 1 sess., 26-27.

566 *Ibid.*, no. 2, 36 Cong., 1 sess., I, 741-747 (ser. no. 1023).

government would have to adopt some new policy for handling the Indian problem in this section.

Major Dodge was the first Indian agent in western Utah
to select areas on which to settle the Indians. He set off three
sections of fertile lands for their exclusive use, where they
would be more or less isolated from the white settlements.
He believed that with some help from the government
the Indian could be made self-supporting on these reservations. In 1859 there was only one man living on what is now
the Truckee Meadows. Dodge believed that the government
could buy him out easily.[567] On these beautiful grassy
meadows he thought he could place the Washoes and some
of the Paiutes. In attempting this arrangement, Dodge was
not acquainted with the former relations of these two tribes,
which had been enemies for many generations. In the hostilities the Washoes had been the losers. They had been
greatly reduced in numbers; they had been driven to the high
country around Tahoe and Honey lakes, the sources of the
Truckee, Carson, and Walker rivers; and they had been
forced to agree that no member of the tribe could ever own
or ride a horse. Hence, nothing came of his plans for this
reservation.

The Washoes were so humbled by these wars, and so
reduced in numbers by an epidemic of smallpox that they had
very little fight left in them. They were miserably poor and
wretchedly degraded.[568] Very few depredations or attacks
by them on the white people were ever reported to the government officials. They were never settled on a definite reservation.

In 1860 Dodge, in charge of the Carson agency, employed
Warren Wasson to assist him in marking off the Walker
and Pyramid Lake reservations. Dodge left for Washington
in the same year, and remained until the outbreak of the
Civil War. He joined the army and lost his life in the second
year of the war. Wasson became acting agent, holding the
position for several years and continuing Dodge's plan
of two Paiute reservations. The Truckee-Pyramid Reservation was intended at first to include a large portion of the

[567] *Report Commissioner Indian Affairs*, 1861, 113.
[568] J. P. Doolittle, *Condition of the Indian Tribes*, 518-520.

bottom land between Wadsworth and Pyramid Lake. Along the river's edge there was a great deal of timber which he planned to have cut, so that the Indian might put up houses and other reservation buildings. There was sufficient land in this area, if it were cultivated, to keep the Indian without very much help from the government. Unfortunately, the Truckee-Pyramid Reservation was cut down six miles when the projected route of the Central Pacific Railroad was decided. After the secretary of the interior had expended $25,000 for the construction of a sawmill, it was sold, and the privilege of cutting the timber was granted to a lumberman.[569] The reason given for such a move was that the expense exceeded the benefits to be expected from the enterprise.

The Walker Lake Reservation, designed for the Paiutes also, contained many acres of grassy lands. A kind of a bulbous root, called tabooza, which grew in this section, together with the abundant pine nut crop in the Pine Nut range on the upper Walker river, the meal made from the seed of the bunch grass, and the great quantities of fish in Walker Lake, gave the Indians a plentiful supply of food, but it was difficult to induce the Paiutes to remain on the reservation. Anyone who promised to remain and cultivate a plot of ground was rewarded with gifts. The first buildings for the Carson agency were constructed on the Walker River Reservation — a stable, and a three roomed farmhouse (one room used for an office, one for a kitchen, and one for a store room).[570]

As the winter of 1859-1860 was an unusually hard one, suffering among the Indians was intense. Isaac Roop, governor of the provisional territory of Nevada reported:

The Indians in Truckee Meadows are freezing and starving to death by scores. In one cabin the governor found three children dead and dying. The whites are doing all they can to alleviate the miseries of the poor Washoes. They have sent out and built fires for them, and offered them bread and other provisions. But in many instances the starving Indians refused to eat, fearing that the food is poisoned. They attribute the se-

---

[569] *Report Commissioner Indian Affairs,* 1861, 113; Charles Royce, *Indian land cessions,* 832-833.

[570] *Report Commissioner Indian Affairs,* 1864, 149.

verity of the winter to the whites. . . The Truckee river is frozen over hard enough to bear up loaded teams.[571]

In March, 1859, Peter Lassen, veteran trail blazer and station keeper, went out with two companions to prospect in the Black Rock Desert country. After they had camped a short time about twenty-six miles northwest of the Black Rock Cape, Lassen and Clapper were murdered. The crime occurred near a very large boulder just south of Alum Creek; "Murder Rock" has ever since been a landmark.[572]

In the spring of 1860 there were many depredations and outrages committed by the Indians on the people living along the overland trails, and in the settlements of western Utah. The brutal murder by Paiutes on January 13, 1860, of Dexter E. Demming on his ranch in Willow Creek Valley, just north of Honey Lake Valley, incensed the citizens to such an extent that they demanded protection from the federal government.[573] Almost one hundred citizens of Susanville petitioned Roop to send out a military force to chastise the Indians for the murder of Demming. Roop immediately sent a detachment of volunteers under Lieutenant U. J. Tutt to hunt out the murderers. On January 24, the lieutenant reported that he had tracked them to the Paiute camp. Four days later the governor appointed two commissioners to visit Chief Winnemucca and demand the murderers, in accordance with a treaty by which he had agreed to deliver up from his tribe the murderer of a white man. Although he acknowledged the stipulation in the treaty, Chief Winnemucca not only refused to interpose his authority to hunt out the murderer, but demanded that the settlers of Honey Lake Valley pay $16,000 to the Paiutes for the valley. How the chief arrived at that price is puzzling. Some "squaw man" living among the Paiutes may have told him to ask that much.[574]

When the Paiutes became defiant over the Demming affair,

---

[571] *Territorial Enterprise,* December, 1859, quoted in Angel, *op. cit.,* 148.

[572] Angel, *op. cit.,* 148; "Murder Rock" is shown on DeGroot's "Map of 1863," manuscript map in Bancroft Library, University of California.

[573] Angel, *op. cit.* Honey Lake Valley was at that time considered a part of Utah.

[574] Angel, *op. cit.,* 149. The murder of Mr. Demming made the eighth murder in that vicinity within a few months.

Governor Roop asked the federal government for assistance, and dispatched an appeal to General Clarke, commander of the Pacific department, to send troops to Honey Lake Valley at once to protect the citizens from the inevitable war between the whites and the Indians. He also asked that if it were not possible to send a company of men, at least to send arms, ammunition, and a four or six pound cannon. General Clarke sent no troops, nor did he furnish any arms. His inaction aggravated the bloodiness of the outbreak.[575] The federal government was forced to adopt another policy toward the Indian — force of arms had to be used before the red man could be subdued in Nevada.

---

[575] *Loc. cit.*

# The Last Stand of the Nevada Indian

The Nevada Indian wars were the inevitable outcome of the rush of people to western Utah in the spring of 1860. So long as the white settlements were few and the emigrant season short, complete loss of the Indians' hunting and grazing grounds was not threatened. When, however, the prospector, the rancher, and the mail company station keepers preëmpted lands, a serious situation developed. The Indians attacked the white people from the time they came into the Great Basin, but there was no general uprising until 1860. In the spring of that year, the Indians went to Pyramid Lake for a war parley. In addition to the Paiutes, there were a number of Pit River, Bannock, and Shoshone Indians who, having been driven from their northern homes by the severe winter, were permitted to remain at the Pyramid Lake Reservation for the season.

Governor Roop and a few other cautious citizens in the Honey Lake region feared the danger that might ensue from the Indian meeting, but the prospectors, farmers, and station keepers did not seem especially alarmed. The Indians' "big talk" began in the latter part of April; it was still in progress on May 7, when the news of the attack on the station of James O. Williams, on the Carson river, was brought into Virginia City and neighboring towns.[576] Williams' Station was on the Overland Trail about ten miles northeast of Buckland's Station or bridge across the Carson, and twenty-five miles east of Dayton. Williams had prospered from the trade with the emigrants on their way across the Forty-six mile Desert. With him at the time of the attack on the station were his two brothers, Oscar and David, and three other men, Samuel Sullivan, James Fleming, and another man known as "Dutch Phil." The first three men were shot by

---

[576] Bancroft, *History of Nevada, Colorado, and Wyoming*, 208-209.

the Indians; the other two were burned to death when the Indians set fire to the buildings.[577]

The real reason for the attack on Williams' Station is not known definitely at this late date. A generally accepted story, however, circulated at the time, declared that it was a matter of personal revenge for the capture of two young Indian women by the men at the station. The young Bannock squaws were supposed to have been shut up for two or three days in a cave near the station. The husbands finally traced their wives to this station, but when they demanded their surrender, the men drove them off. The bucks tried to induce the Paiutes to help them recover their wives, but the Paiutes refused. Thirty Bannock warriors volunteered, however, to go to the station to free the women; it is believed that it was they who burned the station.[578]

The Indians' version of the story was told to a correspondent of a San Francisco newspaper. It was as follows:

A Pah-ute had tied his horse along Carson river for a few moments, while he was fishing some white man came along and took off the horse and sold him to Williams, of whom the Pah-ute demanded him. Williams refused to give him up; whereupon the Indian went off to his chief, Winnemucca, at Pyramid Lake, complaining of his loss. The chief told him that he must not resent the injury; that he had himself lost many horses and never complained. The Indian who lost the horse was not satisfied; so he told his grievances to some bands of Pit River and Bannock Indians, who, driven from their own country by severe cold, had, by permission of Winnemucca, encamped at Pyramid Lake. The Pit River Indians numbered fifty, and the Bannocks over one hundred. These tribes offered to send some of their number with the Pah-utes to regain his horse. Accordingly, seventeen of them started to Williams' Station, with three Pah-utes. Williams, giving them no satisfaction concerning the horse, the Indians burned the station.[579]

In most accounts of the Indian outbreaks of 1860, very little mention was made of the gross outrages committed against the Indians by the white men. There was a set of fellows who kept little "grog shops" called trading posts along the routes of travel, in which the chief stock in trade was whisky. Since there was practically no government at all in

---

[577] Angel, *History of Nevada*, 152.
[578] Dan De Quille (William Wright), *The Big Bonanza*, 118.
[579] *San Francisco Herald*, May 25, 1860.

western Utah in 1860, these white men took advantage of conditions to commit the most outrageous crimes, well knowing they would never be punished. The Indians, exasperated at these repeated injustices, took matters in their own hands. The attack on Williams' Station was only the eruption of a pent-up wrath.

When news of the destruction of Williams' Station and the murder of the five men was brought to the settlements, runners were sent out in all directions to warn the ranchers and prospectors. From all the settlements volunteers gathered at Buckland's Station where they organized on the morning of May 9. Altogether there were one hundred and five men, divided into four companies, who set out to drive the marauding Indians out of the country. Major William M. Ormsby, in command of the Carson detachment, urged that a commander-in-chief for the expedition be chosen. His suggestion was not followed, but each group of volunteers went forward with a commander from its own community.[580]

The expedition arrived at Williams' Station on May 10 where it camped for the night. After the bodies of the two Williams men and Samuel Sullivan were buried, a council was held, after which a vote was taken on whether they would pursue the murderers or disband, resulting in a unanimous decision to pursue the Indians. Accordingly, on the following morning, the entire number of volunteers marched north to the Big Bend of the Truckee river, and camped on the site of Wadsworth on the eleventh of May.

Although no Indians had been seen, they had nevertheless been watching the movements of the expedition from the time it had been organized. Unnoticed by the white men, they had kept to the ridges of the mountains. On May 12, the expedition started down the trail along the east side of the Truckee river some fifty feet above the banks. Every move of the army was observed by Indian runners who reported to young Winnemucca and his warriors gathered on the plain near where the present buildings of the Indian agency now stand at Nixon, Pyramid Lake. The white army proceeded down the river for some fourteen miles without seeing a sign of red men. At this point the trail left the river

580 Angel, op. cit., 153-154.

and dropped down into some thickly wooded meadows, in which the Indians were concealed from the untrained eye of the white men. When the expedition had advanced so far into enemy territory as to make retreat difficult, they saw the first Indians on a low mound which had been used by them for their councils. From this height a view of the entire valley as well as of the approaches from the higher ground could be obtained. When the volunteers saw the Indians they stopped. The Indians, however, began to shoot at them with bows and arrows. The shower of arrows came so quickly and in such number that the whites were forced to retreat. The Indians, anticipating this move, ran ahead to prevent escape, making orderly retreat impossible. The Truckee river was so high from the spring thaw that it could not be crossed. The Indians, taking advantage of the situation, drove off as many of their horses as possible.

At one point in the fighting, which seemed from the many descriptions given of it to have been strung out for some distance along the trail, Major Ormsby assumed command. Although he tried to rally the men, he was supported by only a few of them, five of whom were killed. This maneuver was too late. Ormsby's arms and mouth were wounded during the fighting, the saddle on his mule loosened, and he fell to the ground. He pleaded with the Indians, who surrounded him, not to kill him. Mercilessly they shot him; his body rolled over the ridge and into the gulch below. Among the other well known men killed, was Henry Meredith, a popular young lawyer from Downieville, California. He had just come to Virginia City where he had entered the law office of William M. Stewart.

As to the number of Indians killed in this battle, erroneously called the "Battle of Pyramid Lake" (the lake was four miles away), there is no agreement. An examination of all the sources indicates that forty-six is probably a conservative estimate.[581]

On the morning of May 15, five days after the expedition set out, a few of the men who had escaped with their lives

[581] Angel, *op. cit.*, 158; Bancroft, *History of Nevada, Colorado, and Wyoming*, 209-212.

but had lost their horses began to straggle into Buckland's, and those who had horses rode on quickly to Virginia City, Dayton, and towns farther up the Carson river.

When the story of the battle was told, a panic developed. Women and children were placed in the strongest stone buildings in the towns; defense corps were organized, and sentinels were stationed at vantage points around the cities.[582] The news was flashed to California towns and cities. From Downieville one hundred and sixty-five men, armed and equipped, marched, most of them on foot, to help fight the Indians who had killed the gallant Henry Meredith, their beloved townsman.[583] Volunteers came from many other California towns; San Francisco raised money and arms. Governor John G. Downey of California ordered five hundred Minié muskets and a large quantity of munitions sent.

Major Warren Wasson, then in Genoa, volunteered to carry alone a message from General Clarke, commander at the San Francisco Presidio, to a company of cavalry at Honey Lake Valley, ordering them to proceed at once to Carson City. Wasson, mounted on a powerful and fleet horse, rode the one hundred and ten miles in fourteen hours through the enemy's territory without a change of horses or without seeing an Indian. The orders were delivered, and the cavalry company moved south to aid in the punitive expedition against the Paiutes.

By May 24 the organization known as the Washoe Regiment, consisting of eight companies of infantry and six of cavalry, about five hundred and forty-four altogether, was completed. By mutual consent, Colonel John "Jack" Hays, an old Indian fighter, was placed in command. Among the other prominent officers were Major Daniel Hungerford, father-in-law of John W. Mackay, who was placed on Colonel Hays' staff, and Captain Edward Faris Storey, who headed the Virginia Rifles. General Clarke issued orders to Captain Joseph "Jasper" Stewart of the Third Artillery, at Fort Alcatraz, and Captain F. F. Flint of the

[582] Angel, *op. cit.*, 158.

[583] Henry Meredith's body was taken back to Downieville where a large funeral was held. His grave was marked by an impressive monument.

Sixth Infantry at Benicia Barracks, to advance at once to
join the volunteers and bring two howitzers.[584] On May 31
they met the volunteer forces at the Big Bend of the Truckee.
With such a well organized and disciplined army, there
could be no doubt about the outcome of the impending expedition against the Indians.

On June 2 while the main division was camped on the
Truckee river, a scouting party rode down into the bottom
land about a mile south of where the fighting between the
Ormsby troops and the Paiutes had taken place. They followed along the trail which led toward the Indian village.
On the way down the river they saw many ghastly results of
the fight. Some of the bodies of the slain men had been attacked by wild animals, while others had been stripped of
every stitch of clothing. When the scouts came to the point
where the trail dropped down into the bottom land, they
stopped for consultation. A few scouts who had kept to the
ridges above the river to watch for the enemy, signaled that
the Indians were in sight; orders were hastily given for all
scouts to fall back to the main force, for about three hundred
mounted Indians and many on foot were advancing rapidly.
When the returning scouts observed Colonel Hays coming
forward with the regulars, they decided to make a stand
and turned to face the oncoming Indians. It was here that
a three hour battle took place. Young Winnemucca, the
Paiute war chief, from a high hill which projected from the
mountain, gave his orders, which were unquestioningly
obeyed.

Captain Storey and Captain J. B. Van Hagan, on foot
with part of their command, stormed the Indians' position
on the promontory. Although they were successful in gaining
the position, they found themselves flanked by red warriors
from the direction of the river as well as from the side of
the mountain.

They were relieved from this dilemma of finding themselves inside the
enemy lines by the arrival of the main force. The regulars deployed in
open order as skirmishers and passed to the west of the butte and along
the side of the mountain, driving everything before them, while the volunteers on foot moved forward in the same order to the east of it, firing as

584 Bancroft, *History of Nevada, Colorado, and Wyoming*, 213.

they advanced. In this manner a continuous line about one mile long, extending from the river to near the top of the mountain, was formed, and a general engagement began, the Indians having a corresponding line, to oppose the advance.[585]

Although the Indians resisted stubbornly the advance of the white army, they were driven back. The pursuit of the Indians continued until sundown, by which time most of the red men had fled to the mountains. Captain Storey was mortally wounded by a shot through the lungs from which he died a few days later; two privates from his company were also killed. The other casualties were four wounded in the regular army, and one in the volunteer forces. The Indian losses have never been definitely known. They claimed that they lost only four men, but other sources estimate the number as high as one hundred and sixty killed and an immense number wounded.[586] The Indians may have purposely withheld the truth.

After the battle the Washoe Regiment returned to their temporary breastworks at Fort Storey, which they had erected while in camp before the engagement. On June 5 the main regiment resumed its march toward Pyramid Lake, but the entire valley was deserted. The Indian trail seemed, however, to lead north. One man, William Allen, a scout, was killed from ambush by the Indians.[587] The pursuers decided not to follow them in their flight. On June 7, Colonel Hays returned with his volunteer forces to Virginia City, where they were disbanded. Captain Stewart remained at the lake until the middle of July. During this time earthworks were thrown up which the captain named Fort Haven, in honor of General Haven of California, who had volunteered as a private in Colonel Hays' command.[588]

Following the battles on the Truckee river, the Indians seemed to vent their wrath on the pony express and mail

---

[585] Angel, *op. cit.,* 161.

[586] *Ibid.,* 162.

[587] The vivid account by Captain Robert Lyon of the attempt to save Allen from the Indians is told in Angel, *op. cit.,* 164. The bodies of Captains Ormsby and Storey and the other men were brought back for burial. Storey is buried in Virginia City, Ormsby and Allen in the Carson City graveyard. Three Nevada counties were named after these three heroes, Lyon, Ormsby, and Storey.

[588] Angel, *op. cit.,* 164.

stations along the Humboldt-Carson and the Simpson-Egan trails. They burned many of the stations, killed several of the agents, and drove off live stock. Jay G. Kelly, one of the pony express riders in eastern Nevada during the Indian uprisings in 1860, has told his experience in them. His predecessor had been shot. This particular incident occurred where Kelly had to ride through some quaking aspen trees:

A trail had been cut through these little trees just wide enough to allow horse and rider to pass. As the road was crooked and the branches came together from either side, just above my head when mounted, it was impossible to see ahead more than ten or fifteen yards, and it was two miles through the forest. I expected to have trouble, and prepared for it by dropping my bridle reins on the neck of the horse, put my Sharp's rifle at full cock, kept both spurs into the flanks, and he went through that forest like a "streak of lightning"! At the top of the hill I dismounted to rest my horse, and looking back, saw the bushes moving several places. As there were no cattle or game in that vicinity, I knew the movements must be caused by Indians, and was more positive of it when, after firing several shots at the spot where I saw the bushes moving, all agitation ceased.[589]

Howard R. Egan, another pony express rider, the man for whom Egan cañon was named, and who first demonstrated that the central route across Nevada was the most direct one to Carson Valley, had a thrilling experience which he recorded in his diary:

The express rider at Shell Creek was too sick to undertake the ride, and I volunteered to take his place. The ride at that time was from Shell to Butte. . . I started just at dark and made pretty good time, but being careful not to overdo the pony, but give him frequent breathing spells, at which times I would let him go on the walk, and was doing so when I was about in the middle of Egan canyon and, just before turning a sharp point where I could see the camp. They were on both sides of the road and about in the center of the bend. Well, I had to make up my mind very quickly as to what I should do. Should I turn and go north to another canyon about six or eight miles, where there might be another party of Indians, if they had planned to catch the express rider? . . .

Well, I soon decided to go straight, so taking my pistol in my hand, I rode on as close as I dared, then striking in the spurs and giving an awful yell, a few jumps of the pony brought me to about the middle of the camp. When my gun began to talk, though pointed up in the air, and my yells accompanied each shot. I got a glimpse of several Indians who were doing

[589] Visscher, *Thrilling and Truthful History of the Pony Express*, 41.

FORT CHURCHILL

The fort was declared a military reserve August 7, 1860; formally relinquished June 15, 1871; and was restored as a public park in 1935. From a rare contemporary lithograph.

their best to make themselves scarce, not knowing but there might be a large party of whites after them. When I made the next turn, I was out in the little valley at the head of Egan canyon and had two trails that I could take to finish. I chose the shortest but the roughest and got home all right. . .[590]

Because so many stations had been burned in Nevada, the pony express of May 31, 1860, was not allowed to leave San Francisco, nor did it run until June 9, when twenty picked men accompanied it as far as Salt Lake City. Four expresses from the East, held in Salt Lake City until hostilities were ended, did not reach San Francisco until June 25.[591] The delay in the mails and destruction of the stations cost the express company $75,000.[592]

For some time the Indian agents had been recommending to the federal government that several military posts and camps be established on the overland mail routes across Nevada; but not until the Indians broke out, had killed a number of people, and had fought the two battles on the Truckee river were any steps taken to build a fort. In July, 1860, Captain Joseph Stewart was ordered to erect one on the Carson river. Samuel S. Buckland,[593] who owned the trading station on the south side of the river, persuaded the captain that the hill one mile west of his station on the north side of the river was the best site in that vicinity. On the top of this hill, which commanded a view of the trail in both directions, the construction of Fort Churchill was begun on July 20, 1860.[594] It was named for Captain Charles C. Churchill of the Fourth United States Artillery.

Although the fort, at the time it was founded, was in the territory of Utah, it was placed under the military department of California. However, after the opening of the Civil

---

[590] Egan, *Pioneering the West*, 226.

[591] *San Francisco Daily Bulletin*, May 26, 28, 31, June 2, 9, 25, 1860.

[592] Root and Connelley, *Overland Stage to California*, 122; *infra*, 346.

[593] The Buckland Ranch Station was the source for many of the supplies of the fort. The soldiers used to come down to the ranch for their liquor and good times. The Buckland family is buried in the fort cemetery. There are now a number of things at the ranch house which were once on the fort. Among them are some benches which were in the fort chapel.

[594] The fort was twenty-five miles from Virginia City on the main trail to Sacramento.

War, it was made headquarters for the military district of Nevada.

The land occupied by Fort Churchill was declared a "military reserve" in an army order dated at Fort Churchill, Utah territory, on August 7, 1860. The reserve was nearly in the form of a rhomboid, the acute angles of which were at the northeast and southwest corners, the land lying on both sides of the Carson river. It was never confirmed as a regular military reservation by executive order of the president. When the fort was the military headquarters, orders were sent out from it to the other camps and stations in the state.

The soldiers' barracks, built to accommodate three hundred men, occupied the south side of the square; the six officers' quarters, each costing $16,000, were constructed on the highest ground on the west side; and the barns, stables, and the arsenal were on the north and east sides. The original plans called for buildings suitable for one thousand men, but they had to be curtailed on account of the great cost of building materials in Nevada.

All the buildings were made of adobe; most of them had stone foundations. The government had to keep a large number of cavalry, and quartermasters' horses. When the fort was being built, there were over one hundred work mules, which, in teams of six, were kept busy hauling building materials, fuel, and supplies for the garrison. A great deal of the furniture for the barracks and officers' quarters was made in the carpenter's shop at the fort.[595]

The first garrison of regular troops stationed at Fort Churchill was commanded by Captain Stewart. It consisted of Stewart's own company H of the Third United States Artillery from Alcatraz, a detachment of the same regiment

---

[595] *San Francisco Evening Bulletin,* January 7, 1861; Thomas H. S. Hamersley, *The Complete Regular Army Register of the United States for One Hundred Years* (1779-1879), 128; Fort Churchill was formally relinquished on June 15, 1871. Since the site was never confirmed by executive order, the land reverted to the interior department. It was included later in the Truckee-Carson irrigation project. Through the efforts of the Sagebrush Chapter, Daughters of the American Revolution, two hundred acres on which the ruins of the fort are located were transferred in 1931 to the state of Nevada. The D.A.R. was made custodian of the property. The buildings are being restored through the C.W.A.

from companies I and M from the Presidio in San Francisco, companies A and H of the Sixth United States Infantry from Benicia Barracks, and a detachment from companies A and F, First United States Dragoons. This was the largest force ever at this fort at any one time. Most of the soldiers were called to join the armies of the Union after Fort Sumter was fired on. The Second Regiment California Cavalry Volunteers was then sent to Fort Churchill, where they remained from November, 1861, to September, 1862.[596] At no time after 1861 were there very many regular troops. The force was made up very largely of California and Nevada volunteers.

Fort Churchill, the western terminus for the telegraph line, received the western news where the pony express rider picked it up and took it through to the eastern terminus, Salt Lake City, at which point it was re-telegraphed to far eastern points. Troops were dispatched generally along the trail leading east from the fort, as far as Austin.[597] Distances were too great for the troops at Fort Churchill to protect all the roads and settlements, and many other forts and camps had to be built before the Indian was completely subdued.

When the Indians on the eastern end of the Simpson-Egan Trail became hostile, the military authorities established a post, on September 4, 1862, on the west side of Ruby Valley, known at first as Camp Ruby, later as Fort Ruby. The purpose of having a post at this place was to prevent the Shoshone and Goshute Indians from attacking the emigrants, mail stations, and settlers. The soldiers from Fort Ruby policed the trail both ways — east to Deep Creek Station on

596 The writer is in possession of photostatic copies of the letters filed in the Old Records Division of the adjutant's office of the war department. The descriptions of the forts were obtained from *Outline descriptions of United States Military Posts and Stations in the year 1871*. War department, quartermaster-general's office, Washington, 1871; this information has not been published before.

597 The last troops were at Fort Churchill in September, 1869. The site was abandoned by the army in that year and the general land office assumed jurisdiction over it. In 1933, the Daughters of the American Revolution were made custodians of the ruins of the fort. The fort was offered for sale in 1870. It brought $750. Everything removable was taken away.

the Utah-Nevada line, and west as far as Austin, one hundred and twenty miles distant. The men from Fort Churchill handled the road from Austin through to the Sierra Nevada.

After the second battle on the Truckee river in June, 1860, most of the Indians fled north into the desert, where they almost starved to death. Colonel F. W. Lander, in the surveying service of the federal government, was at that time surveying and constructing a road across the Sierra Nevada in the vicinity of Honey Lake Valley. Early in August, he and about seventy of his men, all armed, had a skirmish with the Indians in the Black Rock Desert country. One of his men was killed; the loss to the enemy was never ascertained. After the Indians were defeated, Colonel Lander held a peace talk with the chief, who said his people were starving. Soon afterward acting-Agent Warren Wasson, left in charge of Indian affairs by Agent Dodge, gathered the Indians together on the Pyramid Lake Reservation. On the last of July, 1860, Wasson posted notices which warned several squatters who had taken up fertile land on the Truckee river, after the soldiers were stationed there, that they must leave. In December, he gave every man in the Paiute tribe around Pyramid Lake a hickory shirt and a pair of blue overalls, and every woman some calico cloth, needles, and thread. The agent won the undying admiration of the tribesmen by pulling off his own shirt to give to an old Indian who had arrived too late to benefit from the gift distribution.[598]

In May and April, 1861, while another uprising similar to the one just described, was being planned in an assemblage of fifteen hundred Indians near the mouth of the Walker river, news of their intentions was conveyed to Wasson by a young Paiute interpreter. The plan was to kill the agent and later attack Fort Churchill. When Wasson learned of these plans, he boldly entered the Indians' camp, where he persuaded them to desist from these intentions.[599]

In July, 1861, Governor Nye arrived to take up his duties as governor of Nevada territory. He was appointed, also, ex-officio superintendent of Indian affairs in his territory,

[598] Angel, *op. cit.*, 165.
[599] *Loc. cit.*

for which he received an additional one thousand dollars.

Governor Nye retained Wasson as agent. He served in this position until May, 1862, when he was appointed United States marshal and commissioner of internal revenue.[600] Governor Nye's first visit to the Paiutes on the Walker river was made shortly after his arrival in July, 1861, with Agent Wasson, under the escort of a company of dragoons from Fort Churchill. He explained to the head chief that a new territory had been created in which the Indian would be treated the same as the white man. Both races would receive the same punishment for a crime. The governor promised the Indians some horses, cattle, and farming tools if they would remain friendly. When he distributed presents, including three beef cattle, they agreed to support him. Nye then proceeded at once to visit the Pyramid Lake Indians, where the same promises and gift distribution were repeated.[601]

The winter of 1861 was another intolerably severe one. Again the Indians suffered intensely from the cold, and again they held the white man responsible. For food, the Mono Indians drove off and killed some cattle belonging to farmers in Owens Valley, California. The nearest settlement was Aurora, Nevada, some distance to the northwest. In retaliation, the cattle owners, assisted by men from Aurora, killed some of the Indians. The red men accepted what they considered a challenge, and killed four white men. In 1862 a small war ensued in which a number of Indians and several white men were killed. Forces went from Fort Churchill and the military department of California. The ultimate outcome of efforts at keeping the Indians in check in this vicinity was the establishment of Fort Independence north of Owens Lake, from which place presents were distributed and peace was at last made. Fort Independence was placed, however, under the direction of the commanding officer of Fort Churchill.[602] In 1865 company c First Infantry, Nevada Volunteers, was stationed at Fort Independence.[603]

[600] J. R. Doolittle, *Report of Condition of Indian Affairs*, 518-519.

[601] *House Ex. Doc.* no. 1, 37 Cong., 2 sess., 717-720 (ser. no. 1117) ; *Report of Governor Nye to Secretary of the Interior*, 1861.

[602] Angel, *op. cit.*, 166-168.

[603] *Old Records Division, Adjutant General's Office, War Department*, Washington, D. C., ms., vol. 4, *Records of Fort Churchill, Nevada*.

In May, 1862, Agent Wasson arranged a conference between Governor Nye and the Paiute Indian chiefs, Old
Winnemucca and Numaga. The governor wished to meet
the chiefs as part of his duties as superintendent of Indian
affairs for the territory of Nevada. He was accompanied to
the lower bend of the Truckee by Captain Price and one
hundred cavalry of the California Volunteers. At that point
on the river the governor's party halted – it had been informed that Chief Winnemucca had positively refused to
allow soldiers to approach any nearer his camping ground
at Pyramid Lake. This fact, however, had been carefully
kept from Captain Price, lest he should resent the hostile
feeling and thereby bring on another war, whereas the governor had come in the spirit of peace.

At this particular time, while Numaga was away in the
north, Winnemucca was "sulking in his tent" on account of
the death of Wahe, who claimed to be a spirit chief. He had
been killed a short time before by two of the Paiute chiefs.
Agent Wasson had persuaded Winnemucca, however, to
come to the conference-ground in grand, barbaric style, with
four hundred of his warriors. During the two-day conference,
these warriors kept up a continuous war dance on live coals;
other feats of pain and endurance were exhibited for the edification and entertainment of the white soldiers. On the third
day Numaga, the diplomat of the tribe, arrived. Although
he and the governor had a long discussion, no specific treaty
was made. Presents were exchanged, however, and the two
parties separated on friendly terms.[604]

On October 25, 1863, another unfortunate occurrence inflamed the Indian against the increasing number of whites
who were cutting down his pine nut trees and disregarding all
his rights. This time it was a chief whose dead body was found
in the Carson river by some of his tribe. In consequence of
the loss of their leader, about thirteen hundred Paiutes assembled at Carson Sink, and dispatched a message to Fort
Churchill demanding redress for the murder of their chief,
who was known to the white people as Captain George.
Lieutenant Oscar Jewett was sent with a messenger to parley
with them. An agreement was decided upon: as damages for

604 Angel, *op. cit.*, 168.

the loss of their chief, they were given a wagonload of provisions and clothing, and $1000 in money.

In 1864 the Indians killed a number of white men who were prospecting in the northwestern part of the state near Paradise Valley. There were also murders reported from many other parts of the territory. It was necessary, therefore, for the army to set out on expeditions to frighten the Indian into submission. At daylight on March 14, 1865, Captain Wells with a company of cavalry surprised a camp of Paiutes on Mud Lake, north of Winnemucca Lake, and killed every Indian in it.[605] Reports were brought to military headquarters of murders and depredations on the Granite Creek Desert north of Pyramid Lake, in Paradise Valley, and on Quinn river.

When rich mines in southern Idaho were discovered, the nearest mail station from the west was Chico, California. The mail road extended from that town to Honey Lake Valley, over into Nevada by the Smoke Creek Desert Route north of Pyramid Lake, to Granite Creek Desert, northeast to the Humboldt river, thence through Paradise Valley and across Quinn river to Idaho. The Indians along this route were particularly hostile to the station keepers, ranchers, and mail carriers. In 1865 almost every settlement in this part of Nevada appealed to the military authorities for protection.

The continued fights between the Indians and whites of western Nevada spread to the Indians in eastern Nevada, where the Shoshones assembled in war array in several places in Lander county. The department of Nevada was called upon to suppress their activities. In the summer of 1865 Colonel Charles McDermit, commander-in-chief of the department of Nevada, took the field. In a number of skirmishes the Indians were routed with a heavy loss of life, while two white men were killed and several wounded. On August 7, 1865, while the colonel was returning to Quinn River Station (later named Camp McDermit), on the line between Idaho and Nevada, he was shot from ambush and lived only four hours. His body was taken to Fort Churchill

---

[605] It was reported by Major McDermit to Governor Blaisdel of Nevada, that thirty-two Indians were killed. Angel, *op. cit.,* 170.

for burial. The army continued its activities in this section for the rest of the summer. The station was renamed for the colonel.

In eastern Nevada it was the same story. In 1861 a most heinous crime was committed against a party of emigrants at Gravelly Ford on the Humboldt river; again in 1862 the emigrant trains reported many depredations. The Goshute war of 1863 was the worst one in eastern Nevada. One of the incidents of that war was illustrative of several acts committed by this tribe. On March 23 the keeper of Eight Mile Station was killed by Goshutes. The story of it was told as follows:

> The overland stage, bound east, contained four passengers, Judge G. N. Mott, of Nevada, an old man and his two little sons. Henry Harper, "Happy Harry," was the driver on this occasion.
>
> As the stage arrived at the scene of the tragedy it was received by a volley from the savages, who were concealed in and about the house, followed by the Indian war whoop. . . Away dashed the frightened horses guided by the unerring hand of the driver, whose life-blood was flowing from a mortal wound. The old man, struck with an arrow, sank into the bottom of the coach-boot, unconscious, and the only chance of escape that remained for any of them rested in the nerve, skill and bravery of the hero inside. Clinging to the lines and fighting against the death that was creeping around his vitals, the driver urged forward those maddened animals in his struggle for the safety of those whose lives were intrusted to his charge, until a film gathering in his eyes, he called to the judge to come out and take his place. While the stage was flying at the top of the horses' speed, Judge Mott made his way by clinging to the sides of the coach to the driver's assistance, and as he grasped the lines "Happy Harry" sank dying under the seat. . .[606]

Judge Mott brought the stage into Deep Creek Station with the dead driver and the passengers. One of the horses died from wounds received in this race for life. Detachments of soldiers from Camp Douglas, Utah, and Fort Ruby scoured the country for the Goshutes and Shoshones who were committing similar atrocities on the overland mail stations. The loss to the Overland Stage Company in Utah and Nevada from the Goshute war was one hundred and fifty horses, seven stations, and sixteen men.[607] By 1866 most of the se-

[606] Angel, op. cit., 180.
[607] Ibid., 183.

FORT McDERMIT, HUMBOLDT COUNTY
From a rare early photograph.

verest Indian hostilities were over.[608] To subdue the red
man in Nevada the federal government had to build and to
maintain thirteen military forts and stations, and keep over
one thousand soldiers in the field most of the time. Due to
the fact that most of the Indian wars in this state were
fought during the Civil War, and the regular soldiers were
called to the East, volunteers had to be recruited from California and Nevada. The Overland Route was the only one
open to the Pacific. Since Indians, urged on in some cases by
copperheads and deserters, threatened to close it, it had to
be policed by soldiers. On three different occasions Brigadier-
general G. Wright, commander-in-chief of the department
of the Pacific with headquarters at the Presidio, called upon
Governor Nye to raise, mount, equip and subsist 1,180 men
for an enlistment period of three years. General Wright
furnished the arms and ammunition, and the federal government furnished the money for the material used in building the
forts. The story of the financial burden thus thrust upon
the young territory of Nevada has been discussed in a previous chapter.[609]

In addition to Fort Churchill, headquarters for the military district of Nevada, several other forts were built. In
northwestern Nevada Fort Winfield Scott was established
on December 12, 1866, forty-five miles north of Winnemucca, at the foot of the Santa Rosa range on the west side
and near the head of Paradise Valley. Quarters for one
hundred men and several officers were made of adobe and
shingled. The storehouses of sod, a hospital of rough stone
with a thatched roof, the guard house of the same material
with one cell and "very insecure," and cavalry and quartermaster's stables built out of willow and cottonwood sticks
and thatched with straw, comprised the remainder of the
buildings.[610]

Thirty-five miles north of Camp Winfield Scott, on the
Idaho-Nevada line, eighty miles north of Winnemucca, Fort
McDermit was built. Although there had been a station at

---

[608] There were small depredations committed by the Indians as late as 1911.

[609] *Supra*, 275-276.

[610] *Outline Descriptions of the Posts and Stations of Troops in the Military
Division of the Pacific commanded by Major John M. Schofield*, 26.

this place on the Quinn river, a fort was not ordered built there until August 14, 1865. It was the largest in northern Nevada. Over ten thousand acres were declared a part of the military reserve for it. Three officers' quarters and two very large barracks, all one story, were built of stone and shingled; a hospital of stone consisting of three rooms, one with a capacity for six beds, and a guard house, comprised the main buildings. The storehouses and stables were very large. One stone building, seventy-five by thirty-four feet, was used for the commissary and quartermaster's storehouse. In addition to the supplies for one company for one year, which were always kept on hand, a considerable amount of food for the Indians was also stored there. One large frame building for forage with capacity for three hundred thousand pounds of grain, and two stables, one of stone and one of frame, were built with a commissary corral of logs in stockade form connecting them.[611]

Camp or Fort McGarry near Summit Lake was built on the Applegate Cutoff to Oregon. Such names in this vicinity as Massacre Lake, Soldier Meadows, and Forty-nine cañon, recall vividly the events that prompted the federal government to establish Fort McGarry on September 9, 1867. The area set aside for this fort was at Summit Lake, north of Soldier Creek in the High Rock cañon territory of western Humboldt county. There were probably few places on the emigrant trails more replete with tragedies of Indian attacks than this. As early as 1844, when Captain Levi Scott and Captain Lindsay Applegate, with a scout named Garrison, were planning the emigrant road through this region to Oregon, two Indians approached them, apparently in a friendly spirit. When close enough to fire, they shot and killed Garrison; Captain Scott's arm was pinned to his side with an arrow. Wounded as he was, he killed one of the Indians; the other fled. Massacre Lake was named for a fearful slaughter of emigrants which took place near there in

---

[611] *Descriptions of Posts and Stations . . .*, 24; Fort McDermit was relinquished December 1, 1886. It was later turned over to the interior department. It is now used as a school and a reservation for the Indians. *United States Military Reservations, National Cemeteries and Military Parks*, 484. On the present maps, "McDermitt" is the form of spelling used.

the summer of 1850, a tragedy concerning which little is known. It seems, however, that this train was a particularly large one composed of several companies. The party had been bothered by the Indians on the Humboldt Trail, and several red men had been killed. Finally the party decided to make a united drive against the Indians, a fatal mistake. Although the Indians were driven back of the train and the white forces returned to their main encampment, the natives were not beaten. Almost at once, they gained on the white train, and attacked the camp when it was not prepared to defend itself. The men of the train finally gained the victory, but not until forty of them had been killed in defense of their wives and children. They were all buried in a common and unmarked grave. Every precaution was taken to obliterate its location lest the Indians disinter and desecrate the bodies.

The Overland Trail led west through High Rock cañon, favorite camping place of many emigrant parties. The good water from the springs, grass for the livestock, and the natural fortification provided by the cañon made it a desirable camping ground in the covered-wagon days. A guard at each end of the cañon kept the emigrants comparatively safe. On one side of the cañon there was a cave, from the ceiling of which at some past time a large smooth slab of rock had fallen and become embedded in perpendicular position in the floor. The names of a number of emigrants, passing through this cañon, were either painted or chiselled on the slab.[612]

In this section of Nevada there are a number of emigrants' and soldiers' graves marked only by mounds of dirt or rock cairns. When the Indians became particularly hostile to the people going through to the Vicksburg mines in the Owyhee river country in southern Idaho in the early sixties, the government was forced to build several forts and establish several stations along the way.

The foregoing description of the forts in 1865 and 1866 has been obtained from records in the war department hitherto unpublished. In December, 1865, and January and Febru-

---

[612] An excellent description of the history of this part of Nevada was given by William S. Brown in the *Sacramento Bee,* March 11, 1931.

ary, 1866, Captain D. J. Williamson, chief quartermaster of the Nevada district with headquarters at Fort Churchill, made a tour of inspection of the posts and stations in northern Nevada. From his report the following descriptions have been obtained. Fort McGarry was only a camp on January 1, 1866. The kitchen and messes were the same as in the field; the bake oven was rudely constructed but answered the purpose well. The perishable stores were preserved from danger by being raised from the ground on poles, and the stables were made of willow and their roofs thatched. The men were living either in Sibley tents or rude huts which they had constructed themselves. Captain Williamson recommended that the camp be improved and a permanent fort built at this point.

Later a number of stone buildings were erected some distance south of Fort McGarry for the men, officers, and soldiers in Soldier Meadows. A short distance south of the fort a stone barn large enough to hold one hundred horses, officers' quarters, and a mess hall and barracks were constructed. Through underground passages the men could go to the barn or from the mess hall to the barracks without exposing themselves. In the latter buildings, whose walls were two feet thick, connections were made between the fireplaces.[613]

In 1863 James A. and R. B. Dun settled on the east side of the Humboldt river, not far from Unionville, Humboldt county. They, in company with one Ragan, drove about five hundred cattle from California, and took up a ranch at Dun Glen where they fed their cattle. The Indians attacked the ranch, killed Ragan, and drove off most of the cattle. In answer to the appeal to the military authorities in Paradise Valley, a detachment of soldiers was sent in pursuit of the Indians. The red men with the cattle were found; the latter were recovered. A post was then established at Dun Glen, and a company of cavalry detailed to that place.[614]

[613] Hamersley, op. cit., 144. Camp McGarry was relinquished March 25, 1871. The area around the camp is now a Paiute and Shoshone Indian reservation.

[614] On January 6, 1866, Captain Williamson inspected Dun Glen. He reported the post to be in good condition. Captain George D. Conrad, Second Cavalry California Volunteers, commanded the post. Old Records Division, MS., vol. IV, 89.

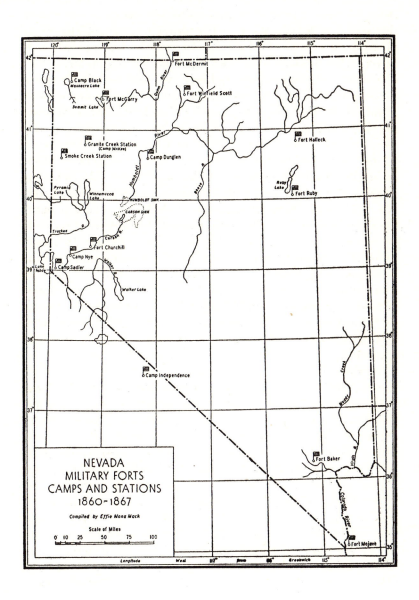

NEVADA
MILITARY FORTS
CAMPS AND STATIONS
1860~1867

Compiled by *Effie Mona Mack*

Scale of Miles

0   10   25      50      75      100

At the time the Chico-Idaho mail road had to be kept open, several camps were maintained in Nevada to protect the stages. The Smoke Creek Station near the California-Nevada line east of Honey Lake Valley was made head-quarters of the sub-district of Nevada. In December, 1865, Captain Williamson inspected this post. Because it was only a temporary camp, he recommended its abandonment and removal of the troops to Granite Creek Station, forty-five miles northeast of Smoke Creek, at the intersection of the road from California by the way of Chico and Susanville to Idaho and Humboldt river county.[615] Granite Creek Station, located north of Winnemucca Lake, was known also as Camp McKee.[616] Camp Black was a floating post. It appears from the records of the war department that there were a number of camps in Nevada by that name. However, there was never more than one Camp Black at any one time. In 1865-1866 there was a Camp Black in Humboldt county estab-lished as an outpost of Fort McDermit.

Two other temporary camps were maintained in western Nevada – Camp Sadler at Carson City, and Camp Nye near the mouth of King's cañon near Carson City. The soldiers and camp equipment for these stations were sent from Fort Churchill.

At the time the surveyors and workmen were constructing the Central Pacific Railroad across Nevada, the federal government helped to protect the workmen in every way. In 1867 the military authorities established Fort Halleck, named for General Henry W. Halleck, twelve miles south of the proposed railroad. When the railroad was completed, the post was thirty miles from Elko, the nearest supply depot; and by wagon seventy miles north of Camp Ruby. The additional reason for establishing a fort at this point was that it could protect both the Humboldt River Route and the Hastings' Cutoff which came through the pass be-tween the east Humboldt range and the Ruby mountains. By executive order, over 10,900 acres were set aside for the military reservation, the largest one in eastern Nevada. Two

[615] *Old Records Division,* vol. IV, MS., 187.

[616] Camp McKee was abandoned and all of the government stores were moved up to Fort McGarry in October, 1866. *Ibid.,* IV, 152.

barracks, one of logs and one adobe, were built to accommodate two hundred men. The four officers' quarters were
of frame and adobe; the storehouses consisted of the quartermaster's and the commissary buildings, and the granary. The
latter building, fifty-nine by twenty-four and one-half feet,
with walls eight feet high, was sufficiently large to hold four
hundred thousand pounds of grain. The adobe hospital of
four rooms, a six cell guard-house built of three inch planks
and bolted with iron, the cavalry and quartermaster's stables
of frame, comprised the rest of the buildings. This post was
supplied with water by a two mile ditch from a spring at the
foot of Ruby range, and by a large stream of water which
ran in the creek bed near the camp from early spring until
July.[617]

There is no way to estimate the number of soldiers stationed in Nevada because the strength of the companies
differed from time to time. There are references to companies of one hundred men each and more. Taking one
hundred men to each company as an average, there were
probably over one thousand soldiers and the necessary officers
to command these troops in Nevada in 1865-1866. The
following is a list of the companies and the forts at which
they were stationed on August 24, 1865:

Company A 1st Inf. Nev. Vols. at Fort Churchill
Company B 1st Inf. Nev. Vols. at Fort Ruby
Company C 1st Inf. Nev. Vols. at Camp Independence
Company D 1st Inf. Nev. Vols. at Camp Nye
Company E 1st Inf. Nev. Vols. at Camp Black (Paradise Valley)
Detachment of
Company F 1st Inf. Nev. Vols. at Fort Churchill
Company B 2nd Cav. Cal. Vols. at Camp Dun Glen
Company D 2nd Cav. Cal. Vols. at Camp Smoke Creek Station
Company I 2nd Cav. Cal. Vols. at Camp McDermit (Quinn's River
Station)
Company D 6th Inf. Cal. Vols. at Camp McDermit (Quinn's River
Station)
Company I 6th Inf. Cal. Vols. at Camp Black (Paradise Valley) [618]

[617] *Outline Description of the Posts and Stations of Troops in the Military
Division of the Pacific commanded by Major General John M. Schofield*, 23.
Fort Halleck was relinquished October 11, 1876. *United States Military Reser-
vations, National Cemeteries and Military Parks*, 481.

[618] *Old Records Division*, adjutant-general's office, vol. IV, records of Fort

Among the many photostatic letters and copies of orders obtained by the writer from the office of the adjutant-general in the war department, there was only one which gave a summary of the activities of the military authorities in Nevada at any particular time. Because this period is a closed chapter, not only in the history of Nevada but of the nation, and because the full significance of the attitude of the military authorities in command of the district of Nevada toward the Indian can be obtained only from the exact wording of the report, the following letter is given in full:

Headquarters, District of Nevada<br>Fort Churchill, Aug. 25th, 1865

Col. R. C. Drum, A.A. Genl. U.S.A.
Hd. Qrs. San Francisco, Cal.

SIR: I have the honor to transmit herewith, for the information of the Major General Commanding the Department, and such further reference as may be deemed proper, a report by Maj. M. O'Brien, 6th Inf. Cal. Vols. of his operations and operations in which he participated from July 16th Ult. to the date of his report, August 18th inst. accompanied by his report of August 2d inst. to the late District Commander, and referred to in his report of the 18th inst. also, official copies of instructions received from the late District Commander for his guidance in constructing a Post at Paradise Valley, also, sub-reports of Lieuts. Osmer and Overend, both of the 2d Cav. Cal. Vols., of operations in which they participated. I would most respectfully invite particular attention to that portion of the reports of Maj. O'Brien and Lieut. Overend relating to the vicinity in which the late much lamented Lt. Col. McDermit was killed. I will here respectfully state for the information of the Commanding General, that that entire Country, surrounding "Camp McDermit," Quinn's River Station, has been thoroughly *searched* and *scoured* in pursuit of Indians, officers and men vieing with each other in their determined eagerness to avenge the death of their late much beloved Commander, and not an Indian can be found at the present time in that portion of this District; it being the general opinion, that they have *all* retired into that wilderness country in the vicinity of Pyramid Lake, disheartened and wearied out, where they will undoubtedly be glad to quietly remain, in their mountain fastnesses, until winter, when as their hoarded stores have been to a great extent captured and destroyed, they will be forced to come out into the valleys and make terms; or should they not come to terms they will then be easily captured or destroyed. And here I deem it proper to respectfully recommend that in case they come to terms, and are disposed to be friendly, and conduct themselves properly, certain provisions should be made to supply them with certain articles of subsistence, that they may not be driven by

Churchill, Nevada, district of Nevada, letters sent, August 18, 1865, to June 13, 1867.

OFFICERS IN FRONT OF THEIR HEADQUARTERS, FORT McDERMIT
Reproduced from the only known copy of this photograph.

hunger and starvation to plunder and pillage upon unprotected whites and in so doing, perhaps, when resisted, resort to murder and arson. Dun Glen, at present a depot of supplies for troops further advanced, and where store-houses, and quarters for troops, are furnished without cost to the Government, would be a good point from which to distribute these supplies to the Indians, as recommended above. I would also invite particular attention to that portion of Major O'Brien's reports having reference to Paradise Valley and the practicability or impracticability of establishing a Post at that point; and would most respectfully state that his report as to the impracticability of obtaining wood for fuel, and timber, or even poles for building purposes is fully corroborated by the reports, formal, informal and verbal of all Officers, men and citizens who have been in that valley from this vicinity; and I shall write under another cover today recommending certain dispositions of troops in *that vicinity,* and enclosing official copies of orders from these Hd. Qrs. holding the troops in readiness for the disposition recommended, should the same meet with the approval of the Maj. Genl. Comdg. the Dept. I also enclose Report of Major L. P. Smith, and would respectfully recommend that two companies, one of Infantry and one of Cavalry, from California, be stationed on the route to Idaho, as recommended by Maj. Smith and that the Q.M. Dept. be authorized to hire buildings at a fair rate of compensation for the protection of Government property and supplies. I also have the honor to report for the information of the Major General Commanding, that on the 23d inst. I had a "big talk" with three of the principal Chiefs of the Piutes, "Capt. Charlie," "Capt. Big George" and "Capt. Ben," who came into Fort Churchill with an interpreter and some of their tribes, "to see their new master the Big Captain," (as they style the District Commander), "they had all heard of the death of their late master, Col. McDermit, who was a good Father to them; all their Tribes had grieved much, men, women and children had shed many tears, and were very anxious as to the treatment they would receive from their new master, who had succeeded their late respected and much loved Father, Col. McDermit. They desired that the most friendly relations should exist between themselves and the whites; all their tribes desired to be at peace with the white people; they would drive all the bad Indians out from among them, would not allow bad or hostile Indians from other tribes to come or remain among them, or within their lines, but would drive them out, and immediately inform the 'Big Captain' or the nearest Captain to them. They hoped their new 'Master' would treat them kindly, and protect them from harm, at the hands of bad white people, and that he would be a good Father to them, like their late master, Col. McDermit." "They had also heard of the death of the 'Great Chief' General Wright, and the sad manner thereof, and had grieved much thereat, he had been a good Chief, whom they had much loved, had treated them kindly, and been a good Father to them." They also desired much to see their Great Father, General McDonell, and had hoped he would come to Fort Churchill that they might see him, and have a "big talk with him." Captain Charley was the principal Chief and spokesman, being very dignified and intelligent. They were told that the new District Commander had heard of them, that they were good Indians, and could be relied on as friends to the white people, that he was glad to see them and shake them cordially by the hand, that he would be a kind Father to all good Indians, would protect them from bad whites who should make them terrible, etc. But that all bad Indians and "bad white men" alike must be brought to punishment and were advised to surrender up to the Civil and Military authorities at once any Indians who may be guilty of committing any depredations whatever, returning or causing to be returned any property that may be or may have been stolen from white people, and that by so doing they would save themselves much trouble, and would be able to maintain friendly relations with the whites, and would be entitled to, and would receive my protection and the protection of all civil and military authorities; and that should they receive bad treatment at the hands of "bad white men," they should not take the matter into their own hands, and resent their injuries, but come to me, or the nearest Commanding Officer, and represent the matter, and they would receive protection, and the "bad white men" would be brought to punishment, and where it was possible be made to make amends, by repairing their injuries or damages.

On taking leave "Captain Charley" expressed much satisfaction at having met the new District Commander, and was glad to know that he would be a kind Father and protector to all good Indians, and that he would go among all the minor Tribes of the Piutes and visit their Chiefs and inform them of what the new District Commander had said, and that his advice would be deeply heeded and carried into effect. And in proof of the sincerity of these Piute Chiefs, I beg leave to state for the information of the Commanding General, that when they first heard that the late Col. McDermit had been killed by hostile Indians, they volunteered and appeared anxious to lead two hundred (200) Piute warriors against the Hostile bands in the Humboldt Country, to avenge his death and their loss; and in this connection I may say that some of these Piute warriors would be no despicable or despisable foe; Capt. Big George stands over six feet three in his moccassins, and must weigh over two hundred and twenty pounds. Before they left the Post, I directed that a few rations of subsistence be issued to them, to which they appeared somewhat indifferent, but for which they expressed many thanks.

Other reports of operations participated in by Officers on detachment service, or in the campaign against the hostile Indians in the Humboldt Country, are in course of preparation, and will be transmitted at the earliest practicable moment, for the information of the Major General Commanding the Department.

I have the honor to remain, Colonel, very respectfully, your obedient servant,

A. E. HOOKER,
Lt. Col. 6th Inf. Cal. Vols. Comdg. District.[619]

619 *Old Records Division,* vol. IV, MS., records of Fort Churchill, Nevada (district of Nevada, letters sent, August 18, 1865, to June 13, 1867).

The coming of the railroad brought the usefulness of most of the western forts to an end. Their history was a part of the story of the continual expansion and consolidation of the American republic. The soldiers were detailed to guard the trails, protect the infant settlements on the frontier, and furnish a fighting force to subdue the attacking Indians.

In Nevada, where the Indians' food was so limited, the army post furnished the red man with food and clothing until the federal government established reservations for him and aided him to be partially self-supporting. Most of the Indian attacks were induced through excessive want and privation. The Indians lost the battle against the forward march of civilization. Although the federal government continued for a short time to keep up the largest forts in Nevada after the coming of the railroad, and although there were intermittent uprisings as late as 1911, there was little need for forts after 1868.

The effect of the soldier on the red man was not entirely wholesome. Much complaint was made by the bucks against the relations of soldiers with the young squaws. The white man furnished the Indians with intoxicating liquors, firearms, and ammunition. The trading in these latter was so common that the Nevada territorial legislature passed a law forbidding the sale of liquors, firearms, and ammunition to Indians, and added a penalty of five hundred dollars fine and six months' imprisonment.[620] To protect the Indian further, the Nevada legislature passed another law which made it a misdemeanor for a white man to marry an Indian, or perform a marriage ceremony between members of the two races. The penalty was a heavy fine and imprisonment of at least a year.[621]

About one hundred thousand dollars was expended in Nevada by the federal government between 1861 and 1864 for food, for clothing, and for supplies for the Indians to use on their farm allotments on the reservations. This amount seemed to the congress very large, but it must be remembered that at that time supplies had to be brought from the East by steamship to San Francisco and freighted over the moun-

[620] *Laws of Nevada Territory,* 1862, 27.
[621] *Laws of Nevada Territory,* 1861, 93.

tains and then taken out to the military posts where distribution was made. Governor Nye made a visit at least once every year to all tribes under his jurisdiction, at which time he distributed the gifts in person. The history of the Indian reservations extends beyond the scope of this work.[622] The Indian fought, but always was forced to retreat, until finally the superior race with better and more effective arms won. Several of the forts were later turned into Indian reservations. Today many Indian children play in and around the buildings which once housed the soldiers sent to subdue their forefathers.

[622] At the present time there are Indian reservations or Indian schools in Nevada near Carson City, Fallon, Fort McDermit, Fort Mojave, Moapa river, Pyramid Lake, Summit Lake, Walker river (Schurz), and Duck Valley.

# From Pack Animal to Railroad

Few communities in the United States were as isolated as the settlements of western Nevada in the period of their earliest history. Steep and almost impassable mountains impeded travel to the west; seven hundred miles of desert and sagebrush separated the people from the nearest communities to the east. Hostile Indians infested most of the routes across the desert. The problem of transportation and communication was greater than in any other frontier community — California not excepted. That state had water communication. Because of this isolated position, some means of communication with the rest of the world had to be made. The conquering of the obstacles in the way of opening the routes, the establishing of means of communication, and providing for the transportation with very little aid from the federal government, were some of the important factors in the development of the western empire. The part played by the first settlements in Nevada in overcoming the physical features of the Great Basin and in hastening to forge the last connecting link in transcontinental communication made a thrilling and romantic story.

The Indians, the trappers, the traders, and the Forty-niners had threaded Nevada with trails before the first permanent settlement was made. In 1851, however, simultaneously with the first permanent settlement, the federal government ordered a monthly mail service between Salt Lake City and Sacramento. Thirty-seven bids were received for a service over this route. They ranged from $20,000 for "horseback or two horse coach service," to $200,000 a year for a service of "135 pack animals with 45 men, divided into three parties." Absalom Woodward and George Chorpenning, having made the lowest bid of $14,000 a year for a thirty-day service, were awarded the contract. The route was to go by the then traveled road,[623] which ran from Sacramento by the way of Folsom and Placerville, thence over the old emigrant trail to Carson Valley, where it followed the Carson-Humboldt-Goose Creek Road to Great Salt Lake City, a distance of about seven hundred and fifty miles.

The first mail carried by this firm, packed on the backs of mules, left Sacramento on May 1, 1851. It took Chorpenning and several men sixteen days and nights to get through the snow in the Sierra Nevada to Carson Valley. In order to open a narrow trail for the animals, the men had to beat down the snow with wooden mauls. When the party reached Carson Valley there was not yet a permanent settlement there, but John Reese and his companions came out from Salt Lake the following July. Chorpenning, being impressed with the splendid wild hay and the adaptability for a mail station, selected a quarter section of land near what later became the townsite of Genoa. He then proceeded eastward with the mail, consuming seven weeks instead of the prescribed thirty days to make the first trip.[624]

The difficulties of this route were too numerous to mention. During the winter, the snow in the mountains on the western end of the route and in the Goose Creek mountains (northeastern Elko county) on the eastern end of the trip fell from ten to twenty feet on the level; it drifted from forty to fifty feet deep in the cañons and gorges. In the spring the Carson and Humboldt rivers were so swollen that they had to be swum. From Stone House Station on the Humboldt river eastward the whole country was infested with hostile bands of Indians who lay in wait to kill and rob the mail parties. In November, 1851, Colonel Woodward, in charge of the mail, and two young companions, John Hawthorne and Oscar Fitzer, were killed by the Indians at Gravel Point near Stone House Station.[625] The snow was so deep in December and January that the mails of 1851 could not be taken through the mountains, but the February mail of 1852 was pushed through in sixty days by way of the Feather river, Beckwourth Pass, Truckee and Humboldt rivers route. The carriers on this

---

[623] House Ex. Doc. no. 56, 32 Cong., 1 sess., pp. 398, 399 (ser. no. 643).
[624] Le Roy R. Hafen, The Overland Mail, 1849-1869, 64.
[625] Angel, History of Nevada, 103.

trip endured dreadful sufferings; their horses having frozen
to death in the Goose Creek mountains, the men walked the
last two hundred miles to Salt Lake City with the mail packed
on their backs.[626] After this frightful trip, the special mail
agent in San Francisco permitted the mail to be carried down
the coast to San Pedro, thence through Cajon Pass and over
the Mormon Trail to Salt Lake City. Thereafter, the Car-
son-Humboldt Route was used during the summer months
only, and the southern route when the passes were closed in
winter. This meant that the people of Carson Valley had to
find some other way to obtain supplies and have communication with the outside world.

In 1853 Fred Bishop and a man named Dritt alternated
with each other in making trips on snowshoes from Placerville to Carson Valley. They were succeeded by George
Pierce and John A. Thompson, the latter a powerful Nor-
wegian, known as "Snowshoe" Thompson. He was to become the hero of the Sierra as a result of his feats on snowshoes. From 1856 until the road was kept free from snow
for the stagecoaches, Thompson provided the only means
of communication available to the ranchers in Carson Valley
and the placer miners in Gold cañon during the winter
months.

In 1851 "Snowshoe" Thompson was smitten with the
gold fever and he went to California. He mined in the vicinity
of Placerville, but, not being satisfied with results, he went
to Putah Creek, Sacramento Valley, where he was a rancher
during 1856 and 1857. He did not like ranching any more
than he did mining; he longed for the snowy peaks of the
mountains with which he had been familiar as a boy in his
native land. Early in the winter of 1856, while he was still
on his Putah Creek ranch, he read in the newspapers about
the trouble the government was having in getting the mails
across the Sierra Nevada. Here was a chance for him to
return to the life he loved so much. He made a pair of snowshoes from some oak timber which he was at that time engaged in splitting.[627] He had no pattern by which to make

[626] Hafen, *op. cit.,* 64.

[627] His original snowshoes are now in Sutter's Fort, Sacramento, among
the souvenirs of the early days.

them except the memory of the ones he had used in Norway. After fashioning his shoes, he set out for Placerville to try them out. He spent several days in practicing, so that when he made his first public appearance he was able to perform stunts which astonished everyone. Mounted upon his snow-shoes and with his long balance pole in his hands, he dashed down the mountain sides at such a terrific speed that many people said he was foolhardy. But Thompson knew what he could do on them; he was satisfied he could carry the mail.

He made his first trip in January, 1856, from Placerville to Carson Valley, a distance of ninety miles with the heavy pack of mail on his back. Having made the first trip success-fully, he went on carrying the mail all of that winter, giving the Nevada settlers communication with the rest of the world. Thompson never failed in all of the time he was pack-ing over the mountains to bring in the mail. No matter how wild the storms he always came through; he never stopped for anything and always set out on the day appointed without regard for the weather. He traveled by night as well as by day. There was no beaten path for him to follow; by day he was guided by the trees and rocks, and by night he looked to the stars with which he was as familiar as ever was Han-steen, the great astronomer of his native country.

For many years he carried the mails across the Sierra Nevada when there was no other way provided. For two years during this time there was no contract to pay for his trips. At each terminal of his route he was promised that an appropriation would be made and that he would be paid for his services, but he received nothing but promises. For the two year service without pay, and for all he had done in the other years he asked only six thousand dollars. His petition to congress was signed by all of the state officials of Nevada and by many other people who appreciated his work. In the winter of 1874 he even went to Washington at his own expense to present his claim, but he never received anything but promises and was paid in the same coin.

"Snowshoe" Thompson was modest throughout his life, and never boasted of his great feats. He looked upon the things he did as belonging to the business of everyday life. He spent his last days on his ranch in Diamond Valley at the foot of his beloved mountains. On May 15, 1876, he died at the early age of forty-nine years; he is still "at home" in a humble grave in the quaint little cemetery at the base of the mountains in Genoa. The snowy peaks of the Sierra Nevada look down on his last resting place "where the voices of the pines are borne to him by every breeze and where the trembling ground often tells of the fall of the avalanche." [628]

Due to the fact that the special mail agent in San Francisco had not explained the reasons for the irregularity of the service to Salt Lake City, the postmaster general annulled the contract with Chorpenning. He then made one with W. L. Blanchard of California.[629] When Chorpenning learned of the Blanchard contract, he went to Washington at once to present his case to his chief. The result was a verbal agreement for him to carry the mail for $30,000 per year until 1858 over the Los Angeles-Salt Lake Route.

In 1854 the legislature of California appointed commissioners to lay out a road from Placerville to Carson Valley. The contract for carrying the mails for four years was again given to Chorpenning, who was joined in the contract by Ben Holladay. These two men were given permission to use a covered wagon and a four-mule team so that passengers could be carried also.[630] This arrangement was convenient for the people of western Utah to go regularly to California or Salt Lake City. Chorpenning and Holladay continued their service until 1857, when J. B. Crandall established a tri-weekly line of stages between Placerville and Genoa. The original contractors had the line from Genoa to the Utah settlements. In 1857, George Brown, one of their mail agents on the Humboldt river and incidentally the backer of the Grosh boys in their silver claims in Gold cañon, was killed by the Indians.

[628] Thompson carried the mail to the placer miners in Gold cañon, Chinatown, and Johntown. He saw the hole in which Peter O'Reilly and Pat McLaughlin struck the first silver ore a short time before the strike was made. He was told by them that they were getting very fair prospects for gold. *A memorial to "Snowshoe" Thompson, hero of the Sierras,* November 14, 1926. Carthay Center, Los Angeles, California (pamphlet).

[629] This contract provided for $50,000 a year, out of which a fortified post in Carson Valley had to be maintained. Hafen, *op. cit.,* 66.

[630] Bancroft, *History of Nevada, Colorado, and Wyoming,* 227.

When the contracts for the mail service west of Salt Lake City were let, George Chorpenning was again the successful bidder. The contract provided for a semi-monthly service at $34,400 a year. A provision in the contract included weekly trips at $130,000 a year.[631] The old emigrant trail was still being used — north of Salt Lake to the Humboldt river and thence by the way of the Carson river and over the Johnson Cutoff to California. Although the Nevada stretch of the road was the most difficult to negotiate, the mail was usually brought in on time. In 1858 a comment on the service was made in a San Francisco newspaper: "The mail leaving Salt Lake on the 16th of July had no change of animals for nearly seven hundred miles, but it made the sink of the Humboldt in twelve days, from whence it is only two days journey to Placerville." [632] In the same year Crandall transferred his Pioneer Stage Line to Lew Brady and Company which instituted a semi-weekly service between Sacramento and Genoa. This company, in turn, connected with the Chorpenning-Holladay overland mail wagons from that city to St. Joseph, Missouri, thereby completing the first mail and stage service between the Missouri and Sacramento rivers.

The first eastward bound coach left Placerville on June 5, 1858; the first arrival from the east at Placerville was on the following July 19.[633] Among the men connected with the line in Genoa was Major William M. Ormsby, who acted as the agent for the Pioneer Stage Company at that place; Mark Hopkins, the later railroad magnate, established several of the mail stations between Placerville and Genoa.[634] The improvement of the road followed almost immediately after the line was inaugurated. Stations were established along the route; the stock was improved, and the amount of mail carried increased rapidly. During the winter of 1858, "Snowshoe" Thompson and J. S. Child started a new stage line between Placerville and Genoa, using sleighs between Strawberry Station and Carson Valley. By these means the road was open all winter for the first time.[635]

---

[631] Hafen, op. cit., 110.

[632] San Francisco Daily Bulletin, August 10, 1858.

[633] Bancroft, History of Nevada, Colorado, and Wyoming, 227.

[634] Angel, op. cit., 104.

[635] Bancroft, History of Nevada, Colorado, and Wyoming, 228.

While the first transcontinental mail line was being established by private enterprise, the federal government was carrying on exploratory work for the most suitable route to the Pacific by the central route. As early as the spring of 1854, Lieutenant E. G. Beckwith was ordered to survey a line west on the forty-second parallel. He succeeded, after some difficulty, in making his reconnaissance from the southern shore of the Great Salt Lake, thence southwest to the Goshute mountains in eastern Nevada, and through the Humboldt mountains to the Humboldt river. The river was followed as far as Lassen's Meadows (Rye Patch) where he turned due west and examined several of the northern passes through the Sierra Nevada. On September 12, he returned to Washington and recommended the forty-first parallel for a railroad. Realizing, however, that it would be many years before a railroad could be built, the citizens of California began to agitate for the speedy construction of good military roads to California protected by forts along the way. In 1854 the first meeting for this purpose was held in San Francisco. The state legislature sent a memorial to congress in which the construction of three or more roads across the northern, central, and southern portions of the state was urged. The federal government was granted the right of way to construct these roads through any portion of the state.[636] Although the memorial was laid on the table, the California delegation in congress introduced a bill for the construction of a military road from some point on the Missouri river by the way of Great Salt Lake and Carson Valley to California. Although the bill was unsuccessful, it inaugurated the movement from which results were soon to come. During the third session of the same congress, $300,000 was appropriated to construct a wagon road from Fort Kearney, Nebraska, by way of South Pass-Humboldt river and Honey Lake Route.[637] Before the road was built, however, more exploratory work had to be done.

By 1855 there were only two traveled routes across the territory from the Great Salt Lake to the Sierra Nevada: the Los Angeles-Salt Lake and the Humboldt river routes.

[636] *California Assembly Journal*, 1856, 35-38.
[637] *Cong. Globe*, 34 Cong., 1 sess., 1485.

There was, however, a third one that had been used by Howard Egan, a major in the Mormon battalion and a well-known guide and mountaineer who had been engaged for some years in driving stock to California. On these trips he had explored a route which lay south of Salt Lake City on the fortieth parallel north latitude until it reached the Hastings' Pass in the Humboldt mountains. At this point it branched off in a southwesterly direction toward Carson Lake, thence it turned up the Carson river to Genoa. This route, Egan maintained, was a much shorter one than either of the traveled routes. In September, 1855, he won a bet by making the round trip from Salt Lake City to Sacramento on mule-back in ten days.[638] Thereafter it was used as a horse or mule trail until October, 1858, when George Chorpenning, with very little work, made the trail usable for mail wagons, and by December had moved his stock, coaches, stands and forts to the Egan route.

In 1859, Captain J. H. Simpson of the topographical engineers was ordered by General Albert Sidney Johnston to explore the Great Basin with a view to finding a direct wagon route from Camp Floyd, Utah, to Genoa, Carson Valley. Simpson's route was practically identical with Egan's as far as Ruby Valley. At this point he turned south, but since there was more grass and water on Egan's route, he recommended that it be used for the entire distance.[639] After this time the Egan-Simpson route became the most traveled highway across Nevada until the building of the railroad. A team and wagon could cover it in a week's time.

Simultaneously with the "rush to Washoe" in the spring of 1860 a fast express across this route was established by the Central Overland Express Company. As early as 1855, Senator William M. Gwin had vainly tried to persuade the federal government to provide such a service for California. In the winter of 1859-1860, William H. Russell, Alexander Majors, and W. B. Waddell established the pony express with the idea of demonstrating the practicability of the central route so as to secure the mail contract from the Missouri river to the Pacific coast. This firm had been oper-

[638] Egan, *Pioneering the West*, 193-197.

[639] J. H. Simpson, *Report of Explorations across the Great Basin of the Territory of Utah.*

ating a semi-monthly mail service between Atchison, Kansas, and Salt Lake City. They had built many stations between the Missouri [640] and the lake, but across the region which was soon to become the territory of Nevada there had to be built some thirty home and change stations at a distance from nine to twenty-five miles apart. The expenditure for the pony express was prodigious – $100,000 in gold at the outset, chiefly to build stations in Nevada, and for purchase of ponies. Before the service could be put into operation at least two men for each station had to be employed; one hundred young men of the proper weight, morals, and courage had to be found to ride the ponies; and a herd of five hundred horses had to be purchased.

On April 3, 1860, in San Francisco, a "clean-limbed hardy little nankeen-colored pony" stood saddled in his flag bedecked stall awaiting his rider. A crowd of people was there to cheer the first pony to leave. He had only to go to the boat which was to carry the express to Sacramento where the real pony express started. The route from this point went by way of Placerville, Carson City, Dayton, Fort Churchill, to Carson Sink, thence over the Simpson-Egan route to Salt Lake City, and on to St. Joseph, Missouri, where on the same day a pony and his rider left for the West. The distance between the two terminals was two thousand miles which had to be ridden in about ten days.

The station houses were built of logs, stone, or adobe, depending upon the material available in the region. There were two kinds of stations: home stations and change stations. The former were larger than the latter, being built to accommodate the riders at the end of their runs. The agent at the home station had a key with which he opened the mail pouches on the arrival of each rider; he counted the number of letters and recorded the rider's arrival and departure. At first the horses were the finest that could be obtained in the West, the California half-mustang. These horses were ridden at the fastest pace they could be made to go, from four to nine miles an hour, depending upon the terrain.

The pony express riders were the finest young men the

[640] The writer was born at Seneca, Kansas, one of the pony express stations about seventy miles west of St. Joseph, Missouri.

frontier could produce. They had to be light of weight, abstemious of habit, and steel of nerve. The boys had to outfit themselves, so there was no uniformity of dress. In general, however, they wore a buckskin hunting shirt, cloth trousers tucked into high boots, and a cap or slouch hat. In stormy weather they wore a complete buckskin suit so as to shed the rain. They provided also their own arms — one or more Colt's six shooters eight inches in length, and an eighteen inch knife. At first a rider's assignment was from twenty-five to thirty miles, but as the service progressed, the distance was increased to from seventy to one hundred miles. Sometimes a rider had to do double duty. If he rode into a station and found that his "relief" had been killed or was ill, he had to take the mail on for him.[641] The best known riders through Nevada were Sam Hamilton, Jay G. Kelly, and Robert H. "Pony Bob" Haslam. The quickest time on record for the express was the one which carried a copy of President Lincoln's first message to congress. It required only five days and eighteen hours — made with double sets of horses, fresh horses at some point between stations, to bring the message from St. Joseph, Missouri, to the legislature of the new territory of Nevada in Carson City, a distance of 1,780 miles. A round trip was made regularly over a run twice a week, for which the rider received from $50 to $150 a month.

The mail was placed in four small leather pouches called *cantinas,* each about six by twelve inches in size. These pouches, sewed on the corners of the large square "machier" (*mochila*), were fitted over the saddle, one letter pouch in front and one behind each leg of the rider. Three of the pouches carried "through mail" and the fourth one contained "way mail." The *mochila* was lifted from the saddle of the incoming rider and transferred to the waiting saddle horse in two minutes. The letters, written on thinnest paper, placed in equally thin envelopes, and bearing the pony express stamp, were wrapped in oilskin in order to keep them dry. At the beginning of the service, $5 for each half ounce or fraction thereof was charged, plus the federal govern-

---

[641] "Buffalo Bill" Cody rode continuously for 320 miles in twenty-one hours and forty minutes. Hafen, *op. cit.,* 178.

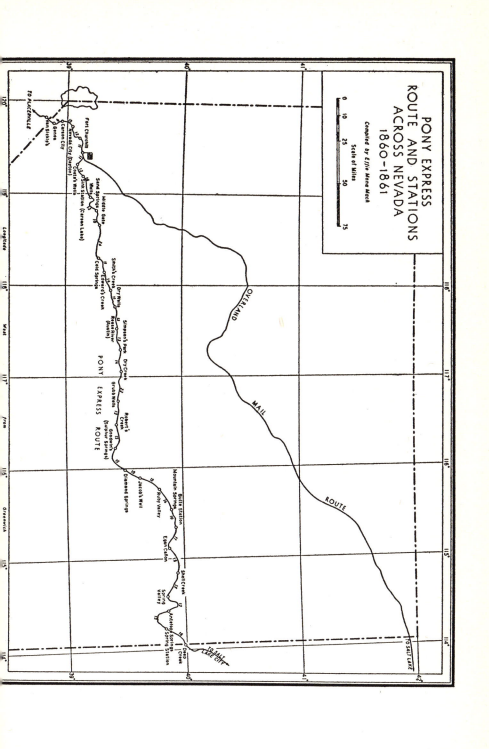

PONY EXPRESS
ROUTE AND STATIONS
ACROSS NEVADA
1860-1861

Compiled by Effie Mona Mack

Scale of Miles

0    10    25         50              75

PONY EXPRESS ROUTE

OVERLAND MAIL ROUTE

TO PLACERVILLE

Fort Churchill
Carson City
Carson City (Dayton)
Genoa
Van Sickle's
Cradlebaugh's Wells
Sink Station (Carson Lake)
Sand Springs Wells
Middle Gate
Cold Springs
Edward's Creek
Smith's Creek
Dry Wells
Simpson's Park
Reese River (Austin)
Dry Creek
Grubb Wells
Robert's Creek
Goodson's (Sulphur Springs)
Diamond Springs
Mountain Springs
Jacob's Well
Ruby Valley
Butte Station
Egan Cañon
Shell Creek
Spring Valley
Antelope Springs
Spring Station
Deep Creek

TO SALT LAKE CITY
TO SALT LAKE

Longitude    West    from    Greenwich

ment's tax of ten cents. As the service progressed, the fee
was gradually reduced to one dollar per half ounce. Twenty
pounds of mail was the maximum any rider was required
to carry.

Although during the eighteen months existence of the
pony express a total of 29,000 letters were carried, it was
estimated that the firm lost a million and a half dollars in
the enterprise. The service had no sooner been started than
it was to meet its first serious difficulty. During the spring
of 1860, in the Indian uprisings in Nevada, a number of
stations were burned; some of the agents were killed, and
large numbers of their stock were driven off. The stations
were rebuilt of stone or adobe with very thick walls.[642] It
has been estimated this war in Nevada cost the proprietors
of the pony express about $75,000.[643] It required twenty
picked men from Fort Churchill and Ruby Station to accompany the express from Carson City to Salt Lake City.[644]

[642] *Territorial Enterprise,* August 4, 1860.
[643] Glenn D. Bradley, *Story of the Pony Express,* 174.
[644] *San Francisco Daily Bulletin,* June 25, 1860.
The time table from Placerville to Salt Lake City was especially interesting;
the average speed of four miles an hour was made:

| Town | Miles | Hours |
|---|---|---|
| Placerville | 12 | 3 |
| Sportsman's Hall | 12 | 3 |
| Morse's | 12 | 3 |
| Webb's | 12 | 3:15 |
| Strawberry Valley | 14 | 4 |
| Yank's | 12 | 3:15 |
| Rider's (California) | 10 | 2:30 |
| Van Sickle's (Nevada territory) | 9 | 2:15 |
| Carson City | 13 | 3 |
| Nevada City (Dayton) | 12 | 2:15 |
| (?) Station | 11 | 2 |
| Fort Churchill | 11 | 2 |
| Coates' Wells | 12 | 2 |
| Sink Station (Carson Lake) | 16 | 7 |
| Wells | 12 | 3:30 |
| Sand Springs | 10 | 4 |
| Middle Gate | 24 | 7:15 |
| Cold Springs | 11 | 2:45 |
| Edward's Creek | 14 | 4:15 |
| Smith's Creek | 11 | 5:15 |
| Dry Wells | 13 | 3:15 |

Space does not permit dwelling upon the romance and service of the pony express. Although it was a losing undertaking for its owners, at least a part of the purpose for which it was created was realized: the central route was proved to be the most practicable. It was also an invaluable aid in uniting the West and the East at one of the most critical periods in American history. Its passing was regretted.[645]

| Station | | |
|---|---|---|
| Reese river | 13 | 2 |
| Simpson's Park | 14 | 4 |
| Dry Creek | 22 | 8 |
| Grubb Wells | 12 | 4 |
| Robert's Creek | 15 | 3:30 |
| Goodwin's (Sulphur Springs) | 15 | 3:15 |
| Diamond Springs | 10 | 2:30 |
| Jacob's Well | 12 | 3:45 |
| Ruby Valley | 14 | 2:45 |
| Mountain Springs | 10 | 2:30 |
| Butte Station | 11 | 3:30 |
| Egan cañon | 15 | 5:15 |
| Shell Creek | 15 | 3:30 |
| Spring Valley | 12 | 2:35 |
| Antelope Springs | 15 | 2 |
| Spring Station (Nevada) | 16 | 4 |
| Deep Creek (Utah) | 8 | 1:45 |
| Cañon Station | 15 | 3 |
| Willow Springs | 15 | 3:15 |
| Butte or Desert Station | 11 | 3:45 |
| Smith's Springs | 12 | 4:15 |
| Dug Out | 25 | 5 |
| Simpson's Springs | 20 | 4:15 |
| Point Lookout | 15 | 4:15 |
| Rush's Valley | 10 | 2 |
| Camp Floyd | 20 | 4:15 |
| Joe's Dug Out | 10 | 1:30 |
| Fort Rockwell | 14 | 1:30 |
| Travellers' Rest | 14 | 1:30 |
| Salt Lake City | 10 | 1:15 |

*Daily Alta California*, August 28, 1861. Mr. Clel Georgetta, a Reno attorney, now owns the ranch on which the pony express station was formerly built at Spring Station, Nevada, three miles from the Utah-Nevada line.

[645] The more romantic side of the pony express may be read in the following books: Majors, *Seventy Years on the Frontier;* Root and Connelley, *The Overland Stage to California;* W. L. Visscher, *Thrilling and Truthful History of the Pony Express;* the best account of the postal service from the Mississippi to the Pacific can be found in Le Roy R. Hafen, *The Overland Mail.*

An eloquent eulogy to the pony was published in a San Francisco newspaper:

A fast and faithful friend has the pony been to our far-off state. Summer and winter, storm and shine, day and night, he has travelled, bounding like a weaver's shuttle back and forth, till now his work is done. A week ago ended his useful and most memorable career. Good-bye, pony! No proud and star-caparisoned charger in the war-field has ever done so great, so true, and so good a work as thine. No pampered and world-famed racer of the turf will ever win from you the proud fame of the fleet courser of the continent. You came to us often with tidings that made your feet beautiful on the tops of the mountains; tidings of the great world's life; of nations rising for liberty, and winning the days of battles and victories; defeats and reverses. We have looked for you as those who wait for the morning, and how seldom did you fail us; when days were months, and hours weeks, how you thrilled us out of our pain and suspense, to know the worst. You have served us well![646]

It was the telegraph that clicked the pony aside. In May, 1858, Messrs. Bee, Lovell, Bishop, Jones, and Randall organized the Placerville, Humboldt, and Salt Lake Telegraph Company. The people of Carson Valley subscribed $1200 toward the project; they offered to take more stock if necessary to secure the establishment of the line.[647] On July 4, 1858, the first pole was set on the line that was soon to become the transcontinental telegraph; by autumn the first wire to reach Nevada connected Genoa with Placerville; by the spring of 1859 it had reached Carson City; and during the following year the line was stretched to Virginia City. Fred A. Bee was the manager in that city. Because the wires were strung to trees wherever possible, the line became known as "Bee's Grapevine Line."

In June, 1860, congress passed an act for the construction of a telegraph line from the Missouri river to San Francisco. The act directed the secretary of the treasury to advertise for sealed proposals for the use by the government of a line or lines of telegraph to be constructed within two years from July 31, 1860, from some point on the west line of Missouri to San Francisco, for a period of ten years; and to award the contract to the lowest bidder, provided he did not require more than $40,000 per year. All the Pacific coast

646 *Daily Alta California*, November 2, 1861.
647 *Ibid.*, May 20, 1858.

companies availed themselves of this help from the federal government for the construction of a through wire. In consequence the Overland Telegraph Company was organized with a capital of $1,250,000. The distance between the termini was divided into sections of which there were two in Nevada, Salt Lake City to Ruby Valley and Ruby Valley to Carson City. The work in Nevada was begun in May, 1861. It took less than four months to build the line to Salt Lake City where it was connected with the line that was being built from the eastern terminus. In Nevada the line was built along the central route by way of Austin and Ruby Valley; it was operated in connection with the Overland Stage and Mail Line until the completion of the Central Pacific Railroad, when they were both abandoned.[648]

As the building of the telegraph line advanced each way, the distance for the pony to run was lessened – Fort Kearney, Nebraska, was the eastern terminus, Fort Churchill, Nevada, the western one. There was not the speed then in sending telegraphic messages as now. The messages had to be relayed from one point to another – for instance, from Fort Churchill to Carson City there was a continuous line. When the message was received at the latter place it was written down by a single operator, who relayed it to the operator at Placerville, who in turn wrote it down and re-telegraphed it to San Francisco.[649]

At the opening of the Civil War, the Butterfield Company moved their Southern Daily Overland Mail, established in 1859 through northern Texas, New Mexico, Arizona to California, to the central route through Nevada. Since there was no mail going to California by the way of South America or the Isthmus of Panama, the only transcontinental mail and telegraph service passed through Nevada. Congress gave the Butterfield Company a million-dollar contract to carry six hundred pounds a trip, twenty days, for eight months; and twenty-three days, for the other four months. This line operated six days a week.[650]

The Pioneer Stage Line was the sub-contractor for the

[648] Angel, *op. cit.,* 106.

[649] *Daily Evening Bulletin,* May 25, 1861.

[650] *Sen. Ex. Doc.* no. 1, 37 Cong., 2 sess., 555, 560 (ser. no. 1119).

Overland Company from Virginia City to points in California. After the "rush to Washoe" and the opening of other mining camps in western Nevada, there was so much business that it required many stations, seventy-five coaches, thirty drivers, and two hundred and sixty-eight horses. In the postmaster-general's report this line was numbered route 14,620. Most of the pony express stations were taken over by this line. In addition to these, Fair View, Still Water, and Virginia City were added.[651] On account of the exorbitant cost of hay, grain, and other provisions in Salt Lake City, together with the expense and difficulty of transporting them to the stations along the way, the Overland Stage Company started its own stock and grain farm in Ruby Valley; it was found to be highly profitable. In 1865 the company employed on its farm one hundred men, thirty plows, and ninety yoke of oxen; ninety thousand pounds of grain were sown. It is interesting to note this stage farm was the first land to be cultivated in eastern Nevada.[652] The same company purchased two blocks of ground at Carson City, where it erected stables, blacksmith and coach shops. Before the Civil War was over there was a continuous stage and telegraph connection across the United States.

The most famous piece of this stage line was the short stretch between Virginia City, Nevada, and Placerville, California. After the discovery of the Comstock Lode, it became the "Main Street" of the far West. The Pioneer Stage Company operated this stretch of the road. To put it into proper shape, it cost its owners $500,000 to build, and $5,000 a mile per year to maintain. This short distance was so remunerative in its business that sub-leases were granted for shorter distances along the way. Over this highway thousands of people traveled, and millions of pounds of freight were carried. Some idea of the colossal amount of freighting over this road may be obtained from the statement of one firm in Virginia City in 1861. In a single month, November of that year, one firm alone, Kelly, Mott and

651 *House Ex. Doc.* no. 24, 38 Cong., 2 sess., 10, 11 (ser. no. 1223).

652 Angel, *op. cit.*, 106. In 1865 the yield was 8,575 bushels of oats, 1,655 bushels of potatoes, 1,854 bushels of turnips, 1,000 bushels of carrots, and 78 bushels of beets.

Company, a hardware firm in Virginia City, received 390,817 pounds of merchandise; the freight charge on this amount was $17,591.26.[653] In the same year, 25,000 passengers went over this line.[654] By 1863, to serve the freighting demands alone of the mining towns in Nevada, 15,000 mules and horses and 3,000 men were employed.

From 1860 to the building of the Central Pacific Railroad, this highway was truly the Main Street of America. In no other part of the United States was there the traffic, the excitement, or the efficiency which was present on this short stretch of one hundred and fifty miles. Over it freighting teams, stagecoaches, droves of sheep and hogs, wild Mexican cattle, pack trains, miners on foot or on burros passed continuously. There were in the neighborhood of one hundred stations, each with a stable, saloon, a general merchandise store, and a hotel or lodging house. The stages ran day and night so that a passenger could travel through to his destination without staying over. It took but eighteen hours to make the trip from Virginia City to Sacramento; a record trip of twelve hours and twenty-three minutes was made when three Virginia City miners chartered a stagecoach.

The coaches used came from the factories of Abbott, Downing Company, of Concord, New Hampshire. Each coach, designed to carry nine passengers, cost in the neighborhood of $1,000 delivered; a set of six harness cost about $225. The six horses used to draw the coach were the best obtainable. The team was matched as to size, color, and endurance – the wheelers, those next to the coach, were larger than the leaders. Two men, the conductor or express messenger and the driver, accompanied each coach. The former had complete charge of the mail and express for his run of about two hundred miles. He rode on top with the driver, whose run was generally about fifty miles, or from one home station to another. Home stations, about fifty miles apart, had a hotel, telegraph, and a blacksmith shop;

---

[653] *Territorial Enterprise,* November 1, 1861. It has been estimated that during the early sixties over 100,000,000 pounds of freight passed and at least half that much went over the Henness Pass Road.

[654] *Daily Alta California,* July 26, 1861.

division stations at about ten mile intervals had repair shops only.

The messenger sat on top in his dickey-seat with a revolver in each hand, and a finger on each trigger cocked, in readiness to shoot the first bandit who might jump from the bushes or from behind rocks to rob him of his precious cargo. The driver was the hero of the age. He, his conveyance, his chargers, and his highway have been described:

. . . A sprinkled road over which dashed six fine sleek horses before an elegant Concord coach, the lines in the hands of an expert, whose light hat and linen duster and lemon-colored gloves betokened a good salary and exacting company, and who timed his grooms and his passengers by a heavy gold chronometer watch, held carelessly, if not conspicuously, on the tips of his fingers.[655]

The arrival of one of these stagecoaches was the occasion for the entire populace to turn out, if possible, to see it come in. It was at that moment the driver became the object of admiration. With the fast click-clack of the galloping horses, the cannon crack of the whip, the familiar "Hi! Hi!" to his steeds, the scream of the brakes as he pulled back on the reins to bring the rearing leaders and lurching coach to a sudden stop, this important personage brought in his cargo and passengers. "Hank" Monk, one of the most colorful stage drivers of the West, has been immortalized by Mark Twain in *Roughing It* when the humorist described how Hank drove Horace Greeley up this "city street" at a breakneck speed to meet a speaking engagement in Placerville.[656] From a more sober pen came the description of the experience in a ride over this same route by Samuel Bowles, editor of the *Springfield Republican*, and Vice-president Schuyler Colfax:

The ride over the mountains, down their western slopes, on to the ocean, was a succession of delights and surprises. The surging and soughing of the wind among the tall pines of the Sierras came like sweetest music, laden with memories of home and friends and youth. . . The pines of these mountains, indeed, seemed to us monsters - three, four, five feet through, and running up to heaven for light, straight and clear as an arrow by the hundred feet . . . along and far below the road on which our horses galloped up hill and down at a fearful pace. . . To keep the road hard and

[655] Bancroft, *History of Nevada, Colorado, and Wyoming,* 230.
[656] Mark Twain, *Roughing It.*

in repair as well as to allay the fearful dust that would otherwise have made the ride a trial rather than a pleasure, nearly the whole line was artificially watered during the long, dry summer. Luxurious as this seems - the daily sprinkling of one hundred and fifty miles of mountain road - and expensive as it was, it was found to be the simplest and cheapest mode of keeping the road in good repair. The stages were drawn by six fleet, gay horses, changed every ten miles, without the driver's even leaving his seat.

Thus munificently prepared, and amid the finest mountain scenery in the world, we swept up the hills at a round trot, and rolled down again at the sharpest gallop, turning abrupt corners without a pull-up, twisting among and past the loaded teams of freight toiling over into Nevada, and running along the edge of high precipices, all as deftly as the skater flies or the steam car runs; though for many a moment we held our fainting breath at what seemed great risks or dare-devil performances.[657]

Vice-president Colfax well said, in one of his western speeches, that "it required more talent to be a justice of the peace in the country, so he was sure much more was necessary to drive a stagecoach down the Sierras as we were driven, than to be a member of congress."

The freighting over this stretch of road was one of the most interesting and unusual in the history of transportation. On account of the very steep grades and the heavy machinery that had to be hauled over them, especially strong wagons had to be built. The "Washoe wagon," as it was known, was made in Stockton and Placerville. John M. Studebaker, a founder of the Studebaker factories, was a Placerville wagon maker. An imported hickory and ash and very strong wrought iron were used in their construction. They had very powerful brakes, stronger and heavier frames and deeper beds than those built in the East. The average load of twenty-four tons was placed into three of these wagons which in turn were fastened together and pulled by a sixteen-mule team. The best drivers were the bullwhackers of the early emigrant days. They had a curious character – they were very large and strong with long unkempt hair and a face covered with a stiff beard. These teams were not driven in the usual manner – the driver either walked, rode the swing mule, or sat in the wagon box. The mules were not guided by reins. With a long whip and equally long oaths, of which it has been said they were the longest in the world, the mules were made to know the direction

[657] Samuel Bowles, *Our New West,* 51-52.

to go or the thing to do. To the handle of the whip, about three feet in length, was attached a twenty foot braided rawhide lash. The slightest move of the handle or the crack of the whip, stopped, started, and turned the team. At certain intervals along the road, spaces protected by a rock wall were built. They were large enough to turn the long equipage around. The mule teams, horse drawn vehicles, and pack mules announced their approach by a string of small bright brass bells hung on a metal arch over the bearskin fur collar of the harness.[658]

During the first few years after the discovery of the Comstock, the Placerville road collected an average of $693,000 a year in tolls for freight teams alone; the passenger tolls were proportionately higher. Five million dollars was the estimated value of all the transportation facilities used on this road.

From state line on the Nevada-California boundary, to Placerville, gray granite milestone markers resembling the old-fashioned tombstone, indicated the distance. On the center of each stone was a feathered arrow pointing westward, below the arrow there was the letter "P" for Placerville, and above the arrow, the number of miles between the marker and Placerville. Opposite the marker and in the center of the road, was placed a level block of granite.[659]

From the main line many roads radiated from Virginia City and Carson City. During the territorial period the federal government was very liberal in establishing postal roads, the most important of which ran to Aurora, Susanville, Star City, and Unionville.[660] Almost all were toll roads.

So many petitions were granted by the territorial legislatures that Mark Twain said that they "hung over the

---

[658] The writer has gained most of this information from old pioneers with whom she has talked. There are a number of these old teamsters left to tell of the many thrilling and interesting freighting days.

[659] Most of these markers are still in place. They can be seen where the new highway follows the old toll road. Each one was set exactly one mile from the other. The old and new highway are practically identical from Kyburz Station to Lake Tahoe.

[660] *House Misc. Doc.* no. 19, 36 Cong., 1 sess. (ser. no. 1064) ; *ibid.,* no. 80 (ser. no. 1065) ; *ibid.,* nos. 101, 103, 105, 39 Cong., 1 sess. (ser. no. 1271) ; *Cong. Globe,* 38 Cong., 1 sess., app. 239; *U.S. Statutes,* 38 Cong., 3 sess., 663.

edge like a fringe." In 1862 the territorial legislature granted thirty permits (including bridges) ; in 1864, thirty-two more. Many of these roads exhibited great engineering skill; among the best known were the road from Virginia City through the Devil's Gate to Silver City and Dayton, and the Geiger Grade from Virginia City to Steamboat Springs. One of the charters granted by the first territorial legislature was to C. W. Fuller of Susanville, who in March of 1860 settled on the Truckee river on the site of the present Riverside Hotel in Reno. This particular spot on the river had been a fording place used by the early emigrants.[661] There he built a rude log hotel and constructed a bridge across the river. On either side of the bridge he built a road, the northern part four miles in length connected with the Beckwourth road; the southern one connected with the Glendale road at Huffaker's. Fuller's bridge took three months to build, at a cost of $3,000.[662] Stone and Gates and Company commenced a bridge over the Truckee near Glendale a short time after. This company also applied for a franchise. The legislature granted it, but stipulated that no bridge could be built within three miles of Fuller's or the Stone and Gates' bridges. The territory and later the state received ten per cent of all of the money collected from the franchises granted for roads and bridges. The Fuller bridge carried most of the traffic which went to the Comstock and nearby towns over the Dutch Flat, and Henness Pass roads.

Although the Placerville Route to California was the most

[661] The ford was a diagonal one. It passed from the site of the present postoffice on Mill Street to the back of the Elks' Home, from which point the road angled off to the west. Church Lane, north of the Baptist Church, was a part of this old road. Statement of Mrs. D. B. Boyd to the writer, September 25, 1930.

[662] The legislature gave Fuller permission to charge the following tolls across his bridge:

| | |
|---|---|
| Pack animals or loose stock | $ .10 a head |
| Footmen | .25 a person |
| Horsemen | .50 a person |
| One or two horse wagon or pleasure carriage | 1.00 |
| Four horse or ox wagon | 1.25 |
| For every additional span of horses and yoke of oxen | .25 |

William M. Stewart was the attorney for the petitioner. *Territorial Records,* MS., office of the secretary of state, Carson City, Nevada, drawer 6.

famous and widely traveled, there were a number of other
roads from California to the Nevada mining towns – the
Big Tree Route through Sonora Pass to Carson City was
favored by the heavy freight teams but it was closed during
the winter; and the Henness Pass Road from the Nevada
City, Grass Valley, and Downieville region was used by the
people coming from that portion of California. When the
Central Pacific Railroad built its line as far as Dutch Flat
in 1864, the railroad company built a wagon road from that
point to Virginia City. Most of the freight was carried as
far as the railroad went, and then transferred to wagons
and thus it was freighted the rest of the way. The railroad
service took most of the business from the Placerville road;
the days of famous highways were over.[663]

In the spring of 1860 the Wells Fargo Express Company
purchased the Pioneer Stage Line from Genoa to Placerville. From two to seven cents an ounce in addition to the
regular postage rates were charged. To this company was
intrusted the safe transportation of the gold dust, silver
bullion, and coin. Before a bank was established in the territory of Nevada this company collected all the negotiable
instruments, notes, drafts, and bills. Some idea of the services
of the company to this frontier community may be gained
from the fact that the Wells Fargo Company carried $12,-
000,000 worth of bullion and money in the year 1863 for
the citizens of Nevada.[664]

To provide for the expanding commerce of a growing
territory, the ingenuity of the frontiersman was ever manifest. This characteristic was particularly true in the rugged
and inaccessible regions of the Great Basin. Although the
southernmost part of Nevada did not become an integral
part of the state until 1866,[665] its history, nevertheless, belongs to it. In the early sixties a number of Mormon families
settled on the Muddy river and along the Virgin river between its confluence with the Muddy and its mouth in the

---

663 *Infra,* 370.

664 *Virginia Daily Union,* March 14, 1864.

665 This section was first a part of the territory of New Mexico; in 1864
it became a part of the territory of Arizona; and in 1866 it was given to
Nevada.

Colorado river. Believing there was going to be a large increase of Zionites in this vicinity, the head of the church
ordered Anson B. Call in 1864 to build a fort at the head
of navigation on the Colorado. In obedience to his orders,
Call erected several dwellings, two warehouses, and a number of corrals. The small community that grew up around
this settlement (about three miles below the site of the
present Boulder cañon dam), was called Fort Callville.
The purpose of the fort was to receive the supplies and prose-
lytes brought by steamer from Mexican and California towns
lower down the river. At Callville they were transported by
wagons to the southern Nevada and the Utah settlements.
A steamer, the "Esmeralda," was procured to ply between
Mazatlán and Callville. At the former place goods consigned to the Utah settlements from eastern points, brought
around the horn as far as Mexico, were transferred to the
river boat, where they were brought up the Colorado river
to the Nevada fort. It was intended that the products of the
Mormons could be sold, and carried out by this river route.
In order to gain a passage for the "Esmeralda" through the
rapids just below Callville, a large bolt was set in an enormous reddish gray boulder on the Nevada side of the river
bank. Fastened to the bolt was a ring about twelve inches in
diameter. As the vessel approached or departed from the
"Ring Bolt Rapids," the tow line run through the ring was
wound or unwound by the steam winch on the deck. Navigation on the Colorado continued until the building of the
railroad ended the isolation of southern Nevada. Several
attempts to gain help from the federal government to remove the obstacles from the Colorado river bed were futile.
Several mail routes, however, were established from Utah
points to southern Nevada.[666]

To transport the large quantities of salt, needed by the
mills for reduction of the quartz, the waterless wastes
of the Nevada deserts had to be overcome. Camels were
brought to the state for this purpose. Experiments in camel
transportation in New Mexico and California by the war

[666] Angel, *op. cit.*, 489; *Message of Honorable Richard C. McCormick*, acting-governor of the territory of Arizona, to the second legislature, Prescott,
Arizona, December 11, 1865, 7.

department were made as early as 1855, most of them being
unsuccessful. In 1860 one of these experiments was made by
Captain Hancock. He started a camel express from Los
Angeles to Fort Mojave,[667] a distance of three hundred
miles. This line was known as the "Dromedary Line." After
a few trips it was discontinued, for the camels made no better
time than the government mules; they were more difficult
to handle,[668] and more expensive to maintain. There was one
use, however, to which the camels were put which was declared a success. In February, 1860, when the boundary line
between California and Nevada was being run from the
35th to the 37th parallel, three camels were taken from
Fort Tejon by Lieutenant Mowry, who was in charge of
the survey, and stationed at Fort Mojave. Dr. J. R. N. Owen
and fourteen men used them to establish supply depots for
the surveying parties between Fort Mojave and Lake Tahoe.
On leaving Mojave, the three camels in charge of Haga Ali,
a Turk who came over with the first shipment of camels
from Egypt, were loaded with fourteen hundred pounds of
water, food, and supplies.[669]

During the Civil War, Secretary Edward Stanton having
little time to give to the different reports concerning the
camel experiment, ordered them sold at public auction on
September 9, 1863. At that time there were thirty-five
camels in the different army camps in southern California. A
herd was taken to Benicia Barracks, where they were sold
on February 28, 1864, to Samuel McLeneghan who had
formerly been one of the caretakers. McLeneghan, in turn,
sold most of the animals in California. He selected, however,
ten of the best camels to constitute a train to carry freight
from Sacramento to points in Nevada territory. Of these
ten, seven had been born in California; they were from two
to four years old. "Old Tule," however, was thirty-five
years of age, and "Mary" was old, too. She had been one of

[667] Fort Mojave is just across the river from Nevada in Arizona. Part of
the Mohave Reservation is in the southernmost part of Nevada.

[668] Native Turks were brought along with the camels. A good account
of the camel experiment is given by Gray, Farquhar, and Lewis, *Camels in
Western America.*

[669] *Hayes Collection,* southern California, 1860-63, VIII, doc. 159.

BACTRIAN CAMELS IN NEVADA, 1861

Nine Bactrian camels were brought to Nevada in 1861 to carry salt from the marshes at the forks of Walker river to the mills of the Comstock Lode. This encampment is in Carson Valley.

the camels presented to the United States government by the sultan of Turkey in the first shipment in 1855.[670]

On March 31 nine camels (no mention was made of what happened to the tenth one) arrived in Sacramento en route to Nevada. When they reached the California capital the owners found the state fair in progress, so they decided to make some money by exhibiting the camels and racing them on the track. The exhibition and race were held, but from them there was little or no financial gain. The day after the race McLeneghan set out for Nevada, where he sold the camels to a mining company in Austin to carry salt from the marshes, southeast of Walker Lake, to the quartz mills. Edwin Franklin Morse, who spent a number of years in Nevada mining towns, said, "I have often seen trains of half a dozen camels coming into Austin with their loads."

The experiments by the federal government in testing out camels for transportation in California stimulated the organization of private companies to import them for similar purposes. In the spring of 1860, Otto Esche, a merchant in San Francisco, believing that camels were going to be in great demand in the mining sections of Nevada once they were introduced, went into the heart of China to obtain his herd. He was successful in negotiating for thirty-two Bactrian camels at Nicolaevsky, Mongolia, in the Amur river country.[671] Of the thirty-two purchased, only fifteen arrived in San Francisco, the others having died en route. The survivors were auctioned off, nine of which were purchased for the purpose of packing loads over the Sierra, and to run as regular camel transports to and from Placerville and the silver mining districts of Nevada.

These camels, however, were not used for anything other than to carry salt to the mills in the vicinity of Virginia City and along the Carson river. Each camel carried about five hundred and fifty pounds of salt.[672] These camels were driven by Mexicans "who seem not to know the difference between a mule and a camel." [673] They were not particularly well

[670] *Sacramento Daily Union*, April 2, 1864.
[671] Gray, Farquhar, and Lewis, *Camels in Western America*, 14.
[672] *Daily Evening Bulletin*, August 9, 1861.
[673] Gray, Farquhar, and Lewis, *op. cit.*, 16, fn. 55.

cared for. In 1865 a professor from Yale University reported
that during a trip through Nevada he saw some of these
camels near Virginia City. He said, "Their backs had not
been cared for, and they had been used in packing heavy loads
of salt from the deserts. Salt water and alkali had accumulated in the long hair of their humps, and great loathsome
sores nearly covered the parts touched by the saddles." [674]
The camels continued to carry salt to Virginia City from
the Esmeralda marshes until this product was found at Leeteville on the Carson river some sixty miles from the mills. [675]
It was no longer profitable to use them in this service so they
were turned out to roam. [676] However, as late as 1876, mention of them was made in the Virginia City newspaper when
it described a train of eight camels carrying wood to within
one hundred and fifty feet of the summit of Mount Davidson,
an altitude of nine thousand feet, for the purpose of making
a huge bonfire to celebrate the one hundredth anniversary
of independence.

The camel experiment in the West was the last one made
in transportation before the coming of the railroad. In 1862,
when President Lincoln signed the bill to construct a railroad from the Missouri river to the Pacific coast, the age
of the pony, the stagecoach, and the camel was doomed. It
was six years, however, before Nevada was crossed by rails.
By this time a transcontinental telegraph line had been built
and the Overland Stage and Wells Fargo Express companies
had instituted dependable and safe transportation facilities
across the broad western empire.

---

[674] Lewis Burt Lesley, *Uncle Sam's Camels*, 127.

[675] The camels became so troublesome on the highways in frightening teams,
that the Nevada legislature passed an act to prohibit camels and dromedaries
from running at large on or about the public highways of Nevada. This act was
repealed in March, 1899. *Nevada State Journal*, June 10, 1909.

[676] *Territorial Enterprise*, June 28, 1876.

# The Central Pacific Railroad crosses Nevada

On May 10, 1869, the impressive ceremony of joining the rails of the two great railroad lines at Promontory Point, territory of Utah, ended the long struggle for a transcontinental railroad. The long contest in congress over the route of the road, the great service rendered the Central Pacific Company by William M. Stewart, United States senator from Nevada, and the thrilling race between the Union and Central Pacific railroads, the former building westward from the Missouri, and the latter building eastward from California across the Nevada and Utah deserts, were some of the sensational episodes in this national drama. The participation of Nevada in this great enterprise was both geographic and political. To build a line directly from California to the Missouri river, Nevada had to be crossed.

Communication from coast to coast was a part of the process of the Americanization of the continent by the federal government. The origin of this idea has been attributed to Thomas Jefferson, whose part in bringing it about was his sending out of the Lewis and Clark expedition in 1804. The explorations made by this party proved that there were no insurmountable barriers to the establishment of a wagon road to the Pacific ocean by the way of the Columbia river. Discussion over such a road led to other government expeditions to the western mountain ranges which had to be crossed in such a project. The congress did not, however, have to aid the building of such a road. This work was begun by the trappers when they opened a trail to and beyond South Pass; it was finished by the emigrants who widened the trappers' trail for their wagons when the first settlers went through to Oregon and California.[677] Although

---

[677] Bancroft, *History of California,* VII, 495-497.

150,000 Americans had migrated over this road to the territory beyond the Rocky mountains by 1849, the federal government had not given aid to construction of a single mile
of wagon road west of Fort Leavenworth, Kansas. Many
routes across the plains and deserts, and many passes through
the mountains were explored during the gold rush days.
The most traveled wagon road across Nevada was the
Humboldt-Truckee Route explored by trappers, and used
by emigrants; the railroad engineers found no better route.
The Salt Lake-Los Angeles Route across southern Nevada
was explored similarly and a railroad later built along it.

When the federal government found it had no need to
build a wagon road, it turned its attention toward the building of a railroad. The task of finding the most feasible route
across the continent was given to the war department. A
number of surveys were conducted by this department, the
reports of which were presented to the congress with the
recommendations of the engineers in charge. Because most
of the secretaries of war during this period were southerners, the greater number of the routes were upon lines directly
west of the southern states. It is beyond the scope of this
work to discuss the routes proposed for a continental railroad.
The question of routes, however, delayed the actual construction. It was natural that every section of the country,
for selfish reasons chiefly, should advance the one route
which favored its own district, and disapprove of lines
proposed for other sections. It was the acquisition of the
Mexican territory in 1848 and the great rush of people to
central California that determined the route and the terminus
of the transcontinental railroad.

One more question had to be settled before actual work
was begun. Should the railroad traverse the northern or
southern part of the United States, and a branch line be
built to central California from either of these sections, or
should it be built directly across the United States? If the
question were settled in favor of the northern or southern
routes, Nevada would not be crossed; if the central route
were adopted, Nevada had to be crossed.

The results of the exploring expeditions of 1853 sent out
by Jefferson Davis, secretary of war, to ascertain the most

practicable and economical route for a railroad from the
Missouri river to the Pacific ocean, narrowed the choice to
five routes over which reconnaissances were to be made.
The ones selected were the northern trail between the forty-
seventh and forty-ninth parallels, the route between the
forty-first and forty-second parallels, the Benton "Buffalo
Trail" between the thirty-ninth and thirty-eighth parallels,
the thirty-fifth parallel trail, and the southern trail near the
thirty-second parallel.[678] Three of these crossed Nevada.
The route along the forty-second parallel from the Great
Salt Lake to Sacramento was explored by Lieutenant E. G.
Beckwith. He ran his survey line, however, along the forty-
first parallel from south of the Great Salt Lake to the Humboldt river, thence along the river to its sink, where instead
of turning south to run his line to the Truckee river, he
turned west and explored two routes through the Sierra
Nevada; first through the Madeline Pass, across Round
Valley, down Pit river cañon to Fort Reading, California;
and second, through the Noble Pass near Honey Lake, down
Battle Creek to Fort Reading, and thence to Sacramento
and Benicia. He estimated that it was a distance of 1,410
miles in a straight line, but 2,032 miles by the route he proposed; the sum of the ascents and descents was 29,120 feet,
and the estimated cost was $116,095,000.[679]

During the time the federal government was working on
the best route, the people in California, especially in the
central part, were anxious for their state to have quicker
and better means of transportation than that afforded by
water and wagon road. The state legislature, the local newspapers, and many other organizations became very active in
agitating for a railroad. There were sectional rivalries in
California, also, but the Sierra Nevada mountains helped
them to settle the question of location of the road.

The completion of a railroad might have been delayed
indefinitely had not the needs created by the Civil War forced
the issue. The federal government realized that a transcontinental railroad must be built to keep the western states
and territories in the Union. The Civil War determined,

[678] *Report of the Secretary of War*, February 27, 1855.
[679] *Pacific Railroad Report*, I, 31.

also, the route that was to be followed; a road could not be built through the seceded southern states. Thus war and secession ended the long struggle over choice of the route for a transcontinental railroad.

On July 1, 1862, President Lincoln signed the Pacific Railroad Bill,[680] which had two main provisions. The first one gave the Union Pacific Company the right to "locate, construct, furnish, maintain, and enjoy a continuous railroad and telegraph appurtenances from a point on the one hundredth meridian of longitude west from Greenwich, between the south margin of the Republican river, and the north margin of the valley of the Platte river, in the territory of Nebraska, to the western boundary of Nevada territory." The second section authorized the Central Pacific Railroad Company of California to construct a railroad and telegraphic line from the Pacific coast, at or near San Francisco, or the navigable waters of the Sacramento river, to the eastern boundary of California to connect with the main railroad and telegraph lines.

The successful completion of these railroads was considered of such great national importance that the congress, for the purpose of aiding their construction, gave to each company extensive grants of land. Under the Pacific Railroad Acts passed on July 1, 1862, and July 2, 1864, there was granted to the two companies every alternate section of public land, designated by odd numbers, within twenty miles of its road bed, excepting, however, mineral lands and tracts to which preëmption and homestead claims had legally been attached. These land grants were equivalent to twenty sections to each mile, or 12,800 acres. On the reserved mineral lands within ten miles on each side of the line, the timber was granted also to the company. These acts were in terms of a gift, and were, therefore, a full and perfect conveyance from the original source of the land title, the federal government. Since in Nevada there was very little land preëmpted, the Central Pacific Company received about five million acres of land.[681]

---

[680] Bancroft, *History of California*, VII, 495-549; *United States Statutes at Large*, XIV, 489-498.

[681] In making these surveys, Mount Diablo, a prominent peak near the junction of the Sacramento and the San Joaquin rivers, was selected as the

In addition to these munificent grants the federal government gave the two companies, through the railroad bills, United States treasury bonds of $1,000 each, to the amount of $16,000 per mile of constructed road. These bonds bore six per cent interest, and were payable in thirty years. For one hundred and fifty miles in the Rocky and Sierra Nevada mountains, the bonds were trebled to $48,000; and between these two ranges (that is, across the Great Basin in Nevada and Utah) the federal aid was doubled to $32,000 per mile for every twenty miles constructed. The track was to be of uniform width and gauge, to be determined by the president of the United States. A continuous railroad must be built from the Missouri river to the Sacramento river by July 1, 1876, or all privileges and aid from the government were to be forfeited.

It is the purpose of this narrative to relate only the most important features of the building of the Central Pacific Railroad across Nevada, hence the story will be limited to that which is necessary to assist the reader to understand this part of the project.[682]

"The Central Pacific Railroad found its origin in the enthusiasm of one man, and owed its completion to the determination and shrewdness of four." [683] The one man was Theodore D. Judah, organizer of the company and pioneer of the project. After he had made twenty-two examinations, some of them in the severest part of winter, of possible routes across the Sierra Nevada, he went east in the interest of the company; but while he was on this mission he fell ill and died. The four men were Leland Stanford, Republican governor of California, who was chosen president of the company; Collis Potter Huntington, vice-president; Mark Hopkins, treasurer; and Charles Crocker, in charge of the construction of the road. James Bailey was made secretary at first, but was soon succeeded by Edward H. Miller, a

initial or starting point. From this point four lines were run, two north and south called meridian lines, and two east and west called base lines, and from these lines the townships were surveyed east to Nevada. The railroad was given the odd numbered sections.

[682] A good account of the construction of the railroad is given in Edwin L. Sabin, *Building the Pacific Railway;* and Bancroft, *History of California,* VII.

[683] Reprinted from Cleland, *op. cit.,* 383, fn. 8, by permission of The Macmillan Company.

partner of Hopkins.[684] Edwin B. Crocker, justice of the supreme court of California, and brother of Charles, was a silent member of the firm. They formed a perfect combination – none of them was rich, but each had some money, and all had been accustomed to the hardships of the frontier. The work was divided among them. Huntington went east, where he handled the necessary legislation in the national capital, and where he purchased the building material; Charles Crocker was superintendent in charge of the actual construction of the line; Stanford handled the legislation in California; Judge Crocker gave the company the necessary legal advice; and Hopkins, assisting Stanford with the details in California, acted as the adviser to all of them.[685]

In addition to the federal, state, and county subsidies, the company expected to monopolize the enormous amount of freight going to and from the Comstock and the other mining towns in Nevada. Some idea of the revenue of that freight may be gained from Judah's report in 1862. He checked the number of tons hauled over the Placerville-Carson road for that year, and found that about one hundred and twenty tons of freight, at rates from six to eight cents a pound, were carried daily, or an annual income of $5,250,000; $500,000 a year was gained from passenger fares; while the Wells Fargo Company carried $12,000,000 of bullion for the year 1863.[686]

The legislation and affairs of Nevada, as well as of California, needed attention. When the first constitutional convention of Nevada was in session an attempt was made to incorporate a clause permitting the legislature to give to the first railroad to connect Nevada with navigable waters $3,000,000 in state bonds. To prevent this donation from going into Nevada's organic law, Governor Stanford came over to Carson City to appear before the constitution framers. He pled with them to give this money directly to his company. But the subsidy for any road was voted down.[687] During this first session of the Nevada state legislature in

[684] Bancroft, *History of California*, VII, 546-547.
[685] *Ibid.,* 545.
[686] *Virginia Daily Union,* March 14, 1864.
[687] Bancroft, *op. cit.,* 560.

1864 there was a series of resolutions introduced, the purpose of which was to request the federal government to give
United States bonds to the first railroad to build a continuous
line from Sacramento to western Nevada. All of these resolutions were lost, but they served to hasten the construction
of the Central Pacific Railroad across the state.[688] In 1866
Nevada granted the Central Pacific Company the right of
way across the state, but never consented to aid the corporation in any other way.

Their isolation gave the citizens of Nevada peculiar interest in any railroad enterprise; indeed as early as 1861
the territorial legislature granted four franchises to build
railroads. A charter was granted to the Nevada Railroad
Company to build a road from the eastern to the western
boundary. To the Virginia, Carson, and Truckee Railroad,[689]
to the Aurora, East Walker Line, and to the Virginia City
and Washoe Railroad franchises were also given.[690] In 1862
a franchise was granted to the Lake Bigler and Virginia
Railroad, but this line was never built.[691]

The story of the struggle for the location of the railroad
over the Sierra Nevada may not belong properly to this
narrative, but the final decision was of utmost importance
to the future of Nevada. There were three routes proposed:
one to pass through El Dorado county, California, and into
Douglas county, Nevada; another to go through Nevada
county, California, and over the Henness Pass to the Truckee
river, thence down the cañon of that river to the Nevada
desert; a third route was to follow the old emigrant road
from Sacramento to Clipper Gap, Illinois Town (Colfax),
Dutch Flat, over Donner Pass and down the Truckee river.
Theodore Judah favored the last route, for the selection of
which he gave thirty reasons.[692] It was the easy grade down
the Truckee cañon to the level plains of the Great Salt Lake

---

[688] Loc. cit.

[689] The Virginia and Truckee Railroad was built between Carson City and
Virginia City in 1869; in November, 1871, it was built from Reno to Steam-
boat Springs, and in August, 1872, it was completed from Steamboat to Carson
City. Angel, op. cit., 280.

[690] Neither of these lines was built.

[691] Laws of Nevada Territory, 1862, 168, 172.

[692] Bancroft, op. cit., 547.

Basin upon which Judah finally won his point. It was planned first to build the road as far as Dutch Flat, and then build a wagon road to Carson Valley, thereby turning the immense freight business from the Placerville road to the Central Pacific, so that the receipts from the Comstock freighting would help to pay for the road.

The decision to build the railroad as far as Dutch Flat brought bitter assault upon the Central Pacific Company from the rival railroads in California, and from the newspapers in the state. It was dubbed by the latter the "Dutch Flat swindle." Some editors maintained that since the Central Pacific did not have the means to build the line into Nevada, it should be content to serve that state with the Dutch Flat-Carson Valley wagon road, but the critics of this railroad did not correctly estimate the political acumen of the officers and directors of the Central Pacific Railroad. In 1863, no less than seven different legislative acts were passed by the California legislature and approved by Governor Stanford to assist this company. These acts practically forced the people of California to pay for the construction of the first forty miles of the road.[693] In 1864, however, the amended Pacific Railroad Act passed by the congress made it possible for the Central Pacific to continue building its line independently of state subsidy. By this act the United States became virtual endorser of the bonds of the company for the full amount of its own subsidy of $48,000 or $96,000 per mile upon which the company could draw for each mile of road constructed.

By the act of 1864, the 1862 act restricting the Central Pacific from building farther east than the California-Nevada line, was amended to permit it to build eastward one hundred and fifty miles into Nevada, or about as far as the Humboldt Sink near Lovelock. By this act the Union Pacific lost the exclusive right to build across Nevada, but retained the privilege to do so if it could reach the proposed junction of the two lines ahead of the Central Pacific, an accomplishment which the Central Pacific never intended to allow if it were possible to prevent, as they did not intend to permit the Union Pacific to get the Salt Lake trade. The latter

[693] Bancroft, *History of California*, VII, 565.

THE FIRST CENTRAL PACIFIC TRAIN ARRIVES AT ELKO, 1868
Reproduced from an exceedingly rare photograph.

company had no such master politician in Washington as the Central Pacific's Collis P. Huntington. In 1866, largely through the efforts of United States Senator William M. Stewart of Nevada, a bill was passed which amended the act of 1864, which in turn amended the act of 1862. By the 1866 railroad bill, the Central Pacific secured a release from its limitation to one hundred and fifty miles into the Nevada desert, and was allowed to build eastward across Nevada until it should meet the Union Pacific, wherever that point might be.[694]

When this favorable legislation was granted there began the most spectacular race recorded in the history of the nation. The building of the railroad through the Sierra Nevada was a colossal task. This company not only had to lay one hundred and fifty miles of track, but also to grade the road from sea level to an elevation of 7,000 feet. To accomplish this herculean task, mountain sides were cut away, innumerable trestles and culverts were built, and a number of tunnels cut. As the line progressed, a telegraph line, snowsheds, depots, and water tanks were constructed. Not the least of the task was the maintenance of an army of workmen and hundreds of horses and mules. Materials for construction of all these projects were contracted for in the East, loaded on to steamships that went around the horn to San Francisco, and thence carried along the line for the workmen.

On December 13, 1867, the California-Nevada line was crossed at a place where the railroad "emerged from its windings among the eternal hills." The Central Pacific entered upon the race for the trade of Utah as well as for the bonds and lands granted by the federal government. There was still a gap, however, in the Sierra Nevada which was not yet completed; that part was finished when the snows melted in the following spring. The engine and other materials needed to build on into Nevada were brought over by ox teams.[695]

Indeed, this was the grandest race ever run to complete

---

[694] Brown, *op. cit.,* 334-335; Bancroft, *History of California,* VII, 550, 565, 570.

[695] *Carson Daily Appeal,* June 28, 1868.

the most stupendous work that man had ever conceived, of the most far-reaching results. When the race began the Union Pacific had constructed five hundred and fifty miles of roadbed over the plains of Nebraska and Wyoming – but it had yet to cross the Rocky and Wasatch mountains before it reached Utah. The Central Pacific Company had crossed its mountain barrier successfully, and was heading for the Utah trade by way of the Truckee desert and the Humboldt Valley – easy grade most of the way. As early as 1863 the Central Pacific had sent surveyors eastward as far as the Big Bend of the Humboldt river (Winnemucca). In January, 1867, they ran their line by the way of Humboldt Wells and thence two hundred and thirty miles to the mouth of Weber cañon in Utah. They even went farther through Weber and Echo cañons, across the Wasatch mountains and to Fort Bridger on the western slope of the Rocky mountains. They set their flags and stakes beside those of the oncoming Union Pacific.[696]

The Union Pacific, then building a mile of track a day, boasted that it would meet the Central Pacific at the California-Nevada line. It threw out graders as far west as the Humboldt Wells; many miles of track were laid; but the gap between that portion of its work and the continuous track was never filled, although a round million was spent on this work in Nevada. Such a challenge was all Superintendent Crocker needed. To win his race, Crocker employed 10,000 workmen, Chinese coolie laborers and white men; he had 1,000 horses, mules, and oxen to help. The Chinese were imported from China by the Six Companies in San Francisco, who received one dollar a head for them from the Contract and Finance Company.[697]

These Orientals really won the race for the Central Pacific. They were very agreeable and tractable workmen who could endure great hardships. The Union Pacific had to depend upon white labor, whose wages were higher and who were difficult to obtain and to handle. The work across Nevada was contracted by the mile to Sisson, Crocker and

[696] Bancroft, *History of California,* VII, 571.

[697] The Six Companies had to guarantee the Chinaman burial in China if he died after leaving there.

Company, formerly Sisson, Egbert, Crocker and Company. The Chinese were divided into groups of forty to fifty men headed by a Chinese boss who could speak some English. They in turn were under "riding bosses" who had eight or ten foremen under them. Each gang was known by the name of its Chinese boss. It was his duty to keep the record of each workman's time which he posted in a conspicuous place so that each man could see it. In California the Chinese railroad workers received about $26 a month, in Nevada about $35 a month. There was one white man among the riding bosses, Sam Thayer, who could understand several Chinese dialects, whose duty it was to mingle with the Orientals to listen for trouble or discontent. The Chinese were forced to purchase their supplies from the contracting company. Their food consisted chiefly of rice which they ate out of powder kegs sawed off for the purpose. They wore American clothes: blue denim overalls and shirts, but insisted upon having Chinese coolie hats for the extreme heat of the desert.[698]

The Union Pacific had a good deal of difficulty with the Indians while the Central Pacific had very little. Crocker let the Paiutes ride on the trains free of charge. When the road was constructed as far as Wadsworth, Nevada, the bosses made friends with young Winnemucca and his sister Sarah. Old Chief Winnemucca was given a pass to ride on passenger cars, and the other Indians were allowed to ride the box cars. The Indians enjoyed the train and frequently availed themselves of their privileges.

But the Chinese and the Indians did not get along well. The two races began to see much of each other; soon the red man found that the Oriental was very superstitious. A story was related to the writer of how the Indians told the Chinese that there were snakes out on the desert east of Wadsworth, so large that they could swallow a Chinaman in one gulp. The Chinese became so frightened that a large number of them struck and started to walk back to San Francisco.

[698] The writer had a very interesting interview with Mr. Joseph Madison Graham of Berkeley, California, on August 1, 1931. Graham was one of the surveyors of the Central Pacific. A great deal of the material for this chapter was given to the writer from data he had in his diary. He surveyed the townsites of Reno and Wadsworth.

Whereupon, the riding bosses were ordered to get horses as quickly as possible and pursue the fleeing Chinese, and if necessary to whip them back to their jobs. The Orientals had not gone very far when they were found trudging along the road. When they were told that they had to choose between the whips and the snakes, the Chinese took their chances with the Nevada dragons. One day a Paiute was seen to be sharpening a large knife, and when he was asked what he was going to do with such a sharp knife, he said, "Make Chinamen heap sick." The railroad officials were fearful a serious clash might result, so precautions were taken to keep the races apart.

In constructing the line across Nevada, very little attention was paid to finishing the roadbed. After the grading was done, the ties were laid and the rails fastened down as quickly as possible. When the Union Pacific was slowed up in its construction over the Rocky and Wasatch mountains and it became apparent that the Central Pacific was going to win the race, the former sent its surveyors and workmen into eastern Nevada to grade and prepare the roadbed for the laying of the track in that section. For some distance in Elko county the two roadbeds paralleled each other. When Superintendent Crocker thought he did not have sufficient workmen to win the race he appealed to Brigham Young for several hundred young Mormon boys to build the road into Utah. For this the Mormon church received a substantial block of stock in the Central Pacific Company. Crocker was a driver, very blunt and abrupt in his manner, but he got results. Some years later he said, "Why, I used to go up and down that road in my car like a mad bull, stopping along wherever there was anything amiss, and raising Old Nick with the boys that were not up to time." [699]

Beginning at the summit of the mountains and continuing eastward, construction camps were built by the Central Pacific. Each camp was numbered from west to east across the state. "Camp number 1" was at the summit of the Sierra Nevada mountains. Some of the camps became permanent towns; others were taken up and moved along as the track was built. To keep the building material and supplies going

699 "Crocker's Railroad Building," MS., Bancroft Library, University of California.

THE FIRST CENTRAL PACIFIC DEPOT, RENO

The depot was built in 1869 and burned March 2, 1879.

forward "to the front," from seven hundred to one thousand cars were on the tracks all the time. At noon on May 4, 1868, the track and telegraph line were complete to Reno, where stage lines had already been waiting to connect the railroad with the Comstock and nearby towns. When the railroad reached Lake's Crossing, Reno, Crocker bargained with Lake, who claimed two hundred three and one-half acres on both sides of the river, for eighty acres on the north side of the Truckee river, on condition that a station be established on it; to Lake he agreed to deed every alternate lot as the town was laid out. The agreement was made in March, 1868, but the auction of the first lots was not held until May 9, or five days after the railroad reached the town. The track, however, was not yet continuous; the first through train from Sacramento to Reno arrived on June 18, 1868. Reno sprang into existence overnight. On the day the auction of lots was held great crowds flocked from the neighboring towns, many of whom slept in the sagebrush to be on hand to bid for a lot. Over two hundred lots were sold the first day at ten per cent down and the balance in the next ten days. The lot on the east corner of Commercial Row and Virginia Street was the first sold; it brought six hundred dollars. Houses, saloons, and business blocks sprang up over night. By August, three months later, the town was described as a

. . . mushroom town which sprang up in a single night. . . It lacks age and stability but has great vitality. Mixed stages of civilization from the Paiute squaws with their juvenile encumbrances packed neatly in small packages on their broad backs to the gambler and rough element and the most refined mingle on the street. There is no such thing as rest in Reno. People rush into Reno. The tavern keepers are bent on business, provide no rest and Reno cares nothing. All day the hammer and saw is heard, and all night the fiddles scrape and the glasses clink. No one cares. Busy Reno is on the map, on the railroad and has a big thing. She is bent on making her pile with what speed she can command.[700]

The work across Nevada progressed very rapidly. It was a comparatively easy grade from Reno down the Truckee cañon to the plains across the Truckee Desert. On the edge of this desert and at the last crossing of the Truckee river, the Big Bend, a permanent town, Wadsworth was laid out

---

[700] *Carson Daily Appeal,* August 27, 1868.

and made the base of supplies. A division point with a round-house and machine shop was built, and a townsite was surveyed.[701] Up the Humboldt River Valley was another easy stretch of construction. The fifteen mile cañon through the palisades of the Humboldt river was graded in six weeks. So well trained and so anxious were the workmen to win the race that the record for both companies was broken when ten miles of track were laid in one day. The Central Pacific won the race. The continent was spanned with a rib of steel. Nevada was connected with the East by an overland railroad, and on the west with navigable waters. The story of the changes it wrought in Nevada extends beyond the chronological limitation of this volume. Such a narrative if told in detail would fill several books.

Nevada's part in the ceremony of the uniting of the two roads at Promontory Point, Utah, fifty-three miles west of Ogden, was the presentation of a spike, made from silver of the Comstock, to Vice-president Thomas C. Durant of the Union Pacific Company by F. A. Tritle, commissioner appointed to represent Nevada at the ceremony.[702]

---

[701] Two men, known only as "Joe" and "Pete" had preëmpted the land at the Truckee river crossing, but their rights were disregarded.

[702] Sabin, *Building the Pacific Railway*, 221.

# Geographical Evolution of Nevada

Nevada, seventh largest state in the Union, was not, when admitted, of the size and shape it now is. It evolved from Carson county, territory of Utah, cut off in 1855 from the western portion of the counties of Millard, Iron, and Juab, to embrace finally in 1866 the largest part of Utah territory, and a portion of the territory of Arizona. The boundaries of states are usually taken for granted. Unless a particular study is made of them, they are generally regarded as an adjustment made by the congress when the state was admitted. It is the historically illustrated tendency of a developing territory to expand to its "natural" boundaries, often at the expense of the neighbor. Such was the case of Nevada, whose natural boundaries were derived from the physical features of the Great Basin. In this area the lack of agricultural lands was acute. To expand eastward, northward, or southward meant more desert land; to the west there were rich agricultural lands, but the powerful, rich, and politically strong state of California blocked development in that direction.

The northern boundary of Nevada, the forty-second degree north latitude, was the oldest one. Its demarcation dates from the purchase of Louisiana territory in 1803. Thomas Jefferson, president at the time of the purchase and great proponent of "Manifest Destiny," declared that the purchase included Oregon territory also. After Jefferson had determined with more or less accuracy, by sending out the Lewis and Clark expedition, the sources of the rivers that flowed into the Mississippi and those that flowed into the Pacific northwest, he conceived the line between Oregon territory and the Spanish possessions to the south to be at the forty-second degree.[703] Although at that time the claim

---

[703] Marshall, *A History of the Western Boundary of the Louisiana Purchase, 1819-1841*, map 4.

of the United States to Oregon was shadowy and the boundary line mythical it is interesting to note that the forty-
second degree line became definitive by the Treaty of 1819
between Spain and the United States.[704] This line was taken
because it was supposed to be the source of the Snake river;
the forty-second degree was kept as the boundary when
Mexico became independent in 1821; it remained at this
point, when by the Mexican cession provided for in the
Treaty of Guadalupe Hidalgo of 1848, Alta California became part of the United States; in 1850 congress made it
the northern boundary of the state of California and of the
territory of Utah; and in 1861 it was fixed finally as the
northern boundary of the territory and later the state of
Nevada.

The remaining boundary lines of Nevada were determined
by several elements: by the character of the people brought
in by the mining industry, by the topographical features of
the Great Basin area, and by the inaccurate knowledge which
the congress had of the western part of the United States.
Two important factors entered into the fixation of the western and eastern boundaries: first, the fact that California
was the first far western state to be created and have its
boundaries fixed, prevented Nevada from expanding westward; second, Nevada, detached from the western part of
the territory of Utah, took advantage of the prejudice
against the Mormon state to expand eastward.

The northern and southern boundaries of California were
fixed by international agreement, its eastern boundary was
defined when it was admitted as a state in 1850. In that
direction there was a vast undetermined area known to the
Spanish and Mexican authorities as Alta California. The
character of its soil and physical features were no better
known by the members of congress. When the people of
California applied for statehood, the eastern boundary had
not been fixed. The debate over a large and small state of
California has been discussed in a former chapter.[705] The

---

[704] William M. Malloy, ed., *Treaties, Conventions, International Acts,
Protocols, and Agreements between the United States and other Powers, 1776-
1902*, II, 1651; Marshall, *op. cit.*, 46-70.

[705] *Supra*, 145-146.

eastern boundary was finally fixed by the constitutional convention at the summit of the Sierra Nevada. But in the bill
which admitted California to the Union the congress defined
the eastern boundary to begin:

> . . . at the point of intersection of the 42nd degree north latitude with
> 120 degrees of west longitude west from Greenwich and running south
> on the line of said 120 degrees of west longitude until it intersects the 39
> degree of north latitude; thence running in a straight line in a southeast-
> erly direction to the Colorado river at a point where it intersects the
> 35th degree of north latitude.[706]

The territory of Utah, created about the same time, was
bounded on the west by the state of California, on the north
by the territory of Oregon, on the east by the Rocky mountains, and on the south by the 37th degree north latitude.[707]
In fixing the boundary between Utah and California, the
congress, on account of its inaccurate knowledge of the geography of the country, failed to make a distinction between
mountainous and desert country. Natural boundaries could
have been recognized; instead, the state line traversed deserts, valleys, and mountains. There was no logical reason
why this arbitrary division was made. On the eastern side
of the Sierra Nevada there were a number of fertile valleys,
Honey Lake, and the Truckee Meadows, north of Lake
Tahoe, and Carson, Walker, and Smith valleys south of the
lake. The California-Utah line, as fixed by congress, inter-
cepted most of these valleys. It was natural for their residents to have interests with the communities that could be
most easily reached — those of western Utah, but the seat
of that government, Salt Lake City, was too far away, so
they sought to be annexed to California. Some efforts were
made by them and some encouragement was received from
the California state legislature. As time went on and the
settlers of these valleys wanted to have the titles to their
farm and mining claims secure, they sought to set up their
own government. This effort was likewise thwarted.

As a result the people in the vicinity of Honey Lake Valley had maintained for some time a spirit of independence
regarding the jurisdiction of California law. In 1856 a num-

[706] *Constitution of California*, art. VII; *Laws of California*, 1850-1853, 58.
[707] *United States Public Laws*, 31 Cong., 1 sess., 453-458.

ber of the settlers organized an independent territory which they called "Nataqua," [708] the boundaries of which included the more populous regions farther south and to the east, whose people they believed had many things in common with them. This area was a part of the territory of Utah; since 1855 it had been organized into Carson county, over which the Utah authorities were exercising a strong control. Honey Lake Valley had been included in Carson county, Utah, and the California officials made no protest. Although nothing came of Nataqua territory, it was indicative of the spirit of independence of this community.

Efforts to bring these valleys under the authority of California were made again when mining became active on the eastern slope of the Sierra Nevada. In 1860 there was a move to include a large area east of the California line and to create "Washoe county" out of it. The new territory was to be attached to El Dorado county, California, until formally organized. The argument advanced in favor of adding this county to California was the sudden increase of the population to ten thousand, the largest number of which were Californians, and the expectation of four or five times this number in a short time. A bill was introduced and passed in the California assembly to change the El Dorado-Amador county boundary line, but it failed to pass in the senate.[709]

When the attempts to add the valleys and mining regions east of the mountains to California failed, the territory of Nevada was organized in 1861. This territory claimed the summit of the Sierra Nevada as its western boundary; the most northern county, Roop, included the Honey Lake country. This same area had been made also a part of Plumas county, California, whose county seat was in Quincy, on the other side of the range. A steep summit, the road over which was closed most of the winter, separated the people in Susanville, Honey Lake Valley, from Quincy. The attempts of the governments, both of Plumas county, California, and Roop county, Nevada, to exercise authority over the people

[708] Fairfield, *Pioneer History of Lassen County, California,* 46-50.

[709] *California Assembly Journal,* 11 session, 1860, 537, 696ff.; *California Senate Journal,* 11 session (1860), 746, 772.

on the east side of the mountains brought on a clash between the officials of both counties, which became known as the "Sagebrush" or "Border line War," [710] the story of which will be told later.

The first attempt to determine the boundary between Utah and California was made in 1852, when the surveyor-general of California went to Placerville to make the preliminary observations. In his report to the California state legislature, he stated that:

While here we computed a sufficient number of observations to satisfy ourselves as to one position approximately, and finding that Placerville was about forty-six miles from the angle of the state boundary at that intersection of the 120th meridian and the 39th parallel, and that the lowest estimate of the airline distance from Placerville to Mormon Station in Carson Valley was sixty miles, I was reluctantly forced to the conclusion that the valley was from twelve to fifteen miles out of the state.[711]

Shortly after this report was made, forty-three citizens of Carson Valley petitioned the California legislature for annexation to California for judicial purposes until congress should otherwise provide.[712] The select committee to which the petition was referred was favorably disposed. A memorial was sent, therefore, to the congress, setting forth the reasons why Carson Valley should be added to California. It was proposed by the memorial committee that the eastern boundary of California be extended from the intersection of the 120th degree of longitude and the 42nd degree north latitude to the intersection of the 35th parallel and the Colorado river. The area thus defined would have included all of the valleys east of the mountains and a considerable portion of New Mexico. The memorial passed the senate, but opposition to bringing any part of the Mormon state under the control of California developed in the assembly, and it failed to pass that body.[713] Just what action the congress would have taken is doubtful.

In 1855 the territory of Utah created Carson county.[714]

[710] Coy, *California County Boundaries*, 22-23.

[711] *California Senate Journal*, 1853, 4 session, appendix, doc. 3, pp. 13-14.

[712] *Ibid.*, doc. 46.

[713] *Loc. cit.*

[714] *Utah Acts*, 1855, 261.

When the officials arrived to perfect the organization, the settlers were still divided as to who held jurisdiction over them. The gentiles maintained they were in El Dorado county, California; the Mormons declared they were under the jurisdiction of Utah. The Utah officials did not want to go on with the proceedings until they were sure of their authority. In this same year the California legislature passed a bill authorizing the building of a wagon road to the eastern boundary of the state. It was necessary, therefore, to determine that boundary. In consequence the surveyor-general of California, Seneca H. Marlette, appointed George H. Goddard to act in conjunction with the Carson Valley authorities in surveying the line. Goddard found that the apex of the obtuse angle of the California boundary was in the southeastern part of Lake Tahoe;[715] and therefore Carson Valley was well within Utah territory.

In spite of the Goddard survey, the dissatisfied element of Carson county expressed a preference for the California jurisdiction. In 1856 their persistency created a legal doubt in the mind of the United States District Judge W. W. Drummond, who addressed a communication to the California delegation in congress informing them that the Mormon residents of Carson Valley claimed that they were in the territory of Utah and that a large and respectable portion of the citizens of the valley contended that they were in California. He stated, also, that he had held court in Genoa, believing himself to be in Carson county, but that he was convinced that he was wrong in doing so. An important case which he had heard was appealed to the supreme court of Utah. He was doubtful as to whether the parties to the suit and the property involved in the controversy were in El Dorado county, California, or in Carson county, Utah. In the same communication Drummond described the bitter feeling of the anti-Mormons toward paying a tax to the territory of Utah, which at that time was in open rebellion against the United States. He concluded by recommending to the congress that a boundary commission be appointed.[716]

On November 23, 1855, these same dissatisfied citizens

---

[715] About one-third of Lake Tahoe is in Nevada.

[716] Bancroft, *History of Nevada, Colorado, and Wyoming*, 151-152.

petitioned the California legislature again to be annexed to that state. The committee on federal relations to which it was referred acted favorably on it, and drew up a resolution in which the congress was urged to extend the eastern boundary of California to the 118th meridian.[717] This line would have included all of Carson county and part of the territory of Utah as far north as Oregon territory. The California legislature urged their national representatives to introduce a bill including these provisions.[718] The committee on territories in the house of representatives reported that the solution of the Carson Valley situation did not consist in its being annexed to an already large and unmanageable state, but rather in the correction of poor government in the territory of Utah.[719]

It will be remembered that at this particular time the federal government was confronted with a very difficult situation in the failure of coöperation between the heads of the Mormon church and the officials of the federal government.[720] The important results which affected the communities in western Utah were the removal of Brigham Young as territorial governor and the appointment of Alfred Cumming in his place, the disorganization of Carson county (reduced to an election precinct and attached to Salt Lake county), the advancement of a division of the United States army to Utah, and the withdrawal of most of the Mormon settlers to Salt Lake City. Before the Zionites were all gone from Carson, Washoe, and Eagle valleys and the Truckee Meadows, the movement for a separate territorial government was inaugurated, which did not terminate until the territory of Nevada was created four years later. Although previous efforts to be annexed to California had not been successful, the authorities of that state were eager to help

---

[717] *Sen. Misc. Doc.* no. 48, 34 Cong., 1 sess.; *Sen. Journal,* 34 Cong., 1 sess., 296; *House Com. Report* no. 116, 34 Cong., 3 sess.; *California Assembly Journal,* 1855, 7 sess., 387-388.

[718] It is of interest to note that at the time the California legislature was asking congress to enlarge their state by the annexation of Carson Valley, there was a bill before it to divide California into three states because it was too large.

[719] *House Committee Reports,* 34 Cong., 1 sess., no. 116, pp. 1-2 (ser. no. 940).
[720] *Supra,* 168.

the gentiles of Carson Valley to separate from Utah. The Carson Valley memorial, sent to California, was favorably received. Governor John B. Weller and the California legislature forwarded the memorial to President Buchanan with the following addendum: "February 2, 1858. The president will see that this subject has received the favorable action of our state legislature. I recommend this memorial to your favorable consideration." [721] A resolution from the California state legislature accompanied the memorial which recommended a territorial government for Carson Valley "with such boundaries as circumstances may warrant and require." [722] It was presented to the senate on March 1, 1858.[723] James M. Crane, the delegate chosen by the Carson Valley people to plead their cause in Washington, wrote to his constituents that he was certain of the creation of a new territory to be "bounded on the east by Goose Creek mountains, on the west by the Sierra Nevada or eastern line of California, on the north by the Oregon line, and on the south by the Colorado river." [724]

It is interesting to note that these proposed boundaries were approximately the ultimate limits of the state of Nevada.[725] Crane's memorial was referred to the committee on territories. This committee reported a bill on May 13, 1858, "to organize a territorial government of Nevada." [726] The bill provided that Nevada should be bounded by:

California on the west, commencing at a point where it leaves the Colorado, thence with said line on the latitude of 42 degree north, east to the 114th degree of longitude to the Goose Creek mountains; thence southerly with said range to the headwaters of Lake Nicollet; thence down the stream formed by said waters to said lake and through the same to the nearest range of mountains running southerly until it shall

721 *House Ex. Doc.* no. 96, 35 Cong., 1 sess., 102.

722 *California Senate Journal,* 1858, 9 sess., 111, 140; *California Assembly Journal,* 1858, 9 sess., 114, 158; *Statutes of California,* 1858, 350; Bancroft, *History of Nevada, Colorado, and Wyoming,* 83.

723 *Senate Journal,* 35 Cong., 1 sess., 590; *Sen. Misc. Doc.* no. 181, 35 Cong., 1 sess., III.

724 Crane's letter is reprinted in full in Angel, *op. cit.,* 46.

725 *Infra,* 408.

726 *House Journal,* 35 Cong., 1 sess., 789, 1221; *House Reports,* 35 Cong., 1 sess., III, 375; Bancroft, *History of Nevada, Colorado, and Wyoming,* 83, fn. 47; Angel, *op. cit.,* 46.

reach Cedar City at or near the 114th degree; thence with the most conspicuous landmarks to the headwaters of the Virgin river; thence down
said stream to its intersection with the Colorado; thence down said river
to the beginning.[727]

The area thus defined would have been larger than the
present site of Nevada; it would have included also some
very valuable agricultural land; and it sought to reach some
natural boundary on the east. The bill was debated in the
committee of the whole; opposition, however, from the
southern states toward adding any more territories resulted
in its defeat.[728] It served, however, to acquaint the members
of congress with the dissatisfaction of the people of western
Utah; in addition, it gave the national government some idea
of the geography of the Great Basin.

Although the federal government denied the citizens of
Carson Valley a separate territorial government, the settlers
were not daunted in their determination to be free from
Mormon domination. At a convention held in Genoa from
July 18 to 28, 1859, a "Declaration of Independence" from
Utah was formulated; a territorial constitution was framed;
and the election of officers for the new territory was authorized. The convention described the boundaries of the new
territory as:

Commencing at a point on the Sierra Nevada mountains where the
42nd degree of north latitude touches the summit of said mountains, thence
southerly with said summit to the 35th degree of north latitude; thence
east on the said parallel to the Colorado river; thence up said river to
its junction with the Rio Virgin; thence up said Rio Virgin to its junction
with the Muddy river; thence due north to the Oregon line; thence west
to the place of beginning.[729]

The members of this convention were residents of all the
valleys west of the mountains. In fact, some of the leading
delegates came from Susanville — Isaac Roop, prominent
rancher and politician, was one of the leaders in this separation movement. The organization of this government was a

[727] *House Report,* 375, 35 Cong., 1 sess., 4-5 (ser. no. 966).

[728] *Cong. Globe,* 35 Cong., 1 sess., 2122; *House Journal,* 35 Cong., 1 sess.,
78 (ser. no. 940).

[729] Article x, "Constitution of proposed Territory of Nevada," *Territorial
Enterprise,* July 30, 1859; facsimile of paper containing the constitution and
convention proceedings are reproduced in Angel, *op. cit.,* 68-73.

means of unifying the people east of the mountains. Counties
were organized: Lake county (northern Washoe county)
included the area in Honey Lake Valley; Susanville was
made its county seat. The authority of Plumas county, California, was ignored completely by the residents and by the
new territory.

When the Carson Valley people first began to be active
for a separate government, the surveyor-general of California recommended to the state legislatures that an official
survey of the boundary between Utah and California be
made. Their arguments were based chiefly on the lack of
revenue from the taxes which were being paid to the Utah
government; the uncertainty of court jurisdiction was disturbing, too. Knowing that it would be very expensive to
survey this great distance, the California delegation in congress sought national legislation for this purpose. The eloquent and forceful David C. Broderick, United States senator
from California, introduced legislation to this effect, but
the congress was indifferent.[730] In 1858 Governor Weller in
his message to the California state legislature requested
urgently that money be appropriated for a joint California
and United States boundary commission. This request was
incorporated in a resolution which passed both houses of the
legislature. It read:

> Whereas, no portion of the boundary between the state of California
> and the territory of Utah has ever been definitely ascertained by actual
> survey under the authority of the government of the United States; and
> in consequence thereof conflicting claims exist between said state and
> territory as to the jurisdiction over lands and their inhabitants situated
> near the boundary line; therefore, be it resolved by the assembly, the
> senate concurring, that our senators be instructed and our representatives
> in congress be requested to procure at an early date the passage of a bill
> authorizing the survey of the boundary between the state of California
> and the territory of Utah, to be designated by appropriate monuments.
> The said survey to conform to the boundary line now established by law
> of congress between said state and territory.[731]

This statement indicated clearly that California would

[730] *California Assembly Journal*, 1857, app., doc. no. 4, 23; *House Journal*,
35 Cong., 1 sess., 977-978 (ser. no. 940); *Senate Journal*, 35 Cong., 1 sess.,
555, 590 (ser. no. 917).

[731] *Statutes of California*, 1858, 356-357; *Assembly Journal*, 9 sess., 424;
Bancroft, *History of Nevada, Colorado, and Wyoming*, 152.

accept no other line than the original one of 1850. When the resolution reached the congress, it was referred to the committee on territories, but no action was taken.[732] The independent attitude of the Carson Valley settlers in declaring themselves free from the authority of Utah, the rapidly increasing population of western Utah, together with recurring conflicts over jurisdiction, brought forth a second resolution from California to the congress imploring the federal government to approve of a California-United States survey to determine the constitutional line.[733] Again the congress took no action. However, the California legislature appropriated $5,000 for carrying out the provisions of the act. Before anything further was done there occurred the discovery of the great Comstock Lode; a short time later rich silver deposits were discovered on or near the California-Utah (Nevada) line in the Esmeralda mining district. There were now two districts of importance where it was imperative that a boundary line be determined.

Because the congress took no action on the resolutions and requests from the California legislature, California assumed the responsibility of a survey by passing an act on April 13, 1860, which authorized the surveyor-general "to define and establish by astronomical observations and a lineal survey of that portion of the eastern boundary extending from the Mount Diablo base line to the Oregon line." [734] On May 26, 1860, the United States government appropriated $55,000 for making a survey, for erecting suitable monuments, and for paying the expenses of the men employed by the United States.[735] To complicate the situation, the California legislature repealed the 1859 act providing for a joint boundary commission and in its place passed another directing the California surveyor-general to run only the northern portion of the eastern boundary line of the state.[736]

---

[732] *Senate Journal*, 35 Cong., 1 sess., 555, 590; *House Journal*, 35 Cong., 1 sess., 977-978.

[733] *California Assembly Journal*, 1858, 424-425; *California Assembly Resolution*, 1858, no. 21, 356-357.

[734] *California Statutes*, 1860, 184-185.

[735] *United States Statutes at Large*, XII, 110; *Cong. Globe*, 36 Cong., 1 sess., 475.

[736] The northern portion meant north of Lake Tahoe. *Statutes of California*, 1860, 184-185; Bancroft, *History of Nevada, Colorado, and Wyoming*, 152-153.

The reason for this changed attitude may be found in the development of the Comstock mines and the rush to the Esmeralda district (Aurora). California was beginning to look covetously on the very rich strip of territory directly east of the mountains.

In 1861 the message of John G. Downey, governor of California, stated that the people in the mining regions were anxious to be annexed to California; he recommended that the congress be memorialized to grant the right to California to extend her boundary to the 118th degree of longitude. California lost her opportunity to have this territory added when the people of Carson Valley were pleading and beseeching the legislature of that state to annex them. At this same time, 1860, there was a bill before the congress providing for the creation of the territory of Nevada.[737]

The United States surveying party, under the direction of Lieutenant Mowry, was in the field by the fall of 1860 to run the line between California and Utah. By April 1 of the following year, in addition to having spent $37,551.19 of the $55,000 appropriated, he had incurred further liabilities of $34,416.21. In other words, it had cost the federal government $71,967.40 to determine two points, the point where the Colorado river intersects the 35th degree and the location in the southeastern corner of Lake Tahoe of the angle formed by the oblique line extended from the Colorado river point to its junction with the 120th meridian. It was true that these two points were the most difficult of the entire section to locate, but the cost of determining them seemed out of proportion to other surveying projects.[738] On account of his large expenditures, Lieutenant Mowry was removed and the work was transferred directly to the general land office.

On August 30, 1861, Lieutenant Butler Ives, the astronomer for the Mowry surveying party, resigned. He stated in his report to the United States surveyor-general that after the two initial points had been fixed any surveyor could run the boundary line between them.[739]

[737] Bancroft, *History of Nevada, Colorado, and Wyoming,* 153.
[738] *Sen. Ex. Doc.* no. 1, 37 Cong., 2 sess., 447 (ser. no. 1117).
[739] *Report of Interior Department,* 1861-1862, 490.

In summarizing the first work of the federal government toward the establishment of official boundaries between the western states and territories, it may be stated that the members of the congress exhibited a woeful ignorance of topography and frontier conditions. The interior department made the first mistake when it did not submit the project to bids and let the work out by contract. The extremely rugged character of the country to be traversed made it a very expensive undertaking. Lieutenant Mowry may have been a poor business executive, but the congressmen were three thousand miles away. It would have been impossible, for instance, for them to have comprehended why Lieutenant Mowry had to spend so much money in trinkets to be used in pacifying the hostile Indians. Nor could they understand the expense entailed in the necessity of having his base of supplies at Visalia, California, on the western side of the Sierra. To reach either of the places where he could begin observations, supplies had to be hauled up the steep grades, over the Sierra, and thence across difficult desert country. Water for the men and the animals had to be hauled in some cases for many miles. The following comment on the surveying work was made in a Visalia paper:

The party of reconnaissance sent out by Lieutenant Mowry, United States commissioner, arrived in Visalia on Sunday, after having examined the country for about 200 miles along the line. From what we can gather from the gentlemen composing the expedition, they passed through a very desolate, rough, and sterile region. After leaving the Colorado, they proceeded in a northwesterly direction, toward Lake Bigler. The line runs west of the Las Vegas mountains and through Ash Plain about 70 miles above. Westward from this plain is the sink of the Amargosa, a stream that rises in the upper part of Ash Plain and running southward, sweeps around to the northward again, and after a course of 200 miles or upwards, sinks into an extensive marsh of salt and alkali within 15 miles of its source. This marsh is in a valley of great length, running nearly north and south. One of its remarkable features is its great depression being not less than 400 feet below the level of the sea, as indicated by barometrical measurement. At about the level of the sea, a small stream of fresh water runs out. This remarkable plain has been called Death Valley. The entire region they traversed is nearly destitute of vegetation. Indications of silver, gold, and other minerals are frequently met with but the nature of the surrounding country, the difficulties attending the transportation and the general uninviting aspects of the region, would be sufficient to deter any class of people, except Californians, from attempting to work mines or even prospect them.[740]

Events in the spring of 1861 changed the entire aspect of the boundary question. In addition to the fact that another congressional appropriation would have to be made before further work could be done, the Civil War had broken out, and the territory of Nevada had been created.

In the organic act of March 2, 1861, the boundaries for the territory of Nevada were defined as follows:

> Beginning at the point of intersection of the 42nd degree north latitude and the 39th degree longitude west from Washington, south on the 39th degree west longitude until it intersects the northern boundary line of the territory of New Mexico, thence west to the dividing ridge separating the waters of Carson Valley from those that flow to the Pacific, thence on said dividing ridge north to the 41st degree north latitude; thence due north to the southern boundary of Oregon, thence due east to the place of beginning.[741]

The "dividing ridge" of the Sierra Nevada was made the provisional western boundary. A clause was added "that so much of the said territory as is within the present limits of California shall not be included until California assents to the same." [742] When this description of the new territory of Nevada was made, the federal government withdrew from the boundary dispute. The question of ceding the area devolved upon the state of California, and the first step had to be taken by the legislature of that state: it must vote favorably to relinquish all of the land west of the mountains. Then, after that question was settled, there still remained the difficult adjustment of the "dividing ridge." As a result of this clause in the organic act, the settlement of the California-Nevada line opened a very unpleasant issue which was not concluded for four years.

The first move was made by Nevada territory when Governor Nye, through a message to the legislature, recommended the appointment of a committee to be empowered to visit the California state legislature at its next session and to urge

---

[740] *Visalia Delta,* May 13, 1861, quoted in the *Daily Evening Bulletin,* May 25, 1861.

[741] A. J. Marsh, *Official Reports* [*Nevada*] *Constitutional Convention,* ii.

[742] Angel, *op. cit.,* 100; Bancroft, *op. cit.,* 151.

the expediency of ceding to Nevada the area suggested by the Nevada territorial organic act. Governor Nye's message inferred that if the Nevada boundary commission approached the California legislature in a friendly manner, that state would be willing to yield a portion of her vast domain. A natural boundary was much more advisable for harmonious relationships between the two commonwealths than an artificial and arbitrary one.[743] Governor Nye had some difficulty in finding the necessary power to appoint the commission. A law was finally passed after several postponements by a joint session of the two houses on November 9, 1861, in which two commissioners were to be selected for that purpose. The governor was to nominate them; the two houses were to make the final selections.[744] Of the eight nominees submitted, Isaac Roop, territorial councilman from Susanville and formerly provisional governor of Nevada territory, and R. M. Ford, representative from Silver City, were appointed. In addition to the two thousand dollars appropriated to defray the expenses of the commissioners,[745] the sum of $350 was appropriated to survey the boundary line from Lake Bigler (Tahoe) to Honey Lake.[746] It was believed that it would be an aid to the Nevada commissioners in the presentation of their memorial if the line were surveyed. John F. Kidder, deputy United States surveyor, was instructed to run the line as described in the Nevada territorial organic act, but instead of following "the dividing ridge," or summit of the Sierra Nevada, he ran the survey according to the California constitutional line. On November 29, the Nevada legislature appropriated one thousand dollars for the survey of the boundary south from Lake Bigler to the Esmeralda mining district.

At this particular time, many of the citizens of Nevada territory were already thinking of a state government. The two districts under dispute, Honey Lake and the Esmeralda mining district, would be a great aid in advancing this cause. It was believed by many miners that the Esmeralda mining

[743] *Nevada Council Journal*, 1861, 97, 113, 115.

[744] *Laws of Nevada Territory*, 1861, res. no. II, 513-514.

[745] *Nevada Council Journal*, 1861, 215.

[746] *Statutes of Nevada*, 1861, 132.

district might be richer than the Comstock region. The Esmeralda miners were mostly Californians; many of the residents, therefore, wished to be under the jurisdiction of that state and many of the companies had been organized under the laws of California. The people desirous of having California control these regions found a responsive attitude in the California press, which started a vigorous campaign against Nevada's desire for the Sierra Nevada summit boundary line.[747]

Before Governor Nye and Commissioners Roop and Ford proceeded to Sacramento, the Nevada legislature forwarded a resolution and a memorial to the California legislature. The tone of these documents was suppliant; in them "the people of Nevada beseeched their generous and powerful neighbor to grant the prayers of a weaker commonwealth." [748] When the Nevada representatives arrived at the California capital they were accorded every courtesy; the privilege of the floor of the assembly was extended to them. A special joint session of the two houses was held on the evening of March 21, 1862, to hear the arguments presented by the Nevada commissioners. Ford spoke first — he read the Nevada memorial; Roop followed with a lengthy discussion of the question. Although he dwelt upon the northern boundary, with which he was the most familiar, he presented a petition from some of the residents of the Esmeralda district in which they requested to be annexed to Nevada. Governor Nye, relying upon his persuasive oratory, closed the arguments. He touched upon the desirability of natural boundaries, the inadequacy of the $55,000 federal appropriation to make the preliminary survey, the conflicts over the jurisdiction of the courts, and the failure of either Nevada or California to control the criminal element on the bordering counties. In conclusion, Nye contrasted the great sea coast of California with the barren desert lands, from whence came the millions of dollars to make San Francisco prosperous. "Why shouldn't a magnanimous neighbor sur-

[747] *Daily Alta California,* March 22, 1862; *San Francisco Daily Bulletin,* November 1, 14, 1861, March 22, 25, 1862.

[748] *Laws of Nevada Territory,* 1862, concurrent resolution VI, 195; *California Senate Journal,* 1862, 387.

render a narrow strip of land in exchange for the silver of the Nevada mines?" [749] The appeal of the Nevada commissioners was incorporated into a report forwarded to congress.[750]

The result of Nevada's appeal was the introduction of a bill in the California legislature to cede to the Nevada territory all of the land east of the dividing range of the Sierra Nevada. For the consideration of the bill, a special committee of legislators, one from each of the bordering counties: Shasta, Plumas, Sierra, Nevada, Placer, El Dorado, Mono, Calaveras, and Tuolumne, was appointed.[751]

Although some of the members of the California legislature were willing to cede this strip, they maintained that they were powerless to do so, for the 120th meridian had been the boundary line when the state was admitted; this line had been incorporated into the California constitution and accepted by the federal government; an amendment to the California constitution would therefore be needed before it could be changed.[752] Governor Nye answered all these arguments by stating that the federal government had power over the state government: "that so much of the said territory as is within the present limits of California shall not be included until California assents to the same," [753] and since the congress and the territory of Nevada agreed, it remained only for California to give consent to the "dividing ridge." These arguments were not effective; California did not want to lose the possibility of the revenues from the Esmeralda mines, nor did the border counties want to yield any of their land. After the special committee reported unfavorably nothing more was done at the session, and the Nevada commissioners had to return to Nevada with the adverse report that the entire matter had been "indefinitely postponed." [754] Governor Nye, being anxious to find out the exact location of Aurora in the Esmeralda mining district,

---

[749] *Daily Alta California*, March 22, 1862.

[750] *House Ex. Doc.* no. 26, 37 Cong., 3 sess., vol. v, 12 (ser. no. 1161).

[751] Lassen, Alpine, and Inyo counties were not yet created.

[752] It took three years to amend the constitution of California.

[753] *Supra*, 394.

[754] "Message of Governor Nye to the Nevada Legislature," *Nevada Assembly Journal*, 2 sess., 1862.

appointed Butler Ives and John F. Kidder to survey the
part of the boundary line from Lake Bigler to the southern
boundary line of the territory. Although Aurora was found
to be well on the Nevada side, California would not recognize the Kidder-Ives survey.

The failure of the two legislatures to settle the matter
peaceably brought on a civil war between Plumas county,
California, and Roop county, Nevada. The origin of this
conflict dated from the time when Peter Lassen built his
cutoff on the Humboldt River-Lassen Meadows (Rye
Patch) to his ranch on the Yuba river. A number of settlers
began to take up lands along the route. One of the most
desirable locations on Lassen's route was on the Susan river
which flowed into Honey Lake; the Lassen trail went through
what is now the main street of Susanville, California, located
on the east side of the mountains. Although Honey Lake
Valley was over one hundred miles from Carson Valley,
there were no impassable mountains separating the two
communities. Because they could have communications the
year round, and because their valleys were in the Great
Basin their industrial, political, and social problems were
similar. When the territory of Nevada was organized, it
was natural, therefore, for these people in Honey Lake
Valley to want to be incorporated into the political subdivisions of Nevada where they could take part in all activities.
Isaac Roop, one of the earliest and most prominent residents of Susanville, was very active in the organization of
Nevada territory.[755] The county seat of Lake county, Nevada
(changed to Roop county on December 2, 1862), was located at Susanville. This county included approximately all
the present Washoe county, Nevada, north of the mouth of
the Truckee river, and all of Modoc, Lassen, and Plumas
counties, east of the dividing ridge of the Sierra Nevada.
There were only two fertile areas in it, Honey Lake and
Surprise valleys; most of the remaining lands were mountains, barren deserts, and mud flats, inhabited by hostile
Indian bands. It will be seen, then, that the future existence
of Roop county depended almost entirely upon these two
valleys which lay between the divide and the 120th meridian.

---

[755] This area was made the ninth council district of Nevada territory.

Although Roop county was one of the original nine counties of Nevada territory created in July, 1861, it was not officially organized until the election of county officers on September 3, 1862.[756] On December 14 and 15, Governor Nye issued the commissions to all the newly elected county officers. Five days later, the Nevada legislature ordered Judge Mott to hold a special term of the first district court in Susanville on the third Monday in January, 1863. This was a bold step for the young territory to take in view of the fact that it was acting contrary to the federal act, and in opposition to the sentiment of the California legislature; it was extending its jurisdiction over territory which had not been transferred to Nevada. There was naturally an immediate reaction from Plumas county which claimed jurisdiction over Honey Lake Valley.[757] Although most of the residents of that valley were hardy, resolute, self-reliant, law-abiding citizens, they became very adroit in the evasion of taxes; they declared allegiance to Nevada or California according to the dates that taxes were due to the respective commonwealths. Many of the citizens of the Susanville region refused to submit to California jurisdiction until the boundary question should be settled. They gave as their chief reason that an almost impassable summit separated them from the county seat at Quincy, California, and that they were several hundred miles from Sacramento, while they had their own county seat under Nevada laws and were a comparatively short distance from Carson City on a road that was open practically all the year.

As a preliminary to the special term of court which Judge Mott was to hold in Susanville, the Nevada legislature passed an act which legalized all of the previous rights and pending court actions acquired under the laws of California.[758] Although the judge found no actions to be heard, the Plumas county officials resented the intrusion of Nevada on their rights. The Plumas county judge issued at once a series of injunctions restraining the Nevada officials from further activity in the collection of taxes. Judge John Ward of Roop

[756] Angel, *op. cit.*, 563.

[757] Plumas county was organized in 1854.

[758] A similar act was passed for legalizing actions concerning the Esmeralda district in the Mono county courts. *Laws of Nevada Territory*, 1862, 37-38.

county issued a writ of injunction restraining Judge William
Young of Plumas county, California, from holding court in
Roop county, Nevada. Judge Young, having ignored the
writ, was arrested, brought before Judge Ward, fined one
hundred dollars and imprisoned.[759] Sheriff E. H. Pierce of
Plumas county upon hearing of the difficulties of the judge
of his county went to Susanville to serve an injunction,
issued by Judge Hogan of Plumas county, against Judge
Ward and Sheriff William H. Naileigh of Roop county.
Judge Ward countered with another injunction against
Sheriff Pierce and his deputies. While the courts were issuing
the injunctions, Sheriff Pierce scored a point by arresting
Sheriff Naileigh and Judge Ward, charging them with usurp-
ation and intrusion into office without authority.

Sheriff Pierce and his deputy started immediately for
Quincy but due to the weather and a heavy snowfall on the
preceding night, the trip was abandoned. Judge Ward was
wrested from the custody of the deputy sheriff by a body of
citizens, of whom Isaac Roop was one, before the abandonment of the trip. The Plumas county sheriff, upon finding that
resistance would be made to service of his warrants, returned
to Quincy the following day, raised a *posse comitatus*
of one hundred and eighty armed men, who with one cannon
returned to Susanville. Previous to this, however, and upon
the first arrival of the sheriff of Plumas in Honey Lake
Valley, proceedings by injunction had been instituted against
all the county officials of Plumas county in the name of the
people of Nevada territory. The writs were served on them
but were completely ignored by the Plumas officer and his
deputy. The sheriff escaped and fled to Quincy, but his deputy
was arrested and brought before the probate judge, who
issued the injunction to answer for contempt of court. The
deputy was released, pending an agreement between him and
the citizens that he would return to Quincy to prevent the
sheriff from bringing over his posse. The Plumas sheriff
intended to serve an injunction upon all the county officials
of Roop county, which when served, he intended to have
carried out until the supreme court of California should

[759] He was released almost immediately.

finally pass upon the question of jurisdiction. A heavy snow prevented the deputy from returning to Quincy.

On the arrival of Sheriff Pierce of Plumas county with his posse, the same citizens who made the agreement with his deputy were called together at the request of Sheriff Pierce, who informed them that he did not concur in the agreement and was therefore not bound by it. Judge Ward and Sheriff Naileigh of Roop county were arrested at once, but were not placed in jail. During the same evening they were both taken by a body of Susanville citizens and placed in a log cabin closely guarded. Runners were then sent out in every direction to inform the people of the contemplated arrests. By the next morning, a large body of armed men had congregated at Honey Lake, had fortified the log cabin, provided themselves with munitions of war, and put in a supply of provisions. It was really a declaration that no arrests by California officers under the laws of that state could be made in Honey Lake Valley.

On February 15, when Sheriff Pierce saw the large number of Nevada people, he marched his men to a large barn nearly opposite the cabin occupied by the Roop county men, and they, too, began to fortify the barn with some large hewn logs. While they were so engaged, the Honey Lake men ordered them to stop. The order was repeated, but when it was disobeyed the third time, the Roop county men fired; one man was seriously wounded. The fight then became general and continued for several hours, but with no serious injuries other than the wounding of several persons, among whom was Judge Ward.

A cessation of hostilities was then agreed upon until nine o'clock the next morning. A mass of the citizens assembled and demanded that the two sheriffs come before them. Sheriff Pierce made a proposal: "That each of the parties should disband their forces, appoint a committee of conference and correspondence consisting of four persons (2 from each) to represent the circumstances to their respective governors, to request them to settle, if possible the boundary between the two governments. That all jurisdiction should cease until a settlement was made or authorized to proceed." [760] The agreement was signed; the Plumas county posse returned to Quincy, and the miniature war was over.

When Governor Leland Stanford received news of the war, he appointed Judge Robert Robinson of Sacramento to go to Nevada on March 4 to investigate, and, if possible, to settle the matter with the Nevada officials.[761] Acting-governor Clemens appointed John E. Lovejoy as commissioner to proceed to Susanville and to report to him the unfortunate affair; he was to coöperate with Judge Robinson by calling a council of the territorial officers to hear the California emissary present the California case.

Lovejoy's report was characteristic of the frontier. It expressed the indignity and the grievances the citizens of Roop county suffered at the hands of the California officials. After summarizing the status of affairs he continued to give the governor his opinion of the underlying causes for the trouble:

The settlers of Honey Lake Valley from its earliest history, have been of a peculiar character, fearless, self-reliant, hospitable, willing at all times to render justice to all connected with them, and ready (it may be too much so) to avenge promptly, a wrong committed upon themselves or those who may be connected with them. This character is as necessary as gunpowder in the protection of our frontiers and has been the bulwark which has since the earliest period of our territorial history, defended us repeatedly and promptly from the depredations of our savage and marauding neighbors, within and contiguous to our territorial limits - the Paiutes, Bannocks, Shoshones. . .

The mass of citizens of Honey Lake Valley and the settlements contiguous thereto, have ever from its earliest settlement claimed that they were and of full and first right ought to be citizens of first, Utah territory (the laws of which were thrown over them), and secondly, Nevada territory, the legislature of which, at its last session took decisive steps by throwing her laws over them, in accordance with the expressed wishes of almost the entire body of that people, as well as in the belief that even should they prove to be within the jurisdiction of California will be just and magnanimous enough . . . to cede the same, and cease to persecute them with their onerous jurisdiction. . .

First, they are called oftentimes by the authorities of Plumas county

[760] This summary of the sagebrush war was taken from the report made by Sheriff William Hill Naileigh to Governor Nye. All of the correspondence concerning this affair is among the territorial records in the secretary of state's office in Carson City.

[761] *California Senate Journal,* 1863, app. no. 34, 3-12.

to travel over the mountains, a distance of forty miles, as jurors, or witnesses at all seasons of the year . . . thereby suffering great loss and creating confusion and derangement in all their affairs both financially and socially.

They have been and are socially, financially and geographically, connected with this territory, its people and its every interest by an almost impassable mountain barrier between themselves and their source of judicial and executive authority at California, so much so that as to render the execution of law either criminal or civil, burdensome to them. . .

That even though they should be within the jurisdiction of California . . . the formation of a new county under the jurisdiction of California . . . would so burden them, owing to the sparseness of the population, over the portion of territory proposed, that to support a county government would render taxation unbearable. . .

Independent of these facts, should the authority of Plumas county attempt to enforce her jurisdiction in the least matter, they will immediately come in collision with as brave and determined a body of men as ever raised a rifle; and the sequence will be a bloody warfare of the most desperate character. . .[762]

At this meeting Robinson stated very definitely that California would not consider the "dividing ridge" boundary. After some discussion of the situation Acting-governor Clemens intimated that perhaps Nevada had acted too hastily in organizing Roop county before California consented to the summit boundary, and was for that reason the aggressor in the sagebrush war. The final agreement was made in which each state was to appoint a commissioner to run the boundary line during the year. The Nevada officials proposed that if it were agreeable to California, a tentative line would be considered, placing Honey Lake Valley in California, and Aurora, Esmeralda county, in Nevada.[763] This arrangement was not acceptable to California, but it did provoke the California legislature to pass an act "to survey and to establish the eastern boundary of the state of California and to request the governor of Nevada to join in the survey." [764] The California surveyor-general was authorized to begin work by June 1, 1863, to define the eastern boundary of California from the intersection of the 35th

[762] This report is in the territorial records in the office of the secretary of state in Carson City, Nevada. It was made February 28, 1863.

[763] Bancroft, *History of Nevada, Colorado, and Wyoming*, 154; Angel, *op. cit.*, 101-102; *Sacramento Daily Union*, March 19, 1863.

[764] *Statutes of California*, 1863, 619.

degree north latitude and the Colorado river to the Oregon line, and to mark it with suitable monuments. The cost of the survey to California was not to exceed $25,000; Nevada was to pay her surveyor. The survey was to be made in sixty days, after which time three copies of the maps and the field notes were to be filed together with a complete report to the state legislature.

Governor Nye proceeded more cautiously in organizing Esmeralda county; California controlled Aurora until September, 1863, the date of the September election and the time for the report of the boundary survey to be submitted. However, when Governor Nye learned that the initial point of the 1863 survey placed Aurora in Nevada, he made this city the county seat, appointed the county officials, and sent Judge Turner to that place to hold court. Upon arrival, Turner found Judge Baldwin of Mono county in Aurora holding court. There was no conflict of jurisdiction between the judges because the Esmeralda district had been incorporated under the laws of California as a part of Mono county. Since Aurora was the county seat of Mono county, the records belonged to California.

The general territorial elections of Nevada were set for September 2, but the survey had not yet reached the Esmeralda district. Governor Nye agreed tactfully to permit two elections to be held in Aurora at the same time. The result of this situation was without parallel perhaps in the history of the United States. Thomas N. Machin of Aurora was chosen a representative to the California assembly where he was elected speaker of the lower house; Dr. Thomas W. Pugh, also a resident of Aurora, was elected a delegate to the Nevada assembly, and he, too, was chosen speaker of the lower house. Thus, there existed the singular coincidence of the lower house of the two adjoining states having its speaker come from the same town and elected practically by the same constituents.[765]

Butler Ives was appointed surveyor for Nevada by Acting-governor Clemens. John Kidder was to serve California in a like capacity. Their task was stupendous in face of the topographical difficulties to be overcome; first, they had to find

---

[765] Angel, *op. cit.*, 102.

the initial point in Lake Tahoe, and from that point run a line north to the Oregon line, a distance of two hundred and ten miles, and then run another to the Colorado river, four hundred and fifteen miles to the southeast. A glance at the list of articles in their equipment is sufficient to understand what conditions they anticipated. There were in addition to the necessary astronomical and surveying instruments, sailboats, snowshoes, toboggans, pack mules, guns, swords, mosquito nets, innumerable gifts for the Indians, and the most unusual item on the list, perhaps, the sum of money set aside for the hire of camels to carry their equipment on the desert.

Surveyor-general Houghton of California met Surveyors Ives and Kidder at Lake Tahoe with the maps and notes of the Mowry survey. They took the initial point [766] again, which they found to be one and one-half miles west of the former survey. By these measurements they ascertained Lake Tahoe to be twenty-six miles long instead of forty, as had been stated in the Mowry report.

On June 6 twelve men with twenty-five pack animals started out to run the northern line. With the exception of some hostile demonstrations of the Modoc Indians, suppressed quickly by troops sent out by Acting-governor Clemens, there were no great difficulties. Most of the Honey Lake Valley was found to be in the state of California.[767]

The southern survey was begun on July 24. Scarcity of water, hostilities with the Mono Indians, shortage of supplies and a heavy snowstorm prevented the completion of the survey; it extended to within one mile of the 38th degree north latitude, but had been run far enough, however, to determine the fact that Aurora was in Nevada. When this became known, the county records were transferred immediately to Bridgeport, California; the Esmeralda county officials were permitted to copy all the records relating to the Nevada county. The Kidder-Ives line was marked with pine-posts which could easily be found.[768] The location of Honey

---

[766] The angle formed by the intersection of the oblique line extended northwest from the point where the 35th parallel intersects the Colorado river and the 120th meridian.

[767] *California Assembly Journal,* 15 sess., app. 42.

[768] In 1873 the line was run by A. W. von Schmidt which took some more

Lake Valley in California and the Esmeralda mining district in Nevada ended practically the deep-rooted boundary dispute.[769] The California legislature accepted the report on April 4, 1864; the legislature of the state of Nevada did likewise on February 7, 1865.

The question of the eastern boundary of Nevada was more readily adjusted, as in that direction there was no powerful state to resist expansion; on the contrary, the congress was quite willing to reduce the frontiers of Utah territory. Territorial Delegate Cradlebaugh presented a memorial from Governor Nye and the legislature asking for one degree of territory to the east. On July 14, 1862, congress granted the request. The eastern boundary of Nevada territory was extended sixty miles.[770] This addition was compensation for the loss of Honey Lake Valley; it included the rich mining district around Austin.

When Nevada was admitted to statehood the following boundaries were incorporated in the organic act:

Commencing at a point formed by the intersection of the 38th degree of longitude west from Washington with the 37th degree north latitude, thence due west along the said 37th degree north latitude to the eastern boundary of California; thence in a northwesterly direction along said east boundary of California to the 43d degree north latitude to point formed by its intersection with aforesaid 38th degree longitude west from Washington thence due south down 38th degree north longitude to place of beginning.[771]

Since the western boundary was given as the "eastern boundary of the state of California," Nevada tacitly relinquished the "dividing ridge" boundary in the territorial act. Oregon territory bounded Nevada on the north, Utah territory on the east, Arizona territory on the south.

As soon as the first United States senators from Nevada,

territory from Nevada; in 1889, another series of surveys began which finally culminated in the United States geodetic survey line. It cut more land from Nevada. In 1903 this survey was completed and accepted by Nevada.

[769] The part of Roop county left in Nevada was attached to Washoe county and the name Roop was dropped entirely. Nevada made a futile attempt to reopen the question with California in 1871. *Laws of Nevada,* 1871.

[770] *United States Statutes at Large,* 37 Cong., 2 sess., vol. XII, chapter CLXXIII, 575; *Cong. Globe,* 37 Cong., 2 sess., app. 408.

[771] *Statutes of Nevada,* 1864-1865, 35, 60.

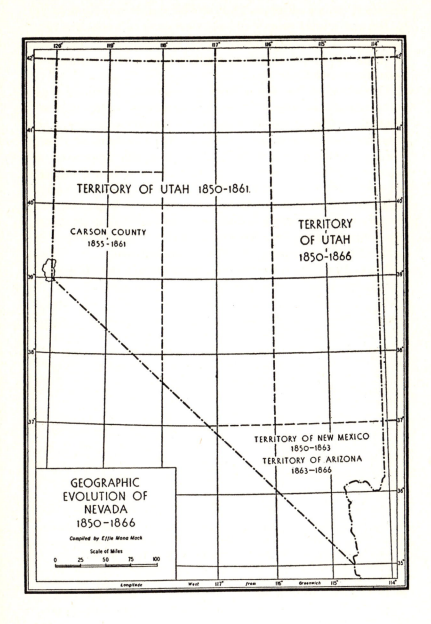

TERRITORY OF UTAH 1850-1861.

CARSON COUNTY
1855-1861

TERRITORY
OF UTAH
1850-1866

TERRITORY OF NEW MEXICO
1850-1863

TERRITORY OF ARIZONA
1863-1866

GEOGRAPHIC
EVOLUTION OF
NEVADA
1850-1866

Compiled by Effie Mona Mack

Scale of Miles

0    25    50    75    100

Longitude          West    117°    from    116°    Greenwich    115°          114°

William M. Stewart and James W. Nye, took their seats
in congress, they began at once to extend the boundaries of
Nevada, introducing a bill to amend the Nevada Enabling
Act to include an additional degree of longitude on the east.
The bill passed the senate at that session, but failed to receive action in the house because of lack of time. At the
next session another bill was introduced to "extend the eastern and southern boundaries of Nevada." It provided for
the extension of the boundary to the 37th meridian west
from Washington, and the southern boundary to the Colorado river.[772] The area thus included took large sections
from the territories of Utah and Arizona.[773] The delegates
from both of these territories resisted vigorously, but the
congress had the power to adjust these lines without asking
the consent of either of them.[774]

Although the state of Nevada finally evolved a very
much larger state than when created a territory, there was
no natural reason, with the exception of the Colorado river,
for any of its boundaries. The northern line, the 42nd degree
north latitude, cut the Snake river drainage basin when a
natural boundary could have been located at the watershed
of the Humboldt-Snake rivers; and the dividing ridge of
the Sierra Nevada could have been made the western boundary. A natural boundary on the east could have been determined also. So far as either eastern or western boundary
lines marking any cleavage between the areas bordering
Utah or California were concerned, both of them were
mythical. The interests of the citizens of Modoc, Lassen,
and Plumas counties were unalterably connected in many
ways with the interests of Nevada; Inyo and Mono counties

[772] This area included the present counties of Elko, White Pine, Lincoln,
Clark and a large part of Nye.

[773] *Cong. Globe,* 38 Cong., 2 sess., 663-665, 671-672; *Statutes at Large,* xiv,
ch. LXXIII, 43; *Senate Journal,* 38 Cong., 2 sess., 235 (ser. no. 1208); *Laws of
Nevada,* 1865; Arizona refers to the southern part of Nevada as "the lost
county of Pah-Ute." John R. Murdock, *The Constitution of Arizona,* 27.

[774] A conflict over the jurisdiction of Nevada and Utah authorities arose
in Lincoln county, Nevada, the story of which extends beyond the dates fixed
for this volume. In brief, when the Mormons on the Virgin and Muddy rivers
found they were in Nevada, most of them left and took up land in Utah.
Angel, *op. cit.,* 79.

were closer to Nevada centers of industry than to those of
California, and Alpine county was commercially and socially
a part of Douglas county, Nevada. The eastern counties
of Nevada have no particular or cogent reason for being in
this state. They were added to reduce the Mormon lands,
yet the people of Utah were more extensively interested in
that area than any other group. All of which went to prove
that the federal government in her relations with the western
territories exhibited regrettable ignorance of geography,
and an apathetic attitude toward the problems of the frontier
communities.

# Nevada, a Land of Wide Open Spaces

By the terms of the Mexican cession to the United States, 522,568 square miles were added to the national domain. As soon as the United States took possession of this land the congress extended the laws of the United States over it. All of Nevada, 110,690 square miles, or somewhat less than one-fourth of the former Mexican lands, had to be disposed of by the federal government. A very small portion of this land was cultivable; the greatest part of it was mountainous and arid; a very little of it was timber land; most of it was covered with sagebrush and greasewood.

Of the 70,641,600 acres in Nevada, about 12,000,000 acres have been withdrawn for Indians, forests, stock driveways, reclamation, game refuges, and historic spots – Fort Churchill, the Lost City, the Valley of Fire, the Cathedral Gorge, and Lehman Cave. Of the remaining area, 51,000,-000 acres are open and reserved public lands. Less than fifteen per cent of the land in Nevada is privately owned, and one-half of that belongs to the railroads. For these reasons, the federal government has had a great deal to do with the survey, sale, and disposition of the land embraced within the state.[775]

At the time the United States acquired the land which later became Nevada there were no settlements on it, but in the following year, 1849, a trading post was set up at the eastern base of the Sierra Nevada in Carson Valley, on the road to California, for the purpose of selling supplies to the Forty-niners. In 1851 this trading station became a permanent settlement through the efforts of John Reese, who came out that summer with a number of men and a large quantity of supplies and seed. He cultivated a number of

---

[775] Donaldson, *The Public Domain, its history with statistics*, 134. Hereafter this book will be cited as *Sen. Ex. Doc.* no. 52, 51 Cong., 1 sess.

acres of land – turnips were the chief crop.[776] Reese took up a number of acres for his own use, and several of the men in his party did likewise. On November 12 of the same year about twenty of the settlers in Carson Valley held a meeting. Absalom Woodward of the mail company, who had taken up some land for a mail station in the spring of that year, presided over it. The purpose was to regulate the taking up and the holding of land claims. In the business transacted at this meeting was the provision for the survey of land claims and the appointment of a surveyor. James H. Haynes was made surveyor; the amount of land each person could take was fixed at one quarter section, which was to be recorded in a book.[777] A week later, a second meeting, presided over by John Reese, was held for the purpose of regulating further the distribution of land. This pioneer legislature resolved to give the land claimants permission to sell their claims and take up new ones. It required further that improvements to the amount of five dollars must be made on any land claim before the expiration of six months. It gave authority, also, to companies to take land claims for each member. The privilege to prove up on an entire claim owned by a company by doing all of the work on one claim was allowed. To regulate the taking up of timber land, of which there were many acres bordering on Carson Valley, it was voted that all wooded lands should be held in common by everyone except a sawmill owner, who was to be limited to a certain amount of land.[778]

It may be wondered why the holding of land by a company should be regulated when there were so many millions of acres of land available. This action was taken so that John and Enoch Reese of the J. and E. Reese Company of Salt Lake City could hold a large amount of land. From the meager data obtainable it appears that Enoch Reese of Brooklyn, New York, brother of Colonel John Reese of Carson Valley, was the capitalist who financed the Reese Company of Salt Lake City.[779] The trading station on the

[776] Supra, 149-150.
[777] Bancroft, History of Nevada, Colorado, and Wyoming, 69.
[778] Bancroft, History of Nevada, Colorado, and Wyoming, 70.
[779] Loc. cit.

site of the later town of Genoa was a branch of the Utah company.

In the Nevada territorial records on file in the office of the secretary of state there is the book in which were recorded the land claims in Carson Valley. At that time land was described by metes and bounds. "Ranch no. 1," taken up by John Reese, was the first land claim recorded in Nevada, then under the government of the territory of Utah. It extended from his trading house (located on the east side of the main street of Genoa)[780] south to a lone tree, and it included all of the land bounded by the Carson river to the east and the Sierra Nevada on the west. "Ranch no. 2" was surveyed for Hampden S. Beatie, clerk in the Reese store in Salt Lake City.[781]

As the population of the valley began to increase the land laws became more strict. At a citizens' meeting held in 1853 it was decided that a person intending to take up a land claim must first give notice of his intention. A married man was permitted to take up one section. The length of time, however, in which the assessment work could be done was shortened to sixty days, but the improvements must be worth one hundred dollars.[782] Many Mormon settlers came to the valley north of Carson Valley,[783] and land claims in Washoe, Pleasant, and Steamboat valleys, and the Truckee Meadows were taken up. When Carson county, Utah, was created, these claims were recorded with the county officials.

In 1851 six placer miners came over from California to look for gold in Carson Valley, but not finding any rich deposits they took up land in Eagle Valley, now the site of Carson City. These men either did not take the trouble to learn the rules and regulations of taking up land in western Utah, or paid no attention to the self-constituted government in Carson Valley, for they claimed all of the land in Eagle Valley. Although these would-be placer miners took up all of the land, the first ranch in the record book for Eagle

---

[780] The log house built by Reese was the first one to be built in Nevada. It burned in 1916.

[781] *Et supra*, 147-148.

[782] Bancroft, *History of Nevada, Colorado, and Wyoming*, 71.

[783] Jack's Valley north of Carson Valley was settled by Mormons.

Valley was surveyed for Dr. B. L. King, who in 1852 took up a fertile piece of land at the mouth of the cañon (King's cañon) to the west of what is now Carson City. In the fall of the same year, one, Clark, selected a piece of land in Washoe Valley under the shelter of a timbered spur of the Sierra Nevada through which flowed a small stream of water. It was near the site of the present Franktown. Although he named his place "The Garden of Eden," it could not have been very idyllic, for he deserted it after a short time. In the book of surveys "Ranch no. 1" in Washoe Valley belonged to Jacob H. Rose; "Ranch no. 2" in the same valley was surveyed for John Campbell. Local interest and sentiment were attached to the Campbell ranch; it was to become a few years later the property of Alison "Ellen" Orrum Hunter Cowan Bowers. In May, 1856, one undivided half of this ranch in Washoe (Wassau) Valley was sold for $100 to Alexander Cowan, second husband of Mrs. Bowers. It consisted of three hundred and twenty acres. (In this same record book, the writer found an account of the divorce Mrs. Cowan obtained from her Mormon husband.)[784] The court granted this land to Mrs. Cowan. In 1860 this same land was surveyed for Lemuel S. Bowers, the third and last husband of Alison Orrum. By 1857, the year of the "Utah War" when Brigham Young called all Zionites back to Salt Lake City to resist the United States soldiers, most of the Mormons sold out to the apostates and gentiles for whatever they could get for their lands and improvements. It was estimated that nine hundred and eighty-five Mormons, men, women, and children left western Utah.[785] The Mormons gave to their purchasers or leasees the best title they possessed. Most of the ranches were recorded in a book kept by Stephen A. Kinsey.[786] All of this land had been preëmpted, but the preëmption laws of the United States had not been extended over this territory.[787] The first legislature of the territory of Nevada rejected these titles.[788]

[784] Territorial Record Book, MS., office of the secretary of state, Carson City, Nevada.

[785] Daily Alta California, October 8, 1857.

[786] Supra, 232.

[787] San Francisco Evening Bulletin, February 15, 1860.

[788] Laws of Nevada Territory, 1861, 231.

By the middle of the nineteenth century, the United States had developed a more or less well-defined public land policy. It consisted in the main of making liberal grants to the new states for the promotion of education, internal improvements, and sale of the national domain on liberal terms.[789] The congress gave also to all of the states from two to five per cent of the net proceeds of the sale of public lands within the state.[790] These generous donations from the federal government were made on condition that the states would not tax the lands sold by the United States for a period of five years after the date of the sale. In 1841 the Preëmption Law gave *bona fide* citizens the right to settle on surveyed lands offered or not offered for sale, and to purchase their holdings, not exceeding one hundred and sixty acres at the minimum price of one dollar and twenty-five cents an acre. All of the land taken up in Nevada before the Homestead Act of 1862 was passed had been preëmpted. There must have been a considerable amount of land taken up after the passage of that act, but there were no homestead entries before 1864. In that year there were forty-three applications for homesteads totaling 6,452.07 acres; for the next two years there was only one entry a year — forty acres in 1865 and eighty acres in 1866.[791]

The surveyor-general for the territory of Nevada was John W. North of Minnesota. He took up his duties on June 22, 1861, and served until September 14, 1863, when he was appointed federal judge of the first judicial district.[792] As soon as he opened his office in Carson City, he made a tour of the surrounding valleys, Carson, Washoe, Walker, and the Truckee Meadows, and of the leading settlements, Virginia City, Gold Hill, Dayton, and Silver City, in order that he might determine what his policy should be. Land problems in Nevada were comparatively easy; there were no land grants, and the population was more or less concentrated in the western part of the territory. The courts of the territory

---

[789] *United States Statutes at Large*, IX, 330.

[790] *Sen. Ex. Doc.* no. 52, 31 Cong., 1 sess., 239.

[791] *Sen. Ex. Doc.* no. 52, 31 Cong., 1 sess., 205.

[792] North was known to hold an opinion favorable to the Chollar Mining Company; Judge Mott was induced to resign and North was appointed in his place. Bancroft, *History of Nevada, Colorado, and Wyoming*, 173; *supra*, 260.

of Utah had for several years permitted the settlers to hold
as much land as they could fence. Because it was difficult to
get timber for fence purposes most of the farmers had
cleared their lands of stones and had piled them up for
fences.[793] Many of the ranch owners had been able to include
one thousand acres, some had three thousand. The first surveyor elected for Carson county, Utah, was Henry W. Niles,
chosen at the first election to be held in western Utah on
September 20, 1854. He had surveyed, without any official
approval by the surveyor-general, some of the lands in Carson county, but since no guide or base lines had been established, and since all of the land had been taken up without
the extension of the preëmption laws, all the land claims
were illegal and invalid.[794] The settlers on these lands had
been duly notified. They were anxious to have an official
survey made so that they could confirm the extent of their
holdings with the correct government lines. But before the
survey was accomplished in December, 1860, one hundred
and ninety of them petitioned the surveying district.[795]

When Surveyor North took up his duties, he followed
the instructions of the interior department to extend the
Mount Diablo base line, by which the surveys of central and
northern California had been made, to Carson Valley; and
then to establish a guide meridian down Carson river with
standard parallels thirty miles apart. By surveying this part
first, he was reaching the most thickly settled agricultural
lands.[796] The surveyor-general's office assisted in establishing
the boundaries of Nevada, especially on the west during the
dispute between California and Nevada. In his report for
1862-1863, he indicated that he had surveyed 147,584 acres;
during the following year the report showed 269,849 acres
surveyed, or a total of 417,433 acres surveyed during the
territorial period.[797] In the year 1863-1864, he coöperated

---

[793] A number of these fences may be seen in Carson Valley at the present
time.

[794] *Sen. Ex. Doc.* no. 1, 36 Cong., 2 sess., 62 (ser. no. 1078).

[795] *Sen. Ex. Doc.* no. 1, 37 Cong., 2 sess., 467, 617 (ser. no. 1117).

[796] *Sen. Ex. Doc.* no. 52, 37 Cong., 1 sess., 181; *Report Commissioner General Land Office,* 1862, 112-113.

[797] *Ibid.,* 1863, 43; *House Ex. Doc.* no. 1, 37 Cong., 3 sess., 44-45 (ser. no.
1157).

with the railroad surveyors in selecting a route for the proposed Pacific Railroad down the Truckee river cañon and the Humboldt River Valley. In his report, after having gone over the Humboldt river route, he came to the conclusion that it would not be practicable to extend the standard lines north so as to include the land along the river, but rather to establish the sixtieth parallel northward by transverse lines as a basis for surveying in this district. This recommendation by North was rejected by the congress.[798] The surveys were not entirely satisfactory. Constant complaints were being made to the general land office. That office, however, had given very indefinite orders to the territorial authorities. Territorial Delegate Cradlebaugh criticised the waste of money in useless surveys of alkali flats and deserts, money which was necessary for the survey of the fertile sections.[799]

The clouded titles to the lands taken up under the Utah government, and the desire to hasten the sale of agricultural lands in western Nevada, brought about on July 2, 1862, the establishment of a Nevada land district. This step brought all of the public lands of the United States in Nevada territory under the control of that office.[800] It was also provided that a resident registrar and a receiver be appointed by the president. It was provided that the preëmption laws of the district should be applied and that all of the townships in the range of the regular surveys were open to measurement with the exception of the mineral lands which were reserved to the government.[801] The citizens who wished the services of the land office had to file written applications, accompanied by a deposit large enough to defray the cost of the survey. On March 11, 1863, the land office opened at Carson City. Just as it had begun to get organized, the office was ordered closed on June 1, 1863, for the reasons of economy. The Nevada records were ordered removed to California,

[798] Report Commissioner General Land Office, 1864, 29.

[799] Cong. Globe, 37 Cong., 2 sess., 527, 1862; Report Commissioner General Land Office, 1864, 97-98.

[800] Cong. Globe, 37 Cong., 2 sess., 2871, 2987, 3082; Sen. Journal, 37 Cong., 2 sess., 695, 735, 748 (ser. no. 1116).

[801] Cong. Globe, 37 Cong., 2 sess., app. 385-386; House Journal, 37 Cong., 2 sess., 377-378 (ser. no. 1126); U.S. Statutes at Large, 2 sess., 503.

and the surveyor-general of that state was instructed to serve for both California and Nevada.[802]

A memorial was sent to the congress by the citizens of Nevada protesting this action. They pointed out that owing to the increasing demand for timber lands, it was necessary for Nevada to have a land office. The demand for agricultural lands as soon as the Central Pacific Railroad was completed across the state was anticipated also. They supported their contentions with facts to prove that there would be many sales of these lands, thereby justifying the establishment of a Nevada land district.[803] The federal government not only disregarded this request on July 2, 1865, but also separated Nevada from the California district and attached it to the surveying district of the territory of Colorado. However, as soon as Nevada had been made a state and its representatives had reached Washington their efforts resulted in Nevada's becoming a separate district in July, 1866.[804]

During the territorial period, there was no definite settled policy of the federal government concerning the mineral lands. Several attempts to offer them for sale or to lease them were made. Petitions from the Nevada mine owners were sent to the congress requesting that nothing be done about these lands until the Nevada representatives could reach Washington. In short, the federal government tacitly permitted the prospector to go upon the public domain and search out the precious metals without restricting or regulating the way in which he was to hold his land. In 1866 the National Mining Law was passed which incorporated in the main part the rules and regulations adopted by the miners themselves.[805] The interior department was very active in this matter. A number of suggestions were made but none of them was adopted.[806]

After the Paiute war of 1860, the federal government

[802] *Cong. Globe,* 37 Cong., 2 sess., app., 345; *House Ex. Doc.* no. 1, 37 Cong., 3 sess., 45 (ser. no. 1157).

[803] *Laws of Nevada Territory,* 1862, app., 193-194.

[804] *Sen. Ex. Doc.* no. 52, 51 Cong., 1 sess., 195.

[805] *Infra,* 434.

[806] It was suggested that the mineral land be divided into five and forty acre tracts and leased to the miners.

took steps to settle the Indians of Nevada on reservations. The Indians had claimed the fertile land along the rivers and the lakes. The trouble between the whites and the Indians had been largely due to trespassing by the white man. Governor Nye, ex-officio superintendent of Indian affairs, arranged for the settling of this trouble by agreements with the tribes that they should have the exclusive use of certain definite areas. Indian reservations were established at the mouth of the Truckee river at Pyramid Lake to be used by all of the Indians. Small reservations were made on Walker Lake also.[807]

On the eastern side of the Sierra Nevada there was a very luxuriant growth of cedar and pine, but on the basin ranges to the east there was little or no timber. The land was covered, however, with sagebrush, which burns readily, but it was soon grubbed off by the first people who went to the silver rush. The great demand for firewood, for fence posts, and for fuel for the boilers in the mills led to the beginning of cutting the timber on the public domain. The federal government brought suit against Ephraim Briggs; the decision of the supreme court made it illegal for anyone to cut timber on the public domain and made the offender liable to punishment. To take care of the needs of the people, the department of the interior established a number of lumber agencies in Nevada and placed the administration of the timber lands in the hands of the surveyor-general. The preëmptors under the Utah laws were permitted to cut timber on their own land for building, fencing and firewood, but they were not permitted to sell their land unless they had resided on it for five years.[808] The lumber business was one of the greatest industries of the early years of Nevada history. The mountains to the west of Nevada were almost denuded of timber to furnish wood for the mines and for the people. Hundreds of people were engaged in some de-

---

[807] *Sen. Ex. Doc.* no. 1, 37 Cong., 2 sess., 617 (ser. no. 1117). Reservations were made later in Duck Valley and western Shoshone, Elko county, Fort Mojave, Moapa river, Clark county, Pyramid Lake, Washoe county, Paiute and Shoshone, Walker river, Churchill, Mineral, and Lyon counties, Elko and Humboldt counties; and Winnemucca in Humboldt and Lander counties. *Supra,* 314.

[808] *Report of General Land Office,* 1864, 21, 97.

partment of lumbering during the boom days of the Comstock.[809]

Although the Homestead Law went into effect on January 1, 1863, there was not a single entry under that act for that year; in 1864 there were less than fifty applications; and during the following two years there was but one entry for each year. The reason for the lack of interest in agricultural lands was due probably to the desire of most of the people to engage in mining. The farmers, however, received high prices for their products.

After the first rush to Washoe in 1859 and the following years, after it had become reasonably apparent that there were going to be a number of permanent cities and towns; some expedient to meet temporary needs had to be made. The Townsite Law of 1863 permitted a person to "squat" on a town lot under the preëmption law, and after some formality, to claim it as his own. There was much ambiguity in this law, inasmuch as it cost almost as much to obtain a lot as it did one hundred and sixty acres of land.[810] Where a town was already in existence it was difficult to obtain a title to property in the manner and form in which a man owned it. When a "squatter" acquired a town lot he owned the surface of the land only; the owner of the mining claim owned the minerals below it. Virginia City had two hundred and fifty blocks reserved under the Townlot Act, and Gold Hill had one hundred and seventy-nine. Many of the early towns in Nevada took advantage of this act. The person taking up the lot obtained his title by applying to the land office, by furnishing certain proof that he had taken up the land and by the payment of a small fee.[811]

The federal government was very liberal in its policy of granting large tracts of land to states having large areas of public domain. Congress had by several acts granted to the several states containing public lands, the sixteenth

809 *Infra*, 442-444.

810 *Sen. Ex. Doc.* no. 52, 31 Cong., 305.

811 In 1870 the law was modified so that the authorities of the town could enter the townsite and could obtain a patent for the benefit of the lot owner at a dollar and a quarter an acre. This law would ordinarily not cost the tenant more than two or three dollars for his title. *Sen. Ex. Doc.* no. 52, 51 Cong., 1 sess., 305.

and thirty-sixth sections in each township. In Nevada this amounted to 3,925,333 acres, which the state chose to use for school purposes. Twenty complete sections, 12,800 acres to be selected by the state legislature by January 1, 1868, in legal subdivisions of not less than one hundred and sixty acres, were donated for the erection of state buildings at the capital at Carson City, for legislative and judicial purposes; a like amount was set aside for a state penitentiary.[812] Under the Internal Improvement Act of September 4, 1841, Nevada was granted 500,000 acres of land. By the Morrill Act of July 2, 1862, the several states were allowed 30,000 acres of land for each senator and representative, to establish a college of agriculture and mechanics. Nevada received 90,-000 acres by this act.[813] Altogether, the state received from the federal government on her admission three million and a half acres of land.[814] In addition to these lands, Nevada was given five per cent of the net proceeds of the sales of the public land within the state. These allowances were in lieu of the state taxation of United States public lands. The law took effect from the date of admission of the state into the Union.

Surveying lands was very costly. The request to survey the fertile lands, which were widely scattered, required a number of lines to be run. Water and fuel were scarce; supplies were expensive; and the time and work required to run the standard parallel lines across the mountains made the cost mount very high. The appropriations were never large enough to meet the needs of the surveyor-general. His salary was only $3885; and the salaries of the registrar and receiver were $2500. The former asked the congress generally for about $100,000; from $10,000 to $20,000 exclusive of salaries was usually granted. It was impossible for the congress to realize that surveying in Nevada was any different from surveying in the more level and accessible regions of the United States.[815]

Nevada was and still is a state of wide open spaces. When

[812] A. J. Marsh, *Constitutional Debates*, 1864, sec. 16, ix, sec. xi.
[813] *Congressional Globe*, 37 Cong., 2 sess., app., 336.
[814] H. G. Blaisdel, *First Biennial Message*, 1867, 12-13.
[815] *Report of Commissioner General Land Office*, 1862, 22-23; 1863, 163.

the boundary dispute between California and the territory
of Nevada was terminated in 1863 there was estimated to be
62,880 square miles, or 40,243,200 acres; and when Nevada
was admitted as a state there were approximately 81,539
square miles within it, or 52,184,960 acres. By the act of
May 5, 1866, 18,325 square miles or 11,728,000 acres of
land belonging to the territory of Utah, and 12,225 miles
or 7,824,000 acres of land belonging to the territory of
Arizona, were added to Nevada.[816] Of the 70,000,000 acres
in Nevada, there are a total of 51,399,296 acres of unappropriated and unreserved lands, of which 21,265,652 are un-
surveyed at this late date. Most of this land, however, is
mountainous and suitable for grazing purposes only.[817]

---

[816] *United States Statutes at Large*, 1866, 43.
[817] *Report of Surveyor-general and State Land Registrar, Nevada*, 1931-
1932, 49.

# From Preëmption to Ownership

Whenever the history of the Pacific coast is told the mining period is emphasized. The history of California is always thought to hinge on the gold rush; it is no less a tradition, when the history of Nevada is mentioned, to base it on the silver rush to Washoe. Every section of the United States has contributed its part to the process of nationalizing our American people. One of the most important contributions which the mining frontier of California and Nevada made to this process was the affirmation of the right of the American citizen to go onto the public domain and search for precious metal for his own use. The discovery of gold in California brought about the birth of a distinctive mining law;[818] the discovery of silver in Nevada carried to completion the adoption of the National Mining Law of 1866.

Before the discovery of gold in California the federal government had had very little experience in regulating disposal of the mineral lands. In the absence of any American law on that question the government adopted first the system used in some European countries of reserving the mineral lands for the federal government subject to lease by the miners, who were required to pay a rent. Collection of rent cost the government more money than the revenue derived. In 1847 the leasing system was abolished, and the mineral lands were offered for sale.[819] When gold was discovered in California the following year and thousands of men flocked to the gold fields, there was no law to regulate the mineral lands.

California was under military law, but the army officers in command were powerless to handle the situation. Indeed, many of them rushed to the gold fields themselves to win

[818] William E. Colby, "The Extra-lateral Right – shall it be Abolished?" in *California Law Review*, IV, 437.
[819] *United States Statutes at Large*, IX, 146, 147, 179.

quick fortunes by being first on the ground. Colonel Richard B. Mason, military governor in 1849, recommended granting licenses to mine small tracts of land, about one hundred yards square, at a rent ranging from $100 to $1000 a year; or else selling the lands in tracts of twenty to forty acres at public auction to the highest bidder.[820] After President Polk had received Colonel Mason's report, he recommended that congress either reserve the mineral lands of the Pacific coast for the United States government, or sell them in small tracts at a minimum fixed price.[821] In compliance with the president's request, the senate public lands committee reported a bill which provided for division of the mineral lands into tracts of about two acres to be offered for sale at public auction, the minimum price to be $1.25 an acre. Senator Thomas Hart Benton opposed this plan, offering in its place a bill which provided that agents grant permits for working mineral lands without any compensation to the government. It will be remembered that Senator Benton was the father-in-law of General Frémont, who had acquired large acreages in the California mining districts. Neither of these plans was adopted, nor was anything done about the situation during Polk's administration. But the miners did not wait for the federal government to devise a system for the regulation of the mines; they made rules and regulations themselves. Every day brought thousands of men into the gulches, cañons, and river beds on the slope of the Sierra Nevada, along a distance of six hundred miles more or less. Every day thousands of dollars worth of gold were being placered out of the sand and gravel on lands that belonged to the United States. Because there were no laws to regulate this activity, and because the military officials who had charge of government property had no instructions, the federal officials took a *laissez faire* attitude toward the question.

However, the first California legislature of 1850 discussed the mining situation at some length. There were several proposals advocated to regulate the mineral lands. One legislator suggested that the right to mine on national lands be restricted to American citizens and to certain for-

[820] *House Ex. Doc.* no. 17, 31 Cong., 1 sess., 532-533.
[821] Richardson, *Messages and Papers of the Presidents,* IV, 643.

eigners who had declared their intention to become citizens. Another proposed to lease or to sell the lands outright, or to permit American citizens to work the mines freely except for a small leasing tax to secure some protection to the miners. The legislature adopted the last suggestion, and it was incorporated into a bill which Senator Frémont introduced in the senate. He wanted the proceeds of mining revenues to be divided between the federal and the state governments. The bill was opposed on the ground that the leasing system had been adopted and had been found impracticable. A substitute bill was offered which provided that the federal government sanction a policy of the freedom of the mines without any regulations. Although this bill was not adopted and many other suggestions and bills were introduced in subsequent congresses, the policy which it proposed was actually followed until the adoption of the National Mining Law of 1866.[822]

The *laissez faire* attitude of the federal government was perhaps best, since it gave the miners the opportunity to work out for themselves a fair system of rules and regulations. From the many miners' codes at first adopted there evolved eventually a more or less uniform set of rules. The National Mining Act of 1866 legalized these rules and regulations, thereby giving rise to the first federal statutes on this subject. Nevada, as both territory and state, and William M. Stewart, senator from the state for thirty years, took a very important part in the passage of that act.

The first mining in the West was placer mining, seasonal and short-lived. The miners who engaged in it floated from place to place with the news of "rich diggings." For a group of legislators in the national capital, many of whom had never seen a mine and had never had any experience with a mining population, to attempt to legislate for the mines and miners, and then to have expected the laws to be enforced, was as absurd as it would have been for the federal government to try to control that first excited mass of humanity which rushed to the gold fields. No laws could have been enforced except those which the miners made themselves, simple laws, symptomatic of the rugged individualism

[822] *Cong. Globe,* 31 Cong., 1 sess., 1815, 1869, 2018, 2029-2030.

of the frontier, and the synthesis of the experiences of hard headed fortune seekers from every part of the world.

"Miners came from the lead mines of Michigan, from the gold mines of Virginia, Georgia, and the Carolinas, from the mines of Cornwall, the lead mines of Derbyshire, the silver and gold mines of Mexico and Peru, and in fact from every known mining community." [823] The contributions to legislation of these miners brought about one of the most remarkable and purely democratic governmental institutions in the history of the world.[824] Whenever a group of miners rushed to a rich field a meeting was called. Every miner in the vicinity was his own representative. The meeting place was out in the open or in a miner's rude cabin. The size of the district was determined and its boundaries defined, generally by metes and bounds. Officers, usually a chairman, a secretary, and a recorder, were elected, after which a simple code of rules, by which mining in that district was to be carried on, was adopted. At first when there was no law in force, the code included other civil rights and the punishment of crimes.[825]

In brief, from their knowledge of existing codes in Germany, Cornwall, Mexico, and Peru, these miners fixed the boundaries of the district, the size of the claims, the manner in which each was to be marked and recorded, the amount of work which a miner had to do on his claim to secure title to it, and the circumstances under which a claim could be jumped.[826] These rules and regulations were enforced by the miners themselves, and were recognized by the courts and legislatures of California; they spread to the other western states and territories as new mining discoveries were made in them. The right to appropriate the use of water in the streams of California was also made part of these codes.

When the miners discovered quartz ledges, a more extensive code had to be framed to cover a new type of mining.

[823] Colby, *op. cit.,* 437.

[824] A good account of the rise and development of mining codes may be found in Charles H. Shinn, *Mining Camps; a study in American frontier government.*

[825] Angel, *op. cit.,* 62.

[826] Colby, *op. cit.,* 439.

It was, however, closely related to the placer mining codes. There was another factor to be considered in quartz mining. It required very little capital to engage in placer mining, whereas quartz mining required large investments for excavation and extraction.

The discovery of extensive veins of gold and silver ore in Nevada attracted the attention of the federal government during the Civil War. Why could not the national government liquidate the Civil War debt by the sale of these lands to the highest bidder? And why could not the army police and enforce the sale and lease of these lands? At least an attempt was made to pass laws to do so, but the representatives from the mining states forestalled such action.

When the federal government began to discuss the possibility of regulating the mineral lands, the mining interests in Nevada became very fearful lest all of their claims might be confiscated. Many millions of dollars had been expended in mining and mill machinery. The national government must recognize the miners' rules and regulations, as the western states and territories had done. These investments must not be lost. The mining interests found a champion in William Morris Stewart, United States senator from Nevada.

The mine owners of Nevada could not have sent to congress a man better equipped with knowledge of their situation than Senator Stewart. From the time he arrived in the West he had been connected with the mining industry. In 1850 he engaged in placer mining in Nevada county, California; [827] in November, 1852, he was chairman of the committee which drew up the first rules and regulations for quartz mining in California; [828] in the same year he was appointed district attorney of Nevada county, California, and as such made a systematic study of mining law. From that time until he followed the rush to Washoe he was engaged in politics and the practice of mining law in several places in California. Stewart's successful record in winning mining suits in California followed him to the Comstock, and in consequence he was employed as counsel by the owners of the most extensive mining interests on the lode. In fact,

[827] Oscar T. Shuck, *Representative and Leading Men of the Pacific*, 636.
[828] *Ibid.*, 532.

Stewart and his partner, Alexander Baldwin, during the early litigation, were the leading law firm in Virginia City from 1860 to 1864. They were opposed by the most prominent lawyers from the Pacific coast and other parts of the United States. Stewart had given particular and special study to the possessory rights of the miners. In all of his pleadings:

. . . his statements were as clear and straightforward as possible, avoid, ing carefully any semblance of legal quibble or trick. He placed himself on the level of the juries, spoke to their crude sense of justice and fairness and strove to convey the idea that his clients were entitled to a verdict in equity even more than by law. His opponents protested that he was endowed with a faculty of imposing the sublimest absurdities upon juries as pure and spotless truth, but the success of his method was grumblingly admired.[829]

In his associate and his auxiliary aides he had a corps of experts which made his firm an exceedingly formidable one with which to cope. He was always referred to as the "great leader of the Washoe bar." The same writer said, "No one ever gets the advantage of him and few ever try it. The most ambitious are content with the glory of preventing Stewart from getting advantage of them. I am a veteran lawyer, and when I have made a drawn game with him, I am satisfied." [830] The counsel fees in the cases which he prosecuted or defended were enormous for those times. His income from his practice for the years from 1860 to 1865 amounted to $200,000 annually.[831]

By 1864 most of the important litigation on the Comstock had been settled. In October of that year when Nevada became a state, Stewart was elected the first United States senator from Nevada. It was now his privilege to carry this mining question to the congress, and to bring it before the supreme court.

---

[829] Eliot Lord, *Comstock Mining and Miners* (U.S. Geological Survey monograph, IV), 147.

[830] There were 304 civil cases for the court term commencing March 7, 1864, 217 of which were mining suits. *Virginia Union,* March 6, 1864.

[831] Some examples of the individual fees which Stewart and Baldwin received from the mining companies they represented may be gained from the reports of the companies: Gould and Curry Mining Company, $31,166.58; Imperial Silver Mining Company, 1864, $76,146.59. *California Miscellany,* v, x, xiv, no. 8. In Bancroft Library.

The two senators from Nevada, Stewart and Nye, were sworn into office on February 1, 1865. Nevada was allotted a two and a four year term; Nye drew the former, Stewart the latter. It took some time, however, for them to reach Washington. The question of the confiscation of the mines by the federal government was already before congress. The secretary of the interior recommended to congress that some action be taken for securing revenue from the proceeds of the sale or lease of the mines.[832] George W. Julian of Indiana was elected twice to the house of representatives on a platform to sell the mineral lands at auction in order to pay the expenses of the Civil War. On account of his activity on this question, he was made chairman of the committee on public lands. As such, he became the chief opponent of the miners in the fight for their rights to the possessory and fee titles to their claims. The Nevada mine owners became so alarmed over the discussion that they petitioned the Nevada legislature to forward a resolution to congress requesting that no action be taken on the bill to tax the mines on the public domain until Nevada's representatives could reach the capital.[833]

Soon after Senator Stewart took his seat he made a long speech against the bill then pending to tax gold and silver ore. He was successful in defeating it. Thus, this first bill with a provision to burden the mine owners with a heavy federal tax was prevented, but it made the western congressmen realize that they would have to be constantly alert to prevent further adverse legislation.[834] On February 10, Senator Stewart requested in a resolution that a committee on mines and mining be added to the list of senate committees. The resolution was not acted upon then, but on March 8 the resolution was again introduced, and this time it was adopted. The first members of the mining committee in the senate were John Conness of California, chairman, and Senators Stewart, Chandler, Morgan, Fessenden, Buckalew, and Guthrie. The creation of this committee was a distinct tri-

---

[832] House Ex. Doc. no. 25, 38 Cong., 2 sess., 1220.

[833] Cong. Globe, 38 Cong., 2 sess., 562, 587, 595, 687; George W. Julian, Political Recollections, 256.

[834] Sen. Journal, 38 Cong., 310-311; Cong. Globe, app., 38 Cong., 2 sess., 11.

umph for the mining industry. All bills relating to mining had necessarily to be referred to it. There were two western senators on it, Stewart and Conness.

When Nevada was proclaimed a state there was no provision made for a United States district court. A bill for the creation of a judicial district for Nevada was introduced by Henry G. Worthington, representative of Nevada. The bill passed the house successfully. When it reached the senate, Stewart added an amendment: "That in actions respecting mining claims the customs and regulations of the miners shall be regarded as law, and enforced by the courts of the United States; provided, this shall not be construed so as to affect in any way the right of ownership of the United States to the same." [835] In this amendment Senator Stewart was opposed by Senator Conness of California, who said:

> I do not like altogether the amendment proposed by Senator Stewart. . . I think we are hardly ready at this time to declare by a statute of the United States that all local customs and regulations shall be law, because the local rules and regulations are as multifarious, as numerous as different and as many as there are localities and communities.[836]

Senator Stewart answered this statement in a masterful speech in which he won the support of Senator Davis of Kentucky and Senator Kendricks of Indiana. A second amendment to the same bill was offered by Stewart, in which he asked that the possessory title as stated in the miners' rules and regulations be recognized. This amendment read:

> And be it further enacted, that no possessory action between individuals in any of the courts of the United States, for the recovery of any mining title or for damage to any such title shall be affected by the fact that the paramount title to the land on which such mines are, is in the United States, but each case shall be adjusted by the law of possession.[837]

Both of Senator Stewart's amendments were adopted and added to the Nevada Court Bill. They were incorporated later in the National Mining Law of 1866. The special correspondent of a California newspaper commented on the second amendment:

> This section, it will be seen, recognizes the principle that individuals have "possessory rights" in mining property, and hence for the first time

[835] *Cong. Globe,* 38 Cong., 2 sess., 949.
[836] *Ibid.,* 950.
[837] *Statutes at Large,* XIII, 441.

we shall now see that right recognized in a United States court. Senator Stewart and Representatives Worthington and Higby deserve a great deal of praise for their indefatigable efforts to secure this wise proviso in the bill, as well as for the salvation of the bill itself.[838]

The first case in which the legality of the Court Bill was tested was the one referred to above, appealed from Storey county, Nevada. The action brought in Sparrow *versus* Strong for the recovery of a certain mining claim on land belonging to the United States government was started when Nevada was still a territory. Stewart argued for the plaintiff that the territorial legislature of Nevada, with the implied sanction of the federal government, recognized indirectly the possessory mining claims as property without interference of the national authority. He alleged further that the national government through the federal courts could not dismiss the writ of error, because the controversy concerning the possessory right to a mining claim was capable of being valued in money.[839] Chief Justice Chase gave a lengthy opinion in which he sustained the principles set forth by Stewart in his amendments to, and his arguments upon, the Court Bill. Justice Chase wrote in part:

. . . that history informs us that under this legislation, and, not only without interference by the national government, but under its implied sanction, vast mining interests have grown up employing millions of capital, and contributing largely to the prosperity and improvement of the whole country. . .

A special kind of law, a sort of common law of the miners, the offspring of a nation's irrepressible march - lawless in some senses, yet clothed with dignity by a conception of the immense social results mingled with the fortunes of these bold investigators - has sprung up on the Pacific coast, and presents in the value of a "mining right" a novel and peculiar question of jurisdiction for this court.[840]

The same justice quoted at length from Stewart's open letter to Senator Alexander Ramsey from Minnesota on the rights of miners. The letter was incorporated entirely in Justice Chase's written opinion.[841] Thus Stewart was responsible

---

[838] *Sacramento Daily Union*, April 10, 1865.

[839] Gregory Yale, *Legal Titles to Mining Claims and Water Rights*, 95; Sparrow *versus* Strong, 1865, 70, U.S. 97, 18 L. Ed., 49.

[840] John W. Wallace, *Reports of the United States Supreme Court*, III, app. no. 1, 90-100.

[841] *Cases argued and adjusted in the Supreme Court of the United States*, December term, 1865, III, 1870.

for obtaining recognition by the United States supreme court of the "possessory mining rights" – an accomplishment of which he was very proud.[842]

The "possessory rights" gained through the Court Bill satisfied the placer miners, but they did not completely meet the needs of the quartz mining interests. The former knew their possession of the claim was necessary only for the short time in which they were placering the surface dirt. The equipment for working these claims was small, returns were quick, and the claim was abandoned as soon as placered out. In fact, the placer miner did not wish to have any further responsibility toward his claim after it had yielded its potential values. Not so with the quartz miner. Surface indications did not always improve with depth. Deep mining, irregularities in ledge placements, and possible litigation necessitated the expenditure of a large amount of money before any profit was realized. The uncertainties which might arise over a possessory title during the development of a mine hindered the investment of capital unless the title was secure.

The character of mining in Nevada made it necessary to invest millions of dollars in machinery, mills, tunneling, and timbering in order to reach the ore bodies. Stewart had fought successfully in the territorial courts for the rights of the original locators of mining claims. He had prevented the incorporation of a measure in the first constitution of Nevada to tax the miners' "shafts, tunnels, and bedrock," and he had secured the recognition of congress and the supreme court of possessory titles to mining claims. One more fight had to be made before the quartz miners were protected fully: they must be guaranteed a fee title to their claims.

On April 9, 1866, Senator John T. Sherman, chairman of the finance committee of the senate, introduced a bill which had been framed by the secretary of the treasury, for the regulation and occupation of mineral lands.[843] The object of this bill was to survey the mineral lands in legal subdivisions, and sell them to the highest bidder without regard to the rights of those who had discovered or had developed

---

[842] Statement of Jackson H. Ralston to writer, December 3, 1928.

[843] *Sen. Journal,* 39 Cong., 1 sess., 321; *Cong. Globe,* 39 Cong., 1 sess., 2851; Yale, *op. cit.,* 10-11.

them. The bill was referred to the committee on mines and mining. The two western members of the committee, Stewart and Conness, were directed to make a study of the bill for the committee. They disregarded Sherman's bill entirely; as a substitute, Stewart drafted a mining bill. On June 18 he introduced his bill and explained its merits in a set speech. He said in part:

> . . . that these equities had been secured by the pioneers who had developed the mineral regions of the Pacific coast by their energy and industry. While the local governments sanctioned their possessory rights and the government acquiesced by its silence, the miners relied upon the good faith of the United States that their property rights thus acquired would be respected.[844]

He portrayed in glowing language "the rapid development of the mining regions by the most energetic and self-sacrificing race of men that ever occupied a new country." [845] He called attention to the fact that the credit of the nation had been sustained through the production of gold and silver by the pioneers of the Pacific coast at a time when the federal government sanctioned the occupancy of the mineral lands by its non-action and silence. Stewart's bill had two strong advocates, Stewart and Conness. Every argument advanced against it was so forcefully and logically answered by them that it passed the senate on June 28. On the same day it was sent to the house of representatives.

The Stewart-Conness mining bill should have been referred to the house committee on mines and mining. Instead, Representative Julian, who had advocated sale of the mineral lands on the public domain to the highest bidder, had sufficient influence to have it referred to the committee on public lands, of which he was chairman. When the bill was being discussed in committee, Stewart went before it to defend his proposal and explain its merits.[846]

About the time the mining bill was under discussion in the house, Representative Higby of California introduced a bill designed to grant right of way for ditches and canals over the public domain. This bill passed the house [847] and went to

---

[844] *Cong. Globe,* 39 Cong., 1 sess., 926, 945-946.
[845] *Loc. cit.; Stewart Scraps,* II, 77. In Nevada Historical Library, Reno.
[846] Yale, *op. cit.,* II.
[847] *House Journal,* 39 Cong., 1 sess., 375, 388, 831.

the senate, where it was referred to the committee on public lands, of which Stewart was a member. When the bill was discussed in this committee, Stewart was sufficiently influential to have all of the bill struck out except the enacting clause. He substituted, then, his mining bill which contained some of the provisions in the ditch and canal bill.[848] The senate public lands committee reported favorably the ditch and canal bill with the mining bill attached thereto. It was readily adopted. When it went to the house it was placed on the calendar as a house bill with a senate amendment. It could not, therefore, be referred to the committee on public lands without the vote of the house.[849] In the meantime, Julian introduced in the house a bill for the confiscation of the mines which was endorsed by the committee on public lands; but when it came up for discussion he found to his surprise that sentiment had changed. This change had been effected by Stewart, who had visited personally every member of the house and explained the mining situation in the West. On July 26, 1866, the Stewart-Conness mining bill passed the house by a two-thirds majority. It became law, however, under the odd title: "An Act granting the Right of Way to Ditch and Canal Owners over the Public Lands, and for other Purposes."

The eleven sections of the bill declared the mineral lands of the United States free and open to exploration by citizens of the United States. It permitted the federal government to issue patents to a person or a company of persons who had expended one thousand dollars in improvements and actual labor on the mineral lands, according to the local customs in each mining district. The bill provided further for the right of way for the construction of highways over the public lands not reserved for public uses. It protected, also, the right to use the water for mining, agricultural and other purposes where such rights have vested and accrued; and it confirmed the right of way for the construction of ditches and canals for the same purposes. The bill gave protection to persons who had homesteaded on mineral land, but it made provision for the secretary of the interior to

[848] Yale, *op. cit.*, 13; *Stewart Scraps*, II, 77.
[849] *Cong. Globe*, 39 Cong., 1 sess., 4022.

designate the more purely agricultural lands for settlement.[850]

Those who were present at the time declared that the work of Stewart in convincing the members of the house by private interviews of the justice of his cause was the most earnest and effective they ever witnessed.

In the course of the debate the senator made a number of very convincing speeches in which he pled for the free and unlimited right of the prospector to go upon the public domain and to search out the precious metal for himself.[851]

Representative Julian was very much disturbed over the defeat of his bill and the passage of the mining bill. He said that "when Stewart found that his bill was going to be defeated in the house by referring it to the committee on public lands, he resorted to sharp practice," and when the bill finally passed, Julian scored him and referred to his indecent haste to obtain legislation under false pretenses. For his uncomplimentary remarks he was called to order by the speaker.[852] Stewart said "that the miners would prize fee title above all else." [853]

This escape from complete confiscation of the mines was very narrow. The miners and the mining industry owed a great deal to Stewart and his colleague for waging an unceasing and successful fight in their behalf.[854] An estimate of the work of Stewart and Conness was made by the Honorable H. F. Dunne of Nevada:

Fortunately, the mining interest was ably represented in congress, led by Senators Stewart of Nevada and Conness of California, both masters of the subject. They grappled the question with all their power, knowing it was a matter of life or death to the regions they represented, and, after a desperate struggle, defeated the highest bidder plan, and achieved a complete victory for the principles most anxiously desired by the miners,

---

[850] *Statutes at Large,* XIV, 251-253.

[851] Appendix no. 1, 70 U.S., 779, 780.

[852] *Cong. Globe,* 39 Cong., 1 sess., 4049.

[853] *Stewart Scraps,* II, 77.

[854] The Mining Act of 1866 was not satisfactory in every detail. In 1870 and again in 1872 important changes were made to the mining laws. A complete account of the laws concerning mining passed by the United States from 1785 to 1915 may be found in the *Report of the Department of the Interior, Bureau of Mines,* I-II.

namely, the recognition of their mining laws, and the right of the discoverer of a mine to purchase the title from the government at a reasonable
price. No matter how defective the bill may be in detail; no matter how
many points it leaves entirely untouched; the miners will ever be grateful
for its passage, for in that, to them, memorable session, it was not a question of detail nor perfection, but a struggle between two great conflicting
principles and the policy desired by the miners prevailed.[855]

The National Mining Act of 1866 quieted the uneasiness
of the capitalists who wished to invest money in the development of the great silver veins on the Comstock Lode. It
brought to an end another important chapter in the relations
of Nevada and the federal government. The future existence
of this state was assured; the great silver veins which ribbed
many of the mountains in Nevada could be explored; they
could be developed without federal interference. It ushered
in Nevada's thrilling age of silver.

---

[855] Extract from a letter written by Judge Dunne to Dr. R. W. Raymond,
December 20, 1869, which is printed in Raymond, *Mineral Resources*, 423.

# Nevada's Age of Silver

By 1866 most of the important federal relations with the state of Nevada were settled. By the extraordinary combination of the circumstances of the discovery of large deposits of silver and gold and subsequent rush of people to the scene of the discovery with the urgent necessity for the admission of another state so as to legalize the Proclamation of Emancipation, new threads were woven into the pattern of American history. It is difficult to estimate the influence of these federal relations upon the history of the United States; it is not so difficult to determine the effect of the settlement of these relations on the mining industry, which in turn had important consequences not only to the United States but to the world. It is worth while to set forth with greater fullness the story of the mines during Nevada's age of silver.

For two decades, 1859 to 1879, the production of the Nevada mines fixed the attention of the world. The output of silver and gold from the Comstock, Eureka, Aurora, Austin and many regions of lesser importance in these few years exceeded the output at any previous time in the history of the United States. It challenged the wonderment of all ages. Hundreds were attracted to the Nevada mining rushes; thousands of dollars poured into the state for the many industries necessary to extract the metal from the quartz. The men who developed these riches met truly on a "field of the cloth of gold."

In the years between the discovery of the Comstock Lode and the demonetization of silver which closed most of the Nevada mines, more than half a billion dollars were produced. It has been said that the Comstock Lode alone made more fortunes than any other area of equal length in the world. By putting hundreds of dollars into the channels of trade, transcontinental railroads were built, great steamship lines were established, telegraphic cables were laid across the ocean, great newspapers were financed, and palaces and castles were built in France and in Italy. A multitude of industries on the Pacific coast profited during the development of the Comstock Lode and the other Nevada silver mines. It laid the foundation of the resplendent San Francisco, it perpetuated also in history a host of names made great during Nevada's age of silver.

To dig the precious metals from the bowels of the earth, the greatest engineering skill in the world was challenged. To compose an *Iliad* of the pulsating life of Nevada's age of silver would require the master pen of a Homer. It would be necessary to write volumes to describe adequately the incidents which made up the diverse patterns of life during these years. The parts of the story of this age which stand out predominantly above all of the others must be briefly told.

After the discovery of the Comstock Lode and the finding of other silver ledges, the original locators in most cases sold out their interests to the first speculators to arrive. They received usually very small amounts for their claims, and soon were as poor as ever. James Finney, or Fennimore, alias "Old Virginia," to whom more than to any other person the credit for the discovery of the Comstock was given, sold his interest in the ledge for an old horse, worth about $40, and a few dollars in cash. He died, poor, on July 6, 1861, in Dayton, two years after the discovery was made.[856] H. T. P. Comstock sold out for much more than Finney did, but his money went into business adventures, the management of which he was incapable of handling. He committed suicide or was killed while returning to Montana in 1870, after having been called to Virginia City to testify in a mining suit over a claim he had formerly owned.[857] Out of the thousands of claims located, about twenty became producing mines, each of them located on the outcroppings of the lode.

[856] *San Francisco Daily Evening Bulletin*, July 6, 1861.

[857] William Jennings, "Carson Valley," MS., 3; Dan De Quille (William Wright), *History of the Big Bonanza*, 82-87. The writer owns Dan De Quille's original copy of this book. It contains a number of marginal notes made by the author.

VIRGINIA CITY, 1865

From a rare contemporary photograph.

At first the ore was freighted to San Francisco, but it cost $24,000 to ship the first forty tons. In 1859 the ore was worked in *arrastras* run by water-power from the Carson river. Then a horse-power four-stamp battery mill was built, which was followed the next year with two steam quartz mills. As soon as possible, stamps, settling pans, engines, boilers, and other machinery were made in the San Francisco foundries, the parts transported to Virginia City in two and three broad-tired wagons drawn by twelve, fourteen, and sixteen mules. The steam mills were located at first in Gold Hill and Six Mile cañon. When it became too expensive to haul the wood fuel, the mills were built in Washoe Valley. The ore was hauled from the mines down the steep Ophir grade over a causeway built across Washoe Lake to the mills. Several mills were located on the east and north end of the lake, also. When the Virginia and Truckee Railroad was built in 1869 from Carson City to Virginia City, most of the mills were moved to the Carson river or were built in Virginia City. The wood for the mines formed the load from Carson City to Virginia City and the ore from the mines was carried from Virginia City to the mills on the river.[858]

It became manifest very early, as the development of the lode progressed, that there were five principal needs: mining timber, lumber for houses, cord wood for the steam hoists, water, and improved machinery. To obtain the first, the forests of the West yielded millions of feet of timber. From as far north as Oregon and Puget Sound the very hard timbers were obtained. On the eastern slope of the Sierra Nevada very good timber was available. At first it was cut and hauled to the mines and mills, but the cost of road repairing each year, after the winter storms were over, was too expensive; hence, fluming the wood was resorted to. There was a time when seventy-two million five hundred thousand feet of lumber went annually into the caverns and drifts of the lode. Millions of feet of lumber were used for buildings above the ground. Two hundred and fifty thousand cords of wood were burned under the boilers that supplied power for the hoists and mills. These

[858] Bancroft, *History of Nevada, Colorado, and Wyoming*, 110-116.

figures are not mere metaphors of immensity; they are obtained from the reports of the mine superintendents.

To cut the wood on the slopes of the Sierra Nevada and get it to the railroad, a "V" shaped trough or flume, the invention of J. W. Haines, of Genoa, was built deep enough to carry logs of considerable size. There were ten of these flumes in operation in 1880 with a total length of eighty miles. Two million feet of timbers and thirty-three million feet of cut lumber were used in constructing one of them. Seventy-one thousand cords of wood passed through the flumes in one year. For a distance of fifty or sixty miles along the eastern slope the mountains were denuded of timber for use in the mines. Even the roots were pulled out and made into charcoal. After the lumbermen cut the wood on the eastern side of the mountains they reached over to the California side of the range, where the trees were felled, rafted across Lake Tahoe or were rolled or flumed down to flat ground and hauled to the mines. The next move was to erect sawmills far up in the mountains, and construct large flumes leading from them down into the valleys. The flumes, which were built on regular grades, wound around the hills, passed along the sides of steep mountains, crossed deep cañons and were set up in many places on trestle-work of great height. They were sufficiently large to float timbers sixteen inches square and twenty to thirty feet in length. Nearly all the flumes dumped their cargo within reach of the Virginia and Truckee Railroad. In many of the pictures still extant of this industry, thousands upon thousands of cords of wood and millions of feet of lumber are shown in dumps near the railroad.

In 1874 one of the largest flumes, that of the Pacific Wood, Lumber and Flume Company, was built by the "big four," James C. Flood, James G. Fair, John W. Mackay, and W. S. O'Brien, who were also owners of the controlling interests in the Consolidated Virginia and California, Hale and Norcross, Gould and Curry, Best and Belcher, and Utah mines. These mines used one million feet of lumber a month underground; and they burned forty thousand cords of wood a year. As there was no wood available in the mountains near Virginia City, this firm acquired twelve thousand acres of heavy pine forest in the mountains northwest of Washoe

Lake, and within fifteen miles of Reno. Judging from the description of this flume it must have been a wonderful piece of engineering. The "V" shaped flume was made of two-inch plank nailed together. Across the top it was about two and one-half feet in width. The ends were carefully fitted together so that there was no unevenness, for timbers flying through the flume at the rate of fifteen to sixty miles per hour had to have a clear road.

In this trough, water from Hunter's Creek, situated about twenty miles from the terminus of the flume, carried the wood to Huffaker's, a few miles south of Reno. Near this terminus an iron break which slanted toward one side was placed in the trough so that when the timber came down, fifty or one hundred pieces, one after the other, each piece was turned over the side and the men at the break with a dexterous use of the crowbar sent them bounding to the ground. A printing telegraph extended along the whole line of the flume, by which means orders were transmitted to the men stationed at intervals. Two lumber mills were built, one in the lower belt of timber and the other on the middle fork of Evans Creek two miles higher up. In five minutes' time a log from two to three feet in diameter was reduced to lumber, planks, scantling, boards, and square timber in these mills. Sometimes one log gave three or four kinds of lumber.

The flume was built entirely upon trestle-work and stringers. The grade was so heavy, between sixteen hundred and two thousand feet from the top to the lower end, in a distance of fifteen miles, that there was little danger of a jam. The trestle-work was substantial enough to support a narrow gauge railway. The flume ran over foothills, through valleys, around mountains and across cañons. In one place it was seventy feet high. On an air line from beginning to end it was eight miles long; the additional seven miles were in turns and twists. The trestle-work was thoroughly braced, longitudinally and across, so that no break could extend farther than a single box, which was sixteen feet. All the main supports, which were five feet apart, were firmly set in mud-sills. The boxes or troughs rested in brackets four feet apart; these again rested upon substantial stringers.

There were two reservoirs made by damming the water

from Hunter's Creek. One of them was eleven hundred feet
in length. A ditch, nearly two miles long, took the water to
the first reservoir, whence it was conveyed three and one-
fourth miles to the flume through a feeder capable of carrying four hundred and fifty inches of water. The entire flume
was constructed in ten weeks, between four and five hundred
men working on this enterprise alone.[859]

There were a number of smaller mills and flumes built
in the timber belt along the east side of the Sierra. After
most of the timber had been cut on this side of the mountains the lumber firms began on the California side. Glenbrook, on the southeast side of Lake Tahoe, was the principal lumber manufacturing place in the state of Nevada.
There were fifty thousand acres of timber and wood lands
in this vicinity. The place was first settled in 1860; in the
following year a water power sawmill was erected, and in
1864 a steam mill was built, soon to be followed by a number of mills in this section of the mountains. In 1873 the
lumber firm of Yerington and Bliss built a narrow-gauge
railroad from their sawmills on the shore of Lake Tahoe
to the head of Clear Creek. The road, eight miles in length,
was used to transport lumber from the mills to their large
flume at the head of Clear Creek, which flowed into Carson
river. In order to reach the head of the flume, a tunnel of
five hundred feet was built for the railroad, after which
the lumber was flumed down Clear Creek to Carson Valley.
The Sierra Nevada, facing the Great Basin and on the western side of Lake Tahoe, were practically denuded during the
years in which the mines and mills devoured this stupendous
quantity of wood and lumber.[860]

To provide Virginia City, Gold Hill, and several other
small settlements with pure water an artificial lake in the
Sierra Nevada had to be built. For the first few miners who
came to the Comstock, the natural springs at the base of
Mount Davidson and in the ravines were sufficient. Later a
few wells were sunk; then, when water began to flow from
the mining tunnels, it was gathered into large wooden tanks
and distributed through pipes. But as the towns grew, this

[859] Wright, op. cit., 238-246; Angel, op. cit., 188-191.
[860] Angel, op. cit., 380.

supply was not only inadequate, but the sources became exhausted as the tunnels ran dry. In 1872 the Virginia and Gold Hill Water Company, after having spent thousands of dollars to keep these communities supplied with water from the underground wells, determined to go into the Sierra Nevada twenty-five miles away, to bring it into Virginia City. The company sent for H. Schussler, engineer for the Spring Valley Water Works of San Francisco, to help solve its water problem. After examining the terrain over which the water had to be conveyed, he said it could be done, though with great difficulty. To conduct the water from the Sierra Nevada to the Virginia range, on the slopes of which Virginia City and Gold Hill were built, Washoe Valley had to be crossed. A depression in this valley of one thousand seven hundred and twenty feet, at its lowest point not far from the Lake View Hill, had to be spanned. It was a feat of hydraulic engineering which had never been attempted before. A year was required to make the wrought iron pipe for carrying the water across this depression.

The engineer furnished the pipe manufacturers with an exact plan of the shape of the pipe necessitated by the rocky points. Deep and narrow ravines which had to be crossed required the curving and shaping of each piece of pipe. The entire length of the pipe was over seven miles; the diameter, twelve inches, was capable of delivering 2,200,000 gallons of water every twenty-four hours. The pipe, laid across Washoe Valley, was in the form of an inverted siphon. The end in which the water was received rested in a spur of the main Sierra Nevada west of Washoe Lake; its outlet was on the crest of the Virginia range east of Lake View Hill. Because the inlet was four hundred and sixty-five feet higher than the outlet, the great pressure forced the water rapidly through the pipe.

At first the water sent through this pipe came from Hobart Creek. In 1875, a second pipe ten inches in diameter was laid beside the first one. This same year the supply flume was extended eight and one-half miles to Marlette Lake, artificially made on the east side of the Lake Tahoe basin, a total distance of thirty-one and one-half miles from Virginia City. The lake, from thirty to forty feet deep, covered three hundred acres. In order to reach the lake, a tunnel three thousand feet long beneath the dividing ridge of the Tahoe and the Great Basin had to be dug. Connected with the water works several reservoirs were built to hold many million gallons of water. Since Marlette Lake was fifteen hundred feet above the main street in Virginia City, the pressure was sufficiently great to carry the water into every part of the community. The cost of this project was two million dollars. When this water supply reached the Comstock on August 1, 1873, there was great rejoicing; the Frémont cannon was fired, bands paraded the streets, and rockets were sent up all over the city. The mines, mills, and homes were amply supplied with water from that time on.[861]

There were about eighteen paying mines on the lode.[862] The ore from some of these mines was hoisted to the surface through perpendicular shafts, from others through inclines that followed the dip of the vein. As the shafts were sunk deeper, and as crosscuts and tunnels were extended for many miles, the difficulties and problems of mining increased. In most of the mines bonanzas were found. They were masses of very high grade ore of lenticular shape, some of which, such as "The Big Bonanza" in the Consolidated California, were hundreds of feet in length and from two to three hundred feet in width at the broadest part.[863] This high grade ore was generally so soft that pillars of it could not be left to support the great weight above it. To find a way to keep the mountain from caving in, to replace the heavy timbers when they were broken, and to guard against fire, challenged the ablest engineers of the age. The man who was equal to the task was Philip Diedesheimer, a German educated in a

[861] Wright, *op. cit.*, 231-237; Angel, *op. cit.*, 600-602.

[862] The leading mines on the Comstock Lode were the Utah, Sierra Nevada, Union Consolidated, Mexican, Ophir, California, Consolidated Virginia, Best and Belcher, Gould and Curry, Savage, Hale and Norcross, Chollar-Potosí, Bullion, Exchequer, Alpha, Yellow Jacket, Kentuck, Crown Point, Overman and Caledonia.

[863] For the reports on the geology and resources of the Comstock Lode consult George F. Becker, *Geology of the Comstock Lode;* J. Ross Browne, *Mineral Resources of the States and Territories west of the Rocky Mountains;* Eliot Lord, *Comstock Mining and Miners;* Baron F. Richthofen, *The Comstock Lode.*

technical school, who went to California in 1852, and to
Nevada in 1860. The Ophir Company appealed to Diedesheimer to invent some system to prevent the sinking of the
roof of the mine. After three weeks of study and observation he devised a plan of square sets, a system of timbering
without which the Comstock mines could not have been
developed to any great depth. It was a simple idea of forming timber cribs four by six feet square which could be set
one upon the other to any required height. They could be
made to conform to any circumstances, whether lateral or
downward pressure. Since the cribs were hollow, the waste
ore could be dumped into them, thereby making practically
solid pillars from the bottom to the top of the mine.[864]

Another great obstacle against which a constant vigil had
to be kept was water. There were great underground reservoirs of very hot water which had to be pumped out. As the
mines grew deeper the power of the pumps had to be increased. The fifteen horse power pump of the Ophir mine
on the north end of the lode had to be replaced in a short
time by one of forty-five horse power; and that one, in turn,
by others of still greater power, until machines of even
one thousand horse power were used to lift the water from
the lowest depths of the mines. Soon it was seen that if the
bottom of the lode was to be reached, pumps could no longer
handle the water. Again a problem confronted the mine
superintendent, and again a German, Adolph Heinrich
Joseph Sutro, an Austrian Jew, who went to California in
the gold rush days and to Nevada in March, 1860, solved
it. Even at that early date, Sutro recognized the necessity
of finding a less expensive way of draining the mines than
by pumping, and a more effective way of ventilating them.
He proposed to drive a tunnel nearly four miles long from
the floor of the Carson Valley to strike the lode some eighteen hundred feet below the surface. The purpose of the
tunnel was to drain the mines and to permit ore to be taken
out through it.

At first the mine owners approved Sutro's plan. They
even went so far as to make contracts with him in which
they agreed to pay him two dollars a ton royalty on all of

---

[864] Bancroft, *op. cit.*, 113, 114; Angel, *op. cit.*, 573.

the ore mined. Encouraged by these contracts, he set out
to raise from four to five million dollars for the construction
of the tunnel. A company was formed; the authority of the
state of Nevada and of the United States was procured.
Everything seemed to be favorable for the prosecution of
the project, when the mine owners suddenly changed their
minds. They revoked their contracts, and even began to
oppose the enterprise.

For nine years Adolph Sutro, with the assiduity of his
nationality, labored to overcome this opposition. During
this time, success and failure alternated with each attempt
to build the tunnel. At first some New York capitalists
promised to aid him, then they retracted their bargain. He
applied to congress for a loan or a guarantee for his bonds,
which for a time seemed likely to succeed; but the support
was not granted. He went to Europe to ask financial help
from capitalists interested in American investments. They
were favorably impressed with the idea at first; then they
grew indifferent to it. As a last resort, he appealed to the
miners themselves whose future jobs depended on the successful handling of the water problem. They answered his
appeal with a contribution of $50,000 paid regularly from
their wages. With this small amount of money he began on
October 19, 1865, to drive the tunnel.

A few years later he obtained $2,100,000 from subscrip-
tions in the United States and in Europe. The work on the
tunnel was then pushed with all possible speed. In 1878
Sutro's dream was nearing realization — the men working
in the tunnel could hear the miners at work with their drills
in the Savage mine, the shaft nearest the tunnel. Finally,
on July 8, 1878, a round of powder broke the last remaining
wall between the tunnel and the shaft. Sutro himself was
there when the last shot was fired. He was the first to crawl
through the opening. It was said the rush of air from the
shaft into the tunnel was so great that it sucked Sutro through
the hole with such a terrific force that he was hurled to
the other side of the shaft. He was picked up bruised, bleed-
ing, and almost unconscious. Although he was almost overcome with excitement and with the extreme heat of the
tunnel he was able to shout with joy. The main tunnel

measured 20,480 feet in length and cost $2,096,556.41, exclusive of the expenses incurred by Sutro in the carrying out of his plan.[865]

Although the tunnel was completed, he had no contract with the mine owners to use it. They still insisted they had no use for it. The Savage Company, whose shaft the tunnel had penetrated, did not remonstrate with him; the other companies, however, tried to drain their mines through the Savage shaft without paying for the use of it. To stop this use of the tunnel without compensation he started a drainway which would turn the incoming water back into a lower level of the Savage mine from which it was pumped, only to return again. When this scheme was discovered in February, 1879, the workmen were arrested, and the nearly completed work on the drain shaft was stopped. The men were released immediately, but the court restrained Sutro from completing the drain. A sudden rise of water in the Hale and Norcross mine caused an overflow in the combination shaft used by several of the mines. To keep the great flow of water in check it was pumped into the Sutro Tunnel in such quantities that it drove the men from their work. Sutro then threatened to seal the tunnel hermetically. To do so, he had built and had placed two immense solid oak doors which formed a water-tight bulkhead when closed. The water would then be turned back into the mines and flood them. The mine owners were beaten into a compromise. A new contract was made whereby the companies agreed to furnish him with sufficient money to extend the lateral branches of the tunnel and to pay him for the ore taken through the tunnel, according to its value. In addition to the ore that was taken out of the tunnel in ore cars drawn by mules, there was discharged daily in 1880, 3,500,000 gallons of water.[866]

Nevada's age of silver ushered in the first speculative adventures on the Pacific coast . The fame and wealth of the Comstock Lode and of the other mines in the state spread

[865] *Daily Alta California,* April 20, 1860; Sutro, *Closing Argument of Adolph Sutro on the bill before the Congress to aid the Sutro Tunnel, delivered before the Committee on Mines and Mining of the House of Representatives of the United States of America, Monday, April 22, 1872,* Washington, D.C., 1872; Bancroft, *op. cit.,* 141-147.

[866] Bancroft, *History of Nevada, Colorado, and Wyoming,* 146.

rapidly. Soon there were many people who wished to share in the potential wealth of the products of the mine. According to the rules, made by the miners themselves, the size of the claims were fixed at fifty feet square. Speculators began to come into the mining camps. They bought up claims; they consolidated them; and, then, they began to sell feet or "shares" in them. Speculation in feet and inches was begun in the camps, and spread to San Francisco, where on September 11, 1862, there was organized the San Francisco Stock and Exchange Board with forty members, the first on the Pacific coast, and second only to the New York Stock Exchange. For two decades this exchange became "the vortex of a feverish speculative mining boom." Everyone began to invest in the Nevada mines, and in the Comstock Lode especially. So eager at one period of the boom was the public to buy Comstock shares, that police had to guard the doors of the exchange. An example of the rapidity of the rise and fall in mining shares may be seen in the race to control the Hale and Norcross mine. In 1868, the price of a "foot" increased from $2,825 to $7,100 in one week. A month later the stock had fallen to $2,900 a foot. On January 7, 1875, the peak of the excitement, the total value of the shares of Comstock mines listed on the exchange was in the neighborhood of $300,000,000; six years later it was less than $7,000,000.[867]

Between 1859 and 1872 there had been twelve small bonanzas found along the lode, but there was one bonanza still undiscovered. This one became known as "The Big Bonanza." Before 1872 there were 1310 feet on the lode upon which considerable money had been spent, but the ore extracted therefrom had not paid well. Messrs. Fair and Mackay in company with Messrs. Flood and O'Brien,[868] formerly saloon keepers in San Francisco, bought the control of the Consolidated Virginia Mining Company, which had suspended operations for want of funds. These four men decided to drive a drift from the Gould and Curry mine through the Best and Belcher at a depth of 1,167 feet.

[867] Angel, *op. cit.,* 620.

[868] F. M. Walker was one of the original partners, but Mackay bought him out thereby giving him a two-fifths interest in the mine.

When they had gone some distance they cut the top of a very rich and large body of ore. To meet their drift from the Gould and Curry they sank a shaft. At a depth of 1500 feet they came upon the rich ore body. A cross cut was made to determine its width. Across the vein the ore assayed $630 a ton. It was this bonanza that gave national and international fame to the Comstock Lode. In 1875 the California and Virginia mine took out 169,307 tons of ore valued at $16,717,394; in two years the mine management had speeded up the extraction of ore to 217,432 tons valued at $18,924,850.27.

In 1866 Senator Stewart succeeded in having an appropriation made by congress for the establishment of a mint at Carson City. By the fall of 1869 it was ready to coin all denominations of United States money and the "trade dollar" used in the Orient.[869] The mine owners no longer had to pay transportation charges on their bullion to the San Francisco mint.

A description of the mining and mill buildings, machinery, and processes of extraction belongs more to a scientific treatise than to a history. But it must be mentioned that the different devices for silver mining invented to extract the ore from the Comstock Lode made history not only in the field of engineering but also in many other sciences. The army of workmen who were employed not only in the Comstock mines, but in the others in Nevada, came from the four corners of the earth. They were men of superb muscular equipment capable of doing eight hours of the heaviest kind of work under the most difficult conditions imaginable. When the Comstock mines were producing the most in the middle seventies, thousands of men were employed in the mines, mills, iron works, and other industries necessary to furnish the equipment and products for the mining and milling processes.

The miners worked in three shifts of eight hours each. Upon reaching the different stations of the mines, through cages lowered from the surface, the men stripped themselves of almost all clothing. In the intense heat many wore only a breech clout, a hat to protect their heads from falling stone

---

[869] Angel, *op. cit.,* 557.

or sand, and heavy shoes to protect their feet from jagged rocks or from the heat. In some of the particularly hot spots of the mine a spray of cold water played on the miners' backs. Under these conditions they worked for fifteen minutes; then they rested briefly or went to cooling stations where there were huge tubs of ice. Towels or rags dipped in the ice water were thrown over their bodies. It was not surprising that the men often died of miner's consumption, caused by this abuse of the body and by the breathing of the dust caused by the drills. For these eight hours of work they received generally four dollars a day. In the peak of the production the mines were lighted with candles and oil-lamps. Each miner upon descending into the mine took his lantern with him.[870] At a later period the mines were electrically lighted.

Some idea of the vast amount of material consumed by the mines may be gained from mentioning several of the more important ones. The California Consolidated Mining Company alone purchased 1,957,402 pounds of ice in one year for the cooling stations in its mine. Consumption of salt for the extracting of the silver from the ore was enormous. In the heyday of the Comstock mines, when the big mines were going full blast, San Francisco was the greatest quicksilver market in the world. In the seventies the storage vaults of Messrs. Barron held as much as fifty thousand flasks of quicksilver, hauled from the mines in the Santa Cruz mountains, most of them to be sent to the Nevada mills for the amalgamating process. In 1875 the Consolidated Virginia mine alone used each month the following amounts of material:

Feet of timber per month, 500,000; cords of wood, 550; boxes of candles, 350; giant-powder, 2 tons; 100 gallons of coal oil, 200 gallons of lard-oil; 800 pounds of tallow; 20,000 feet of fuse; 37 tons of ice; 3,000 bushels of charcoal; 1½ tons of steel; 5 tons of round and square iron; 4 tons of hard coal; 50 kegs of nails; and a thousand and one other articles in the same proportion.[871]

It must be remembered there were about twenty profitable mines during the peak of production, each consuming a proportionate amount of materials.

[870] Wright, *op. cit.*, 293-309.
[871] *Ibid.*, 325.

Sometimes the miners were kept in their hot subterranean chambers two weeks at a time. The reason was to prevent the news of the underground developments from being brought to the surface after each shift was through work. In this way the owners could manipulate the rise or fall of the shares in their mines as they chose. The mine superintendents gave these miners whatever they wished. No item on the bill of fare of the best hotel in the city was denied these men.

It has been said that "California drew to her golden shores the pick of the world. Nevada drew to herself the pick of California." Nevada's age of silver produced Titans. Whether lawyers, politicians, doctors, mine superintendents, newspaper reporters, stage drivers, or teamsters, they had to be the best. The man who was not an expert simply could not meet the demands of those exciting days of silver. If he produced the "goods" he was paid whatever price he asked.

A number of names connected with the Comstock were stamped indelibly in history in almost every field of human activity. Many of the great Comstock tycoons were household names, such as James Flood, Alvinza Hayward, Adolph Sutro, Mark Requa, "Sandy" L. S. Bowers, and William Sharon. The politics of the period could not be discussed without mentioning William Morris Stewart and John Percival Jones, both United States senators from Nevada. In the field of journalism the tone of the press was set by a host of men such as Dan De Quille (William Wright), Mark Twain (Samuel Clemens), J. Ross Browne, C. C. Goodwin, Joseph T. Goodman, Rollin M. Daggett, Wells Drury, Arthur McEwen, and Harry Mighels.

The task of collecting the literature of Nevada's age of silver is an undertaking which awaits some future historian. The first description of the great rush to Washoe was written by J. Ross Browne [872] in the fall of 1860. An article, entitled

_____

[872] This article had appeared in the form of letters in the *San Francisco Bulletin*. John Ross Browne has never been given the credit he deserves in the books on this period of western history. He was born February 11, 1821, at Beggar's Bush, near Dublin, Ireland. He came to America with his family in 1833. The family settled in Kentucky. He started on his travels in 1842. In 1848 he was appointed to the revenue service in California, but when he arrived in San Francisco he found his appointment had been withdrawn by the change in administration. He was, however, made inspector of postal

"A peep at Washoe," appeared in the *Harper's Monthly*
for December of that year and January and February of
1861. Browne was an ubiquitous assayer and a wandering
journalist who wrote many other articles for newspapers
and magazines descriptive of the life and mines in Nevada.
The best-known writer of the early period of the Comstock
days was Mark Twain. In his book, *Roughing It,* he has
given a pictorial description of the years he spent in Nevada,
though parts of it were taken from other works published
or tales that were told before he came to the West. It is
not the intention of this volume to "debunk" Mark Twain,
but it is a matter of history that he borrowed stories and
was greatly influenced by the writings of J. Ross Browne,
and from his co-reporter on the *Virginia City Territorial
Enterprise,* Dan De Quille. The yarn of the "Jumping Frog
of Calaveras" was told by W. E. Townsend, better known
as "Lying Jim" or "Truthful James," years before Mark
Twain published it. It was first entitled "Jim and his Jumping Frog." [873]

It would be difficult to picture the activities of the underground working of the mines in a few words. Each level
was like a city, with many miles of streets. On the floor of
each level tracks were laid over which the ore cars traveled
from one stope to the other, gathering up their cargoes of
ore or waste rock, each of which was hoisted to the surface,
the one to be taken to the mill, the other to be sent to the

service instead. In 1849 he became secretary of the California Constitutional
Convention. He came to Nevada in the fall of 1859. The writings of Browne
concerning Nevada were: "A peep at Washoe," December, 1860, January and
February, 1861; "Washoe revisited," May, June, and July, 1865; "A trip
to Bodie Bluff and the Dead Sea of the West," August and September, 1865;
"The Reese River Country," June, 1865; "The Walker River Country," November, 1865, all in *Harper's Monthly Magazine; Report on the Mineral
Resources of the States and Territories west of the Rocky Mountains; Adventures in the Apache Country; A tour through Arizona and Sonora, with notes
on the Silver Regions of Nevada; Bodie and Esmeralda: being an account
of the revival of affairs in two singularly interesting and important mining
districts.* A complete list of his writings may be found in *Check-list of First
Editions of the Works of John Ross Browne, California Pioneer, with a
chronology, 1821-1875,* compiled by Emma Miriam Lone. Lathrop C. Harper,
New York, 1930.

[873] Statement of Alfred Chartz in the *Reno Evening Gazette,* June 20, 1933;
*The Californian,* October 13, 1866.

dump. Every man underground and everyone above the mine had to be an expert in his line of work, whether mine superintendent or lowly mucker.

San Francisco was the residuary legatee of the gold of California and the silver of Nevada. The wealth and the spirit reminiscent of California's El Dorado and Nevada's Silverado days were carried to that city. The silver from Nevada built San Francisco's first beautiful hotels; it erected the first spacious homes on Nob Hill; it founded San Francisco's Stock Exchange; it financed its first large banks and hundreds of other businesses. It developed large tracts of real estate around the San Francisco Bay region. The spirit of cordiality, conviviality, generosity, and democracy of the mining days was salvaged by the people of San Francisco; these characteristics of the early mining society have never ceased to exist in the mining towns of Nevada. In Nevada's age of silver there seemed to be an ecstasy of living which marked a summit beyond which the art of living could not be carried. In the towns of Nevada and in San Francisco the expenditure of money by the *bons vivants* was prodigious. The finest viands and liquors the world could produce were demanded by them. In no less degree was money spent for clothes, jewels, *objets d'art,* and furnishings for their homes.

The influence of Nevada's production of silver was not exerted solely upon the Pacific coast; it was felt throughout the entire world. The greatest effect of all perhaps was on the international monetary systems. In a preceding chapter, there was discussed briefly the unsuccessful attempt made by congress to sell the mines to the highest bidder and thereby liquidate the Civil War debt. The vast production of silver disturbed the ratio of gold and silver. It attracted the attention of Emperor Louis Napoleon. Could he not, by acquiring the gold and silver mines of California and Nevada, emulate his illustrious uncle, whose great military expeditions had been financed by the silver and gold of Mexico? At least he wanted to know the extent of the wealth of these mines. In 1864 he sent M. E. Guillemin Tarayre to California and Nevada. In his report, this agent of Emperor Napoleon said:

The silver mines of Nevada, and especially those of the Washoe district offered a novel attraction and one of distinct importance; I have found on the other side of the California range, on the uncultivated and desolated plateaus, a population taking hold with difficulties that a new country presents. On September 3, I arrived at the center of the most productive mines, Virginia City. . .

During the three months of September, October, and November, 1864, I went through the regions which I have enumerated above, discovering in each locality the groups of veins, studying their mode of formation, the composition of the minerals and soil, their relation with the outcropping rocks and the structural faults of the country. The means of extraction and the methods of metallurgical treatment engaged my attention particularly. A mineralogical and geological collection designed for a description of the Nevada mines has been collected and addressed to your Excellency on the first three months of 1865 with the notes and maps to support them.[874]

Farther on in Tarayre's report he made an important statement concerning the estimated production and richness of the Nevada mines:

The forty thousand people settled in the state of Nevada have already shown an example of unusual perseverance; they have brought about in a few years an annual extraction of four hundred tons of silver, a production which rivals the mines of Mexico, an important figure, far from diminishing, growing from year to year and to increase by better means in the ways of transportation.[875]

The European nations, especially France and England, who had gold for their standard, had been heavy purchasers of Civil War bonds. As the production of silver increased the apprehensions of bankers and bondholders grew. They feared the bonds and the interest on them would be paid in silver instead of gold. Something had to be done in order that these countries might hold their commanding position in the monetary circles of the world.

The upshot of the Tarayre report and of the position in which the European bondholders were placed was the calling of the first international monetary conference by Emperor Napoleon in 1867 in Paris. Especially were the English financiers interested in making money dearer by making it scarcer, a theory advanced by Sir Thomas Gresham. The production of gold was declining; silver production was increasing rapidly. If England and France could

[874] E. Guillemin Tarayre, *Exploration Mineralogique des regions Mexicaines,* 4-7. The report is written entirely in French.
[875] *Ibid.,* 17.

effect the demonetization of silver their bonds would be worth more.

John Sherman, United States representative from Ohio, was the chairman of the ways and means committee during the early part of the Civil War. In 1863 he was appointed to the senate, to fill the unexpired term of Salmon Portland Chase who had been made secretary of the treasury. Sherman was made the chairman of the finance committee of the senate. He was also appointed in 1867 the delegate from the United States to the international monetary conference in Paris. On his way to France he visited London, where he had a conference with the English bankers who were holding large blocks of Civil War bonds. It was Sherman who introduced the resolution at the conference which pledged the representatives to return to their respective countries to establish the gold standard. As soon as he returned to the United States he began to carry out the terms of the resolution.

In order that the United States might be put on the gold standard, the mint and coinage laws had to be revised completely. The first step in this direction was the preparation of a long bill which codified the mint laws. It was written by John Jay Knox, comptroller of the currency. This bill, entitled "An Act Revising and Amending the Laws Relative to Mints, Assay-offices and Coinage of the United States," [876] "The Mint Bill," as it was popularly known, was the origin of the controversy which is still being waged in behalf of silver. It was the beginning of "The Crime of '73," when the silver dollar was surreptitiously omitted from the bill by "stealth or fraud," "accident, mistake or design," or by "expert routine."

The complete history of the demonetization of silver by the passage of the Mint Bill is a long one. When it was first introduced by Senator Sherman on April 25, 1870, this famous bill contained sixty-eight sections, four of which referred to gold and silver dollars. Section sixteen defined silver coins, which included the dollar. The bill was printed, reported, amended, debated, recommitted, and re-introduced

[876] *Cong. Record,* 53 Cong., special sess., "History of the Demonetization of Silver."

nine times in the senate and ten times in the house of representatives before it went to the conference committee and became a law on February 12, 1873. During its legislative course many interesting events happened. The most interesting was the visit of John Sherman and his party to the Comstock mines.[877]

In July, 1872, after the bill had passed the house of representatives with a number of amendments, Senator John T. Sherman, the Honorable W. H. Rinehart of Rome, and James W. Wilson of London, European representatives of the Rothschild interests, Colonel Thomas Scott, interested in railroads, and several other prominent men and women, seventeen altogether, made a trip to the Pacific coast in the private cars of August Belmont, the American agent of the Rothschilds. Among the places visited by the party was Virginia City. The party went down into the mines; they visited the Sutro Tunnel and spent three days on the Comstock. Did Senator Sherman and the Rothschild representatives plan at this time the way to curb the flood of silver that was about to be let loose from the "Big Bonanza?" The answer to this question may be found in the Mint Bill as it was printed in the senate when Sherman returned to congress that fall. When the bill was reported on December 16, 1872, section sixteen, containing the provision for the coinage of the silver dollar, had been shuffled or juggled out by clever manipulation of the numbering of the sections. The bill, it will be remembered, contained sixty-eight sections. The sections which defined the coins in the United States monetary system were:

SECTION 14. That the gold coins of the United States shall be a one-dollar piece, which at the standard weight of twenty-five and eight-tenths grains, shall be the unit of value; a quarter eagle, or two-and-a-half-dollar piece; a half eagle, or five dollar piece; an eagle, or ten dollar piece; and a double eagle, or twenty-dollar piece. . .

SECTION 15. That the silver coins of the United States shall be a trade dollar, a half dollar, or fifty-cent piece, a quarter-dollar, or twenty-five cent piece, a dime, or ten-cent piece; and the weight of the trade dollar shall be four hundred and twenty grains troy. . .

SECTION 16. Reënacts the provisions of the existing laws defining the

[877] The writer is now preparing a monograph description of "The Crime of '73."

silver coins and their weights, respectively, except in relation to the silver dollar, which is reduced in weight from 412½ grains to 384 grains, thus making it a subsidiary coin in harmony with the silver coins of less denominations, to secure its concurrent circulation with them. . .

SECTION 17. That no coins, either of gold or minor coinage, shall hereafter be issued from the mint other than those of the denominations, standards, and weight herein set forth. . .

The legislative trick was accomplished by the following device used in printing the bill:

> Section 14
> Section 15
> Section [17] 16
> Section [18] 17

The omission of the provision for the silver dollar escaped the notice of the senators and representatives of Nevada and of the other silver states. It was passed without detection of the omission of section sixteen by the leading members of the congress. President Grant, who later declared he did not know that the bill omitted the silver dollar, signed the bill at once.[878]

The evidence found in the reports indicated that the omission was made possible by the hasty passage of the bill through the senate. The fraud was more easily perpetrated because of the number of times the bill was reported, amended, printed, debated, and recommitted.[879] It was given its final form in a conference committee which was appointed

---

[878] *Statutes at Large*, 16, 424.

[879] The bill was submitted by the secretary of the treasury on April 25, 1870; referred to senate finance committee April 28, 1870; five hundred copies printed May 2, 1870; submitted to house June 25, 1870; reported, amended, and ordered printed in the senate December 19, 1870; debated in the senate January 9, 1871; passed by a vote of 36 to 14 in the senate; senate bill ordered printed January 13, 1871; bill reported with substitute, and recommitted February 25, 1871; original bill reintroduced and printed March 9, 1871; reported and debated January 9, 1872; recommitted January 10, 1872; reported back, amended, and printed February 13, 1872; debated in the house April 9, 1872; amended, and passed by a vote of 110 to 13 in the house May 27, 1872; printed in the senate May 29, 1872; reported, amended, and printed in the senate December 16, 1872; (section 16 omitted) passed the senate January 17, 1873; printed with amendments in the house January 21, 1873; conference committee appointed; became a law February 12, 1873. It is said it became a law without the yeas and nays being called for. Senator John Sherman was the chairman of the senate finance committee and the conference committee.

on January 21, 1873, and became a law, as has been said, on February 12 of the same year. It was said that the English banking interests so much desired the demonetization that they spent large quantities of money to accomplish this.

The effect of this bill on the silver industry was disastrous. The price of the metal began to decline shortly after it was passed. In 1873 silver was worth over a dollar an ounce; in 1895 it had reached the low level of fifty cents an ounce; the story of the silver question from 1895 to 1935 is well known. The fall in the price of silver closed most of the mines, and the industries dependent on them were forced to shut down. Nevada's age of silver was at an end.

# Appendix A

## TERRITORIAL GOVERNORS OF NEVADA [880]

### Military Governors of New Mexico, 1845-1863 [881]

Kearny, Stephen W. .............................August 19, 1846
Bent, Charles [882] ...............................September 22, 1846
Vigil, Donaciano [883] ............................January 17, 1847
Vigil, Donaciano ...............................December 17, 1847
Washington, J. M.[884] ...........................October 11, 1848
Munroe, John ...................................October 11, 1849

### Territorial Governors of New Mexico

Calhoun, James S.[885]..........................................1851
Lane, William Carr .........................................1852
Meriwether, David .........................................1853
Rencher, Abraham ..........................................1857
Connelly, Henry ...........................................1861

### Territorial Governors of Utah

Young, Brigham [886].............................January 3, 1851
Cumming, Alfred ....................................July, 1857

### Territorial Governor of Nevada

Nye, James W. ....................................July 11, 1861

### Territorial Governors of Arizona [887]

Gurley, John A.[888]..................................March, 1863
Goodwin, John N. ..............................August 21, 1863

[880] All of the state of Nevada between the 37th and the 35th degrees north latitude was under the control of the territory of New Mexico from the time the United States occupied Santa Fé, New Mexico, to 1863.

[881] The military governors were the officers in command of the United States army in New Mexico.

[882] Assassinated January 17, 1847.

[883] Acting-governor from January 17, 1847, to December 17, 1847.

[884] Commandant of the department.

[885] Inaugurated the first governor of New Mexico under the organic act. He was a kinsman of John C. Calhoun.

[886] All of Nevada between the 37th degree and the 42nd degree north latitude was a part of the territory of Utah from 1850 to 1861; the area between the 116th and the 114th meridians was a part of the same territory between 1850 and 1866. Young was elected governor of the unofficial state of Deseret, March 12, 1849. The congress never recognized this state. He was appointed the governor of Utah territory in 1851.

[887] In 1863 the territory of Arizona was organized. The same area of Nevada which had been under the jurisdiction of the territory of New Mexico came under the control of Arizona.

[888] Gurley died August 18, 1863. John N. Goodwin, chief justice of the supreme court of Arizona, was appointed his successor August 21, 1863.

# Appendix B

## TERRITORIAL DELEGATES OF NEVADA

### Territory of New Mexico, Delegates to Congress

Messervy, William S.........thirty-first congress ...........1849-1851
Weightman, R. H...........thirty-second congress .........1851-1853
Gallegos, Manuel José.......thirty-fourth congress .........1853-1855
Otero, Miguel A............thirty-fourth congress .........1855-1857
Otero, Miguel A............thirty-fifth congress ...........1857-1859
Otero, Miguel A............thirty-sixth congress ...........1859-1861
Watts, John S..............thirty-seventh congress ........1861-1863

### Territory of Utah, Delegates to Congress

Babbitt, Almon W.[889]......thirty-first congress ...........1849-
Bernhisel, John M..........thirty-first congress ...........1850-1851
Bernhisel, John M..........thirty-second congress .........1851-1853
Bernhisel, John M..........thirty-third congress ...........1853-1855
Bernhisel, John M..........thirty-fourth congress .........1855-1857
Bernhisel, John M..........thirty-fifth congress ...........1857-1859
Hooper, William H.........thirty-sixth congress ...........1859-1861

### Territory of Nevada, Delegates to Congress

Cradlebaugh, John [890]......thirty-seventh congress ........1861-1862
Mott, Gordon N...........thirty-seventh congress ........1862-1863

### Territory of Arizona, Delegate to Congress

Poston, Charles D.........thirty-eighth congress .........1863-1865

---

[889] Babbitt was elected by the senate and house of representatives of the state of Deseret, but he was not seated by the congress.
[890] Resigned to join the Union forces.

# Appendix C

## STATE OF NEVADA SENATORS

Nye, James W., Rep. ...................................1865-1867
Stewart, William M., Rep. ...........................1865-1869
Nye, James W., Rep. ...................................1867-1873
Stewart, William M., Rep. ...........................1869-1875
Jones, John P., Rep. ...................................1873-1879
Sharon, William, Rep. .................................1875-1881
Fair, James G., Dem. ..................................1881-1887
Jones, John P., Rep. ...................................1885-1891
Stewart, William M., Rep. ...........................1887-1893
Jones, John P., Rep. ...................................1891-1897
Stewart, William M., Silver ..........................1893-1899
Jones, John P., Silver .................................1897-1903
Stewart, William M., Silver ..........................1899-1905
Newlands, Francis G., Dem. ...........................1903-1909
Nixon, George S., Rep. ................................1905-1911
Newlands, Francis G., Dem. ...........................1909-1915
Nixon, George S., Rep.[891] ..........................1911-1912
Massey, W. A., Rep., appointed July 1, 1912...........1912-1913
Pittman, Key, Dem. ....................................1913-1917
Newlands, Francis G., Dem.[892] ......................1915-1917
Pittman, Key, Dem. ....................................1917-1923
Henderson, Charles B., Dem., appointed January 4, 1918......1918-1919
Henderson, Charles B., Dem. ..........................1919-1921
Oddie, Tasker L., Rep. ................................1921-1927
Pittman, Key, Dem. ....................................1923-1929
Oddie, Tasker L., Rep. ................................1927-1933
Pittman, Key, Dem. ....................................1929-1935
McCarran, Patrick, Dem. ..............................1933-
Pittman, Key, Dem. ...................................1935-

[891] Died June 5, 1912.
[892] Died December 24, 1917.

# Appendix D

## REPRESENTATIVES TO CONGRESS FROM NEVADA

Worthington, H. G.,[893] Rep. . . . . . . . . thirty-eighth congress . . . 1864-1865
Ashley, Delos R., Rep. . . . . . . . . . . . . thirty-ninth congress . . . . 1865-1867
Ashley, Delos R., Rep. . . . . . . . . . . . . fortieth congress . . . . . . . 1867-1869
Fitch, Thomas, Rep. . . . . . . . . . . . . . . forty-first congress . . . . . 1869-1871
Kendall, Charles W., Rep. . . . . . . . . . forty-second congress . . . 1871-1873
Kendall, Charles W., Rep. . . . . . . . . . forty-third congress . . . . 1873-1875
Woodburn, William, Rep. . . . . . . . . . . forty-fourth congress . . . 1875-1877
Wren, Thomas, Rep. . . . . . . . . . . . . . . forty-fifth congress . . . . . 1877-1879
Daggett, Rollin M., Rep. . . . . . . . . . . . forty-sixth congress . . . . 1879-1881
Cassidy, George W., Dem. . . . . . . . . . forty-seventh congress . . 1881-1883
Cassidy, George W., Dem. . . . . . . . . . forty-eighth congress . . . 1883-1885
Woodburn, William, Rep. . . . . . . . . . . forty-ninth congress . . . 1885-1887
Woodburn, William, Rep. . . . . . . . . . . fiftieth congress . . . . . . . 1887-1889
Bartine, Horace F., Rep. . . . . . . . . . . . fifty-first congress . . . . . 1889-1891
Bartine, Horace F., Rep. . . . . . . . . . . . fifty-second congress . . . 1891-1893
Newlands, Francis G., Silver . . . . . . . fifty-third congress . . . . . 1893-1895
Newlands, Francis G., Silver . . . . . . . fifty-fourth congress . . . . 1895-1897
Newlands, Francis G., Silver-Dem. . . fifty-fifth congress . . . . . 1897-1899
Newlands, Francis G., Silver-Dem. . . fifty-sixth congress . . . . . 1899-1901
Newlands, Francis G., Dem.-Silver . . fifty-seventh congress . . . 1901-1903
Van Duser, Clarence D., Silver-Dem. . fifty-eighth congress . . . . 1903-1905
Van Duser, Clarence D., Silver-Dem. . fifty-ninth congress . . . . . 1905-1907
Bartlett, George A., Dem. . . . . . . . . . . sixtieth congress . . . . . . . 1907-1909
Bartlett, George A., Dem. . . . . . . . . . . sixty-first congress . . . . . . 1909-1911
Roberts, E. E., Rep. . . . . . . . . . . . . . . . sixty-second congress . . . 1911-1913
Roberts, E. E., Rep. . . . . . . . . . . . . . . . sixty-third congress . . . . 1913-1915
Roberts, E. E., Rep. . . . . . . . . . . . . . . . sixty-fourth congress . . . 1915-1917
Roberts, E. E., Rep. . . . . . . . . . . . . . . . sixty-fifth congress . . . . 1917-1919
Evans, Charles R., Dem. . . . . . . . . . . . sixty-sixth congress . . . . 1919-1921
Arentz, Samuel S., Rep. . . . . . . . . . . . sixty-seventh congress . . 1921-1923
Richards, Charles L., Dem. . . . . . . . . sixty-eighth congress . . . 1923-1925
Arentz, Samuel S., Rep. . . . . . . . . . . . sixty-ninth congress . . . . 1925-1927
Arentz, Samuel S., Rep. . . . . . . . . . . . seventieth congress . . . . . 1927-1929
Arentz, Samuel S., Rep. . . . . . . . . . . . seventy-first congress . . . 1929-1931
Arentz, Samuel S., Rep. . . . . . . . . . . . seventy-second congress . 1931-1933
Scrugham, James G., Dem. . . . . . . . . seventy-third congress . . 1933-1935

[893] Worthington was elected a representative to congress to fill the unexpired term from December, 1864, to March 3, 1865.

# Appendix E

## GOVERNORS OF NEVADA

Blaisdel, H. G., Rep. ....................................1865-1870
Bradley, L. R., Dem. .....................................1871-1878
Kinkead, John H., Rep. .................................1879-1882
Adams, Jewett W., Dem. ..............................1883-1886
Stevenson, C. C., Rep.[894]............................1887-1890
Bell, Frank, Rep. (acting from September 21, 1890).........1890-
Colcord, R. K., Rep. ....................................1891-1894
Jones, John E.,[895] Silver Party ...........................1895-1896
Sadler, Reinhold, Silver Party (acting-governor)...........1896-1898
Sadler, Reinhold, Silver Party ...........................1899-1902
Sparks, John, [896] Silver-Dem. ..........................1903-1908
Dickerson, D. S., Dem.-Silver (acting-governor)...........1908-1910
Oddie, Tasker L., Rep. ..................................1911-1914
Boyle, Emmett D., Dem. ................................1915-1922
Scrugham, J. G., Dem. .................................1923-1926
Balzar, Fred B.,[897] Rep. ...............................1927-1934
Griswold, Morley, Rep. (acting-governor)................1934-1935
Kirman, Richard, Dem. ................................1935-

---

[894] Died September 21, 1890, and Frank Bell became acting-governor by virtue of his office as lieutenant-governor.

[895] Died April 10, 1896, and R. Sadler became acting-governor by virtue of his office as lieutenant-governor.

[896] Died May 22, 1908, and D. S. Dickerson became acting-governor.

[897] Died March 21, 1934, and Morley Griswold became acting-governor.

# Bibliography

## MANUSCRIPTS

ARCHIVO del Arzobispado de San Francisco, collected by Dr. A. S. Taylor, 1859. MS. in the Bancroft Library.

ASHLEY, Delos R. Documents for the history of California, 1827-1860. MS. in the Bancroft Library.

BEATIE, Hampden S. First in Nevada, 1884. MS. in the Bancroft Library.

BIGLER, William Henry. Diary of a Mormon in California, 1872. MS. in the Bancroft Library.

CARSON, Christopher. Kit Carson's story as told by himself. MS. in the Bancroft Library.

CRADLEBAUGH, William M. Nevada biography, 1883. MS. in the Bancroft Library.

DAVIES, Jessie Hughes. The expedition of Peter Skene Ogden in the Snake river region, with a brief survey of previous travel and exploration in that region. MS., University of California, 1926. M.A. thesis.

HALL, E. Raymond. A study of the food habits of the white pelican at Pyramid Lake, Nevada. MS., University of California, 1925. M.A. thesis.

HIXON, Jasper Morris. A gold hunter; the itinerary across the continent in 1849. MS. (quoted in Coy, The Great Trek).

JENNINGS, William. Carson Valley, 1884. MS. in the Bancroft Library.

[NEVADA] Territorial record books, 1861-1865. MS. in the office of the secretary of state of Nevada, Carson City.

NEVERS, Samuel A. Nevada pioneers, 1884. MS. in the Bancroft Library.

REESE, John. Mormon station, 1884. MS. in the Bancroft Library.

STEWART, William Morris. Stewart scraps, 1887-1905. MS. and newspaper clippings in the Nevada Historical Library, Reno. 17 vols.

VAN SICKLE, H. Utah desperadoes, 1883. MS. in the Bancroft Library.

## GOVERNMENT DOCUMENTS

ARIZONA (TERR.) GOVERNOR. Message . . . 1864-65. Prescott, 1865.

CALIFORNIA, ADJUTANT-GENERAL'S OFFICE. Records of California men in the War of the Rebellion, 1861 to 1867. Revised and compiled by Brig.-gen. Richard H. Orton . . . Sacramento, 1890.

CALIFORNIA, GEOLOGICAL SURVEY. Geological survey of California. [Various places], 1864-82. 13 vols.

CALIFORNIA, LAWS, STATUTES, ETC. California statutes, 1860. Sacramento, 1860.

CALIFORNIA, LEGISLATURE. Journal of the Assembly . . . 4th to 16th sessions. Sacramento, 1853-1865.

CALIFORNIA, LEGISLATURE. Journal of the Senate . . . 4th to 16th sessions. Sacramento, 1853-1865.

NEVADA (TERR.) LAWS, STATUTES, ETC. Laws . . . 1861-64. [Various places], 1862-65.

NEVADA (TERR.) LEGISLATURE. Journal of the Council and Proceedings of the House, 1861. San Francisco, 1862.

NEVADA (STATE) GOVERNOR. Message . . . 1865-67. Carson City, 1867.

NEVADA (STATE) LAWS, STATUTES, ETC. Laws . . . 1864-1873. Carson City, 1865-73.

NEVADA (STATE) SURVEYOR-GENERAL'S OFFICE. Report . . . 1931-32. Carson City, 1932.

BECKER, George Ferdinand. . . . Geology of the Comstock Lode and the Washoe district . . . Washington, 1882. 1 vol. and atlas. (U.S. geological survey. Monographs, III.)

DONALDSON, Thomas. The public domain: its history, with statistics . . . Washington, 1884. (U.S. public land commission, 1879-80. Cf. serial 1975.)

HODGE, Frederick Webb. Handbook of American Indians north of Mexico. Washington, 1907-10. 2 vols. (U.S. Bureau of American Ethnology. Bulletin 30.)

LORD, Eliot. Comstock mining and miners. Washington, 1883. (U.S. geological survey. Monographs, IV.)

MALLOY, William M. Treaties, conventions, international acts, protocols and agreements between the United States and other powers, 1776-19—. Washington, 1910-    . (In progress.)

ROYCE, Charles. Indian land cessions in the United States . . . Washington, 1899. (U.S. Bureau of American Ethnology. Annual report, 1896-97.)

RUSSELL, Israel Cook. Geological survey of Lake Lahontan; a quaternary lake of northwestern Nevada. Washington, 1885. (U.S. geological survey. Monographs, XI.)

SIMPSON, James Hervey. Report of explorations across the Great Basin of the territory of Utah for a direct wagon-route from Camp Floyd to Genoa, in Carson Valley, in 1859 . . . Washington, 1876.

U.S. CONGRESS. Congressional Globe, 31st to 40th Congress. Washington, 1849-67.

U.S. CONGRESS, HOUSE. Committee reports, 34th Cong., 1st sess. (serial 940); Committee reports, 35th Cong., 1st sess. (serial 966); Executive documents, 32d Cong., 1st sess., no. 56 (serial 643); Executive documents, 33d Cong., 1st sess., no. 2 (serial 714); Executive documents, 34th Cong., 3d sess., no. 37 (serial 899); Executive documents, 35th Cong., 1st sess., no. 96 (serial 957); Executive documents, 36th Cong., 2d sess., no. 40 (serial 1097); Executive documents, 37th Cong., 2d sess., no. 1 (serial 1157); Executive documents, 38th Cong., 2d sess., nos. 24-25 (serials 1222-23); Executive documents, 46th Cong., 3d sess., no. 47 (serial 1975); Executive documents, 51st Cong., 2d sess., no. 287 (serial 2868); Journal, 31st Cong., 1st sess. (serial 556); Journal, 35th Cong., 1st sess. (serial 1126); Journal, 37th Cong., 2d sess. (serial 1155).

U.S. CONGRESS, SENATE. Executive documents, 31st Cong., 1st sess., no. 1 (serials 549-51); Executive documents, 31st Cong., 1st sess., no. 18 (serial 554); Executive documents, 31st Cong., 1st sess., no. 52 (serial 612); Executive documents, 32d Cong., 2d sess., no. 1 (serial 658); Executive documents, 33d Cong., 1st sess., no. 1 (serials 690-93); Executive documents, 35th Cong., 2d sess., no. 1 (serials 974-78); Executive documents, 36th Cong., 1st sess., nos. 1-2 (serial 1023); Executive documents, 37th Cong., 2d sess., no. 1 (serial 1117); Executive documents, 37th Cong., 2d sess., no. 36 (serial 1122); Executive documents, 51st Cong., 1st sess., no. 52 (serial 2682); Journal, 34th Cong., 1st sess. (serial 809); Journal, 36th Cong., 1st sess. (serial 1022); Journal, 37th Cong., 1st sess. (serial 1116); Journal, 37th Cong., 3d sess. (serial 1148); Miscellaneous documents, 35th Cong., 1st sess., nos. 181, 201, 240 (serial 936).

U.S. CONGRESS. Miscellaneous documents, 36th Cong., 1st sess., no. 19 (serial 1064); Miscellaneous documents, 36th Cong., 1st sess., no. 80 (serial 1065); Miscellaneous documents, 37th Cong., 2d sess., no. 70 (serial 1141); Miscellaneous documents, 37th Cong., 3d sess., no. 26 (serial 1171); Miscellaneous documents, 39th Cong., 1st sess., no. 101 (serial 1271).

U.S. DEPT. OF THE INTERIOR. Report, 1861-64. Washington, 1861-64.

U.S. DEPT. OF THE INTERIOR. Report . . . communicating reports upon the Pacific wagon roads constructed under the direction of that department . . . [Washington, 1859]. (U.S. 35th Cong., 2d sess., Senate Ex. Doc. 35, serial 984.)

U.S. GENERAL LAND OFFICE. Report . . . 1861-66. Washington, 1861-66.

U.S. OFFICE OF INDIAN AFFAIRS. Report . . . 1849-65. Washington, 1850-66.

U.S. QUARTERMASTER'S DEPT. List of military posts, etc., established in the United States from its earliest settlement to the present time. Washington, 1902.

U.S. QUARTERMASTER'S DEPT. Outline description of the posts and stations of troops in the military Division of the Pacific commanded by Major-general John M. Schofield. Washington, 1872.

U.S. QUARTERMASTER'S DEPT. Outline descriptions of United States military posts and stations in the year 1871. Washington, 1872.

U.S. SUPREME COURT. Reports . . . vol. III, appendix no. 1. Washington, 1870.

U.S. SURGEON-GENERAL'S OFFICE. Report on the hygiene of the United States army, with description of military posts. Washington, 1875.

U.S. WAR DEPT. Report . . . 1861-65. Washington, 1861-65.

U.S. WAR DEPT. Reports of explorations and surveys to ascertain the most practicable and economical route for a railroad from the Mississippi river to the Pacific ocean, made . . . in 1853-56. . . Washington, 1855-60. 12 vols. in 13.

U.S. WAR DEPT. The war of the rebellion: a compilation of the official records of the Union and Confederate armies. Washington, 1860-1907. 70 vols.

## PRINTED BOOKS, NEWSPAPER FILES, AND ARTICLES

ANGEL, Myron. History of Nevada, with illustrations and biographical sketches of its prominent men and pioneers. Oakland, 1881.

ARMSTRONG, Margaret Neilson. Field book of plants as a source of drinking water. New York, 1915.

[AUSTIN, Nevada] Reese River Reveille, 1864.

BANCROFT, HUBERT HOWE. History of Arizona and New Mexico, 1530-1888. San Francisco, 1889.

────── History of California. San Francisco, 1884-90. 7 vols.

────── History of Nevada, Colorado, and Wyoming, 1540-1888. San Francisco, 1890.

────── History of Utah. San Francisco, 1889.

BEAN, Edwin F. History and directory of Nevada county, California. [Nevada City, 1859.]

BECKWOURTH, James P. The life and adventures of James P. Beckwourth, in the wild west, written from his own dictation, by T. D. Bonner. New York, 1856.

BIDWELL, John. Echoes of the past: an account of the first emigrant train to California, Frémont in the conquest of California, the discovery of gold and early reminiscences . . . Chico, [19—].

BIRNEY, Hoffman. Zealots of Zion. Philadelphia, [1931].

BOLTON, Herbert Eugene. Anza's California expeditions. Berkeley, 1930. 5 vols.

────── Outpost of empire. New York, 1931.

BOWLES, Samuel. Our new west; records of travel between the Mississippi river and the Pacific ocean . . . Hartford, New York, 1869.

BRADLEY, Glenn D. Story of the pony express, an account of the most remarkable mail service ever in existence, and its place in history. Chicago, 1913.

BROWN, William S. "Northwestern Nevada – Land of enchantment," in The Sacramento Bee, March 11, 1931.

BROWNE, John Ross. "A peep at Washoe," in Harper's Monthly Magazine, vol. 22, New York, December, 1860-February, 1861.

────── Report . . . on the mineral resources of the states and territories west of the Rocky mountains [1867], Washington, [1868].

BRYANT, Edwin. What I saw in California . . . New York, Philadelphia, 1848.

BRYANT, W. C. The silver mines of Nevada. New York, 1864.

CALIFORNIA MISCELLANY. [A collection of pamphlets in the Bancroft Library], 14 vols.

[CARSON CITY, Nevada] Daily Appeal, 1868.

[CARSON CITY], Nevada Democrat, 1861.

[CARSON CITY, Nevada] Silver Age, 1861.

CHAPMAN, Charles Edward. A history of California: the Spanish period. New York, 1921.

CHITTENDEN, Hiram Martin. The American fur-trade of the far west. . . New York, 1902. 3 vols.

CLELAND, Robert Glass. A history of California: the American period. New York, 1922.

CLEMENS, Samuel Langhorne. Roughing it. Hartford, 1891.

COHN, Mrs. C. Amy. "Arts and crafts of the Nevada Indians," in Nevada Historical Society Biennial Report, 1907-08. Carson, 1908.

COLBY, William E. "The extralateral right – Shall it be abolished?" in the California Law Review, vol. 5, nos. 1, 4, Berkeley, November, 1916, May, 1917.

COMO, [Nevada] Sentinel, 1864.

COOKE, Lucy Rutledge. Crossing the plains in 1852 . . . Modesto, 1923.

COY, Owen Cochran. California county boundaries: a study of the division of the state into counties and the subsequent changes in their boundaries . . . Publication of the California historical survey commission, Berkeley, 1923. Sacramento, 1923.

—— The great trek. Los Angeles, San Francisco, [1931].

DALE, Harrison Clifford. The Ashley-Smith explorations and the discovery of a central route to the Pacific, 1822-1829, with the original documents . . . Cleveland, 1918.

DANA, Charles Anderson. Recollections of the Civil War; with the leaders in the field in the sixties. New York, 1902.

DANGBERG, Grace. "Washo texts," in the University of California publications in American archaeology and ethnology, vol. XXII, no. 3, Berkeley, 1927.

DAVIS, Sam P. The history of Nevada, 2 vols. Reno, Los Angeles, 1913.

[DAYTON, Nevada] Lyon county Sentinel, 1864.

DELANO, Alonzo. Life on the plains and among the diggings; being scenes and adventures of an overland journey to California . . . Auburn, Buffalo, 1854.

DELLENBAUGH, Frederick Samuel. Breaking the wilderness; the story of the conquest of the far west . . . New York, London, 1905.

DEWEY, Squire P. The bonanza mines and bonanza kings of California, their 5 years' reign: 1875-1879 . . . [San Francisco, c. 1880].

DOOLITTLE, James Rood. Condition of the Indian tribes. Washington, 1867.

DUTCHER, B. H. "Piñon gathering among the Panamint Indians," in the American Anthropologist, vol. 6, no. 4, Washington, October, 1893.

EGAN, William M. Pioneering the west, 1846 to 1878. Richmond, Utah, 1917.

ELDREDGE, Zöeth Skinner. History of California. New York, 1915. 5 vols.

ELLISON, Joseph. California and the nation, 1850-1869; a study of the relations of a frontier community with the federal government. Berkeley, 1927. (University of California publications in history, vol. XVI).

FAIRFIELD, Asa. Fairfield's pioneer history of Lassen county, California . . . San Francisco, [1916].

FREMONT, John Charles. Memoirs of my life, including in the narrative five journeys of western exploration, during the years 1842, 1843-4, 1845-6-7, 1848-9, 1853-4 . . . Chicago, New York, 1887.

—— Report of the exploring expedition to the Rocky mountains in the year 1842, and to Oregon and North California in the years 1843-44 . . . Washington, 1845.

GALLATIN, Albert. A synopsis of the Indian tribes within the United States east of the Rocky mountains and in the British and Russian possessions of North America. Cambridge, 1836. (Archaeological Americana. Transactions and Collections of the American Antiquarian Society, vol. 2.)

GARCES, Francisco Tomás Hermenegildo. On the trail of a Spanish pioneer; the diary and itinerary of Francisco Garcés . . . in his travels through Sonora, Arizona, and California, 1775-1776, tr. . . . and ed. . . . by Elliott Coues . . . New York, 1900. 2 vols.

GOLD HILL, [Nevada] Evening News, 1864.

GRAY, A. A. Camels in western America, by A. A. Gray, Francis P. Farquhar and William S. Lewis. Three articles and a bibliography reprinted from the Quarterly of the California historical society, vol. IX, no. 4, December, 1930. San Francisco, 1930.

GREGG, Josiah. Commerce of the prairies; or, the journal of a Santa Fé trader during eight expeditions across the great western prairies and a residence of nearly nine years in northern Mexico. New York, 1844. 2 vols.

HAFEN, Le Roy R. The overland mail, 1849-1869, promoter of settlement, precursor of railroads. Cleveland, 1926.

HAMERSLEY, Thomas Holaup Stevens. . . . Complete regular army register of the United States for one hundred years (1779-1879) . . . Washington, 1880.

HARRINGTON, Mark Raymond. Archaeological explorations in southern Nevada. Los Angeles, 1930. (Southwest Museum, Papers, no. 4.)

—— Paiute caves. Los Angeles, 1930. (Southwest Museum, Papers, no. 4.)

HASTINGS, Lansford Warren. Emigrant's guide to Oregon and California . . . Cincinnati, 1845.

HAYDEN, Irwin. Mesa house. Los Angeles, 1930. (Southwest Museum, Papers, no. 4.)

—— "Nevada cavemen: rich archaeological find reveals amazing details of life among American troglodytes throughout a thirty-century period," in Touring Topics, vol. XXII, no. 2, Los Angeles, February, 1930.

HAYES, Benjamin. Hayes Scrap Book, 138 vols. In Bancroft Library.

HEAP, Gwinn Harris. Central route to the Pacific from the valley of the Mississippi to California: journal of the expedition of E. F. Beale . . . and Gwinn Harris Heap from Missouri to California in 1853. Philadelphia, 1854.

HILL, Joseph John. "The Old Spanish trail," in the Hispanic American Historical Review, vol. IV, no. 3, Durham, August, 1924.

—— "Spanish and Mexican exploration and trade northwest from New Mexico into the Great Basin," in the Utah Historical Quarterly, vol. III, no. 1, Salt Lake City, January, 1930.

—— "Ewing Young in the fur-trade of the far southwest, 1822-1834," in the Oregon Historical Quarterly, vol. XXIV, no. 1, Eugene, March, 1923.

HOPKINS, Sarah Winnemucca. Life among the Paiutes; their wrongs and claims . . . ed. by Mrs. Horace Mann . . . Boston, New York, 1883.

HORN, Hosea B. Horn's overland guide from the U.S. Indian sub-agency, Council Bluffs . . . to the city of Sacramento, in California, . . . New York, 1852.

INGALLS, Eleaser. Journal of a trip to California by the overland route across the plains in 1850-51. Waukegan, Ill., 1852.

JOHNSTON, Philip. "The Valley of fire," in Touring Topics, vol. XXI, no. 1, Los Angeles, January, 1929.

JONES, J. Claude. "Age of Lake Lahontan," in the Bulletin of the Geologic Society of America, vol. 40, no. 3, Washington, 1929.

―――― The geologic history of Lake Lahontan. Chicago, 1925. (University of Chicago Abstracts of Theses series.)

JULIAN, George Washington. Political recollections, 1840-1872. Chicago, 1884.

KELLY, Charles. Salt Desert trails; a history of the Hastings Cutoff and other early trails which crossed the great salt desert seeking a shorter road to California. Salt Lake City, 1930.

KELLY, J. Wells. . . Directory of Nevada territory . . . San Francisco, 1862.

KING, Joseph L. History of the San Francisco stock and exchange board . . . San Francisco, 1910.

KROEBER, Alfred L. "The Washo language of east central California and Nevada," in University of California Publications in American Archaeology and Ethnology, vol. IV, no. 5, Berkeley, 1907.

LAMBOURNE, Alfred. The pioneer trail. Salt Lake City, 1913.

LEE, Bourke. Death Valley. New York, 1930.

LEEPER, David Rohrer. The argonauts of Forty-nine . . . South Bend, Ind., 1894.

LEONARD, Zenas. Leonard's narrative; adventures of Zenas Leonard, furtrader and trapper, 1831-1846. Reprinted from the rare original of 1839; ed. by W. F. Wagner. Cleveland, 1904.

LESLEY, Lewis Burt. Uncle Sam's Camels. The journal of May Humphreys Stacey supplemented by the report of Edward Fitzgerald Beale (1857-1858). Cambridge, 1929.

LINN, William Alexander. The story of the Mormons. New York, 1902.

[LIVERPOOL, England] The Latter-Day Saints' Millennial Star, 1850-65.

LONE, Emma Miriam. Check-list of first editions of the works of John Ross Browne, California pioneer; with a chronology, 1821-1872 [i.e., 1875]. New York, 1930.

LOOMIS, Leander V. A journal of the Birmingham emigrating company . . . ed. by Edgar M. Ledyard. Salt Lake City, 1928.

LYMAN, George Dunlap. John Marsh, pioneer; the life story of a trailblazer on six frontiers. New York, 1930.

MACK, Effie Mona. "William Morris Stewart, empire builder," in Proceedings of the Pacific Coast Branch of the American Historical Association. [Los Angeles], 1930.

MAJORS, Alexander. Seventy years on the frontier . . . Chicago, New York, 1893.

MANLY, William Lewis. Death Valley in '49 . . . the autobiography of a pioneer . . . San Jose, 1894.

MARCY, Randolph B. The prairie traveler: a handbook for overland expeditions with maps, illustrations and itineraries of the principal routes between the Mississippi and the Pacific. New York, 1859.

MARSHALL, Thomas Maitland. A history of the western boundary of the Louisiana Purchase, 1819-1841. Berkeley, 1914. (University of California Publications in History, vol. 2.)

MAXWELL, William Audley. Crossing the plains; days of '57; a narrative of early emigrant travel to California by the ox-team method. [San Francisco, 1915.]

McGLASHAN, C. F. History of the Donner party; a tragedy of the Sierra. San Francisco, 1880.

MEXICO [CITY]. Registro oficial del gobierno de los Estados Unidos Mexicanos, 1830.

MUIR, John. Steep trails: California, Utah, Nevada, Washington, Oregon, the Grand Canyon. Boston, New York, 1918.

MURDOCK, John R. The Constitution of Arizona. Tempe, Arizona, 1929.

NEIHARDT, John Gneisenau. The splendid wayfaring; the story of the exploits and adventures of Jedediah Smith and his comrades, the Ashley-Henry men, discoverers and explorers of the great central route from the Missouri river to the Pacific ocean, 1822-1831. New York, 1920.

NEVADA HISTORICAL SOCIETY. Biennial report, 1909-10. Carson City, 1911.

NEVADA HISTORICAL SOCIETY. Papers, vol. IV, 1923-24. Carson City, 1924.

NEVINS, Allen. Frémont, the west's greatest adventurer; being a biography from certain hitherto unpublished sources of General John C. Frémont, together with his wife, Jessie Benton Frémont, and some account of the period of expansion which found a brilliant leader in the Pathfinder. New York, London, 1928. 2 vols.

NEW YORK TRIBUNE Almanac and Political Register, 1838-68. New York, 1838-68.

OGDEN, Peter Skene. "The Peter Skene Ogden journals; editorial notes by T. C. Elliott," in the Oregon Historical Quarterly, vol. XI, no. 2, Portland, 1910.

PAINE, Swift. Eilley Orrum, queen of the Comstock. Indianapolis, 1929.

PURKITT, J. H. "Nevada territory," in the San Francisco Evening Bulletin, February, 1860.

RENO, [Nevada] Evening Gazette, 1930.

RICHARDSON, James D., comp. A compilation of the messages and papers of the presidents. Washington, 1889. 10 vols.

RICHTHOFEN, Ferdinand Paul Wilhelm, freiherr von. The Comstock Lode, its character, and the probable mode of its continuance in depth. San Francisco, 1866.

ROBERTS, Brigham Henry. The Mormon Battalion, its history and achievements. Salt Lake City, 1919.

ROOT, Frank Albert. The overland stage to California; personal reminiscences and authentic history of the great overland stage line and pony express . . . By Frank A. Root and William Elsey Connelley . . . Topeka, 1901.

RUF, Peter. "Dat-so-la-lee," in the California Christian Advocate, vol. LXXV, no. 3, San Francisco, 1926.

SABIN, Edwin Legrand. Building the Pacific railway . . . Philadelphia, London, 1919.

[SACRAMENTO, California] Daily Union, 1860.

[SAN FRANCISCO, California] Daily Alta California, 1851-66.

[SAN FRANCISCO, California] Daily Evening Bulletin, 1860-66.

SAN JOSE, [California] Pioneer, 1877.

SAWYER, Lorenzo. Way sketches; containing incidents of travel across the plains from St. Joseph to California in 1850, with letters describing life and conditions in the gold region . . . with historical notes . . . and an introduction by Edward Eberstadt. New York, 1926.

SHELLBACH, Louis. An unusual burial in Mesa ruins. Los Angeles, 1930. (Southwest Museum, Papers, no. 4.)

SHINN, Charles Howard. Mining-camps: a study in American frontier government. New York, 1885.

—— The story of the mine as illustrated by the great Comstock Lode of Nevada. New York, 1896.

SHIVELY, J. M. Route and distances to Oregon and California, with a description of watering places, crossings, dangerous Indians, &c., &c. . . . Washington, 1846.

SHUCK, Oscar Tully. Representative and leading men of the Pacific: being original sketches of the lives and characters of the principal men . . . San Francisco, 1870.

SMITH, C. W. Journal of a trip to California across the continent from Weston, Mo., to Weber Creek, Cal., in the summer of 1850. Edited, with introduction and notes, by W. R. G. Vail . . . New York, [1920].

STENHOUSE, Thomas B. H. Rocky mountain saints: a full and complete history of the Mormons . . . and the development of the great commercial wealth of the territory of Utah . . . New York, 1873.

STEWART, William Morris. Reminiscences . . . edited by George Rothwell Brown. New York, Washington, 1908.

—— Stewart Scrap Books. In Nevada Historical Library.

SUTRO, Adolph Heinrich Joseph. Closing argument . . . on the bill before Congress to aid the Sutro Tunnel, delivered before the committee on mines and mining of the House of Representatives . . . April 22, 1872. Washington, 1872.

SWIFT, John Franklin. Robert Greathouse. New York, 1870.

SWISHER, Charles Brent. Stephen J. Field, craftsman of the law. Washington, 1930. (Brookings Institution.)

TARAYRE, E. Guillemin. Exploration mineralogique des regions Mexicaines suivie de notes archéologiques et ethnographiques . . . Paris, 1869. (Extrait du tome III des Archives de la Commission scientifique du Mexique.)

THISSELL, G. W. Crossing the plains in '49. Oakland, 1903.

THWAITES, Reuben Gold, ed. Early western travels, 1748-1846; a series of annotated reprints . . . Cleveland, 1904-1907. 32 vols.

TIDESTROM, Ivar. Flora of Utah and Nevada. Washington, 1928.

TRAMP, J. C. Prairie and Rocky mountain adventures. [N.p.], 1870.

TRIBUTE to the memory of Reuel Colt Gridley – compiled and published for the purpose of raising money to aid in building a monument to his memory and establishing a fund for his family. Stockton, 1883.

TYLER, Daniel. A concise history of the Mormon Battalion in the Mexican War, 1846-1847. Salt Lake City, 1881.

UDELL, John. Incidents of travel to California across the great plains, together with the return trips through Central America and Jamaica . . . Jefferson, Ohio, 1856.

VAN DYKE, Walter. "Overland to Los Angeles by the Salt Lake route in 1849," in the Annual Publication of the Historical Society of Southern California, vol. 3, Los Angeles, 1894.

VIRGINIA [CITY, Nevada] Daily Union, 1864.

VISALIA, [California] Delta, 1861.

VISSCHER, William Lightfoot. A thrilling and truthful history of the pony express; or, blazing the westward way . . . Chicago, [1908].

WERNER, Robert Morris. Brigham Young. New York, [1925].

WHITNEY, Orson F. History of Utah. Salt Lake City, 1892-1904. 4 vols.

WREN, Thomas. A history of the state of Nevada, its resources and people; the late Hon. Thomas Wren . . . editor-in-chief . . . New York, Chicago, 1904.

WRIGHT, William [Dan De Quille, pseud.]. History of the big bonanza: an authentic account of the discovery, history, and working of the . . . Comstock silver lode . . . Hartford, San Francisco, 1876.

YALE, Gregory. Legal titles to mining claims and water rights in California . . . San Francisco, New York, 1866.

# Index

# Date Due